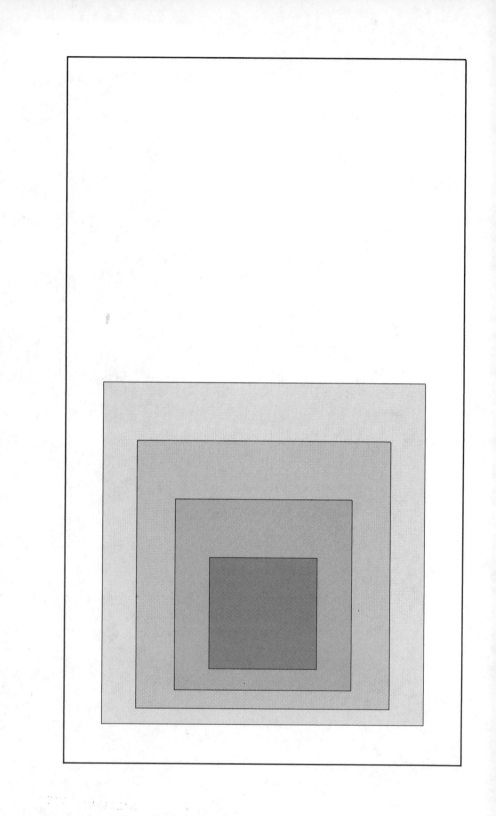

SOCIOLOGY of OCCUPATIONS
AND
PROFESSIONS

SECOND EDITION

RONALD M. PAVALKO
UNIVERSITY OF WISCONSIN — PARKSIDE

WITHDRAWN

F. E. PEACOCK PUBLISHERS, INC.
ITASCA, ILLINOIS

HT
675
.P38
1988

TO LINDA, FRED, LIZA, PETER, AND HELEN

PREFACE

M ANY DECADES of sociological research and writing have produced a rich literature dealing with occupations. The present review of this work is necessarily selective. I have organized the book around what appear to me to be the main topics, problems, and controversies that have emerged from past work. I have also attempted to be sensitive to issues that are likely to be major concerns of the sociological study of occupations in the future.

This book is intended primarily for use as a text in college and university courses dealing with the *sociology of occupations and professions*, or the *sociology of work*. It also deals with topics that are part of the field of *industrial sociology*. A good deal of the material also is relevant to courses on vocational guidance and career counseling, particularly the material dealing with occupational choice, careers, and the future of the American labor force.

In writing this book I have assumed that the reader would be familiar with basic sociological concepts, assumptions, and terminology, typically by having taken an introductory college level course in sociology. Nevertheless, I have tried to be conscientious about defining and explaining major concepts, albeit usually briefly, as they are introduced.

I would like to express a personal debt of intellectual gratitude to Professor Raymond J. Murphy of the University of Rochester. He was a faculty member in the Department of Sociology at the University of California at Los Angeles when I did my graduate work there in the early 1960s. He first introduced me to the sociology of occupations and professions and made it a lively and exciting area of scholarly interest.

I can only hope that this book will kindle similar kinds of interest and awareness.

There are several other contributions to this book that I would like to acknowledge. I would like to thank the Regents of the University of Wisconsin for granting me sabbatical leave during the fall semester of 1985 to begin work on the book. Professors Joel E. Gerstl of Temple University and Harry Gold of Oakland University provided valuable critiques of the first draft of the manuscript. I appreciate very much the suggestions they made. Robert Gorelik, my undergraduate student assistant at the University of Wisconsin—Parkside, provided valuable library assistance and comments on the manuscript from a student-reader perspective. Finally, the support and enthusiasm of Ted Peacock, President of F. E. Peacock Publishers, was a crucial ingredient in the completion of this project.

RONALD M. PAVALKO
Racine, Wisconsin
March, 1987

CONTENTS

CHAPTER 1

An Introduction to the Study of Work

T HIS INTRODUCTORY CHAPTER has four objectives. *First,* we want to identify and discuss the kinds of assumptions sociologists make in studying work and occupations. In other words, it is necessary to spell out what we mean by work as a social phenomenon in contrast to, for example, an economic phenomenon or a physical activity. A *second* task is to discuss why it is important to study work. This involves the identification of assumptions about the importance of work in the lives of individuals and the nature of occupational roles as an element of social structure. The *third* purpose of this introductory chapter is to locate the study of occupations within the field of sociology. To accomplish this, we need to identify the unique issues and problems that this specialty addresses and discuss its relationship to other specialties such as industrial sociology, social stratification, and the study of complex organizations. The *fourth* objective is to explain the plan and rationale for the organization of the remainder of the book.

WORK AS A SOCIAL PHENOMENON

Work is an activity that is taken for granted in the lives of most adult members of contemporary society. Its sheer pervasiveness poses analytic problems. With what aspects of work should we be concerned? What

1

kinds of questions should we ask about work? What do we want to find out about work and occupations? Any social scientist seeking to describe and analyze human society must sooner or later come to grip with the fact that most adults spend more time working than in any other activity except perhaps sleeping. However, what is done with this observation varies considerably within the social sciences.

The economist, for example, might look upon work as one of several input variables in the economic system. Economists concern themselves with such questions as the supply of people with particular work skills and the demand for those skills. They are also interested in questions of worker productivity, factors related to unemployment, the growth and decline of different industries and the jobs within them, and the contribution of different industries to the gross national product. The psychologist, on the other hand, may be concerned with such questions as the kinds of satisfactions and dissatisfactions that individuals derive from their work, why they are motivated to enter and perform different kinds of work, job related stress, and the effect of work on mental health. Industrial and personnel psychologists have also attempted to devise tests that measure the extent to which individuals possess a variety of cognitive, motor, and visual skills in order to match people with specific job requirements. They are also interested in such issues as worker morale and the relationship between work and personality.[1]

In addition to being of interest to social scientists, work also may be approached as a physiological activity. Thus, biologists might be interested in the relationship of work to various neurological, muscular, and respiratory states. Occupational hazards that represent a threat to physical health are also of concern to medical scientists and others in the field of public health. An interest in work is not limited to scientists, either. Philosophers have dealt with the meaning that work has had for people in different periods of human history.[2] Furthermore, the workplace is frequently the setting in which novelists and playwrights locate their plots and characters.

WORK AS A SOCIAL ROLE

While sociologists frequently deal with some of the concerns mentioned above, they approach the study of work with other primary interests and are guided by a number of key assumptions. For the sociologist, the most important thing about work is the fact that it is a social activity. Occupations are a type of *social role*. As such, they locate their incumbents in a network of social relationships. Once we realize that occupations are social roles, a number of questions arise. Since occupational roles are achieved rather than ascribed (as age and sex roles are), how do individuals decide to enter one rather than another occupational role? How are occupational roles learned? What are the personal and social consequences of performing one rather than another occupational role? How does the behavior expected in occupational roles conflict with behavior expected in other (e.g., familial) roles? How do individuals come to change occupational role expectations and how are they, in turn, changed by virtue of occupying a particular occupational role? These, of course, are questions that can be asked about any social role. Once we define occupations as roles, they can be analyzed as such.

WORK AS A LINK TO THE SOCIAL STRUCTURE

Another basic assumption made by sociologists who study occupations is that they provide a very fundamental link between individuals and the larger social structure. Except for a few occupations that are performed in isolation (e.g., a night security guard), most work involves interaction with the incumbents of other occupational roles on a regular basis. Occupational roles pattern the basic nature of a great deal of human interaction. They frequently specify the way in which people are supposed to behave in relation to others occupying similar, subordinate, or superordinate roles as well as the way they are supposed to deal with clients or customers. At another level, events far removed from the day-to-day experiences of people affect them through their work. Changes in the international price of gold, the prime interest rate, or the worldwide supply of petroleum have direct and indirect effects on individuals in their work. Occupational roles also link people to political and economic events occurring in national and international political and economic arenas. In other words, they connect our private lives with public events.

WORK AS A SOURCE OF IDENTITY

At a more social psychological level of analysis, occupational roles also are assumed to be a major source of personal identity. This is particularly true in advanced industrial societies such as the United States. Such societies have a high degree of geographic mobility and the nuclear family tends to be the typical family unit. The significance of this becomes evident in comparison to preindustrial societies in which locale and the extended family function as basic sources of identity. In hunting and gathering or agrarian societies work activities are age- and sex-graded and do not serve to differentiate individuals to a very great degree. In such societies, *where* one lives and the extended family of which one is a member define *who* one is. In advanced industrial societies locale becomes a comparatively weak source of identity. It can even be dysfunctional in the sense that geographic mobility may be necessary to take advantage of new employment opportunities. For example, it may be very difficult for a middle-level corporation executive in Boston to identify as a "New Englander" when moves to Dallas, Atlanta, and Denver are likely within the next ten years. Under conditions of high geographic mobility, family membership also becomes a less relevant source of identity. Consequently, the question "Who am I?" is increasingly likely to be answered in occupational terms. In addition, we often use the occupations of other people to identify them. In a preindustrial society two strangers might identify themselves to each other by indicating their village of residence or their location in a kinship network. In a modern industrial society two hypothetical strangers are more likely to "break the ice" by indicating the kind of work they do.

The theme of work as a source of personal identity is also very evident in recent discussions of the changing role of women in contemporary society. The movement of women into the labor force and their entry into traditionally male occupations is one of the most dramatic changes that has occurred in American society since World War II. The topic of women and work will be dealt with at length in chapter 7. At this point we simply want to note that analyses of working women give a great deal of attention to the issue of work as a source of personal identity.

Another illustration of the importance of work as a source of identity can be found in the characterization of late adolescence as a time when young people face a crisis of identity. While discussions of this topic have a heavily psychological and often psychoanalytic tenor, the core of the crisis usually boils down to the transitional and temporary nature of the roles (e.g., student, dependent child) in which young people find themselves. In other words, people in late adolescence, especially college students, are not in stable occupational roles that might serve as a source of personal identity. A lack of occupational identity is especially troublesome in the case of people who have acquired other marks of adulthood such as family roles (i.e., being married, having children). One consequence of increased formal educational requirements for entry into many occupations has been to place many young people "in limbo" between adolescence (a recognized and legitimate social role) and full adulthood (which typically includes the acquisition of an occupational role and an occupational identity).

WHY STUDY WORK? THE UBIQUITY OF WORK IN MODERN SOCIETY

The question posed in the heading of this section has been answered at least partially by the discussion up to this point: A substantial part of people's lives is spent in occupational activities; work serves to link individuals to others and to the broader social structure through work-patterned social interaction; and occupational roles are an important basis of personal identity.

In addition to these, there are several other important reasons for studying the work that people do. Many nonwork activities are directly and indirectly affected by work. It is this sense in which work is ubiquitous or all-pervasive. In one way or another it affects and is affected by a great many of the activities that make up the substance of social life.

One example of this is the fact that a person's occupation is a very good predictor of his or her nonwork life. A wide variety of attitudes, values, and behaviors are correlated with occupation, a topic to be dealt with in chapter 9. Thus, knowing a person's occupation tells us much more than just what the person does for a living. It is a key to understanding how people perceive, interpret, and react to others as well as their orientation to social institutions and public issues. To the extent that social science is concerned with the prediction of human behavior, occupation can be a key predictor variable.[3]

Another reason for being concerned with work is that many sociological concepts and theoretical issues can be and frequently are studied in the context of work. We have already indicated that the concept of *social role*, one of the basic building blocks of sociological analysis, is fundamental to the study of work since occupation is a particular kind of social role. Another distinctive concept of sociology, that of *social norm*, also can be examined within the context of work. For example, many work groups develop norms about how much work should be done in a given amount of time and how fast it should be done. Such norms become binding and individuals may be punished by their co-workers for violating them. Thus, basic mechanisms of *social control* can be studied in the workplace. Another important sociological concept is that of *socialization*. In chapter 4 we will deal with the topic of occupational socialization. The focus here will be on the learning of both roles and norms as a routine aspect of preparation for and working in an occupation. Occupational groups have distinctive subcultures with a variety of shared norms and values. Investigating how they emerge, are learned, and change can contribute to our understanding of the socialization process outside of as well as within the workplace.

Finally, the nonwork years of peoples' lives are affected by work in significant ways. In a sense, most formal schooling during childhood, adolescence, and even young adulthood is preparation for work. While educators debate the relative merits of a vocational versus a liberal arts education, the kind and amount of education people receive have significant effects on their later occupational achievements. Even in the post-work or retirement years, occupational ties may continue, for example, in the form of associations of people who have retired from a particular occupation, organization, or union. Furthermore, as we will see in chapter 9, retirement can be a stressful event to the extent that it involves withdrawal from an occupational role and the loss of an occupational identity. To restate an earlier point, work is such a pervasive phenomenon that to ignore it is to ignore much that is fundamental to life in modern society.

OCCUPATIONS AND OTHER TOPICS OF SOCIOLOGICAL STUDY: AREAS OF OVERLAP AND UNIQUENESS

The evolution of sociology as an academic discipline has resulted in the development of specialties that are the focus of a great deal of research and writing and which come to have their own distinctive literatures. Often the limits and boundaries of these specialties are not clear. While the core issues and literature of a specialty may be clear enough, the edges are blurred and there is considerable overlap with other specialties. This is unfortunate because it can be confusing to students who may find the same specific topic or issue being approached differently in courses and books dealing with different specialty areas. While unfortunate, this problem is probably unavoidable for several reasons including the autonomy of sociology (and other) teachers in structuring courses and deciding how particular topics will be covered. Sociologists have not reached complete consensus on where the boundaries of their specializations should be drawn, and it is not clear that such agreement is necessarily desirable. Perhaps most importantly, this dilemma also exists because the social world is more complex than the subdivisions of sociology would imply. Our specializations are, in effect, an imperfect attempt to impose some order on the vastness, diversity, and complexity of social behavior.

The sociology of occupations is one of those specialties that overlaps with several other specialties, particularly social stratification, industrial sociology, and complex organizations. Pointing out some of these overlaps and hazy areas may be useful as a way of providing a sense of what sociologists who study occupations are concerned with as well as indicating some of the connections between the sociology of occupations and other areas of sociological inquiry.

SOCIOLOGY OF OCCUPATIONS AND SOCIAL STRATIFICATION

The study of *social stratification* is concerned mainly with the arrangement of societies into "hierarchies of positions or strata that command unequal amounts of property, power and honor."[4] It is synonymous with the study of *social inequality* and is often also referred to as the study of *social class*. There are a number of ways in which the sociology of occupations and social stratification overlap.

Occupation, either by itself or in combination with other indicators like education or income, is the most commonly used indicator of position in the stratification system, and when we deal with prestige, the focus is invariably on occupational prestige. Occupation has come to be used extensively in the analysis of stratification for a number of reasons. It is positively correlated with income and educational attainment, both of which are important bases of stratification. Occupation also has a more stable meaning over time than either income or education. The popularity of occupation as an indicator of class position also is due to the fact that information about occupation is readily available and accessible. Social mobility (movement from one to another level of the stratification system over time) is a major topic within the field of social stratification. In studies of mobility the usual strategy is to compare the occupations of people with the occupations of their parents to see how far they have "moved" in a generation. Thus, social mobility has become virtually synonymous with occupational mobility.[5]

SOCIOLOGY OF OCCUPATIONS AND INDUSTRIAL SOCIOLOGY

Industrial sociology is generally concerned with the analysis of the social structure of modern forms of large-scale industrial production. It deals with the way in which the industrial mode of producing goods and delivering services evolved from earlier forms (e.g., the guild system) as well as its continuing evolution as a result of technological innovations such as automation, computerization, and robotics. Industrial sociology also is concerned with the way in which industrialism *as a social system* has shaped and continues to shape other social institutions such as the family and religion, as well as the organization of communities and their political power structures. Relations between management and organized labor as well as problems of coordination and decision making in large work organizations fall within the scope of industrial sociology.

Another distinctive feature of industrial sociology is a matter of perspective. This specialty is usually applied, and has often reflected managerial concerns and problems rather than taking a disinterested view of work.

Industrialism as a way of organizing work has directly or indirectly affected most work activities in advanced industrial societies. Most employed persons are employed by organizations that essentially are modeled after industrial forms of organization. Consequently, the field of industrial sociology has a great deal to offer regardless of the particular perspective taken on the analysis of work.

One difference between industrial sociology and the sociology of occupations is the focus of industrial sociology on the *structure of work organizations* and the conceptualization of industrialism as a social system. Another way of drawing the contrast would be to say that industrial sociology focuses primarily on macrolevel issues while the sociology of occupations places more emphasis on microlevel issues (e.g., socialization, worker-client relationships). Another distinction is that industrial sociologists tend to focus most of their interests on such activities as manufacturing and related support activities including the production of raw materials, transportation, and the distribution of manufactured goods. In the sociology of occupations, a fuller range of work activities (including but not limited to those of industrial sociology) are typically dealt with.

As a specialty within sociology, industrial sociology is changing and will continue to do so. It will be affected by the fact that manufacturing and goods-producing industries are becoming a less important part of the American economy compared to service industries (a topic covered in chapter 10).[6] In many respects the boundary between the sociology of occupations and industrial sociology has become quite blurred. Sociologists who have been identified with both traditions are increasingly dealing with similar questions about the nature of work regardless of whether it is performed in an industrial or nonindustrial context.[7]

SOCIOLOGY OF OCCUPATIONS AND COMPLEX ORGANIZATIONS

To complicate the picture even more, virtually all work organizations that are of interest to industrial sociologists are what we usually refer to as *complex organizations* or bureaucracies. The increasing bureaucratization of work activities means that degree of bureaucratization is a major variable that must at some point be taken into account by the sociologist studying any kind of work.

At the same time, the study of complex organizations has developed into a distinct specialty in its own right. Here the interest is on the sources, degree, and consequences of bureaucratization in a wide range of activities including but extending well beyond just work activities. Thus, the organizational sociologist is interested in the organizational structure of churches, schools and universities, the military, hospitals, government agencies, etc. The main concern is with the organization regardless of the kind of activity going on within it.

Consequently, within the study of complex organizations, the primary emphasis is *on the organization;* the organization is the basic unit of analysis. From the perspective of the sociology of occupations, the occupation is the basic unit. The sociologist of occupations might regard occupations as the key variable to study and see the organization as an important parameter that shapes the way in which occupational roles are performed. On the other hand, the organizational sociologist might be interested in the way in which the occupational composition of an organization is related to the organization's ability to achieve its goals, adapt to a changing environment, resolve conflicts, etc.

Diagram 1.1 is intended to summarize and aid in clarifying the relationships between the sociology of occupations and the other specialties discussed above. Given these relationships and the overlapping nature of these fields, it should be apparent that there is a good deal of arbitrariness and latitude in deciding what does and what does not fall within the scope of the sociology of occupations. In the following section the rationale for the topics included in the remainder of the book is presented. Since some necessarily arbitrary decisions have been made, an effort will be made to point them out rather than leaving them as riddles for the reader to solve.

PLAN OF THE BOOK

Organizing a presentation on the sociology of occupations and professions requires some complex decisions. The occupations at which people work number in the thousands. We are faced with an overabundance of occupational information and behavior that is of potential interest. We could proceed by describing all the different kinds of work that people do. Such an undertaking would probably prove unrewarding, as well as exhausting, since we would end up with a very long list of largely unconnected descriptions of occupations, work activities, and responses to work. This descriptive task has in fact already been done by the U.S. Department of Labor which has compiled a *Dictionary of Occupational Titles* (DOT). In the most recent edition, published in 1977, 28,801 occupational titles were listed.[8]

In studying occupations we face a problem all too common in the social sciences. It is necessary that we *abstract* recurring patterns from the total universe of (in this case occupational) behavior. In a sense, the term "sociology of occupations" is a misnomer since we cannot deal with *every* aspect of *all* occupations. Rather, we are interested in selected aspects of occupations and occupational behavior. Particular *concepts* serve as the guide for selecting some and ignoring other occupational phenomena.

One task is to identify a strategy for organizing the issues, information, and research that fall within the scope of the sociology of occupations. One possibility would be to use the more or less "official" occupational categories used by the U.S. Bureau of the Census and the U.S. Department of Labor for presenting occupational information from the decennial census. For the 1980 Census, the following broad cate-

Diagram 1.1
Relationships and Overlaps Between Social Stratification, the Sociology of
Occupations, Industrial Sociology, and Complex Organizations

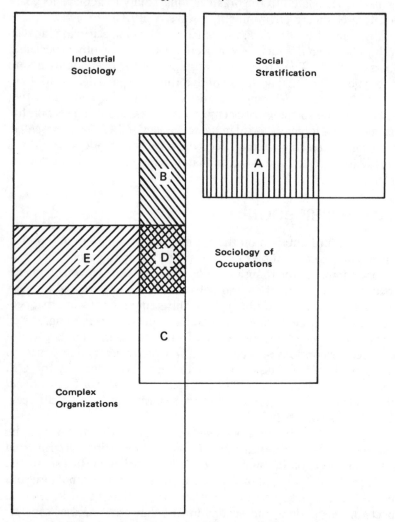

A = Problems common to sociology of occupations and social stratification.
B = Problems common to sociology of occupations and industrial sociology.
C = Problems common to sociology of occupations and complex organizations.
D = Problems common to sociology of occupations, industrial sociology, and complex organizations.
E = Problems common to industrial sociology and complex organizations.

gories, referred to as the Standard Occupational Classification (SOC) system, were used to classify occupations:

1. managerial and professional
2. technical, sales, and administrative support
3. service occupations
4. farming, forestry, and fishing
5. precision production, craft, and repair
6. operators, fabricators, and laborers

Occupational information from earlier Censuses (1940–1970) was reported using a set of categories representing a skill and status hierarchy:

1. professional, technical, and kindred workers
2. managers and administrators, except farm
3. sales workers
4. clerical and kindred workers
5. craft and kindred workers
6. operatives, except transport
7. transport equipment operatives
8. laborers, except farm
9. farmers and farm managers
10. farm laborers and supervisors
11. service workers, except private household
12. private household workers

While much descriptive material could be presented within the categories of either of these schemes, it would give us a rather static picture of occupational behavior. The fact that the categories for classifying occupations changed with the 1980 census requires special attention. Throughout this book, where national data on occupations are presented, the new (1980 census) categories are used whenever possible. However, some government reports issued in the early 1980s use the old categories and these are presented in the book when they can help to illustrate a particular point. National data collected prior to 1980 of course use the old system.

In this book we have chosen an organization that emphasizes *processes* that occur in all segments of the occupational structure. The focus of part 1 will be on processes that crosscut both of the census occupational classification systems presented above.

Part 1 consists of four chapters. Our first concern (chapter 2) will be the development of models for looking at the professions and the processes of professionalization and deprofessionalization. Our concern here is with understanding the sources of occupational differentiation, the motivations and strategies used by occupational groups in the quest for power and prestige in the workplace, and the consequences of achieving or failing to achieve collective power and prestige. While the emphasis here is on the professions, this chapter has implications for nonprofessional occupations, many of which have attempted to imitate the professions. The quest for power and control in the workplace occurs throughout the occupational structure and is very apparent in the case of the professions.

Chapter 3 deals with the process of occupational choice. From the perspective of individuals, occupational choice is basically a decision-making process. However, from a societal perspective, it is simultaneously a process for allocating persons to occupational roles. Our task here will be to examine a variety of theories and models that have been developed for explaining how the process of occupational choice occurs. Since educational decisions have implications for access to occupations, these too must command our attention. Again, we will want to look at the choice process across a broad spectrum of occupations.

Occupational socialization is another process that occurs in all work activities. In chapter 4 our attention will be on the ways in which occupational roles and norms are learned both during the period of preparation for entry into an occupation and in the actual performance of the occupation. Our assumption is that all occupations have a subculture to which their members are socialized. Teachers, colleagues, work groups, and organizations all are agents of socialization that shape individuals' perceptions and understandings of their work roles.

Occupational career processes are another normal and routine aspect of all work activities; these are covered in chapter 5. We will deal mainly with career mobility that involves increases and decreases in occupational status as well as changes in the types of work that people do. Earlier we noted that the study of social mobility is an important part of the field of social stratification. In chapter 5 the focus will be on mobility as it occurs over the occupational lifetimes of individuals and groups rather than occupational mobility between generations.

In part 2 the focus on processes recedes into the background and our emphasis is on occupational issues that are both traditional and contemporary concerns of sociologists who study occupations. However, part 2 continues the theme of examining these issues throughout the occupational structure as much as possible.

In chapter 6 we deal with the variety and diversity of settings, contexts, and environments in which work occurs. Of special interest here are the consequences of industrialization, technological changes, and bureaucratization. These features of the workplace have far-reaching implications for how people work, where they work, and how satisfied or dissatisfied they are with their work. When we take a long-term perspective, it becomes evident that one of the key changes that has occurred in work is increased specialization. Specialization in turn has created problems of coordination and control. The response to this has been the increased bureaucratization of work activities with an emphasis on rules, procedures, close supervision, and a resulting depersonalization of work. Industrialization, specialization, and bureaucratization will be discussed as features of work that define and shape the settings in which people work.

Women and work is the topic of chapter 7. The recent large-scale entry of women into the labor force has a variety of implications for the structure and organization of work activities as well as for the position of women in society. A major concern in this chapter will be the sex segregation of occupations, the sex stereotyping of occupations, and the distinctive career problems of women. We will also deal with the issues of equal opportunity and pay equity.

The position of minority groups in American society is strongly affected by their access to educational and occupational opportunities. In chapter 8 we deal with the occupational position of black Americans, Mexican-Americans, and Asian-Americans. The discussion here will deal with the historical position of these groups in the labor force, various efforts to exclude them from participation in the more rewarding occupations, and their current occupational status.

Chapter 9 deals with the impact of occupation on the nonwork lives of people. Our assumption is that occupational subcultures shape a wide variety of attitudes, beliefs, and behaviors. Occupational participation affects the life-styles of people as well as their life chances. We will be concerned with the effect of work on family life as well as its relationship to such things as longevity, health, divorce, political behavior, and religiosity.

Leisure, another topic dealt with in chapter 9, is often viewed as the opposite of work. Yet, work and leisure are interrelated. We will deal with the meaning of work and leisure, and the way in which the "work ethic" has shaped our perspective on leisure, and the way in which the kinds of work people do affect their leisure behavior.

Chapter 9 also covers the subject of retirement. Although retirement represents the end of work, the way in which it is experienced varies from one occupation to another. Here we will be concerned with this variation.

The final chapter of the book, chapter 10, deals with a number of occupational trends and their implications for the future. Here we will look at basic changes occurring in the American labor force. More specifically, we will focus on the way in which different industries and occupations will be expanding and declining in the years ahead, and some of the reasons for particular patterns of growth and decline.

NOTES

1. For an overview of the psychological approach to work see Walter S. Neff, *Work and Human Behavior*, 3rd ed. (New York: Aldine, 1985).
2. Adriano Tilgher, *Homo Faber: Work Through the Ages* (New York: Harcourt, Brace, and World, 1930).
3. The term prediction is potentially confusing and troublesome because it implies the control of human behavior. A better way of describing this objective would be to talk about making accurate probability statements about behavior. For example, suppose that we found that 90 percent of all women who complete college end up in white-collar occupations. We would then be in a position to predict that there is a .90 probability that women who complete college will end up in white-collar occupations and that there is a .10 probability that those who complete college will end up in other kinds of occupations. Statements of this kind are a far cry from detailed predictions of minute aspects of people's behavior. It would be more accurate to say that sociology is a probabilistic rather than a predicting science.
4. Melvin M. Tumin, *Social Stratification: The Forms and Functions of Inequality*, 2nd ed. (Englewood Cliffs, N.J.: Prentice-Hall, 1985), 1.
5. One of the landmark studies of social mobility in the United States conveys this equation of social and occupational mobility in its very title. See Peter M. Blau and Otis Dudley Duncan, *The American Occupational Structure* (New York: Wiley, 1967).
6. For an informative exchange between four sociologists on the problem of boundaries between industrial sociology and other specialties, see Delbert C. Miller, "Whatever Will Happen to Industrial Sociology," *Sociological Quarterly* 25 (Spring 1984): 251–256; Curt Tausky, "Where is Industrial Sociology Headed?" *Sociological Quarterly* 25 (Spring 1984): 257–260; Eugene V. Schneider, "A Note on Delbert C. Miller's Paper: 'Whatever Will Happen to Industrial Sociology,' "*Sociological Quarterly* 25 (Spring 1984): 261–265; and Charles K. Warriner, "Response to Miller on Industrial Sociology," *Sociological Quarterly* 25 (Spring 1984): 267–271.
7. Robert A. Rothman, *Working: Sociological Perspectives* (Englewood Cliffs, N.J.: Prentice-Hall, 1987), chapter 1.
8. U.S. Department of Labor, *Dictionary of Occupational Titles*, 4th ed. Washington, D.C.: U.S. Government Printing Office, 1977). See also Pamela S. Cain and Donald J. Treiman, "The *Dictionary of Occupational Titles* as a Source of Occupational Data," *American Sociological Review* 46 (June 1981): 253–278.

PART ONE

CHAPTER 2

Models for Studying
the Professions

ONE OF THE most fundamental issues in the sociology of occupations involves the question of how those occupations commonly known as the professions should be studied and interpreted. As we will see, a great deal of controversy has developed over the appropriate answer to this question. However, the analysis of the professions is further complicated by the fact that the terms *profession* and *professional* have a multitude of meanings as they are commonly used in everyday language. By and large, popular usages make invidious distinctions and evaluations of work activities, work groups, and individuals. By looking at popular usages, we are acknowledging that the terms "profession" and "professional" can be thought of as *folk concepts* as well as sociological concepts. In other words, we can ask what the term means to people as they apply it to their own work or to others and their work. After looking at these meanings it will be apparent that the way sociologists use these terms is quite different.

POPULAR MEANINGS OF THE
CONCEPT OF PROFESSION

PROFESSION AS PRESTIGE

In popular usage, the term "profession" is frequently used to convey prestige, respect, and a positive evaluation. To refer to a particular kind

17

of work as a profession is to accord it dignity. To refer to an individual as a professional is to accord him or her a high degree of prestige. This should not be surprising. Some work groups clearly have succeeded in getting their claims to be professions accepted by broad segments of the public. While people may have negative experiences with individual professionals, and good reason to question their lofty claims, the mystique of the professions is nevertheless firmly entrenched as part of the public consciousness and is frequently reflected in the way work is described.

PROFESSION AS FULL-TIME ACTIVITY

The terms "profession" and "professional" are also used to refer to full-time performance of an activity for pay in contrast to engaging in the activity on a part-time basis, as a recreational activity, or without pay. This usage occurs frequently in two areas of entertainment—sports and the theater. For example, people who earn their livings playing games refer to themselves (and are referred to by others) as professional football, baseball, and basketball players, golfers, bowlers, etc. Similarly, actors and actresses are referred to as professionals to distinguish them from *amateurs* who may act solely for their own enjoyment or the enjoyment of others without financial compensation.[1] This usage is not limited to conventional occupations. It also occurs with deviant and illegal activities. Examples would be the use of such terms as professional gambler, professional thief, and professional call girl.

PROFESSION AS COMPETENCE

When people want to convey the idea that they or someone else has great skill or proficiency at performing some task, the term "professional" will often be used. Thus when someone is referred to as a professional mechanic the idea conveyed is that the person knows the trade and is good at the job. Advertisements that promise services of a professional caliber (e.g., professional dry cleaning, professional hairstyling, etc.) are saying, "We know our jobs; we're good and skilled at what we do." Businesses that advertise in this way are attempting to capitalize on popular understandings of the meaning of the term "professional" and turn them to their own commercial advantage. The intent of such claims is to create a sense of confidence and trust among potential customers.

UNPROFESSIONAL AS INSULT

To appreciate this usage it is necessary to switch gears and think of the use of negative prefixes such as *un* and *non* in connection with the words profession and professional. The use of these terms is a form of name-calling. It is a way of insulting a person by raising questions about his or her competence, judgement, commitment, or ethics. To call people unprofessional is to negatively evaluate them and their work, disparage their efforts or lack of accomplishment, or challenge them to change their behavior. It is also a way of putting someone down and, as such, becomes a weapon in struggles for power, control, and advantage. Nicholas Alex's study of black policemen illustrates this. When black policemen said that their white colleagues were not professional, they regarded this as the most critical and negative thing that they could say about them.[2]

THE ATTRIBUTE MODEL: IDENTIFYING THE TRAITS OF THE PROFESSIONS

From its beginnings in the 1930s through the 1960s, the sociological study of the professions was dominated by what has come to be known as the *attribute model*. During the 1970s, several important critiques of the model appeared. Critics challenged its assumptions, the political use of the model by occupational groups, and the kinds of questions to which the model directed inquiry and those that it ignored. The result has been the development of what we will call the *process model*. The process model has come to dominate current thinking about the professions. However, it developed in response to the shortcomings of the attribute model. Consequently, its insights and implications cannot be fully appreciated without first understanding the nature of the attribute model.

The main feature of the attribute model is the effort to identify attributes or traits that can be used to distinguish professions from other kinds of occupations. Sometimes the model is also referred to as a "taxonomy" since it has been used to classify work activities as more or less professional. Sociologists whose work has contributed to the development of this model have asked questions such as: "What is distinctive and different about the professions?" "What do the professions have that other occupations don't have?" An extensive body of literature on the characteristics of the professions has developed in response to these and similar questions. This research and writing include a wide variety of material. It ranges from historical analyses of the development of particular work groups to case studies and surveys of the status and organization of various work activities. Our task here is to identify and summarize the main recurring themes in this literature.

Models of the kind we are developing here are often referred to as *ideal types*. They take some characteristic of a social phenomenon and present it in an exaggerated and extreme form in order to emphasize its significance or to compare it with something else. In model building of this sort, there is always the possibility and danger of misinterpretation. A description of features of the model is sometimes interpreted as an evaluation or advocacy of those features. As we will see, some of the criticisms by proponents of the process model result from this problem. Central to the attribute model is the notion that differences between professions and other occupations are a matter of degree, not a matter of kind. In other words, the professions are seen as quantitatively, not qualitatively, different from other kinds of work groups. Rather, each characteristic of the model should be thought of as a continuum, a scale ranging between two extremes.

DIMENSIONS OF THE MODEL

The attributes and lists of traits that have been used to differentiate professions from other kinds of occupations vary from one author to another. Here, we have summarized and codified these traits under eight major categories or dimensions.[3]

Theory and Intellectual Technique

Theory and intellectual technique comprise one dimension; they refer to the degree to which there is a systematic body of theoretical, abstract, esoteric knowledge on which an occupation is based. According to the attribute model, a profession is an occupation that has developed a complex *knowledge base* that serves as the basis of its members' claim to special expertise. If the professional is an expert it is because this knowledge base has been mastered. Often, but not always, the knowledge base is the product of scientific research. Medicine is a good example of this. It is based on the theory and research of the scientific disciplines of anatomy, biology, neurology, chemistry, etc. The knowledge base of work groups at the profession end of the continuum need not always be scientific, however. For example, the practice of law is based on a highly elaborate and certainly esoteric body of knowledge. But it is hardly scientific. Rather, it is an arbitrary and changing system of rules, customs, and interpretations that are normative and prescriptive, not scientific.[4] Similarly, the work of the clergy, regardless of denomination, is based on an elaborate body of nonscientific rituals, folklore, beliefs, and rules that are also quite normative. Nevertheless, the existence of a sophisticated body of knowledge lies at the heart of the professional's claim to special competence.

　This dimension of the model does not imply that work groups at the opposite end of the continuum are lacking in knowledge or that their knowledge is in some manner inferior. Clearly, all work is based on knowledge of some kind. What the model emphasizes is differences in the *degree* of complexity and elaborateness, and variation between work groups in how abstract and sophisticated the knowledge base is.

Relevance to Social Values

Another characteristic of work is its relationship to important values of a society. In the attribute model, the work of the professions is seen as strongly related to the realization of those values. The extent to which this occurs is seen as a factor that distinguishes professions from other work groups. For example, the relationship of law and medicine to such basic values as justice and health, respectively, would contribute to their stature as professions. While it may be difficult to determine precisely what constitutes a society's basic values, the point is that there is a tendency for work groups to seek their justification in terms of abstract values. The professions claim that their work activities are designed to maximize the realization of such values. One issue here is whether such values exist and the professions develop to meet them, or whether work groups claiming professional status define what those values should be and manipulate them to their own advantage. In other words, professionals have the power to define the society's and their clients' needs in ways that serve their claim to legitimacy and special privilege.[5]

The issue of work and societal values is also involved in how the knowledge and services of a work group get applied to crucial, recurring human problems. Professionals are turned to in times of crisis because it is assumed that they have certain expertise and competencies not available to the layperson and that these competencies can be applied to the solution to those problems. The physician, as one who applies knowledge to the solution of problems that threaten physical well-being and life itself, illustrates this idea. When our property or freedom is threatened by legal action, we may seek the services of a lawyer. In a crisis situation, such as the death of a loved one, we may turn to a clergyperson on the assumption that he or she has the expertise to provide insight, understanding, and solace in a time of trauma.

This aspect of the model is not without its difficulties, however. Given the high degree of occupational specialization that exists in contemporary industrial and postindustrial societies, it can be argued that everyone is dependent on a wide range of occupational experts for the satisfaction of their wants and needs. It is by no means clear which kinds of expertise are most crucial and which can serve to distinguish the professional from others. If I wake up with a toothache and a car that won't run, I desperately need the services of two specialists. Which one is most crucial and should be considered a professional is far from clear. In fact, in this contrived example, the services of the mechanic may be more necessary because without them I won't be able to get to the dentist. On this dimension the attribute model leaves us with the somewhat imprecise notion that work at the professional end of the continuum is that which has the greatest applicability to the most intense crises that people face.

The Training Period

Clearly, all types of work involve training of some kind. This aspect of the attribute model consists of four interrelated but distinct subdimensions. These are the *amount* of training involved, the extent to which it is *specialized,* the degree to which it is symbolic and *ideational,* and the *content* of what is learned during the training period.

Amount of Training. The length of the training period required for entry varies considerably from one occupation to another. According to the model, the greater the amount of training involved, the further toward the professional end of the continuum the work belongs. A major dilemma here revolves around the issue of how much training is essential and how much is contrived. Work groups such as law and medicine claim that long training is necessary in order to assure that the complex knowledge base has been thoroughly mastered. Groups seeking to increase the length of their training period argue that the development of new knowledge and techniques makes it necessary to increase the amount of time spent in training. When such claims are made it is difficult if not impossible to determine how much training is essential for mastery of the relevant knowledge. While educational requirements for occupational entry have increased across the board in recent years, it is by no means clear that this is due to an increase in the knowledge that is needed to practice the occupation.[6]

Specialized Knowledge. According to the attribute model, the extent to which the knowledge required for a particular work activity is specialized is another factor that distinguishes professions from nonprofessions. As we have already pointed out, the occupational structure of contemporary industrial and postindustrial societies reveals a high degree of specialization in all areas of work. Since specialization is so extensive, it is tempting to question the utility or importance of this factor. While specialization may be widespread, the *degree* of specialization in training varies. Specialized knowledge does not stand as an isolated factor. Training at the profession end of the continuum also includes the transmission of abstract and esoteric specialized knowledge.

The Ideational Aspect of Training. Training for work at the professional end of the continuum is seen as strongly ideational and conceptual. There is an emphasis on the importance of mastering the ability to manipulate ideas, symbols, concepts, and principles rather than things and physical objects. Again, the inclusion of this aspect of the model poses difficulties. No work is completely nonideational and none is completely ideational. While a carpenter's work involves mainly the manipulation of things (tools, materials), there are concepts and principles of which one must be aware if the work is to be performed properly. Similarly, the training of physicians and dentists stresses the learning of theories, concepts, and principles. Still, a variety of manual skills and the ability to manipulate machines are also emphasized. The important point is the *degree* to which training is ideational. At the professional end of the continuum there is a primary and extensive emphasis on immersing the would-be member of the occupation in the concepts, principles, and ideas of the field.

The Content of Training. All work involves the acquisition of particular skills and knowledge. The notion here is that professional work involves something more. It involves the learning of an *occupational subculture.* This includes the learning of a distinctive set of values, norms, and beliefs peculiar to the occupation. The attribute model stresses the idea that training for the professions involves the learning of values, norms, and beliefs that are more elaborate and complex than is the case for nonprofessional work. Also, it is assumed that in the professions, the learning of the occupational subculture is seen as more important to workgroup members than it is elsewhere in the occupational structure. Just how useful this aspect of the training period is in distinguishing the professions from other work groups is open to question. Chapter 4, "Occupational Socialization," deals with this topic. As we will see, *all* occupational groups have distinctive subcultures and the training of neophytes includes immersion in them.

Motivation

This dimension of the attribute model involves the contrasting of service and self-interest as motivations for work. The focus here is not on identifying what really motivates people to work. Rather, the concern is the degree to which work groups emphasize the ideal of service to clients and the public as their *primary* objective and as one of the values of the occupational subculture. Also important is the degree to which this claim is at least tacitly accepted by clients and the public. The assumption is that members of work groups at the professional end of the continuum are motivated by the desire to best serve their clients rather than by self-interest and the desire for monetary gain. The latter are seen as distinctly secondary. This difference in orientation is reflected in the restrictions that exist in the subcultures of various work groups against actively seeking out clients. While the norm may be violated, the predominant belief is that the client should take the initiative in seeking out the professional rather than the other way around. The prohibitions against advertising that existed until quite recently among lawyers, physicians, and dentists also illustrate this principle.

This service orientation is linked to other dimensions of the model that already have been identified. People go to professionals in crisis situations because they need their expertise. This puts them in a vulnerable and dependent position vis-a-vis the professional. The belief that the professional has the client's best interest at heart (rather than his or her own self-interest) may create a sense of trust essential to the maintenance of a viable relationship between practitioner and client. Since the client is usually not in a good position to judge how good the professional's advice is, the belief that the professional has the client's best interests at heart may become crucial in determining the credibility of that advice and the likelihood that the client will follow it. At the same time, when clients accept the professional's claim to be motivated solely by service, the professional gains a great deal of power over the client. Under such circumstances it becomes extremely difficult to separate those actions that are self-serving from those that serve the client's needs in the most thorough and competent manner.

The polar opposite of the service motivation is found in business occupations. In the business world a premium is placed on seeking and maintaining customers. Client seeking on the part of the businessperson is expected. It is also clear that the motive for work in business activities is monetary gain and profit. The relationship betwen businessperson and customer is one in which the principle of *caveat emptor* (let the buyer beware) prevails. We enter such relationships assuming that the businessperson is primarily concerned with maximizing monetary gain and that our interests are secondary.

The service orientation has overtones of dedication to lofty principles and ideals. People who enter the clergy often say that they have been "called" to their work or will simply refer to their work as a "calling." By this they mean that they have been called by the deity to enter this work. To a lesser extent and in a somewhat diluted manner this perspective pervades the ideology of other work groups at the professional end of the continuum.[7] The claim of a service motivation need not lead to similar work behavior in all professions. For example, in some branches of the clergy vows of poverty are taken as a symbolic demonstration of the renunciation of worldly, and especially monetary, concerns. The implication is that this gives evidence of one's devotion to serving one's clients. However, in fields like law and medicine, which also claim a service motivation, the argument is made that high incomes are necessary so that a concern with money will not interfere with serving clients in the best possible manner. In addition to being circular, this argument is obviously self-serving.

It is easy and appropriate to be skeptical if not cynical about the sincerity of such claims to a lack of self-interest and a commitment to service. Work groups at the professional end of the continuum are, after all, among the most highly remunerated occupations; they are accorded great prestige; and they exercise considerable power. Critics of this model have argued that the claim to a service motivation is a device that gives professionals control over clients and insulates them from accountability for their actions and their fees. In other words, the claim to a service motivation may be used by professionals to serve their own monetary self-interest. We will return to this issue later in discussing the process model.

Autonomy

Of all the dimensions that make up the attribute model, autonomy is perhaps the most crucial in differentiating work groups. As we will see later, it is also a key factor in stimulating the development of the process model. Autonomy, self-regulation, and self-control are all synonyms for the freedom and power of work groups to regulate their own work behavior and working conditions. As both a sentiment and a structural fact, autonomy is seen as a feature of work at the professional end of the continuum. However, there is variation in the amount of autonomy that work groups and individuals actually have and the extent to which it is a matter of collective concern.

Autonomy is expressed in two distinct but related ways: at the level of the work group and at the individual level. As organized collectivities, work groups seek to control matters of general interest and concern to their members. They may be concerned with specifying and guarding the boundaries of their special sphere of activity or competence. Only those properly schooled in the knowledge and skill of the profession are defined as competent to judge what is and what is not adequate work performance, what fees are appropriate, who is and who is not qualified to practice, etc. Consequently, a great deal of emphasis is placed on maintaining control over access to the profession. This control, in the case of medicine, law, dentistry, nursing, and many other occupations, is often located in legal codes which make it illegal to practice without proper certification or licensing. Certifying and licensing agencies, while ostensibly designed to represent the public interest, are actually private bodies staffed by members of the profession or by persons approved by the profession. The result of this is to add the power of the state to the profession's claim to autonomy.

In addition to collective autonomy, concern with autonomy in the day-to-day work of the individual practitioner is a feature of work at the professional end of the continuum. This concern is expressed, for example, in resistance to supervision, especially supervision by persons from outside the profession. The principle involved here is that the professional's specialized competence makes it appropriate for only those with similar training or competence to judge the quality of the professional's work. Outsiders are seen as unqualified and incapable of making appropriate evaluations. Professionals argue that they provide a nonstandardized service tailored to the unique needs of the client and that they must be given the autonomy to make decisions based on what they believe to be the best course of action. The emphasis on autonomy is also partially responsible for the reluctance of professionals to criticize one another publicly. Rather, they prefer to deal privately with members who may deviate from approved ways of doing things. The principle of autonomy includes the claim that the work group, not outsiders, should control its members.

To the extent that a profession is successful in achieving a high degree of autonomy, it also establishes a *monopoly* over training, the right to perform particular work activities, and the conditions under which work will be performed. The ability to manipulate supply and demand also leads to the ability to determine the fees that will be received for various services. While some skilled trades have achieved a degree of monopoly over who can and cannot practice a particular occupation through such mechanisms as the union shop and local building ordinances, it is substantially less than that of the professions where legal sanctions and severe penalties may be imposed by the state.

Commitment

This dimension of the model involves the kinds of sentiments that people are assumed to have toward their work. At one extreme work may be viewed as a "calling" and approached with an almost religious sense of mission. Membership in the occupation is supposed to be taken very seriously and commitment is assumed to be very strong. Closely related to this is the notion that the commitment to the work is a long-term if not lifelong one. Perhaps the best illustration of this orientation can be found among the clergy, especially the Catholic priesthood. It is assumed that people who enter this occupation will remain in it for their entire lives. The importance of this dimension of the model can be seen in the reaction of members of a work group to the departure or potential departure of a colleague. Among work groups that regard a sense of commit-ment as important, the person who leaves is viewed as a defector or traitor who brings shame and embarrassment to the entire work group. Such departures are viewed as a problem not because they reduce the size of the work group but because they are a potential threat to public and client confidence in the commitment, sincerity, and dedication of the work group as a whole. Consequently, they may threaten the ability of the work group to retain control over how it performs its work activities.

At the other extreme of this dimension there is an absence of a sense of calling and no assumption of a long-term commitment. Work is seen as a means to an end rather than an end in itself. Movement into and out of the occupation may be a common pattern. Even where an occu-pation has a high degree of stability and little turnover, the prevailing attitude is that leaving it for some other type of work is appropriate, or even desirable. Most blue-collar, manual occupations and white-collar, clerical, and managerial occupations exhibit this orientation rather than the assumption of a long-term commitment. As with other dimensions of the model, these sentiments and concerns are rarely found in the stark extremes presented here. Their presence or absence is always a matter of degree.

Sense of Community

Another dimension of the model is the degree to which work groups ex-hibit the characteristics of a community. This is closely related to other dimensions and, as we will see, overlaps and incorporates some of them in certain ways. Still, this aspect of work has received considerable at-tention and needs to be included as a separate dimension. At the heart of the idea of an occupational community is the presence of a sense of *common identity* and *common destiny*. It also includes the idea that oc-cupational groups have distinctive subcultures. The shared norms and values of the subculture serve to reinforce a sense of common identity as well as to control the behavior of members. While these norms operate primarily to shape and control work behavior, they may also extend to nonwork life as well and influence choice of leisure time activities, po-litical orientations, and a wide range of interpersonal relationships.

The concept of an occupational community has been developed by William Goode. According to Goode, there are several features of such communities. Members share and are bound together by a common sense of identity, they share common values (i.e., a subculture), and once peo-ple are in the community few leave it (i.e., there is a strong sense of com-mitment). In addition, the community develops role definitions for members and nonmembers as well as a common language that serves to set members apart from nonmembers. The community is of course a social entity rather than one that exists in spatial and geographic terms. The community has and exercises control over its members. It also produces the next generation by controlling the recruitment and selection of new members and socializing them through its training process. Thus, the occupational community serves as a reference group for its members.[8]

While all occupational groups have some of these features, the attribute model sees them as most fully developed at the profession end of the continuum. At the other extreme, there is less of a sense of identity with others in the same occupation and the occupational culture is more rudimentary and less capable of exerting normative control over the behavior of members.

Codes of Ethics

A final feature of the attribute model is its emphasis on the existence of codes of ethics as a factor that differentiates work groups from one another. Ethical codes may be written or unwritten and may cover a wide range of work issues including practitioner-client and practitioner-public relations, relations among practitioners, and relations between the practitioner and members of other work groups. In a sense, codes of ethics are a system of norms that are part of the occupational subculture noted earlier. While all occupational groups have norms that apply to various aspects of their members' conduct, the norms tend to vary in terms of how elaborate and complex they are, the kinds of behavior they deal with, public awareness of them, and their enforceability. According to the model, elaborate, written codes of ethics tend to be found among work groups at the profession end of the continuum more often than they are at the opposite end. It cannot be emphasized too strongly that this does *not* mean that professionals are more honest, trustworthy, or ethical than members of other work groups. The extent to which complex, written, publicized codes of ethics actually result in ethical behavior on the part of practitioners is an empirical question. There is no evidence to support the conclusion that the existence of codes of ethics among professionals necessarily results in more ethical conduct.

The existence of codes of ethics does tend to reinforce some of the other dimensions of the model, however. For example, the existence of a high degree of specialization means that the professional has power over clients who may be unable to accurately assess the quality of the services rendered. Under such conditions, codes of ethics may be used to reassure the client and the public that a high-quality service is being rendered. Regardless of the actual quality of the service, the existence of codes of ethics may create the belief that the work group will accept

Diagram 2.1
The Nonprofession–Profession Continuum

Dimensions	Nonprofession	Profession
1. Theory, intellectual technique	Absent	Present
2. Relevance to social values	Not relevant	Relevant
3. Training period A	Short	Long
B	Nonspecialized	Specialized
C	Involves things	Involves symbols
D	Subculture not important	Subculture important
4. Motivation	Self-interest	Service
5. Autonomy	Absent	Present
6. Commitment	Short term	Long term
7. Sense of community	Weak	Strong
8. Codes of ethics	Undeveloped	Developed

or tolerate nothing but the best from its members. Codes of ethics also reinforce the service ideal by emphasizing that the practitioner's concern is the client's welfare. Codes of ethics also bolster the work group's claim to autonomy. The argument is that codes of ethics produce effective self-regulation and that external control is unnecessary, inappropriate, and wasteful.

The dimensions of the attribute model are summarized in outline form in diagram 2.1. It should be emphasized again that the model is a heuristic device rather than a description of actual work groups. A work activity exhibiting all these characteristics to a very high degree does not exist, and there is no work activity in which all of these characteristics are entirely absent. In reality, work groups have these characteristics in varying degrees. Before turning to the process model, one final point needs to be made regarding the attribute model. There is no logical or a priori way of determining the relative importance of these dimensions. Various writers have stressed the importance of some and de-emphasized others. Contributors to the development of the attribute model never have settled the question of which (if any) dimensions are *necessary* and which may be *sufficient* conditions for the existence of a profession. In other words, the model leaves us with unanswered questions about how many and which particular dimensions need to be present for a profession to exist and precisely how far along the continuum a work group needs to be in order to be considered a profession.

THE PROCESS MODEL: FOCUSING ON POWER, CONTROL, AND CLAIM-MAKING

As indicated at the beginning of this chapter, the attribute model has been the subject of a good deal of criticism. Out of this criticism has developed what we have chosen to call the process model. The process model must be presented in a different way than the attribute model was presented. The basic points and ideas of the model are contained within the criticisms of the attribute model. At times those points are directly identifiable and at others they are less explicit and must be inferred. Thus, our strategy will be to begin with criticisms of the attribute model and move to an identification of the distinctive points of the process model.[9]

POSITIVE BIAS TOWARD THE PROFESSIONS

One criticism of the attribute model is that it presents the professions in a positive light and, in effect, suggests that the professional form of work organization is good for society and should be encouraged.[10] The professions are seen as service oriented, concerned with the disinterested application of knowledge to the client's problems, guided by codes of ethics, etc. The implication is that if work groups become more professional, clients, and the society as a whole, will be better served. The charge is that the attribute model is a statement of advocacy rather than a mechanism for analyzing work groups.

A process approach would focus on the meaning of such claims (to be ethical or service oriented) for work groups that make them. Thus, attention would be directed to how such claims serve groups in their quest for legitimacy and the value they have in the competition for power and privilege. The attribute model is seen as naive in its identification of such traits as characteristics that *define* a profession. The point is that we should focus on the *process* of claim-making and take a critical and skeptical view of the claims of work groups that they in fact have developed professional attributes.

THE ATTRIBUTE MODEL AS A SCORECARD

The nonprofession-profession continuum can be used as a scale to identify how professional a work group is. Indeed, a number of studies have attempted to measure the location of work groups on the continuum.[11] Furthermore, many work groups have used the traits of the model to assess where they stand on the continuum and to buttress their claims to being professional. But, the assessment of where a work group stands on the scale has political implications. Consequently, according to Douglas Klegon, the attribute model "serves as a standard for determining the degree of power and prestige which an occupation is entitled to enjoy."[12] In a similar vein Julius Roth, a severe critic of the attribute model, argues that sociologists who have developed it have not studied the process of professionalization as much as they have participated in it. According to Roth, they have become "arbiters of occupations on the make, keeping score instead of observing and interpreting the behavior involved in the process of scoring."[13] Clearly, the *process* is seen as the proper subject of sociological inquiry.

IGNORING LINKAGES TO THE CLASS STRUCTURE

Another problem with the attribute model is that it does not deal with connections between the professions and the class structure. This is especially true if one looks at the development of the professions historically. For example, Philip Elliott has pointed out that the three "learned professions" of medicine, law, and the clergy emerged in medieval Europe as what he calls "status professions." They were secure in their high status in the stratification system because of their close association with the ruling landed aristocracy. The coming of industrialization spawned a multitude of "occupational professions" which sought to achieve high status by their claims to special expertise.[14] The attribute model implies that the mastery of expertise leads to professional standing. However, Elliott's analysis suggests that this is a relatively recent phenomenon and the result of the development of a class system based on industrial capitalism. The point is that the attribute model does not sensitize us to the way in which the *process* of claiming professional status on the basis of expert knowledge is shaped by the nature of the class structure. It has also been suggested that the new middle-class occupations that emerged with the development of industrial capitalism claimed to be professions because the name was "connected with the gentlemanly status of the traditional learned professions."[15]

Another important point about the model and the class structure has been made by Dietrich Rueschemeyer. He has pointed out that many of the characteristics of the attribute model used to identify the professions are really characteristics of upper- and upper-middle-class life and their subcultures.[16] Thus, the model may not differentiate professions from nonprofessions as much as it differentiates work groups on the basis of their position in the class structure.

EMPHASIZING INTERNAL AND IGNORING EXTERNAL FACTORS

Douglas Klegon has argued that the attribute model places great emphasis on internal factors but ignores those external to work groups, especially when it comes to explaining their relative position and influence. He uses the idea of an "internal dynamic" to refer to these.[17] Thus, the claim to have the attributes of specialized knowledge, a code of ethics, a self-regulating community, committed and service-oriented practitioners, etc., is an attempt to achieve autonomy, prestige, and control. Such claims are part of a political process in which work groups attempt to advance their interests.[18]

While the attribute model provides us with traits that may be looked at from a claim-making perspective, it still focuses our attention on processes internal to work groups. Klegon also suggests that there is an "external dynamic" that should be examined. This involves looking beyond what is going on within a work group and "relating professional organization and control to other institutional forces and arrangements of power."[19] The role and power of the state is one such external factor. For example, a study of British schoolteachers by N. Parry and J. Parry concluded that their lack of success in claiming professional status is not due to their lack of professional attributes. Rather, it is a result of the fact that they were not organized as professionals (unlike physicians) prior to the etablishment of state control over education.[20] Economic growth and change is another external factor that can affect the success of work groups in claiming professional status. Klegon's analysis of American lawyers is a good example of this. He points out that the late nineteenth-century internal push for professional status among lawyers coincided with crucial external developments. These were the growth of railroads, increased capital investment, and the coming of the corporate form of business organization. As lawyers applied their legal expertise to the needs and problems of large-scale corporate business enterprises, they contributed to the development and stability of those enterprises. This relationship to corporate power enhanced the ability of lawyers to successfully claim professional status.[21]

OVERLOOKING THE IMPLICATIONS OF POWER

The attribute model recognizes the existence of power as an important feature of the professions. The emphasis on collective and individual autonomy indicates that the professions strive to achieve control and domination over both clients and as many aspects of their work activities as possible. Similarly, the professional community exercises strong control over its members. However, the implication of the model is that the professions use their power and authority in many ways that are primarily beneficial to clients and the society as a whole. The emphasis on service motivation, acting in the client's best interests, being guided by a code of ethics, etc., all convey the idea that the professions will exercise their power in altruistic and benevolent ways for the benefit of others. This, critics have pointed out, is simply naive. Professional power creates the situation of a monopoly that can be used to manipulate the supply of practitioners and the demand for their services. Powerful professional associations can and do lobby for favorable legislation that benefits their members. They shape the formulation of public policies that affect their economic well-being. Clearly, legislation and policies favored and promoted by the professions may not be in the public interest and may often run counter to the public interest. Corrine L. Gilb's historical analysis of the development of medicine, dentistry, nursing, law, social work, education, architecture, engineering, accounting, and librarianship indicates that the use of power for the benefit of a profession's own members is a rather common occurrence, and that professional interests are frequently at odds with the public interest.[22]

An example of the use of monopoly power to protect the interests of an occupational group is organized medicine's response to acupuncture. During the early 1970s there was a great deal of popular interest in ancient Chinese acupuncture. This interest was stimulated by the media publicity given to *New York Times* reporter James Reston's treatment for postsurgical discomfort using acupuncture while he was in China.[23] Acupuncture cannot be readily incorporated into the biomedical paradigm on which western medicine is based. It contradicts and conflicts with traditional western medical assumptions about the nature of illness and the functioning of the human body.[24] In the United States, organized medicine's response to acupuncture has been to ridicule and reject it as a legitimate alternative to conventional medical practice. Since it could not be subjugated to and brought under the control of traditional medical practice, it has been relegated to a minor and marginal status within medicine. The medical profession has been successful in severely limiting the practice of acupuncture in all but a few of the states, California being one of them.[25]

The analysis of power—its acquisition and use—is a major emphasis of the process model. The key to understanding the professions is to understand the process by which power is acquired and used vis-a-vis other occupational groups, organizations with which professionals must interact, clients, and the state.[26] Once work groups are conceptualized as engaged in a quest for power and control, we are led to a reinterpretation of the meaning of the traits proposed by the attribute model as features of the professions. Thus, the creation of bodies of esoteric knowledge, the claim to be service motivated and selflessly committed to one's work, the announcement that a code of ethics is operative, etc., can be viewed as *strategic myths* used by work groups in a competitive process of manipulating the environment in advantageous ways.[27] Rather than viewing the attributes as defining what a profession is, they are seen in the process model as *resources* that are used in the competition for rewards and privileges.

Our review of the attribute and process models indicates that we have developed some powerful and useful tools for analyzing occupations. Particularly with the development of the process model, sociological understanding and usage of the concept of profession have become more sophisticated, cautious, and considerably more cynical.

PROFESSIONALIZATION AND DEPROFESSIONALIZATION

The analyses of work that led to the development of the attribute model and, more recently, the process model also include a strong interest in the efforts of work groups to change in the direction of becoming more professional. From the perspective of the attribute model, this involves attempted and actual movement along the continuum toward the profession end. From the perspective of the process model, it involves efforts to acquire power, develop monopolies, and lay claim to the status of profession. From both perspectives, our attention is focused on the dynamic aspect of the life of work groups: change over time through efforts to professionalize.

The emphasis on professionalization deals with change in only one direction, *increases* in professional status. Although the opposite process is clearly a logical possibility, it has received little attention until quite recently. In fact, in 1961, William Goode stated that "There seem to be no examples of professions that lost that status."[28] Yet, recent analyses of a variety of work groups indicate that this does in fact occur. In this section, our task is to develop an understanding of the processes of professionalization and deprofessionalization.

THE PROFESSIONALIZATION PROCESS

Theodore Caplow and Harold L. Wilensky have developed models of the *professionalization process* that attempt to identify major events that represent temporal stages on the road to professionalization in the life history of work groups.

Caplow has identified a sequence involving first the *establishment of a professional association* concerned with defining the criteria for membership in the work group.[29] Second, he points out that there is often a *change in the name* used to identify the group. The function of namechanging is to change the image and identity of the group held by potential clients, the public, and members of the group itself in a manner that implies greater competence, sophistication, and respectability. Examples of such namechanging on the part of groups striving for professional status would include undertakers to morticians, newspaper reporters to journalists, real estate salespeople to realtors, hairdressers to cosmetologists, etc. A third step in the process is the *development of a code of ethics*. This provides a rationale for the usefulness or importance of the work and establishes rules defining what is and is not permissible behavior on the part of members. Codes of ethics also may contain rules that reduce internal competition and create a monopoly over particular activities. The final stage in the process is political agitation for the *enactment of legal restrictions* (e.g., in the form of licensing) on who may perform the work the group claims as its exclusive domain. Caplow sees the establishment of training facilities, directly or indirectly controlled by the group, as occurring concurrently with these stages of the process.

Wilensky has proposed a similar chronology involving five major steps.[30] First, a substantial number of people become engaged on a full-time basis in some activity that needs doing. Second, they establish a training school for the preparation of new practitioners. Next, they form a professional association to promote their collective interests. Fourth, the association engages in political activities to get legislation enacted to protect the group. Finally, they develop a code of ethics.

The differences that exist in Caplow's and Wilensky's models of the professionalization process are minor and are mainly differences in emphasis. While they differ on the order of events, they basically agree on the events that constitute the process.

Wilensky also examined the history and development of eighteen occupations exhibiting varying degrees of professionalization as measured by his model. On the basis of his findings regarding how far through the process these occupations have moved, he proposed a fourfold classification or typology. These are *established* professions, professions *in process or marginal*, *new* professions, and *doubtful* professions.

The established-professions category includes accounting (certified public accounting), architecture, civil engineering, dentistry, law, and medicine. Professions in process, or marginal, includes librarianship, nursing, optometry, pharmacy, school teaching, social work, and veterinary medicine. The new professions category includes city management, city planning, and hospital administration. Finally, the doubtful category includes advertising and funeral direction.

Both Caplow's and Wilensky's models take as given the validity and utility of the attribute model. That is, the professionalization process involves the acquisition of traits at the profession end of the continuum. Patrick B. Forsyth and Thomas J. Danisiewicz have developed a more elaborate scheme for examining the professionalization process in which power, the key variable of the process model, is their central focus.[31] They also place a great deal of emphasis on the image-building activities of occupational groups as a key part of the process. Their model is presented in diagram 2.2.

Diagram 2.2
The Forsyth–Danisiewicz Model of Professionalization

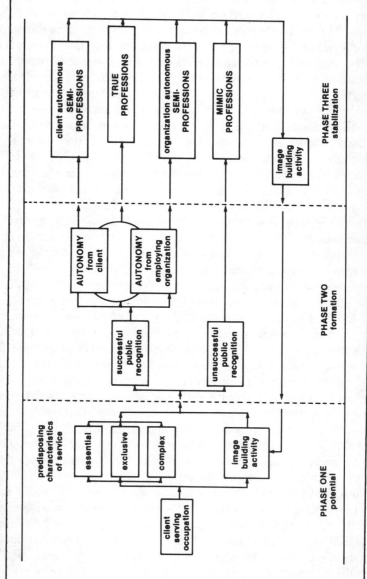

Source: Patrick B. Forsyth and Thomas J. Danisiewicz, "Toward a Theory of Professionalization," *Work and Occupations* 12 (February 1985): 63.

The model is divided into three "phases." In Phase One, a client serving occupation performs a task or provides a service that is *essential*, i.e., of importance to those served. The occupation also has *exclusive* control over the provision of the service. In other words it has a monopoly. The service provided is *complex* in the sense that the work involved is nonroutine and individual practitioners must make judgements about the application of a specialized body of knowledge. This phase of the professionalization process also includes organized efforts on the part of professional associations to promote the work group as a profession. This *image building* activity consists mainly of efforts to convince the public that the work of the group is indeed essential, exclusive, and complex.

Phase Two consists of public acceptance or nonacceptance of the occupation's claims, and the consequences this has for the development of autonomy. In Forsyth's and Danisiewicz's view, autonomy is something that is granted by the public through recognition of the occupation's claims. Although their model presents the recognition of the occupation's claims as a dichotomy (successful-unsuccessful), they recognize that it is in reality a continuum. Forsyth and Danisiewicz deal with autonomy at the level of the individual. They make a very important distinction between two types of autonomy: *autonomy from the client* and *autonomy from the employing organization*. Success in gaining public recognition of the occupation's claims leads to the granting of one or the other or both types of autonomy.

Phase Three deals with the consequences of the kind of autonomy developed in Phase Two. When an occupation acquires *both* autonomy from the client and from the employing organization, we have the development of what Forsyth and Danisiewicz call a *true profession*. Medicine and law would be examples here. When one but not both types of autonomy are granted, the result is the development of a *semiprofession*. Examples of this would be engineering and education (both client autonomous) and nursing and social work (both organization autonomous). When an occupation is unsuccessful in gaining public recognition of its claims and fails to develop either type of autonomy, the result is the development of what they call a *mimic profession*. They suggest that librarianship would be an example of this outcome. In this last phase there may continue to be a substantial amount of image building activity. It may include such things as the development of a code of ethics and efforts to achieve the sanction of the state through the establishment of licensing regulations and the passage of laws to punish those who attempt to practice the occupation without proper certification.

This model represents an important contribution to the analysis of the professionalization process. The interaction between claim-making and public recognition of those claims is clearly an important new factor. The model also presents autonomy as a conditional outcome of the interaction between occupational claims and public response, rather than the result of some unspecified conspiratorial process.

Yet, there are questions that the model, like its predecessors, fails to explain. For example, it is not clear why some occupations that perform essential, exclusive, and complex tasks take the initiative in promoting themselves as professions and others do not. In other words, the predisposing characteristics may exist but they are not exploited by members of the occupation. Why this occurs remains an unanswered question. Another dilemma is why the image building campaigns of some groups are successful and others are not. We need to deal more with the content of those image building activities and the responses of people to them to determine why some are more persuasive than others. Finally, like the earlier models developed by Caplow and Wilensky, this is a one-directional model. That is, it deals with changes from lesser to greater professionalization. What are the conditions under which the process might be reversed? Changes in the direction of decreased professionalization will be dealt with in the following section on deprofessionalization. However, we should ideally be working toward the development of models that deal with both processes simultaneously.

THE PROCESS OF DEPROFESSIONALIZATION

Deprofessionalization is a relatively new topic of interest among sociologists who study occupations. Analyses to date have used two strategies. These involve looking at the loss or decline of a work group on specific characteristics of the attribute model, and looking at threats to the monopoly of work groups and challenges to their autonomy.

Rationalization of the Knowledge Base

Nina Toren has pointed out that changes in the knowledge base of a profession can contribute to deprofessionalization.[32] Much professional work involves the application of specialized knowledge to the unique problems of clients. There is an emphasis on the *nonroutine* nature of these tasks. Toren argues that as the knowledge base of a profession becomes increasingly rational, precise, and specific, the way that knowledge is applied becomes more susceptible to *standardization* and *routinization*. To the extent that work can be reduced to standardized procedures, the profession's claim to unique and mysterious competencies is threatened.

There are a number of examples of this kind of change occurring. In the case of pharmacists, the medications they dispense are increasingly ready-made and less knowledge is needed to prepare them. In medicine, many simple diagnostic and treatment procedures have been routinized and turned over to nurse practitioners and physician's assistants who are also referred to as "physician extenders." The use of audio-visual instruction, instructional television, and computers in education represents a routinization of the work of schoolteachers.

Another example of how such changes can contribute to deprofessionalization is the case of certified public accountancy. Paul D. Montagna argues that the main work of certified public accountants (CPAs), the auditing of firms as required by law, has been reduced to a set of formal, standard, explicit procedures that have changed it from an intellectual to a mechanical task. The result has been to remove much individual judgement and discretion from the work of the CPA.[33]

Robert A. Rothman has identified similar changes within the legal profession.[34] Many legal procedures have become so routine that do-it-yourself legal kits, complete with forms and instructions, have replaced the lawyer's judgement and advice. Electronic data processing has simplified and routinized much legal research and some aspects of juror selection. Such simplification demystifies the work of lawyers and contributes to deprofessionalization.

Challenges to Professional Authority

A number of factors have contributed to an erosion of the traditional authority of professionals, especially in their relationships with clients. One of these is simply the rising educational level of the population. As the amount of formal education attained by people has increased, they have come to know more about the functioning of the human body, the nature of illness and disease, legal processes and procedures, and the like. The knowledge of the professional has become more and more accessible and shared by the general population, if not in its totality, certainly in significant bits and pieces. Consequently, the image of the professional as the all-knowing expert has been undermined. Better informed clients are more likely to ask for explanations of what is being done to them, why a particular course of action was selected, and whether some alternative strategy was considered.[35] Traditionally, the professions' idea of the "good client" has been the person who blindly and unquestioningly obeyed the instructions of the professional. The assumption by professionals was that the client was ignorant, helpless, and totally dependent on them. Clearly, that image has been changed by rising levels of education and the increased amount and variety of information available to people.

Another factor that has undermined professional authority is heightened consumerism. While consumerism flourished in the 1960s, its legacy still affects the authority of the professions. Much of the consumer movement focused on issues of the environment and product safety (e.g., pesticides,[36] automobiles[37]) and issues of consumer fraud.[38] During the 1970s there were also a number of successful challenges to the prohibitions of professional associations against advertising by their members.[39] The rise of private, for-profit medical organizations (hospitals, clinics, and health maintenance organizations) has resulted in increased advertising of health care services and greater consumer choice. The long-term consequence of the consumer movement has been an increased awareness of choice, the development of alternative sources of professional services, and a decrease in the dependence of clients on particular professionals. The result is a subtle erosion of professional authority over the conditions under which professional services are delivered as well as increased client sophistication about the content and substance of those services. During the 1960s many occupational groups also developed internal radical movements that questioned a wide range of traditional practices and assumptions.

Nina Toren has suggested that the service ideal of the professions is threatened by such developments. The service orientation rests on the assumption that concern for what is best for the client guides professional practice. Yet, consumerism means that clients increasingly are playing an important role in defining their needs and how they should be met. Also, governments are using their authority to define the needs of clients and potential clients. The enactment of legislation creating the Medicare and Medicaid programs, for example, represents a governmental definition of how medical care should be delivered to particular segments of the population (the elderly and the poor, respectively) as well as how it should be financed. Such developments can be seen as a challenge to the traditional prerogatives of the medical profession to define the nature of the services needed by clients, and how they will be delivered, financed, etc.[40]

Erosion of the Professional Community

As new knowledge is created and the knowledge base of a work group expands, it creates pressure for specialization.[41] Internal specialization has the potential for creating competing segments within a profession.[42] Internal divisions based on specialization represent a potential threat to the integrity and cohesion of the professional community. To the extent that cohesion is lessened, the ability of the group to exercise control over its members is also lessened.[43]

Another factor contributing to the decline of the professional community is the increased entry of women and minorities into the professions, in part a consequence of internal radical movements noted earlier. Until quite recently, the work groups that had attained the greatest degree of professionalization (e.g., medicine and law) were dominated by white males. The idea of a professional community includes the idea of exclusivity and membership in a group with similar goals, aspirations, concerns, and characteristics. In effect, professional communities exhibit many of the characteristics of private clubs. The entry of women and minorities has changed this. Increased demographic diversity has led to increased attitudinal diversity. For example, women lawyers are more likely than their male counterparts to be supportive of issues such as international human rights, nuclear arms limitations, and gay rights.[44] Black lawyers believe that their professional association should be involved in public policy issues more than white lawyers do, and women lawyers are less likely than male lawyers to be concerned with traditional issues of professional concern such as increasing the status of the profession and preventing unlicensed persons from providing legal services.[45]

The Impact of Organizational Employment

In several respects the spread of bureaucratic organizations is another *potential* source of deprofessionalization. The qualifier "potential" is important here since the research evidence on the effect of bureaucratic employment on professional work is not consistent or unanimous in its conclusions. The topic will be dealt with at greater length in chapter 6. At this point some links between bureaucracy and deprofessionalization can be identified, however.

Bureaucratic organizations place great emphasis on standardizing and routinizing the activities that occur within them. These are characteristics that virtually define bureaucracies. The routinization of professional knowledge, skill, and activity was noted earlier as a source of deprofessionalization. While such routinization can occur independently of the setting in which work occurs, it may be accelerated and intensified where professional work is performed in bureaucratic settings.

In addition, organizational priorities and procedures may place limits on the autonomy of professionals. Opportunities for making independent judgements and taking initiatives may be constrained. Wilensky has suggested that bureaucracy undermines the service ideal of the professions, and Hall's research on professionals in bureaucracies indicated that autonomy, more than any other feature of professions, is inversely related to bureaucratization.[46] As the topic of deprofessionalization is investigated, we need to be sensitive to bureaucratization as one potential factor in the process.

PROFESSIONAL MARGINALITY

The sociological literature on occupations and professions includes extensive use of the concepts of semiprofession, quasi profession, would-be profession, profession in process, and (from Forsyth and Danisiewicz's professionalization model discussed earlier) mimic profession. What they have in common is the notion of incomplete acquisition of the characteristics of a profession or a contradictory location on some characteristics. They imply incomplete professionalization or partial deprofessionalization. While each term conveys a nuance of its own, they are all variants on the more basic concept of *professional marginality*.

The concept of marginality was introduced into the sociological literature by Robert E. Park and extended by Everett Stonequist.[47] They used the concept to refer to the immigrant who sought to disaffiliate from the immigrant group and become a member of the dominant culture. Rebuffed in these attempts and unable to return to the immigrant group (having ostensibly rejected its norms and values), the marginal person remains on the periphery of two social worlds, *in* both but not really a member *of* either. As a result of this, the marginal person experiences a variety of conflicts and behaves in contradictory ways that demonstrate uncertainty as to which group's norms and values should serve as guidelines for organizing life.

Our purpose here is not to exhaustively review the development and use of the concept of marginality in sociology. Suffice it to point out that it has been used to examine such diverse topics as the assimilation of racial and ethnic minority groups, the effects of rural to urban migration, roles that place conflicting demands on their incumbents, the consequences of social mobility, and the etiology of deviant behavior. Basically, the concept has come to refer to the simultaneous occupancy of contradictory positions. Although marginality has been used mainly to examine factors that place strains on individuals, the concept of professional marginality involves a shift to the group level of analysis. Professional marginality refers then to contradictions and inconsistencies in the extent to which work groups exhibit the characteristics of a profession.

There are numerous examples of professional marginality. For example, teaching, nursing, and social work are relatively low in terms of collective and individual autonomy as a result of the fact that these occupations are typically performed in bureaucratic organizations (schools, hospitals, social service agencies).[48] As has already been pointed out, organizational norms and goals limit the degree to which autonomy can be exercised. Goode also sees librarianship as a marginal profession because of the nature of its knowledge base and because codes of ethics do not seem to apply to librarian-client relationships.[49] The concept of professional marginality as well as the broader topic of professionalization can be illustrated by looking in some detail at two work activities, pharmacy and police work.

PHARMACY: MULTIPLE SOURCES OF MARGINALITY

Pharmacy is an extensively researched occupation and a good example of the concept of professional marginality because of the conflict between professional and business norms. Conflict and strain are built into the role of the pharmacist because it contains elements of both the professional and business world.

Since the beginning of this century, pharmacy in the United States has undergone a self-conscious effort to lay claim to professional status. Like many professionalizing occupations, a good deal of effort has gone into increasing and standardizing the formal training of pharmacists. Since 1932, all states have required at least four years of training beyond high school to qualify for a license to practice pharmacy.[50] In recent years, programs leading to graduate degrees with an emphasis on pharmaceutical research have been established at universities in an attempt to increase the knowledge base of pharmacy and to enhance its image as a profession. Training programs that include work in the natural and physical sciences and place an emphasis on research have created a model of the pharmacist presented to students closely paralleling that of the disinterested research scientist.

However, there is a discontinuity between this model presented to students and the actual working conditions experienced by many pharmacy graduates. The transition from school to work may be relatively smooth for those who enter pharmaceutical research and development roles in, for example, large pharmaceutical companies, research hospitals, or universities. The conception of work as a pharmacist developed during training in such cases is compatible with the role expectations that people find in these work environments. The situation is quite different for those who work as salaried employees of chain drug stores or as independent entrepreneurs. In these cases there are many opportunities for the development of conflict between the professional norms to which the pharmacist has been socialized and the business norms that permeate the work environment.

The way the strains created by this conflict are resolved has been examined by Earl R. Quinney in a study of pharmacists working in retail drug stores.[51] He suggests that pharmacy has failed to institutionalize a single occupational role but rather shares two divergent roles (the professional and business). Individuals resolve the dilemma by organizing their work behavior in terms of one or the other role. That is, he assumes that the conflict cannot be tolerated indefinitely and that a state of equilibrium eventually must be reached by developing an orientation that is more toward one than the other role. Quinney's study of eighty pharmacists found that there is in fact variation in the relative emphasis on the two roles, but the conflict is not completely eliminated. However, the more professionally oriented pharmacists report that they experience the normative conflicts more than those oriented primarily toward the business role.

Another study of pharmacists by Carol Kronus suggests that the conflict and strain depicted by Quinney may be overdrawn.[52] In her study of fifty-three pharmacists she found that business-oriented and professionally oriented pharmacists both subscribed to business and professional values. Furthermore, those who had this dual orientation were least likely to be motivated by a concern for extrinsic rewards such as high income. Retail pharmacists also expressed stronger service values than did pharmacists working in hospitals, despite the fact that the latter were the most professionally oriented. Her findings suggest that working in a business setting is not necessarily detrimental to subscription to professional values and that the business-professional conflict need not always create unresolvable role strain.

A different set of concerns has prompted Norman K. Denzin to conclude that pharmacy represents a case of "incomplete professionalization."[53] By this he means that pharmacy has failed to recruit people strongly committed to professional norms, to develop a set of values anchored in the principle of service, and to become self-regulating and self-governing. Most importantly, pharmacy has failed to maintain control over the development, production, and application of the use of drugs, the basic object that justifies its existence. The implication of Denzin's discussion is that these conditions do not necessarily represent an unchangeable state of affairs resulting in permanent marginality. Rather, they describe the occupation at a particular point in time as having failed to complete the professionalization process. However, domination of the development and production of drugs by the pharmaceutical industry and control over the prescribing of drugs by physicians place the occupation of pharmacy in a dependent position with clear limits on its autonomy.

THE POLICE

An attempt to attain professional status has been a very self-conscious activity on the part of spokespersons for the police. The goal of professionalization has been articulated and sought largely by police administrators. Police officers have turned to unionization as a means of achieving economic benefits. Yet, the effort to build a public image of the police as professionals has been largely unsuccessful.

While there is a good deal of discussion in police circles about professionalization, Peter Feuille and Hervey A. Juris have pointed out that the way the term is used by the police has some special and very important nuances.[54] In their study of police departments in twenty-two cities, they found that police personnel typically spoke of a "professional department" rather than "the police profession." This illustrates the importance of their organizational location as a constraint on professionalization. The police are after all salaried employees of public administrative bureaucracies.

Feuille and Juris also report some information that illustrates the centrality of image in the issue of police professionalization. While interviewing leaders of a police union in a midwestern city, the latter spoke very positively of the "professional" character of the Los Angeles Police Department which they had just visited. When the interviewers pressed for a definition of "professional," the officers mentioned such things as the lack of interference from city hall, the modern building in which the department was located, shiny new equipment (especially computers), the neat and clean appearance of police officers, and the fact that many jobs in the department were specialized. While things like specialization and political noninterference link into our models of professionalization, the other things mentioned appear more superficial and related primarily to the image and perception of the occupation. In interviews in two eastern cities, police officers referred to previous conditions in their department as "unprofessional." When asked to explain what this meant, ". . . they referred to the slovenly physical appearance of individual offers and the run-down and unkempt state of police buildings."[55] These examples suggest that the term professional may have very different meanings for rank and file police officers than it does for police administrators. They also illustrate how appealing the term "professional" can be to groups concerned with their public image and their image of themselves.

Others who have studied and written about the police also stress the point that "professional" has some distinctive meanings when used by members of this occupation. It includes such things as efficiency, rationality, a nonpolitical approach to law enforcement, personal honesty, and high standards for entry into the work. The emphasis is on an ideology and environment in which universalistic rather than particularistic norms guide decision making. As such, the focus is more on the organization and the department rather than the individual.[56]

A great deal of the discussion of police professionalization revolves around the topic of education and training. What the content of training should be, and how much should be required are pervasive issues and illustrate the marginality of police work on an important dimension of professionalization.

The idea of a well-trained police force is by no means new. In western European nations, extensive training programs for police officers have existed for some time. George H. Brerton has pointed out that the "commissioned" officers of European police forces are recruited to police work from college and university programs in which they have been educated primarily for a career in public service.[57] In the United States the emphasis on education and training was a major issue early in the development of the professionalization movement. In 1923, August Vollmer, a well-known police chief, made several recommendations for raising standards for police officers. His agenda included establishment of high standards of education and training, regular observation of recruits by physicians and psychologists during the training period, and establishment of preparatory and promotional courses for police officers in colleges and universities.[58] Organizations representing police administrators have continued to emphasize the importance of collaboration with educators and institutions of higher education in the development and design of police training programs. Nevertheless, the actual training of police officers remains unstandardized and there is a great deal of variation from one jurisdiction to another in both the content and amount of training required for entry into the occupation.

As noted earlier, a distinction needs to be made between the concerns of police administrators about professionalization and the concerns of rank and file officers. Feuille and Juris conclude that as far as the latter are concerned, the police are not a profession in the conventional sense of the term, police unions have no incentives to support management-initiated professionalization movements, and the goals of police unions are essentially the same as those representing skilled blue-collar workers.[59]

Research on police chiefs indicates that the concept of professionalization may be more relevant to understanding developments in this part of the law enforcement field. John K. Maniha's case study of police chiefs in St. Louis from 1861–1970 concludes that some distinctive changes in the direction of professionalization have occurred. Police chiefs were initially recruited on the basis of community visibility and political patronage, regardless of their expertise in police matters. Later, some policing experience and connection with the department were necessary. Beginning in the mid-1880s, the careers of police chiefs became more orderly and promotion to the position occurred only after a long period of service in the organization. Demonstrated leadership qualities and knowledge of police skills became important criteria for promotion to the position of chief. Since 1925, Maniha concludes, technical knowledge and administrative skill as well as an understanding of and concern with ethical issues have been the primary criteria for a career as a police chief.[60]

While Maniha's study focuses largely on police chiefs and their characteristics, Thomas Keil and Charles Ekstrom suggest that professionalization among police administrators also may be affected by the characteristics of the communities in which they work.[61] Their study of 155 Pennsylvania police chiefs indicated that police chiefs in communities with higher socioeconomic characteristics (particularly higher levels of educational attainment) were more likely to indicate support for various aspects of professionalism. These included such things as use of their professional organization as a reference group, their commitment to colleague control, and a belief in public service. Thus, at least in the case of this occupation, professionalization can be shaped by the community context in which its work takes place.

SUMMARY

The models presented in this chapter represent useful tools for analyzing work and work groups. While the process model dominates current sociological thinking about work, it is clearly linked to the attribute model, having developed out of critiques of the latter. Popular conceptions of the meaning of profession represent a potential for confusion and misuse of the concept. It is clear that work groups of all kinds use the idea of a profession in their quest for power, control, and advantage in the workplace and the marketplace.

The concept of professionalization calls attention to the processes of change continually occurring in the occupational world. The models developed to understand and explain the process of professionalization have emphasized the acquisition of more professional characteristics on the part of work groups. Yet, recent analyses have pointed out the possibility of a reversal of this trend in the form of movement toward less professionalization. Awareness of the possibility of deprofessionalization is an important corrective to the one-directional focus of most thinking about such changes.

While some occupations have been successful in laying claim to professional status, many have clearly failed in their efforts to do so. The idea of professional marginality captures this. Despite concerted efforts at professionalization, many groups are more appropriately seen as semi-professions, quasi professions, or mimic professions. Looking at the barriers to professionalization highlights both the issues that are of concern to work groups, and the problems they face. Our examination of pharmacy and the police as examples of professional marginality illustrates the variety of factors that can operate as obstacles to the development of professionalization as well as the strains and tensions such obstacles produce.

NOTES

1. For an analysis of the concept of amateur, see Robert A. Stebbins, "The Amateur: Two Sociological Definitions," *Pacific Sociological Review* 20 (October 1977): 582–606.
2. Nicholas Alex, *Black in Blue: A Study of the Negro Policeman* (New York: Appleton-Century-Crofts, 1969).
3. This section draws extensively on the following works: A. M. Carr-Saunders and P. A. Wilson, *The Professions* (Oxford: Clarendon Press, 1933); Talcott Parsons, "The Professions and Social Structure," *Social Forces* 17 (May 1939): 457–467; Morris L. Cogan, "The Problem of Defining a Profession," *Annals* 297 (January 1955): 105–111; Ernest Greenwood, "Attributes of a Profession," *Social Work* 2 (July 1957): 45–55; Everett C. Hughes, *Men and Their Work* (New York: Free Press, 1958); William Goode, "Community Within a Community: The Professions," *American Sociological Review* 22 (April 1957): 194–200; "Encroachment, Charlatanism, and the Emerging Profession: Psychology, Medicine, and Sociology," *American Sociological Review* 25 (December 1960): 902-914; "The Librarian: From Occupation to Profession?" *Library Quarterly* 31 (October 1961): 306–318; Edward Gross, *Work and Society* (New York: Crowell, 1958); Bernard Barber, "Some Problems in the Sociology of Professions," *Daedalus* 92 (Fall 1963): 669–688; Harold Wilensky, "The Professionalization of Everyone?" *American Journal of Sociology* 70 (September 1964): 137–158; and Wilbert E. Moore, *The Professions: Roles and Rules* (New York: Russell Sage Foundation, 1970).
4. Dietrich Rueschemeyer, "Doctors and Lawyers: A Comment on the Theory of the Professions," *Canadian Review of Sociology and Anthropology* 1 (February 1964): 17–30.
5. Julius A. Roth, "Professionalism: The Sociologist's Decoy," *Sociology of Work and Occupations* 1 (February 1974): 6–23.
6. Randall Collins, "Functional and Conflict Theories of Educational Stratification," *American Sociological Review* 36 (December 1971): 1002–1019.
7. In the German language the word for occupation is "Beruf." It derives from the verb "berufen" which translates literally as "to call."
8. Goode, "Community Within a Community," 194–200.
9. This section draws extensively on the following works: Roth, "Professionalism," 6–23; Eliot Friedson, ed., *The Professions and Their Prospects*, (Beverly Hills: Sage, 1973); "The Theory of Professions: State of the Art," in *The Sociology of the Professions: Lawyers, Doctors, and Others*, ed. Robert Dingwall and Philip Lewis (New York: St. Martin's Press, 1983), 19–37; Magali Sarfatti Larson, *The Rise of Professionalism: A Sociological Analysis* (Berkeley: University of California Press, 1977); Douglas Klegon, "The Sociology of Pro-

fessions: An Emerging Perspective," *Sociology of Work and Occupations* 5 (August 1978): 259–283; and Richard H. Hall, "Theoretical Trends in the Sociology of Occupations," *Sociological Quarterly* 24 (Winter 1983): 5–23.
10. Klegon, "The Sociology of Professions," 266.
11. Wilensky, "The Professionalization of Everyone," 137–158; Robert Perucci and Joel E. Gerstl, *Profession Without Community: Engineers in American Society* (New York: Random House, 1969); and Richard H. Hall, "Professionalization and Bureaucratization," *American Sociological Review* 33 (February 1968): 92–105.
12. Klegon, "The Sociology of Professions," 266.
13. Roth, "Professionalism," 17.
14. Philip Elliott, *The Sociology of the Professions* (New York: Herder and Herder, 1972).
15. Friedson, "The Theory of the Professions," 24.
16. Rueschemeyer, "Doctors and Lawyers," 17–30.
17. Klegon, "The Sociology of Professions."
18. Eliot Friedson, "Professions and the Occupational Principle," in *The Professions and Their Prospects*, 19–38.
19. Klegon, "The Sociology of Professions," 271.
20. N. Parry and J. Parry, "The Teachers and Professionalism: The Failure of a Strategy," in *Educability, Schools, and Ideology*, ed. M. Flude and J. Ahier (London: Croom Helm, 1974), 160–185.
21. Klegon, "The Sociology of Professions," 273–274.
22. Corrine L. Gilb, *Hidden Hierarchies: The Professions and the Government* (New York: Harper and Row, 1966).
23. Paul Root Wolpe, "The Maintenance of Professional Authority: Acupuncture and the American Physician," *Social Problems* 32 (June 1985): 409–424.
24. For a discussion of the medical philosophy behind acupuncture see Manfred Porkert, *The Theoretical Foundations of Chinese Medicine* (Cambridge, Mass.: MIT Press, 1974).
25. Wolpe, "The Maintenance of Professional Authority," 409–424.
26. Hall, "Theoretical Trends in the Sociology of Occupations," 12.
27. *Ibid.*, 12–13.
28. Goode, "The Librarian: From Occupation to Profession?" 309.
29. Theodore Caplow, *The Sociology of Work* (New York: McGraw-Hill, 1964), 139–140.
30. Wilensky, "The Professionalization of Everyone," 137–158.
31. Patrick B. Forsyth and Thomas J. Danisiewicz, "Toward a Theory of Professionalization," *Work and Occupations* 12 (February 1985): 59–76.
32. Nina Toren, "Deprofessionalization and Its Sources," *Sociology of Work and Occupations* 2 (November 1975): 323–337.
33. Paul D. Montagna, "Professionalization and Bureaucratization in Large Professional Organizations," *American Journal of Sociology* 74 (September 1968): 138–145.
34. Robert A. Rothman, "Deprofessionalization: The Case of Law in America," *Work and Occupations* 11 (May 1984): 183–206.
35. Marie R. Haug, "The Deprofessionalization of Everyone?" *Sociological Focus* 8 (August 1975): 197–213.
36. Rachel Carson, *Silent Spring* (Boston: Houghton Mifflin, 1962).
37. Ralph Nader, *Unsafe at Any Speed* (New York: Grossman, 1965).
38. Jessica Mitford, *The American Way of Death* (New York: Simon and Schuster, 1963).

39. Rothman, "Deprofessionalization," 194–195.
40. Toren, "Deprofessionalization and Its Sources," 332–334. See also Marie Haug and Bebe Lavin, *Consumerism in Medicine: Challenging Physician Authority* (Beverly Hills: Sage, 1983).
41. Eliot Friedson, "The Future of Professionalism," in *Health and the Division of Labor*, ed. M. Stacey, et al. (London: Croom Helm, 1977), 14–38.
42. Rue Bucher and Anselm Strauss, "Professions in Process," *American Journal of Sociology* 66 (January 1961): 325–334.
43. Ronald L. Akers, "Framework for the Comparative Study of Cohesion: The Professions," *Pacific Sociological Review* 13 (Spring 1970): 73–85.
44. Law Poll, "The Organized Bar and Public Issues," *American Bar Association Journal* 64 (January 1978): 41–43.
45. J. P. Heinz, et al., "Diversity, Representation, and Leadership in an Urban Bar: A First Report of the Chicago Bar," *American Bar Foundation Research Journal* (Summer 1976): 717–785.
46. Wilensky, "The Professionalization of Everyone," 137–158; and Hall, "Professionalization and Bureaucratization," 92–105.
47. Robert E. Park, "Human Migration and the Marginal Man," *American Journal of Sociology* 33 (May 1928): 881–893; and Everett Stonequist, *The Marginal Man* (New York: Charles Scribner's Sons, 1937).
48. Amitai Etzioni, ed., *The Semi-Professions and Their Organization: Teachers, Nurses, Social Workers* (New York: Free Press, 1969).
49. Goode, "The Librarian: From Occupation to Profession?" 306–318.
50. Thelma Herman McCormack, "The Druggists' Dilemma: Problems of a Marginal Occupation," *American Journal of Sociology* 61 (January 1956): 308–315.
51. Earl R. Quinney, "Adjustment to Occupational Role Strain: The Case of Retail Pharmacy," *Southwestern Social Science Quarterly* 44 (March 1964): 367–376.
52. Carol Kronus, "Occupational Values, Role Orientations, and Work Settings: The Case of Pharmacy," *Sociological Quarterly* 16 (Spring 1975): 171–183.
53. Norman K. Denzin, "Incomplete Professionalization: The Case of Pharmacy," *Social Forces* 46 (March 1968): 375–381.
54. Peter F. Feuille and Hervey A. Juris, "Police Professionalization and Police Unions," *Sociology of Work and Occupations* 3 (February 1976): 88–113.
55. *Ibid.*, 111.
56. See Jerome Y. Skolnick, *Justice Without Trial: Law Enforcement in Democratic Society* (New York: Wiley, 1966); James Q. Wilson, *Varieties of Police Behavior: The Management of Law and Order in Eight Communities* (Cambridge, Mass.: Harvard University Press, 1968); and Jonathan Rubenstein, *City Police* (New York: Ballantine, 1973).
57. George H. Brerton, "The Importance of Training and Education in the Professionalization of Law Enforcement," *Journal of Criminal Law, Criminology, and Police Science* 52 (May 1961): 111–121.
58. *Ibid.*, 112.
59. Feuille and Juris, "Police Professionalization," 110–111.
60. John K. Maniha, "Structural Supports for the Development of Professionalization Among Police Administrators," *Pacific Sociological Review* 16 (July 1973): 315–343.
61. Thomas Keil and Charles Ekstrom, "Police Chief Professionalism: Community, Departmental, and Career Correlates," *Sociology of Work and Occupations* 5 (November 1978): 470–486.

CHAPTER 3

Occupational Choice

MANY CHARACTERISTICS of work can and do change over time. However, two things that remain constant are the need to continually recruit people to fill work roles and the need for individuals to make decisions about the kind of work they will pursue. From a societal perspective, the problem is one of human resource allocation: assuring an adequate supply of people with the skills needed to carry out the work that needs to be done. For individuals, this fact creates a decision-making problem. Ultimately, the way in which people are distributed among occupational roles is the result of decisions made by individuals. However, those decisions are constrained and shaped by changes in the kinds of jobs that are being created and eliminated as well as by the continually changing demands and needs of the labor market.

The very term occupational "choice" is, in a sense, an unfortunate one. It unduly focuses our attention on the individual and implies that individual choice is the only thing that affects how people are distributed among occupations. Cyril Sofer, a British sociologist, has noted this problem and pointed out that the term implies that people make concrete decisions only after careful and systematic consideration of the alternatives open to them.[1] As we will see, the amount and kind of freedom that people have in making occupational decisions is often limited by a variety of external considerations.

In advanced industrial societies where identity, prestige, income, and life-style are derived in large measure from occupational status, occupational decisions are significant events in people's lives. Increasingly specialized educational prerequisites are continually pushing back the time at which work-related decisions must be made. Consequently, occupational choice is frequently experienced as a major crisis of late adolescence.

In this chapter, our main concern is with identifying the ways in which the process of occupational choice has been interpreted. Following that, we will examine the social origins of people recruited to particular occupations. Finally, we will deal with the reciprocal nature of educational and occupational decisions.

APPROACHES TO THE STUDY OF OCCUPATIONAL CHOICE

Despite the importance of occupational choice for both individuals and society, no single, comprehensive theory of occupational choice has been developed. The sociological, psychological, and vocational guidance literature contains many attempts to investigate, conceptualize, and theorize about occupational choice. These efforts are reviewed below under the labels of the rational decision-making, fortuitous, and sociocultural influence approaches to the study of occupational choice.

THE RATIONAL DECISION-MAKING APPROACH

The distinctive feature of the *rational decision-making* approach is the identification of "stages" or "periods" of occupational interest or decision making which parallel stages in the life cycle of individuals. By and large, the rational decision-making approach focuses on micro level issues and processes internal to the individual while external influences are clearly secondary.

Psychologists took the lead in studying occupational choice. Prior to the 1950s, the analysis of occupational choice was dominated by what C. H. Miller has called a pragmatic "trait-factor" approach to vocational guidance. Basically, this involved matching the traits of individuals with those of occupations. The assumptions of this strategy were that occupational choice is a conscious decision arrived at through a process of reasoning, that there is one right job for each individual, and that individuals actually have choices available to them.[2] Later theories of occupational choice—those that we include in the rational decision-making approach—stress the point that affective as well as cognitive processes are involved and that personality characteristics play a significant role in occupational choice. In the rational decision-making approach, occupational interests and choices are seen as changing as a consequence of increased maturation or movement to another stage of the life cycle.

Developmental psychology is the broader psychological perspective from which the analysis proceeds. The best-known and most influential examples of this approach are the theories of Eli Ginzberg[3] and Donald E. Super.[4]

Ginzberg sees occupational choice as an irreversible process that represents a compromise between a person's interests, capacities, opportunities, and values. The emergence of occupational interests and a concern with values are seen in the context of the individual going through a process of emotional development, change, and maturation. Although the emphasis is on changes occurring within the individual, some external factors are recognized.

According to Ginzberg, the developmental periods through which people are assumed to pass are:

1. *The Fantasy Period* (ages six through eleven). Here the question asked is "What would I like to be as an adult?" This is asked and answered without concern for one's capabilities or the opportunities and limitations that may be experienced at a future point in time.

2. *Period of Tentative Choice* (ages twelve through seventeen). At this stage, the question asked is more likely to be "What kind of work am I best suited for?" During this period there is a recognition that occupational decisions do need to be made. Ginzberg emphasizes that the child's focus is still mainly on subjective factors such as the kinds of interests, abilities, and values that she or he has.

3. *Period of Realistic Choice* (age eighteen plus). During this period initial exploration is followed by the identification of realistic possibilities and an eventual choice. There is a progressive narrowing of alternatives as individuals confront their own limitations and the constraints of the labor market. Occupational choice is ultimately a *compromise* between preferences and the realities that exist.

Within this model, there is a progressive narrowing of the range of occupational choices over time. Ginzberg originally stated that the process is irreversible in the sense that, as time goes on, it is increasingly difficult to undo the consequences of earlier decisions. For example, educational institutions may require people to make decisions that have occupational implications and once a course of action is taken (e.g., beginning an educational program) it may be difficult to abandon it and switch to something else.[5]

Some Problems with the Model

This model makes sense out of many aspects of the occupational decisions of young people and it is consistent with many of our everyday experiences with the dilemmas they face. Yet, there are a number of problems with it as a theory of occupational choice. For example, it is a *culture-bound* conceptualization of occupational choice. The stages and corresponding age spans are closely tied to the American educational system. The choice periods can be viewed as reflecting the times at which the educational system forces students to make decisions (for example, when entering or completing high school). In addition, the approach is *time bound.*[6] Ginzberg's age periods (particularly age eighteen plus for the period of realistic choice) made sense when age eighteen or shortly, thereafter was the age at which most young people took a full-time job. However, a large proportion of high school graduates today postpone a "realistic" choice until approximately age twenty-two by going to college or to an even later age by continuing their education in graduate or professional schools. Finally, the emphasis on the *irreversibility* of the process seems unduly strong. Although the American educational system may force people to make educational decisions with occupational implications, it nevertheless contains a great deal of flexibility and allows them to change, shift, and backtrack extensively in educational programs that prepare them for a variety of occupational pursuits. (As we will illustrate shortly, Ginzberg has recently modified his theory to reduce the rigidity of the process.)

The model of occupational choice developed by Super is similar in its use of developmental stages, but it is considerably more detailed and complex. He identifies six stages of occupational choice:

1. *Adolescence as exploration: developing a self-concept* (roughly comparable to Ginzberg's Period of Tentative Choice).
2. *The transition from school to work: reality testing* (partially comparable to Ginzberg's Period of Realistic Choice).
3. *The floundering or trial process: attempting to implement a self-concept* (partially comparable to Ginzberg's Period of Realistic Choice).
4. *The period of establishment: the self-concept modified or implemented.*
5. *The maintenance period: preserving or being nagged by self-concept.*
6. *The years of decline: adjustment to a new self-concept.*

For Super, vocational development is a lifelong process. While individuals are assumed to pass through these stages, they may do so at different times (ages) and at different rates. Also, the model allows for the possibility of skipping stages. The most important idea in Super's model is that of *self-concept.* The assumption is that individuals make occupational decisions that are consistent with their conception of themselves. The self-concept is defined as a continually changing and developing pattern of attitudes, interests, aspirations, and goals. Occupational choice is seen as an outcome that results from the attempt to attain an equilibrium or balance between the self-concept and the content and demands of work roles. Super assumes that the different abilities, interests, and personalities of individuals suit them for a number of different occupations. While occupations may require a distinctive set of qualities in those who enter them, they can accommodate a wide range of abilities, interests, and personality characteristics. Thus, there is more than just one right occupation for each individual and there is more than just one kind of individual that is right for each occupation.

Ginzberg's and Super's theories were originally published in the early to mid-1950s. One might well ask how relevant and important they are today. There is no doubt that they dominate the practice of vocational guidance and counseling and guide a great deal of research on occupational choice. In the early 1980s, a major symposium on occupational choice included statements from Ginzberg and Super about their theories. Super essentially reaffirmed the basic premises, stages, and assumptions of the original theory.[7]

Ginzberg used the occasion to modify his original theory in some ways. The process of occupational choice need not be confined to the period of early adolescence through young adulthood. Rather, it should be regarded as occurring *throughout a person's working lifetime*. This in effect brings the theory closer to Super's formulation. Ginzberg also modified the principle of *irreversibility*. He recognizes that people are continually discovering new occupational options and new choices are made. Finally, the *compromise* (between interests, capacities, opportunities, and values) is not a onetime occurrence, but rather an ongoing, lifelong activity.[8] Despite these modifications, the basic elements of the theory have remained the same. His concise restatement of the theory is that "occupational choice is a lifelong process of decision making for those who seek major satisfactions from their work. This leads them to reassess repeatedly how they can improve the fit between their changing career goals and the realities of the world of work."[9]

John L. Holland, a vocational psychologist, has developed an interpretation of occupational choice that emphasizes the primacy of personality characteristics. He argues that most people can be classified as one of six personality types: realistic, investigative, artistic, social, enterprising, or conventional. He also assumes that work environments can be classified according to these same six categories. Occupational choice then becomes a matter of attempting to maximize congruence or similarity between personality characteristics and the characteristics of work environments.[10]

Both Super's and Holland's approaches to occupational choice contain a problem that can best be described as the classic "chicken-egg dilemma." While it is possible that individuals may attempt to find work that is compatible with their self-concepts or personalities, it is equally possible that the kinds of work people do can shape their self-concepts and personalities. Whether self-concept and personality are the cause or consequence of occupational choice is open to question. Indeed, there is evidence from research on occupational socialization (to be discussed in chapter 4) to support this alternative interpretation. Super's model also assumes that individuals have considerable freedom to make choices—probably more freedom and discretion than actually exist in the real world. Like all rational decision-making models of occupational choice, it focuses on individuals and gives at best secondary attention to external opportunity structures over which individuals may have little control.[11] The model also implies that people, particularly adolescents, behave in extremely rational ways, systematically seeking occupational information and matching it to their developing self-concepts. Holland also seems to assume that individuals acquire valid information about occupational environments and systematically evaluate it in relation to their personalities. His conception of work environments also seems oversimplified and circular. While he recognizes that occupational environments may contain a variety and mixture of personality types, they are defined in terms of the personality types most frequently found in them.[12]

Another variant on the rational decision-making approach has been presented by Peter M. Blau, a sociologist.[13] His approach is to emphasize a wide variety of factors that need to be taken into account in explaining why people enter the occupations they do. These include biologically conditioned ability, personality characteristics, the historically shaped characteristics of the labor market, the level of technological development, etc. This scheme emphasizes the interaction of individual characteristics and decisions with characteristics of the occupational structure. The latter are seen as "selecting" people for different occupations. Although Blau's model recognizes the importance of factors external to the individual, it fits the rational decision-making approach in two ways. First, from the individual's point of view, choice is seen as deliberate. Individuals are assumed to make a reasoned and well thought-out choice that represents a compromise between their *preference hierarchy* (the kind of occupation they would ideally like to enter) and their *expectancy hierarchy* (the kind of occupation they realistically can expect to attain). Second, there is assumed to be a large measure of rational planning on the part of selection agents (occupational groups, employing organizations, economic sectors) in identifying the kinds of skills, abilities, and personalities they want to recruit.

Two sociologists, Basil Sherlock and Alan Cohen, have proposed another variant on the theme of rational planning and compromise.[14]

They regard occupational choice as a compromise between reward preferences and expectancies of access to particular occupations. They call this a *minimax strategy* to capture the idea that people may minimize one reward preference in order to maximize another. Their study of predental students found that dentistry was chosen because it was seen as offering both high rewards and reasonable ease of access. While medicine might offer greater rewards, it was rejected because it was perceived as more difficult to enter. Conversely, students reported rejecting occupations with similar accessibility to that of dentistry (such as law and university teaching) because they saw them as offering lower rewards than dentistry. While the minimax strategy can help to explain choices between concrete occupational alternatives, it does not explain how individuals develop particular reward preferences to begin with.

THE FORTUITOUS APPROACH

Where the rational decision-making approach sees individuals making purposeful, planned, concrete decisions, the *fortuitous approach* views occupational choice as less structured, purposeful, and rational. Occupational choice is seen as more accidental, due more to chance than to conscious choice. Another way of capturing the emphasis in this perspective would be to say that occupational choice is less a deliberate choice than it is a process in which alternatives are eliminated. The occupations people end up in are "residuals" in the sense that they are what is left after others are eliminated. Some contributors to this perspective have referred to the process as one of occupational "drift" rather than choice to convey the passive rather than active role of the individual in it. Individuals are seen as drifting into decisions and occupations rather than explicitly making decisions and choosing occupations.

This approach may be more appropriate for understanding occupational choice in the case of occupations that require little or no training or preparation or where only a short period of on-the-job training is sufficient. In other words, the prerequisites for entry into occupations may determine how much rational planning has to occur or the extent to which people drift in and out of the occupation. In occupations that have certification requirements or elaborate educational prerequisites, individuals may be forced to engage in rational planning and explicit decision making. In general, rational decision making would be encouraged more by occupations at the profession end of the nonprofession-profession continuum presented in chapter 2, and the fortuitous approach would be expected to occur more often at the other extreme.

While this generalization may be valid, there are some important exceptions that also illustrate how the fortuitous interpretation works.

For example, a number of studies have indicated that the way people enter college teaching fits the fortuitous model better than it fits the rational decision-making model. In one study, John E. Stecklein and Ruth E. Eckert concluded that the college teachers they studied had entered the occupation more by accident than by intent. As undergraduate students they apparently did not anticipate getting into their occupation the way undergraduates who entered other occupations did.[15] Another study of college teachers by John W. Gustad reached a similar conclusion. Gustad found that entry into college teaching was the result of a process of drift and that college teachers did not, as undergraduates, engage in the kind of conscious career planning that typically occurs among people who enter fields like medicine or law.[16]

A study of nursing students by Fred E. Katz and Harry W. Martin offers another example of occupational choice as largely fortuitous. They concluded that occupational choice can be highly spontaneous, nonrational, and influenced by situational pressures. Their study indicated that, at least for some persons, a rational thinking-through of the nature of a career in nursing was of minor importance in their decision to enter nursing compared to the importance of situational contingencies and influences only remotely connected to the occupation.[17]

Theodore Caplow has also pointed out that the basis for an individual's occupational choice is often trivial. For example, a good grade in a history course may lead to the decision to study law because history courses may be required for entry into law school; a student may decide to enter a vocational high school because it offers a course in automobile mechanics and he has been told that automobile mechanics earn good wages; or a high school student may transfer from a college preparatory to a commercial curriculum to be with her best friend.[18] Such spur-of-the-moment decisions and actions may be every bit as common (if not more common) than careful, conscious, rationally planned choices.

Some Observations on the Rational Decision-Making and Fortuitous Models

The rational decision-making and fortuitous approaches to occupational choice clearly represent polar extremes in terms of the underlying assumptions involved. Which perspective is the more accurate description of the process is of course an empirical question. However, it is important to realize that the assumptions made about the process lead to the asking of some questions and preclude the asking of others. Two people investigating occupational choice from these two perspectives simply would not ask the same questions. Being aware of the two approaches enables one to think about the phenomenon of occupational choice in a more comprehensive and thorough manner.

It is also possible that each of these approaches applies more to some types of occupations and individuals than others. As already noted, where elaborate educational prerequisites exist, extensive and deliberate planning by individuals may be essential. However, in many blue-collar occupations where educational credentials and formal entry requirements are less complex, individuals may enter and leave occupations without much planning because such planning is unnecessary. Movement from one semiskilled factory job to another may occur quite casually and routinely.

The relevance of the rational decision-making and fortuitous approaches may also depend on the segment of the class structure with which we are dealing. The idea of rational planning may apply primarily to middle-class youth aspiring to professional and managerial occupations with substantial educational requirements. Decisions may boil down to the question of *which* professional or business occupation one should enter and *which* college or university would best facilitate the achievement of one's goals. Since entry into professional or managerial work requires a substantial investment of both time and money, the decision becomes a crucial one and a dominant concern in these people's lives. Middle-class youth therefore are more likely to engage in a great deal of anticipatory role playing and weighing of the relative advantages, disadvantages, compatibility, and accessibility of a number of high-status occupations.

On the other hand, working-class youth, whose plans are less likely to include college attendance, are more likely to casually drift into an apprenticeship or a semiskilled job where there is not a substantial investment of time or money and where movement to jobs at comparable skill levels may be easy and frequent. It may matter little whether one becomes a machine operator or assembler in an automobile factory or in an electrical appliance factory. Both may be easily entered and easily left. For young people who plan to enter semiskilled blue-collar jobs, it does not make much sense to look at their choices in terms of a model of complex, elaborate planning.

THE SOCIOCULTURAL INFLUENCE APPROACH

A large amount of sociological research has been concerned with identifying and analyzing a number of social characteristics related to occupational choice. The approaches dealt with up to this point focus on the choice process and the decisions of individuals. What we have chosen to call the *sociocultural influence approach* takes a rather different orientation. Choice of occupation is looked at mainly in terms of the *status* and *prestige* of the occupations to which young people aspire. The research of this approach is concerned with the way in which occupational aspirations are affected or shaped by social characteristics such as *social-class background, rural-urban residence, gender,* and *race.* These characteristics are seen as external influences on occupational choice over which individuals have little or no control. They set limits upon and constrain the kinds of choices that individuals can make. In contrast to the rational decision-making and fortuitous approaches, the sociocultural influence approach deals with "macro" level issues and processes.

Social-Class Background

The social-class milieu in which a person is reared, whether measured by family income, parental occupation, or parental education, is a major constraint on occupational aspirations. Numerous studies using national, regional, and local samples conducted in various parts of the United States since the 1940s have consistently demonstrated that family social-class position is directly related to level of occupational aspiration. The higher the social-class level of a young person's family, the more likely he or she is to aspire to more prestigious and rewarding occupational positions.[19]

One of the best-known studies dealing with this topic has been conducted in Wisconsin under the direction of William H. Sewell. In this study, a one-third random sample of the Wisconsin high school graduating class of 1957 (approximately 10,000 people) has been followed through 1975. Students' educational and occupational aspirations and attainments as well as earnings have been the focus of the study. Using such measures of family social-class position as parental income, father's and mother's education, and father's occupation, it is clear that the higher these are, the higher the status of the occupation to which students aspire.[20]

Another study, known as the National Longitudinal Study of Youth, produced similar results in 1979. Using a national sample of 11,400 respondents ages fourteen through twenty-one, this survey asked the question "What would you like to be doing when you are thirty-five years old?" Over three-fourths of the respondents said they would like to be working. Data also were collected about the educational level of their parents. The more education their parents had, the higher the prestige of the occupations to which respondents aspired.[21]

Research on this topic in Canada has produced similar results. Merlin B. Brinkerhoff and David J. Corry asked 949 grade 11 students in Calgary about their occupational aspirations and expectations. Using father's occupation as their measure of family social class, they found that the prestige level of both occupational aspirations and expectations increased as family social class increased.[22]

Rural-Urban Residence

Differences in the occupational aspirations of young people living in rural and urban areas also have been extensively documented. There is a good deal of support for the conclusion that rural and urban environments represent different *opportunity structures* in the sense that urban areas provide more opportunities for becoming acquainted with a broader range of occupational possibilities than do rural areas. Presumably, this greater awareness leads urban youth to aspire to higher-status occupations. While it is possible that the intrusion of the mass media into previously isolated and remote rural areas will diminish the importance of these differences in the future, there is substantial evidence that the size of the community in which people are reared operates as a major influence on their occupational aspirations.[23]

The Wisconsin study referred to above provided data on this relationship. William H. Sewell and Alan M. Orenstein reported that the occupational aspirations of high school seniors change dramatically as we go from farming areas to large cities. For example, only 29.8 percent of the students living on farms aspired to professional and managerial occupations compared to 48.6 percent of those living in large cities.[24] The National Longitudinal Study of Youth referred to above also reported similar results. Using occupational prestige as the measure of aspirations, the study reported that rural residence has a depressing effect on occupational aspirations.[25]

Gender

Research on women's occupational aspirations during the 1950s and 1960s indicated that they were lower than those of men. This relationship between gender and level of occupational aspiration was largely a consequence of traditional cultural norms and expectations regarding gender roles and work roles. For men, attaining and pursuing a full-time occupation has been and still is a very pervasive cultural expectation. A man's social status is largely determined by the kind of work he does and the degree to which he is rewarded for it. Working has not been normatively *expected* of women the way it has been of men. While full- or part-time work is an acceptable and increasingly encouraged activity for women, other options—the traditional wife and mother role—are also available. However, there is some evidence that this is changing as women have come to participate in the labor force in larger numbers, as artificial barriers to women's occupational participation have been challenged, and as issues of sex equality and equal opportunity have become a matter of public policy. In other words, changes in the definition of gender roles are affecting the way in which they operate as a constraint on occupational choice.

Gender and Social Stratification. Conventional sociological thinking about women's work and occupational choices has been influenced to a great extent by theories of social stratification that emphasize the "derived" or "reflected" status of women vis-a-vis their husbands. Kingsley Davis, for example, argued that the family could not perform its function of status ascription if it did not occupy a single position on the stratification scale. Since children acquire their parents' status, the implication is that the parents have a single status to transmit. Thus, for the purpose of their location in the stratification system, husbands and wives are social equals with their joint position based on the position of the husband.[26] Robin M. Williams and Bernard Barber also stressed the necessity of treating the family as the basic unit of the stratification system with husbands and wives seen as occupying a single status.[27] The most influential statement of this view of stratification comes from the work of Talcott Parsons who argued that marital stability depends on husbands and wives being in noncompetitive roles. Since the employment of wives raises the possibility of competition between spouses, he argued that family stability is enhanced by wives not working or working at a noncompetitive occupation. The result would be that they have jobs, rather than careers, that ultimately have little or no impact on the overall position of the family in the stratification system.[28]

Based on his study of Los Angeles high school seniors in the mid-1950s, Ralph H. Turner questioned the appropriateness of comparing the occupational aspirations and choices of young men and women since they were so different. He found that only 3.6 percent of the girls in his study planned on a lifetime occupational career, while 48.4 percent planned to be homemakers exclusively, and 47.9 percent planned to combine a career with homemaking.[29] However, 58.5 percent said that they wanted their future husbands to have occupations in the "professional or large business owner and official" category.[30] Turner concluded that, rather than examining their occupational aspirations, women's ambitions might more appropriately be investigated by looking at the occupational qualifications they seek in their future husbands.

Valerie Kincade Oppenheimer has persuasively argued that this interpretation of the stratification system downplays the significance of women's occupational decisions and participation. Given the tremendous increase in the rate at which married women have entered the labor force in recent years, viewing their status as a reflection of that of their husbands' status distorts our assessment of the relative position of families as well as women in the stratification system. Oppenheimer's analysis of data from the 1970 Census indicated that husbands and wives tend to work in occupations of similar status with the result that wives' occupational status tends to enhance the status of the family. She also concluded that, although wives typically earn less than their husbands, their earnings are a significant contribution to the economic position of the family, sometimes substituting for the husband's mobility or compensating for his relatively low earnings.[31] The implication of Oppenheimer's analysis is that women's occupational choices are significant in their own right and need to be viewed as having important consequences for the position of both individuals and families in the stratification system.

George Psathas has gone so far as to suggest the need for a theory of occupational choice that specifically applies to women.[32] He points out that most theories (Ginzberg, Super, Holland, Blau, etc.) have been developed to explain the occupational choices of men and implicitly incorporate factors that apply primarily to men. He identifies several additional considerations affecting the occupational decisions of women. For one thing, the range of potential occupational choices open to women has been more restricted than that of men. Also, marriage intentions, time of marriage, and childbearing all operate as special constraints on the occupational plans of women. Early marriage, and especially childbearing, are likely to lower the probability of acquiring education that might make it feasible to realistically aspire to higher-status occupations. Psathas also regards family decisions about the allocation of financial resources as having more crucial implications for the occupational choices of women than men. While a family's ability to support or contribute to the education of its children is important for the opportunities of both young men and women, it may become more crucial where the level of resources is marginal and not all children can be so supported. In such cases resources are more likely to be set aside or diverted to facilitate the occupational attainment of male rather than female children. Psathas also suggests that women's occupational choices may be affected by the opportunity to experience upward mobility through marriage. Aspirations for an occupation that requires a college education, for example, may increase a young woman's chances of meeting and marrying a man who will be in a higher-status occupation, simply by virtue of college attendance. Data from the study of Wisconsin high school seniors noted earlier lends support to this argument.[33]

The Convergence of Men's and Women's Occupational Choices. As indicated at the beginning of this section on gender and occupational choice, a great deal of research supports the conclusion that women have aspired to occupations of lower status than have men.[34] There is some recent evidence, albeit mixed, that this relationship is changing, and that the occupational aspiration levels of men and women are becoming more similar. This pattern of *convergence* has been found in a number of studies.

The National Longitudinal Study of Youth found in 1979 that young men and women chose professional occupations at virtually the same rate (36 percent of the women and 37 percent of the men). However, men were more likely than women to choose managerial (12 percent of the men and 5 percent of the women) and skilled craft (19 percent of the men and 2 percent of the women) occupations. Women chose clerical occupations by a margin of 12 percent to 1 percent. This pattern of convergence for professional occupations and continued sex-typing of choices in clerical and skilled craft work recurs in several other studies.[35]

Another example of convergence is found in a 1974 study by Bernard C. Rosen and Carol S. Aneshensel in which some 3,200 students in grades 7 through 12 in three upstate New York communities were asked about their educational and occupational expectations.[36] Students were asked, "What job do you think you'll probably end up having when you are your parent's age?" Only 10 percent of the females said "housewife." When the occupational expectations of the remainder are compared to those of male students, there are both similarities and some differences in their choices. A larger proportion of females (52.2 percent) indicated professional, managerial, and executive occupations compared to 44.7 percent of the males. However, there is also evidence that occupational expectations reflect the traditional pattern of men's and women's choices. While 32.0 percent of the male students indicated major professional and top executive occupations, only 15.7 percent of the females did so. On the other hand, 36.5 percent of the female students expected to be in managerial and "lesser professional" occupations compared to only 12.7 percent of the male students. Further evidence of the sex-stereotyping of occupational expectations is suggested by the finding that 23.7 percent of the males (compared to 3.4 percent of the females) expected to be in skilled manual work. However, clerical and secretarial occupations (traditionally considered as women's work) were indicated by 25.5 percent of the females compared to only 7.0 percent of the males.[37]

Several studies have looked specifically at changes in occupational choices over time. Lloyd B. Lueptow obtained information on the occupational choices of high school seniors in seventeen Wisconsin high schools in 1964.[38] In 1975 the same information was collected from seniors in the same schools. Students were asked what occupation they planned to follow (their expected occupation) and the occupation they would choose if they were absolutely free to go into any kind of work they wanted (their ideal occupation). His focus was on the degree to which the students chose sex-typed occupations. An occupation was defined as sex-typed if it was chosen by at least five students and at least 70 percent of them were of the same sex. In 1964, four-fifths of the female students expected to enter one of twelve occupations that were 88 percent female on the average. By 1975 the percentage expecting to enter the twelve most female sex-typed occupations had dropped substantially to only 49.8 percent. A similar pattern was found for ideal occupational choices. The percentage of females choosing the seventeen predominantly female occupations dropped from 75.9 percent in 1964 to 47.9 percent in 1975. The choices of male students reflect a pattern of both change and stability. The percentage of male students expecting to enter one of eighteen predominantly male white-collar jobs dropped from 91.2 percent in 1964 to 67.1 percent in 1975. However, the proportion expecting to enter one of the twelve predominantly male blue-collar jobs remained essentially the same (98.7 percent in 1964 and 97.0 percent in 1975). A similar pattern held for the ideal occupational choices of male students. While Lueptow's main findings support the convergence hypothesis, he also points out that there is evidence of continuing sex-stereotyping of occupational choices. For example, in 1975 only a very small proportion of males (7.0 percent) expected to enter one of the fifteen predominantly female occupations, and only 1.1 percent of the females expected to enter one of the predominantly male blue-collar occupations. Furthermore, in 1975, *all* of the students whose ideal occupational choice was librarian, bank teller, secretary, or practical nurse were female and *all* of the students whose ideal choice was printer, machinist, carpenter, plumber, appliance mechanic, or welder were male.

Another study focusing on gender and changes over time was done by A. Regula Herzog and deals with the period 1976 through 1980.[39] The findings are based on responses from approximately 3,000 high school seniors in 115 public and 15 private high schools representing a cross section of the United States. Students' occupational expectations were obtained by asking the question, "What kind of work do you think you will be doing when you are thirty years old?" During this relatively short time period there was a modest decrease in male-female differences in occupational expectation. Most notable was a decrease in the proportion of women who expected to be full-time homemakers from 13.2 percent in 1976 to 7.9 percent in 1980. In 1980, 43.1 percent of the men and 39.1 percent of the women expected to be in professional occupations, but the expectations of women were concentrated in traditionally female professions such as nursing, teaching, and social work. Similar proportions expected to be in managerial/administrative work (8.7 percent of the men and 7.3 percent of the women). Skilled craft occupations, however, showed considerable sex-typing with 21.5 percent of the men and only 1.2 percent of the women expecting to enter them. This study also asked students to rate the desirability of different kinds of work settings. Women expressed a preference for schools, social service agencies, police departments, and small businesses, while men preferred self-employment and small partnerships. About the only change that occurred over this time period was an increase in interest in self-employment among women. A final topic dealt with in this study was the kinds of things that the students said they valued about work. Several findings here suggest that young men and women have different priorities with regard to what they look for and value in work. Women placed a higher value than men on such things as contact with other people and the opportunity to assist others. Men placed a greater value on material rewards, status, and opportunities for advancement. By 1980 both men and women attached greater importance to the things they valued in 1976. This increase in importance was slightly larger for women than for men. A final difference was that men placed a greater value on having a job with decision-making responsibility and, surprisingly, a job that allows for vacations and a good deal of free time.

A final example of research looking at trends over time in the occupational choices of men and women comes from the National Center for Education Statistics in the U.S. Department of Education. Based on national surveys of high school seniors in 1972 and 1980, the Center reported that as early as 1972 a larger percentage of females (48.8 percent) than males (41.8 percent) expected to enter professional occupations. By 1980 the difference was even greater. Some 48.7 percent of the females but only 38.8 percent of the males expected to enter professional jobs. Over this eight-year period there was no evidence of male students expressing increased interest in primarily female jobs or females becoming more interested in traditionally male blue-collar jobs. The only additional changes of note were a decrease in the percentage of females expecting to enter clerical jobs (from 25.5 percent in 1972 to 17.7 percent in 1980) and a slight increase of interest on the part of female students in entering managerial/administrative work (from 1.3 percent in 1972 to 6.4 percent in 1980.[40]

In conclusion, recent research on men's and women's occupational choice presents a pattern of both change (congruence) and stability. Compared to a generation ago, young women today are more likely to plan to work and their overall occupational aspirations are higher. In addition, they are more likely to aspire to professional occupations than they did in the past. However, the choice of managerial occupations has not increased dramatically among women, they are not much more likely to aspire to skilled blue-collar occupations than they were in the past, and clerical occupations remain quite popular as an occupational choice. Finally, it should be noted that the changes going on are occurring mainly among women. Young men's occupational choices remain centered on the more established professions, managerial work, and skilled blue-collar occupations. There is no evidence to suggest increased interest among young men in traditionally female professions or in clerical occupations. The occupational choices of young men have remained much more sex-stereotyped than those of young women.

Race

A large number of studies of the occupational choices of black youth have been conducted by sociologists, psychologists, and guidance counselors. Since our concern is with looking at race as a social constraint on occupational choice, we will deal only with those studies that actually compare the occupational choices of blacks and whites. As with other studies of factors related to occupational choice, much of the research summarized here makes a distinction between occupational *aspirations* (what people would *like* to attain) and *expectations* (what they realistically *expect* to attain). Since, as we have already seen, social class and gender are related to occupational choice, it is important that we be alert to the need to assess the independent effect of these factors when making black-white comparisons.

The investigation of black-white differences in occupational choice goes back some thirty years. In the late 1950s R. G. Holloway and Joel V. Berreman examined the effect of both family social class and race on the occupational aspirations and expectations of 313 sixth, seventh, and eighth grade boys in a Pacific northwest city.[41] They concluded that both the aspirations and expectations of white students were higher than those of the black students. Distinguishing between students from middle-class and lower-class backgrounds, they found that white middle-class students had the highest aspirations. The aspirations of middle-class whites were higher than those of lower-class whites, but family class background did not make a difference in the aspirations of the black students. In none of the four race/class groupings was there a difference between occupational aspirations and expectations.

Another study by Jetse Sprey dealt with 2,956 ninth graders in New Haven, Connecticut in 1958 and Harrisburg, Pennsylvania in 1960.[42] The study compared black and white students by gender, father's occupational status, and, for blacks, the region of the country in which they had been reared (North or South). Occupational aspirations and expectations were classified into white collar, skilled manual, and lower manual, as was father's occupational status.

One of the main findings was that black and white girls had similar occupational aspirations, but white boys had higher aspirations than black boys. The effect of class background on aspirations was mixed. For boys, whites from white-collar and lower-manual families had higher occupational aspirations than blacks from comparable family backgrounds. However, among boys from skilled-manual families, the aspirations of blacks and whites were similar. For girls, there was no difference in level of occupational aspiration between whites and blacks when those from each family class level were compared. Black boys of southern origin (born in the South and migrated North with their parents) had lower aspirations and expectations than black boys of northern origin. In other words, black boys who grew up in the North were more like their white counterparts in terms of occupational aspirations and expectations.

The occupational aspirations of 411 high school seniors in three low-income rural counties of northern Florida were the focus of a 1962 study by E. G. Youmans.[43] Surprisingly, a *majority* of blacks and whites of both sexes aspired to occupations broadly defined as professional. Nevertheless, there were some important differences by race. Among boys, blacks were more likely than whites to aspire to skilled-manual occupations (17 percent compared to 8 percent), and whites were more likely than blacks to aspire to professional occupations (61 percent compared to 52 percent). Among girls, blacks were more likely than whites to aspire to professional occupations and less likely to aspire to clerical (office work, sales) jobs. Thus, while black boys had lower occupational aspirations than white boys, the racial difference was just the opposite among girls.

Another Florida study by Russell Middleton and Charles M. Grigg dealt with a sample of 2,183 high school seniors representative of the state's 1955 high school senior population.[44] Overall, whites had higher occupational aspirations than blacks. This pattern held when boys and girls of both races were compared to each other. However, when rural-urban residence was included in the analysis, racial differences in level of aspiration diminished considerably for rural boys. Rural boys of both races had lower aspirations than urban boys. However, rural residence operated as a *greater* depressant on the aspirations of white than black boys. The aspirations of rural black boys were only slightly lower than those of urban black boys. This finding may be an inadvertent consequence of the fact that rural white boys were much more likely to indicate farming as their occupational choice than were rural black boys. Another explanation of this finding might be that rural black boys with very low occupational aspirations are more likely to have dropped out of school before their senior year (compared to urban black boys) and therefore were not included in the sample to begin with.

Is Convergence on the Basis of Race Occurring? Given the educational and economic gains of black Americans in the 1960s and 1970s[45] it is important to ask whether or not there has been a change in occupational aspiration patterns. The changes that have occurred might be expected to produce a shift in the direction of more similar occupational choice patterns analogous to the convergence noted in regard to gender differences in occupational choice. The answer to this question is that there is some support for the convergence hypothesis but there is also evidence that the pattern of generally lower aspirations among blacks compared to whites persists.

Two studies are of particular relevance to this issue. In one, Howard H. Garrison examined the occupational aspirations of male high school seniors in fifty of Virginia's public school districts at two points in time.[46] His sample included 16,270 students in 1967 and 21,465 in 1976. Occupational aspirations were dichotomized into plans for white-collar or blue-collar jobs. In 1967, blacks were more likely to plan on pursuing blue-collar jobs than whites (37.8 percent compared to 30.7 percent), and whites were more likely to aspire to white-collar jobs than blacks (69.3 percent compared to 62.2 percent). By 1976, the aspirations of black and white students were virtually identical. However, this convergence did not occur because of an increase in the occupational aspiration level of blacks. Rather, it was the result of a *decrease* in the proportion of whites aspiring to white-collar occupations and an *increase* in the proportion planning on blue-collar jobs, while the plans of black students remained the same over time.

In another study, Frank M. Howell and Wolfgang Frese collected longitudinal data on 729 students who were fifth and sixth graders in 1969 and whom they were able to follow up six years later in 1975.[47] The students were in schools in five southern states (Kentucky, Mississippi, North Carolina, South Carolina, and Virginia). Their findings are based on the students' aspirations in 1975. The results of this study present evidence of not only convergence, but an actual reversal of race differences in aspirations found in other studies. Overall, blacks had *higher* occupational aspirations than whites. On a scale measuring the status of the occupation to which the students aspired, the mean score for black students was 55.07 compared to 50.52 for whites. Another important finding was that females aspired to higher-status occupations than males, with black females more likely to aspire to higher-status occupations than white females. The results of this study need to be interpreted cautiously. The schools selected for study were in areas with high poverty levels, unemployment rates, and school-dropout rates. They probably are not representative of even the region of the country in which they are located.

SOCIAL ORIGINS OF MEMBERS
OF SPECIFIC OCCUPATIONS

In the literature on the sociology of occupations there is a tradition of research that deals with the *social origins* of people in particular occupations. The focus here is on the extent to which occupations attract or recruit their members from different segments of the social structure and thereby represent, at any given time, a distinctive "mix" in terms of the social origins and backgrounds of their members. Another concern of such studies is the degree to which individuals "inherit" their parents' occupational status, in the sense that they enter the same occupation or one of similar status.

Research on this topic has dealt with social origins by looking at such characteristics as parental occupational status, family social-class origins, rural-urban background, ethnicity, and religious background. Most social-origins research has been done on members of occupations generally regarded as being at the profession end of the nonprofession-profession continuum.

The notion that in a modern industrial society occupational roles are achieved rather than ascribed would lead us to predict that direct occupational inheritance (i.e., people entering the same occupation as their parents) would be comparatively low. Table 3.1 presents data drawn from several studies of different occupations. In all cases, direct occupational inheritance is greater than would be expected on the basis of chance. That is, compared to the proportion of the labor force in these occupations, those with parents in the occupation are overrepresented in it.

Table 3.2 presents data on the parental occupational origins of members of selected occupations in terms of the proportion that come from professional backgrounds. The most appropriate way of interpreting these data is to view them as reflecting the social-class level from which members of these occupations are recruited. With the exception of mental health workers (psychoanalysts, psychiatrists, clinical psychologists, and psychiatric social workers) there is a clear tendency for people in these prestigious professional and semiprofessional occupations to be drawn from the upper levels of the class structure.

These data on social origins reflect more than just selective recruitment on the basis of social-class background. They suggest some influences on occupational choice over and above those considered earlier in this chapter. As part of the normal process of growing up, young people probably learn more about the work and work environment of their parents' occupations than about any other occupation. Furthermore, they probably learn more about them than do people whose parents are not

Table 3.1
Direct Occupational Inheritance

	Percent with Fathers (Mothers) in Same Occupation				
Medicine..	11[a]	19[b]	17[c]	18[d]	14[e]
Medicine (mothers)	6[f]				
Clergy	13[g]				
Military	25[h]				
Lawyers, male	15[i]				
Lawyers, female................................	11[j]				
Dentistry..	8[k]				
Social Work (father or mother)	3[l]				
Police	7[m]				
University Faculty...............................	5[n]				
University Faculty (mothers)	2[o]				

Sources:
[a](Medical Students) Helen H. Gee, "The Student View of the Medical Admissions Process," in *The Appraisal of Applicants to Medical Schools,* ed. Helen H. Gee and John T. Cowles (Evanston, Ill.: Association of American Medical Colleges, 1957), 143.
[b](University of Kansas Medical Students) Howard S. Becker, et. al., *Boys in White: Student Culture in Medical School* (Chicago: University of Chicago Press, 1961), 61.
[c](Medical Students, Eastern University) Wagner Thielens, Jr., "Some Comparisons of Entrants to Medical and Law School," in *The Student Physician,* Robert K. Merton, et. al. (Cambridge, Mass.: Harvard University Press, 1957), 134.
[d](Medical Students) Jane Leserman, *Men and Women in Medical School: How They Change and How They Compare* (New York: Praeger, 1981), 83.
[e](Medical Students, 1974-75) Davis G. Johnson, *Physicians in the Making* (San Francisco: Jossey-Bass, 1983), 107, table 20. The same percentage is also reportedfor first-year medical students at an "Eastern Medical School" in Robert H. Coombs, Mastering Medicine: Professional Socialization in Medical School (New York: Free Press, 1978), 25–26.
[f](Medical Students) Same as note d above.
[g](Protestant Clergymen under age 50 Listed in Who's Who, 1958–59) James Otis Smith and Gideon Sjoberg, "Origins and Career Patters of Leading Protestant Clergymen," *Social Forces* 39 (May 1961): 290–296.
[h](1960 Class of West Point) Morris Janowitz, *The Professional Soldier* (New York: Free Press, 1960) 96.
[i](Law Students) Same as Note c above.
[j](Practicing Lawyers, New York) Cynthia Fuchs Epstein, *Women in Laww* (Garden City, N.Y.: Anchor Books, 1983), 25.
[k](Dental Students) Douglas M. More, "Social Origins of Future Dentists," *The Midwest Sociologist* 21 (July 1959): 69–76.
[l](Social Work Students) Arnulf N. Pins, *Who Chooses Social Work, When and Why?* (New York: Council on Social Work Education, 1963), 44.
[m](New York Police Academy Recruits) Arthur Niederhoffer, *Behind the Shield: The Police in Urban Society* (Garden City, N.Y.: Anchor Books, 1967), 39.
[n]"Characteristics of College and Univeristy Faculty Members," *Chronicle of Higher Education* 31 (December 18, 1985): 26.
[o]Same as Note n above.

members of the occupation. Exposure to and familiarity with the occupation and its surrounding subculture may operate as a very subtle and indirect influence on occupational choice over and above those cases of more overt and direct encouragement to follow a parent's occupation. The relatively professional kinds of work included in tables 3.1 and 3.2 are likely to have fairly well developed subcultures that extend well beyond specific work activities to many aspects of nonwork life as well. Without any overt or intentional planning or intervention on the part of parents or others, people whose parents are in comparatively professionalized occupations grow up in distinctive subcultures about which they become knowledgeable and in which they may function with a great

Table 3.2
Occupational Inheritance in Terms of
Broad Occupational Status Levels

Percent With Father (Mothers) in Professional Occupations			
Medicine	28[a]	22[b]	49[c]
Medicine (mothers)	32[d]		
Clergy			
Catholic	12[e]		
Protestant	36[f]		
Military	50[gh]		
Lawyers, male	10[i]		
Lawyers, female	19[j]		
Lawyers, female (mothers)	20[k]		
Dentistry	24[l]		
Social Work	19[m]		
Teachers	14[n]		
Male Elementary	14[o]		
Male Secondary	22[o]		
Female Elementary	21[o]		
Female Secondary	21[o]		
Engineering	19[p]		
Psychoanalysts	8[q]		
Psychiatrists	8[q]		
Clinical Psychologists	7[q]		
Psychiatric Social Workers	7[q]		
University Faculty	23[r]		
University Faculty (mothers)	18[s]		

Sources:
[a]Same as source a, Table 3.1.
[b]Same as source b, Table 3.1
[c]Same as source d, Table 3.1, p. 82.
[d]Same as source d, Table 3.1.
[e]Joseph H. Fichter, *Religion as an Occupation* (Notre Dame, Ind.: University of Notre Dame Press, 1961), 62.
[f]Same as source g, Table 3.1.
[g]Same as source h, Table 3.1.
[h]Includes professional and managerial.
[i]Jerome Carlin, *Lawyers Ethics: A Survey of the New York City Bar*, (New York: Russell Sage Foundation, 1966).
[j]Same as source j, Table 3.1, p. 26.
[k]Same as source j, Table 3.1, p. 27.
[l]Same as source k, Table 3.1.
[m]Same as source l, Table 3.1.
[n]*The American Public School Teacher, 1960-61* (Washington, D.C.: National Education Association, 1963), 15.
[o]Michael Betz and James Garland, "Intergenerational Mobility Rates of Urban School Teachers," *Sociology of Education* 47 (Fall 1974): 511-522.
[p]Douglas M. More, "The Derivation of Hypotheses Relating Occupational Mobility and Job Performance," *The Midwest Sociologist* 19 (May 1957): 87–92.
[q]Includes professional and major executive.) William E. Henry, et. al., *The Fifth Profession: Becoming a Psychotherapist* (San Francisco: Jossey-Bass, 1971), 31, table 6.
[r]Same as source n, Table 3.1.
[s]Same as source n, Table 3.1.

deal of ease and comfort. This very fact may operate as an influence on the development of their occupational choices.

The foregoing discussion is clearly speculative. Social origins studies have not conclusively demonstrated that these kinds of influences do in fact occur. Rather, the discussion is intended to suggest hypotheses that might guide and be tested in future investigations of the occupational choice process. A number of studies of lawyers and law students indicate that family influences—in the form of having relatives in addition to one's parents who are lawyers—are common among those recruited to the law. It is almost as if choice of the occupation carries out a mandate to continue a legal heritage.[48] Jane Leserman's study of medical students at three North Carolina schools (Duke University, University of North Carolina at Chapel Hill, and Bowman Gray School of Medicine) also contains evidence that growing up in a medical environment is quite common among people who enter medicine. Over one-third of the medical students in her study were from families in which there was at least one physician.[49]

The kinds of analyses of occupational groups that we have called "social-origins" studies have dealt mainly with patterns of occupational inheritance and the social-class backgrounds of people in a particular occupation. However, several have addressed other origin variables as well, and traced the changing social composition of occupations over time.

Examples of this more comprehensive approach to studying an occupational group are Morris Janowitz's study of the military officer corps and Joseph H. Fichter's analysis of the Catholic priesthood.[50] Janowitz concluded that since the early 1900s there has been a downward shift in the class origins of top military leaders. While people from business and professional family backgrounds are still overrepresented, entry into the military elite has become more open, particularly to those from middle- and lower-middle-class backgrounds. Janowitz also concluded that the military elite has been and continues to be drawn disproportionately from rural areas and southern regional origins. In terms of religious affiliation, the military elite continues to be overwhelmingly Protestant but, as its class base of recruitment has broadened, it has increasingly recruited Catholics to its ranks. Fichter's study of the Catholic priesthood concluded that there was a definite shift in the origins of priests from working-class to middle-class family backgrounds between about 1910 and the late 1950s. This probably reflected the general upward shift in the social class composition of American Catholics from which priests are recruited.

James Otis Smith and Gideon Sjoberg also looked at changes over time in the origins of Protestant clergymen.[51] Even though clergy are drawn disproportionately from families of high occupational status, there has been a downward shift in class origins similar to that reported by Janowitz for military leaders. Smith and Sjoberg also report a shift in rural-urban origins with clergy being recruited more recently from urban backgrounds compared to the more rural origins of their older colleagues.

Other social background characteristics have been dealt with in investigations of occupational groups. A survey of nearly 4,000 psychotherapists in New York, Chicago, and Los Angeles dealt with (among other things) the therapists' religious identification.[52] Respondents were asked to indicate the group (Protestant, Catholic, or Jewish) with which they identified, even if they did not adhere to its religious position and practices. A very large proportion—51.5 percent—indicated a Jewish identification. This was highest among psychoanalysts (62.1 percent) and lowest among psychiatric social workers (48.4 percent) with clinical psychologists (49.8 percent) and psychiatrists (50.5 percent) only slightly higher.[53] The study also reported that the overwhelming majority—nearly 70 percent—had grown up in large metropolitan areas. Psychotherapists are also much more likely to be foreign-born or second generation (native-born of foreign-born parents) than the general population.[54] These findings led the authors of the study to conclude that psychotherapists tend to be recruited from marginal groups in society.

A final illustration of the social origins approach to occupational choice will deal with teachers, a group whose social background characteristics have been the subject of several studies. Research on the social origins of teachers has dealt with both people in the occupation as well as students indicating teaching as their occupational choice.

Several studies have found that teachers are recruited disproportionately from higher social-class backgrounds. Anthony Gary Dworkin found this pattern in a study of teachers in a large southwestern metropolis[55] and a study of Michigan teachers by Michael Betz and James Garland reported similar results.[56] Ronald M. Pavalko's longitudinal study of Wisconsin high school students who became teachers found that they were similarly drawn from higher social class origins.[57] Dworkin also reports that over time the social-class level of the parents of teachers has been increasing. Despite this pattern, the studies by Betz and Garland, Pavalko, and a study of the occupational choices of Kentucky high school students by Harry K. Schwarzweller and Thomas A. Lyson indicate that teaching is an important avenue of upward social mobility for many young people from working class backgrounds.[58]

OCCUPATIONAL CHOICE
AND EDUCATIONAL DECISIONS

To talk about occupational choice without considering educational decisions is to construct a partial picture of reality. Occupational and educational decisions obviously occur simultaneously and interact with one another. In a sense, educational institutions provide the connection between the internal choice process of the rational decision-making and fortuitous models and the external constraints of the sociocultural influ-

Table 3.3
The Relationship between Educational and Occupational Attainment, by Sex, 1984

Percent with:	Mgr. & prof.	Technical, sales & admin.	Service	Precision production, craft & repair	Operators, fabricators and laborers
			Males		
Less than 4 years H.S.	3.7	8.5	27.4	23.7	35.1
4 years H.S.	15.4	34.5	41.0	52.2	49.4
1–3 years college	15.6	27.2	21.0	18.2	12.0
4 years + college	65.3	29.8	10.7	5.9	3.5
Total*	100.0	100.0	100.1	100.0	100.0
			Females		
Less than 4 years H.S.	2.5	7.1	33.3	27.8	40.5
4 years H.S.	19.3	55.9	50.5	52.9	50.2
1–3 years college	19.6	24.6	11.6	12.3	7.2
4 years + college	58.6	12.4	4.5	7.1	2.1
Total*	100.0	100.0	99.9	100.1	100.0

Source: Bureau of the Census, *Statistical Abstract of the United States, 1985* (Washington, D.C.: U.S. Government Printing Office, 1984), 401, table 674.
*Some totals do not equal 100% because of rounding error.

ence model. In effect, educational decisions mediate between the micro and macro processess involved in occupational choice.

In terms of outcomes, it is clear that a strong relationship exists between educational attainment and occupational attainment. Table 3.3 presents data from the 1980 Census on the percentage of men and women over age twenty-five in different occupational categories who have attained different levels of education. It is apparent that those in higher-status occupations have attained more education.

Undoubtedly the most crucial educational decision, in terms of its impact on later occupational options, is the decision concerning college attendance. Once a person enters college, a wide variety of occupational options exist, primarily in professional, technical, managerial, and other white-collar fields. As one proceeds successfully through college, the likelihood of eventually entering a blue-collar or manual occupation decreases.

A continuing debate has raged in American education over the issue of whether or not education (particularly higher education) should be oriented to the preparation of students for occupational roles. The view that it should has been referred to as a "vocational" or "practice-oriented" perspective. This view competes with the idea that higher education should provide a "liberal arts" education that is mainly concerned with communicating an understanding and appreciation of the intellectual heritage of Western civilization. An appropriate analogy would be that of a pendulum swinging back and forth between these two extremes. Where the pendulum is at any given time has implications for the kind and degree of impact education has on the preparation of individuals for occupational careers. During the late 1960s and 1970s the emphasis of American higher education was in the direction of the liberal arts. In the early 1980s there was a return to a concern with vocational preparation, and in the late 1980s there are signs of increasing concern with liberal arts education. It is unfortunate that these two emphases are usually posed as competing and unreconcilable. A recent study of undergraduate students at Stanford University found that students can simultaneously have strong career goals and strong intellectual interests of the kind that a liberal arts education tries to impart.[59]

Nevertheless, regardless of which emphasis prevails at any given time, the acquisition of a college education operates to increase the likelihood of entry into white-collar occupations and reduce the likelihood of entry into blue-collar occupations. Beyond the ability to allocate students to occupations of different statuses, colleges also have linkages to different occupational and economic groups that enable them to shape the occupational goals and interests of their students through the kinds of occupational entry they can credibly promise. David H. Kamens has referred to this sense of what a college can and is supposed to produce as its "charter."[60] The prestige of an institution may affect its charter. For example, prestigious schools may be able to point to the occupational accomplishments of their distinguished graduates. They may also have connections with graduate and professional schools as well as economic and political elites that enable them to sponsor their graduates and use such networks to launch careers. College size is also an important factor that affects the occupational choices of students. Larger schools, Kamens argues, can expose students to a greater diversity of roles and activities than smaller schools can. The greater complexity of larger schools and their connections with graduate and professional schools symbolize their ability to link students with important professional and business roles in the larger society. In a longitudinal study of students at ninety-nine universities and colleges, Kamens found that students at larger schools (over 1,000 students) who as freshmen chose professional occupations (such as law, medicine, the clergy, and engineering) were more likely than students at smaller schools to have professional occupational choices as seniors. On the other hand, at smaller schools freshmen who chose professional occupations were more likely to have switched to the choice of an academic career (college teaching and scientific occupations) as seniors compared to students at larger schools. Although students at both large and small schools switch their occupational choices in both directions, small schools are more effective in recruiting their students to academic/scientific careers and large schools are more effective in recruiting their students to professional careers. In other words, the charter of small schools emphasizes the production of scholars/scientists while that of large schools emphasizes the production of professionals.

In a sense, the educational system is a structure of choices and options with regard to occupational outcomes. As students pass through this maze, choices are explicitly and implicitly forced on them. The initial choice point is usually faced upon completion of junior high school. In larger communities the choice may be whether or not to attend a specialized (vocational, science-oriented) or general, comprehensive high school. In smaller communities or those without specialized high schools, the choice of curriculum (business, college preparatory, general) has later occupational implications. Completion of high school presents another choice point requiring a decision of whether or not to go to college. In addition, the decision of where to go to college is an important one. Usually by the third year of college most students are required to make a decision about a major, a decision that has further occupational implications. College students planning to enter professional schools may be forced to make educational decisions in terms of these future goals at a very early point in their undergraduate work. College graduation represents another choice point regarding whether or not to pursue graduate or professional school programs.

These relationships between educational decisions and occupational alternatives are presented in diagram 3.1. Clearly, the kinds and frequency of decisions that must be made are not evenly distributed throughout the educational process. Rather, major decisions must be made at scheduled times regardless of whether or not individuals are ready to make them.

While the educational system can be portrayed as a series of choice points resulting in various occupational consequences, the portrayal

Diagram 3.1
Educational Decision Points

Educational Decision Point	Decision to Be Made	Occupational Consequence
1. Entering high school	Type of high school	Acquisition of specific occupational skills
	Type of program	Acquisition of prerequisites for college entrance
2. Completion of high school	Go to college?	
	no ─────────►	Blue-collar, low-status clerical, technical work
	yes, where? ─────►	Acquisition of specific occupational skills
		Ease of entering graduate and professional schools
3. Second or third year of college	Major field of study	Restriction of occupational alternatives
4. Completion of college	Go to graduate or professional school?	
	no ─────────►	Occupational entry
	yes ─────────►	Restriction of occupational alternatives
		Preparation for work in specific occupation

should not be overdrawn. The American educational system is by no means a "lock-step" system in which a decision at one point leads to an irreversible series of events at a later point. In fact, a variety of mechanisms have evolved in American higher education that allow people a "second chance" in the form of the opportunity to cycle back and undo the results of earlier decisions.[61] Such mechanisms permit shifting from one educational (and by implication occupational) route to another. Probably the best known such mechanism is the community or junior college which allows the college aspirant who made the "wrong" decisions earlier to acquire the qualifications for college entry. While the record of community colleges in sending their students on to senior colleges is poor, in principle they represent such a "second chance."[62] Most colleges and universities allow undergraduates to change majors almost indiscriminantly. The result is to weaken the binding nature of decisions and allow for some experimentation with alternative educational-occupational paths. A survey of the entering college freshman class in the fall of 1983 found, for example, that 10.1 percent were undecided about the occupation they would eventually enter, and 4.9 percent were undecided about the field in which they would major. In addition, 11.2 percent said there was a very good chance that they would change their occupational choice and 12.0 percent said there was a very good chance they would change their major.[63] In fact, there is evidence to indicate that over a third of all college students change their major at least once between the freshman and senior year.[64] Even in graduate schools (but less often in the case of professional schools), departments frequently admit as probationary or special students those whose academic qualifications may be strong but whose undergraduate education in the field was inadequate for some reason. Switching from one undergraduate to another graduate field of study may be facilitated by allowing the student to take undergraduate or special graduate courses during the probationary period.

One reason why such mechanisms have evolved may be that many of the crucial educational decisions that young people are required to make are made in ignorance of their occupational consequences. Despite the development of educational and vocational counseling programs in high schools and colleges, many educational/occupational decisions may be whimsical, irrational, and based on a lack of information or on misinformation. There is evidence to indicate that high school students have very little accurate information about occupations including the amount and kind of education required for entry into them.[65] A high school student may elect a certain program because a close friend has done so. A college student may decide to major in a particular field because a high grade was earned in the introductory course, or a decision not to major in a particular subject may be made because the kind of work for which it might prepare one may not be apparent. If the argument that educational decisions are made in ignorance of their occupational consequences is correct, mechanisms that permit flexibility and allow for the development of new alternatives may be necessary.

SUMMARY

Occupational choice has been the focus of a great deal of scholarly investigation. Major theories of occupational choice have emerged from the perspective of developmental psychology. This "rational decision-making" model portrays the choice process as one that involves making conscious, thoughtful decisions in which aspects of the individual (self-concept, personality) are matched with the demands and rewards of an occupation. Another perspective on occupational choice, the "fortuitous" model, sees the process as much less rational and essentially unplanned. Individuals are seen as drifting into decisions that have occupational consequences without making conscious choices or developing elaborate strategies. A distinctly sociological model of occupational choice involves looking at how "sociocultural influences" (social class, rural-urban residence, gender, and race) constrain and place limits on the kinds of occupations to which individuals aspire.

Sociologists also have attempted to understand the process of occupational choice by looking at the social background characteristics of persons who enter particular occupations. This "social origins" approach reveals a large overrepresentation of people from upper-middle-class backgrounds in the major professions, as well as a surprising amount of occupational inheritance. The implication is that the occupational environment or subculture in which people are reared can subtly and indirectly shape their occupational interests and choices.

Educational decisions clearly have occupational implications. While the educational system requires individuals to make decisions at particular times, there is also a great deal of flexibility built into it. Within the American educational system, both structures and practices create opportunities for experimentation, changing one's mind, and cycling back to earlier choice points.

NOTES

1. Cyril Sofer, "Introduction," in *Occupational Choice: A Selection of Papers from the Sociological Review*, ed. W. M. Williams (London: George Allen and Unwin, 1974).
2. C. H. Miller, "Career Development Theory in Perspective," in *Vocational Guidance and Human Development*, ed. E. L. Herr, (Boston: Houghton-Mifflin), 1974, pp. 238–239.
3. Eli Ginzberg, et al., *Occupational Choice: An Approach to a General Theory* (New York: Columbia University Press, 1951).
4. Donald E. Super, "A Theory of Vocational Development," *American Psychologist* 8 (1953): 185–190; *The Psychology of Careers: An Introduction to Vocational Development*, (New York: Harper and Row, 1957); "The Critical Ninth Grade: Vocational Choice or Vocational Exploration," *Personnel and Guidance Journal* 39 (1960): 106–109; and Donald E. Super and M. J. Bohn, *Occupational Psychology*, (Monterey, Calif.: Brooks-Cole, 1970).
5. Walter S. Neff, *Work and Human Behavior*, 3rd ed. (New York: Aldine, 1985), 110–113.
6. S. Markham, "I Can be a Bum: Knowledge about Abilities and Life Style in Vocational Behavior," *Journal of Vocational Behavior* 23 (1983): 72–86.
7. Donald E. Super, "Career and Life Development," in *Career Choice and Development*, ed. Duane Brown, et al. (San Francisco: Jossey-Bass, 1984), 192–234.
8. Eli Ginzberg, "Career Development," in Brown, *Career Choice and Development*, 169–191. See also Eli Ginsberg, "Toward a Theory of Occupational Choice: A Restatement," *Vocational Guidance Quarterly* 20 (1972): 169–176.
9. Eli Ginzberg, "Career Development," p. 180.
10. John L. Holland, "Some Explorations of a Theory of Vocational Choice," *Psychological Monographs* 76 (1962); "Explorations of a Theory of Vocational

Choice and Achievement," *Psychological Reports* 12 (1963): 547–594; and *Making Vocational Choices: A Theory of Careers*, (Englewood Cliffs, N.J.: Prentice-Hall, 1973).

11. K. Roberts, "The Social Conditions, Consequences, and Limitations of Career Guidance," *British Journal of Guidance and Counselling* 5 (1977): 1–9.

12. For an extensive critique of Super's and Holland's models, see Neff, "Work and Human Behavior," 105-110 and 116-118. For a review of sixty-three studies related to Holland's approach, see Arnold S. Spokane, "A Review of Research on Person-Environment Congruence in Holland's Theory of Careers," *Journal of Vocational Behavior* 26 (June 1985): 306–343.

13. Peter M. Blau, et al., "Occupational Choice: A Conceptual Framework," *Industrial and Labor Relations Review* 9 (July 1956): 531–543.

14. Basil Sherlock and Alan Cohen, "The Strategy of Occupational Choice: Recruitment to Dentistry," *Social Forces* 44 (March 1966): 303–313.

15. John E. Stecklein and Ruth E. Eckert, *An Exploratory Study of Factors Influencing the Choice of College Teaching as a Career*, (Washington, D.C.: Cooperative Research Program, U.S. Office of Education, 1958), 44.

16. John W. Gustad, *The Career Decisions of College Teachers*, SREB Research Monograph, Series No. 2 (Atlanta, Ga.: Southern Regional Education Board, 1960), 6.

17. Fred E. Katz and Harry W. Martin, "Career Choice Processes," *Social Forces* 41 (December 1962): 149–154.

18. Theodore Caplow, *The Sociology of Work* (Minneapolis: University of Minnesota Press, 1954), 218.

19. The research literature on this topic is overwhelming. Two of the more complete bibliographic identifications of this work can be found in William H. Sewell and Robert M. Hauser, *Education, Occupation and Earnings: Achievement in the Early Career* (New York: Academic Press, 1975); and "The Wisconsin Longitudinal Study of Social and Psychological Factors in Aspirations and Achievements," in *Research in Sociology of Education and Socialization*, ed. Alan Kerckhoff (Greenwich, Conn.: JAI Press, 1980), 59–99.

20. Sewell and Hauser, "The Wisconsin Longitudinal Study of Social and Psychological Factors in Aspirations and Achievements," *Education, Occupation and Earnings*.

21. David Shapiro and Joan E. Crowley, "Aspirations and Expectations of the Youth of the United States: Part 2, Employment Activity," *Youth and Society* 14 (September 1982): 33–58.

22. Merlin B. Brinkerhoff and David J. Corry, "Structural Prisons: Barriers to Occupational and Educational Goals in a Society of 'Equal' Opportunity," *International Journal of Comparative Sociology* 17 (1976): 261–274.

23. There is a substantial literature on this topic. For example, see Lee G. Burchinal, "Differences in Educational and Occupational Aspirations of Farm, Small Town, and City Boys," *Rural Sociology* 26 (June 1961): 107–121; Charles M. Grigg and Russell Middleton, "Community of Orientation and Occupational Aspirations of Ninth Grade Students," *Social Forces* 38 (May 1960): 303–308; and Archibald O. Haller, "Research Problems on the Occupational Achievement Levels of Farm Reared People," *Rural Sociology* 23 (December 1958): 355–362.

24. William H. Sewell and Alan M. Orenstein, "Community of Residence and Occupational Choice," *American Journal of Sociology* 70 (March 1965): 551–563.

25. Shapiro and Crowley, "Aspirations and Expectations of Youth," table 4.

26. Kingsley Davis, *Human Society* (New York: Crowell Collier and Macmillan, 1949), 364.
27. Robin M. Williams, *American Society* (New York: Knopf, 1960), 60; and Bernard Barber, *Social Stratification: A Comparative Analysis of Structure and Process* (New York: Harcourt, Brace, and World, 1957): 73–74.
28. Talcott Parsons, "The Social Structure of the Family," in *The Family: Its Function and Destiny*, ed. Ruth Anshen (New York: Harper and Brothers, 1949), 173–201; and "An Analytical Approach to the Theory of Social Stratification," in Talcott Parsons, *Essays in Sociological Theory* (Glencoe, Ill.: Free Press, 1954), 69–88.
29. Ralph H. Turner, "Some Aspects of Women's Ambition," *American Journal of Sociology* 70 (November 1964): 271–285.
30. Ralph H. Turner, *The Social Context of Ambition* (San Francisco: Chandler, 1962), 40, table 6.
31. Valerie Kincade Oppenheimer, "The Sociology of Women's Economic Role in the Family," *American Sociological Review* 42 (June 1977):387–406.
32. George Psathas, "Toward a Theory of Occupational Choice for Women," *Sociology and Social Research* 52 (January 1958): 254–268.
33. Ronald M. Pavalko and Norma Nager, "Contingencies of Marriage to High Status Men," *Social Forces* 46 (June 1968): 523–531.
34. For a review and summary of this research, see William H. Sewell, et al., "The Educational and Early Occupational Attainment Process," *American Sociological Review* 34 (February 1969): 82–92.
35. Shapiro and Crowley, "Aspirations and Expectations of Youth," 36, table 1.
36. Bernard C. Rosen and Carol S. Aneshensel, Sex Differences in the Educational–Occupational Expectation Process," *Social Forces* 57 (September 1978).
37. *Ibid.*, 171, table 2.
38. Lloyd B. Lueptow, "Sex-Typing and Change in the Occupational Choices of High School Seniors: 1964–1975," *Sociology of Education* 54 (January 1981): 16–24.
39. A. Regula Herzog, "High School Seniors' Occupational Plans and Values: Trends in Sex Differences 1976 Through 1980," *Sociology of Education* 55 (January 1982): 1–13.
40. William B. Fetters, et al., *High School Seniors: A Comparative Study of the Classes of 1972 and 1980* (Washington, D.C.: National Center for Education Statistics, N.D.), p. 32, table 5.4.
41. R. G. Holloway and Joel V. Berreman, "The Educational and Occupational Aspirations and Plans of Negro and White Male Elementary School Students," *Pacific Sociological Review* 2 (Fall 1959): 56–60.
42. Jetse Sprey, "Sex Differences in Occupational Choice Patterns Among Negro Adolescents," *Social Problems* 10 (Summer 1962): 11–22.
43. E. G. Youmans, et al., *After High School What? Highlights of a Study of Career Plans of Negro and White Rural Youth in Three Florida Counties* (Gainesville, Fla.: University of Florida, Cooperative Extension Service, 1965).
44. Russell Middleton and Charles M. Grigg, "Rural-Urban Differences in Aspirations," *Rural Sociology* 24 (December 1959): 347–354.
45. See Reynolds Farley and Albert Hermalin, "The 1960s: A Decade of Progress for Blacks?" *Demography* 9 (1972): 359–370; Reynolds Farley, "Trends in Racial Inequalities: Have the Gains of the 1960's Disappeard in the 1970's?" *American Sociological Review* 42 (1977): 189–207; and David Featherman and Robert M. Hauser, "Changes in the Socioeconomic Stratification of the Races, 1962–1973," *American Journal of Sociology* 82 (1976): 621–651.

46. Howard H. Garrison, "Trends in the Educational and Occupational Aspirations of High School Males: Black-White Comparisons," *Sociology of Education* 55 (January 1982): 53–62.
47. Frank M. Howell and Wolfgang Frese, "Race, Sex, and Aspirations: Evidence for the 'Race Convergence' Hypothesis," *Sociology of Education* 52 (January 1979): 34–46.
48. For a review of these studies, see Cynthia Fuchs Epstein, *Women in Law* (Garden City, N.J.: Anchor Books, 1983), 23–32.
49. Jane Lesserman, *Men and Women in Medical School: How They Change and How They Compare* (New York: Praeger, 1981), 81, table 4.1.
50. Morris Janowitz, *The Professional Soldier* (New York: Free Press, 1960); and Joseph H. Fichter, *Religion as an Occupation* (Notre Dame, Ind.: University of Notre Dame Press, 1961).
51. James Otis Smith and Gideon Sjoberg, "Origins and Career Patterns of Leading Protestant Clergymen," *Social Forces* 39 (May 1961): 290–296.
52. William E. Henry, et al., *The Fifth Profession: Becoming a Psychotherapist* (San Francisco: Jossey-Bass, 1971).
53. *Ibid.*, 11, table 1.
54. *Ibid.*, chapter 2, 9–28.
55. Anthony Gary Dworkin, "The Changing Demography of Public School Teachers: Some Implications for Faculty Turnover in Urban Areas," *Sociology of Education* 53 (April 1980): 65–73.
56. Michael Betz and James Garland, "Intergenerational Mobility Rates of Urban School Teachers," *Sociology of Education* 47 (Fall 1974): 511–522.
57. Ronald M. Pavalko, "Recruitment to Teaching: Patterns of Selection and Retention," *Sociology of Education* 43 (Summer 1970): 340–353.
58. Betz and Garland, "Intergenerational Mobility Rates," 511–522; Ronald M. Pavalko, "Aspirants to Teaching: Some Differences Between High School Senior Boys and Girls Planning on a Career in Teaching," *Sociology and Social Research* 50 (October 1965): 47–62; and Harry K. Schwarzweller and Thomas A. Lyson, "Some Plan to Become Teachers: Determinants of Career Specification Among Rural Youth in Norway, Germany, and the United States," *Sociology of Education* 51 (January 1978): 29–43.
59. Herant A. Katchadourian and John Boli, *Careerism and Intellectualism Among College Students: Patterns of Academic and Career Choice in the Undergraduate Years* (San Francisco: Jossey-Bass, 1985).
60. David H. Kamens, "The College 'Charter' and College Size: Effects on Occupational Choice and College Attrition," *Sociology of Education* 44 (Summer 1971): 270–296.
61. Ralph H. Turner, "Sponsored and Contest Mobility and the School System," *American Sociological Review* 15 (December 1960): 855–867.
62. Richard D. Alba and David E. Lavin, "Community Colleges and Tracking in Higher Education," *Sociology of Education* 54 (October 1981): 223–237.
63. "Freshman Characteristics and Attitudes," *Chronicle of Higher Education* (February 1, 1984): 13.
64. James A. Davis, *Undergraduate Career Decisions* (Chicago: Aldine, 1965).
65. Lois B. DeFleur and Ben A. Menke, "Learning About the Labor Force: Occupational Knowledge Among High School Males," *Sociology of Education* 48 (Summer 1975): 324–345.

CHAPTER 4

Occupational Socialization

A DISTINCTIVE FEATURE of sociology is the assumption that we must understand the nature of human cultures in order to understand human behavior. The possession of culture is what distinguishes humans from other animals. But people do not possess culture at birth; it is learned. *Socialization* refers to the process by which the values, beliefs, norms, roles, assumptions, and practices that make up a culture (or subculture) are learned, and is one of the most basic concepts of sociology. In this chapter our main concern is the process by which occupational subcultures are learned and the consequences of *occupational socialization*.

THE MEANING OF SOCIALIZATION

Before dealing with the occupational socialization process, it is essential to first identify the basic features of socialization as a general phenomenon. Occupational socialization is really just a special case of this more general process.

Most socialization is an unconscious and unintended by-product of routine human interaction. It is often hidden or implicit in the things that people do and say. However, there are situations in which socialization is explicit, intentional, and conscious. The efforts of schools to instill a sense of nationalism and patriotism in young children is such an example. Religious instruction by churches that seeks to inculcate a religious heritage is another example. The basic training of recruits to the

84

military services is an overt and intentional effort to transmit a military subculture and its attendant rules, regulations, definitions of authority, and a new self-concept to the new recruit. When people enter new jobs, there may be a great deal of intentional teaching that is intended to provide the newcomer with an understanding of the organizational culture—its traditions, authority and communication system, expectations of co-workers and supervisors, and the like, as well as the person's specific work tasks. Regardless of how intentional socialization is, the process produces conformity and predictability with regard to shared norms, values, and role expectations.

Definitions of socialization differ mainly in their relative emphasis, either on the *individual* as the recipient or target of the process, or on the *social context* (including other persons) as the agent of socialization. Robert K. Merton has defined socialization in a way that captures both dimensions. He defines it as "the process by which people selectively acquire the values and attitudes, the interests, skills and knowledge—in short, the culture—current in the groups to which they are, or seek to become, a member. It refers to the learning of social roles."[1]

CHILDHOOD AND ADULT SOCIALIZATION

Most discussions of socialization focus on childhood. The learning of norms, values, and roles is usually discussed with a focus on children and adolescents as the targets or recipients of a process of socialization occurring in the context of primary groups such as the family and peer groups, or secondary groups such as schools. Occupational socialization is a special case of adult socialization. The learning of occupational norms, values, and roles involves adults. While there is a basic similarity in both childhood and adult socialization, there also are important differences.

The most important way in which childhood and adult socialization differ is the extent to which the person being socialized can be considered a *tabula rasa* or "blank page." We assume that the child acquires an understanding of norms and roles where none existed previously. In addition, the norms and roles being learned apply to situations with which the child has little prior experience. In the case of adults, socialization frequently involves, in addition to learning new roles and norms, the *unlearning*, relinquishing, modification, or suspension of old roles and norms, as well as sometimes holding conflicting norms and occupying contradictory roles simultaneously. For example, in the military, the new recruit must not only learn the role of soldier but also must give up many aspects of the role of civilian such as discretion in physical appearance, attire, and freedom of expression, to mention only a few very obvious changes required in the transition from civilian to soldier. To the extent that recruits have learned to value egalitarian social interaction, the socialization to military roles requires the acceptance of a conflicting norm that defines superordinate-subordinate interaction based on rank as appropriate, normal, and legitimate. Adult socialization may require changes in previously existing orientations much more frequently than is the case with childhood socialization.

Another way in which childhood and adult socialization differ is the degree to which entry into the process is *voluntary*. The child has little or no control or discretion over the socializing forces that impinge upon him or her. Socialization in families and peer groups happens as a normal and routine aspect of living. Even the socializing influences of schools are difficult to avoid. In childhood, such group memberships are involuntary, and exposure to agents of socialization occurs with the child having little or no control over the process. Adult socialization, on the other hand, is much more voluntary in that adults initiate actions that lead to socializing experiences. The decision to go to college, to enter a particular occupational training program, to seek a promotion, to change jobs, and the like, all involve choices on the part of individuals about the experiences they will or will not have. The counterpart of this is that having voluntarily made such choices, people retain some control over their continued involvement in the situation. While changing a course of action may involve costs, the fact that people can leave college, get out of a training program, change jobs, etc., means that adult socialization experiences are potentially easier to terminate than are those of childhood.

A final difference between childhood and adult socialization involves the distinction between being an *active or passive* participant in the process. Children are relatively passive recipients of the content of socialization. Agents of socialization to which they are exposed in the family (parents) or in schools (teachers) have a great deal of power to determine what is taught, how it is taught, and what is supposed to be learned. This power differential casts the child in a rather dependent role. While adult socialization may also involve power differences, persons being socialized have more room to negotiate. Having voluntarily entered the situation and having prior norms and roles to use as points of comparison, people in adult socialization settings are more able to decide what will and what will not be internalized. They have options and choices regarding such things as their choice of role models, the degree to which they will adhere to norms, and the kinds of exceptions to norms they will tolerate. While adults in such situations may still be dependent on the agents of socialization (e.g., for certification, access to prized positions, or good letters of reference), the degree of dependence and powerlessness is less than in childhood socialization. Within limits, adults are better able to shape their socialization experiences than children are. The consequence of this is that agents of adult socialization are less able to control the outcome of the process compared to the agents of childhood socialization.

ANTICIPATORY SOCIALIZATION

Another important aspect of socialization is the phenomenon of *anticipatory socialization*. Because of their unique ability to manipulate symbols, human beings are able to imagine or anticipate what it would be like to be a member of a group of which they are not presently a member or what it would be like to occupy a role that they do not presently occupy. The latter possibility is also called *role-playing*. Numerous, if prosaic, examples of the phenomenon exist. Young children "playing house" are doing more than just imitating their parents. From a socialization perspective they are trying out in the present roles that they may occupy in the future. Adolescents may similarly imagine what it would be like to be an adult, a parent, a college student, or a member of a particular occupation. The point is that a person need not be a member of a group or an occupant of a role in order for that group or role to have a socializing impact. Since being a member of the group or occupying the role is not necessary for socialization to occur, we also can think of this as *self-socialization*. Individuals may socialize themselves on the basis of their (correct or incorrect) assumptions about the group or role.

Anticipatory socialization has several implications for understanding socialization to occupational roles. People coming into formal occupational training situations may bring with them diverse conceptions (and misconceptions) about the occupation they want to enter. Images of the occupation may be based on information from a variety of sources such as the mass media and people in the occupation. Such information can vary in both its accuracy and completeness. The ready availability of role models such as parents, other relatives, or close friends in an occupation is an important potential source of information. The length of time one has been considering a particular occupation would also affect the amount of anticipatory socialization that has occurred. At one extreme, for example, the person who has grown up in a medical family and decided at an early age to become a physician, has grown up in an environment where exposure to medical role models and access to information about medical work could produce a great deal of anticipatory socialization. At the other extreme, a person with little exposure to the work world of lawyers and who decides late in college to enter law school, is likely to have undergone relatively little anticipatory socialization. As these two examples suggest, people entering occupational training programs may vary a great deal in terms of their prior images and understandings of the occupation. Whether anticipatory socialization aids or hinders occupational socialization depends on how similar the norms and role expectations people have developed are to the content and goals of formal training programs.

Anticipatory socialization occurs during the training process as well as prior to it. The professional or graduate school student has many opportunities for anticipating and "trying out" alternative careers and work styles through the observation of her or his mentors. Anticipatory socialization using information acquired through casual and informal observation of faculty and other practitioners is commonplace during the training period. It involves more than simply imitating those who are already members of the occupation. It may well lead to the seeking of alternative work roles, work styles, and work contexts. For example, in university graduate programs in the arts and sciences, graduate students planning academic careers are routinely exposed to faculty who work in a situation where teaching and research are combined. While such faculty serve as role models for one kind of academic career, students may also develop a preference for a career involving only research in a nonacademic setting or one involving exclusively teaching in, for example, a small liberal arts college. In other words, anticipatory socialization in graduate and professional schools may lead to the *rejection* of norms and roles presented (and the seeking of alternatives) as well as their acceptance and adoption.

REFERENCE GROUPS IN THE SOCIALIZATION PROCESS

The concept of socialization is rooted in the theoretical perspective known as symbolic interaction.[2] From this perspective, a person's self-concept is a reflection of the conception and expectations that others have of the person. In thinking about socialization, it is important to realize that expectations affecting individuals do not just reflect the idiosyncratic ideas of others. These expectations are usually rooted in group norms and values. Thus, the concept of *reference group* becomes relevant to the socialization process.

The concept of reference group has a number of interrelated meanings and implications. It includes the idea that people arrive at subjective judgements about their status by making comparisons with (or "in reference to") some group or individual. Thus, a reference group can be any group to which an individual compares himself or herself in arriving at a judgement about his or her status.[3] There are many dimensions to a person's status (e.g., economic, intellectual, athletic), and more than one reference group may be relevant to a particular dimension. For example, in arriving at a judgement about one's economic status, friends, relatives, people of the same age, or persons in the same occupation may be used as reference groups. Reference groups also may serve a *normative function* in which they set or enforce standards for behavior, or they may serve a *comparison function* as groups against which people evaluate themselves or others.[4]

A reference group may also be a group in which a person seeks to gain or maintain acceptance, a point especially relevant to occupational socialization.[5] Reference groups often provide people with perspectives that they use to deal with a range of situations, problems, and demands. In the broadest sense, the group's perspectives may be used to structure the way in which individual members perceive and interact with the world around them.

There are a number of ways in which these several meanings of the concept of reference group can aid our understanding of the occupational socialization process. The norms of occupational groups can affect individuals at the anticipatory socialization stage insofar as membership in the group is something to which they aspire. In formal training situations, members of the occupation represent a normative reference group because they set and enforce norms and serve as role models. Both faculty and other students may serve as comparative reference groups for the purpose of judging a person's development as a member of the occupation, or the extent to which he or she has mastered the occupation's technical requirements and behavioral nuances. At the end of the process, those who have been through it accept as their own the perspectives of the occupational group on a wide range of occupational and nonoccupational issues.

FORMAL OCCUPATIONAL SOCIALIZATION DURING TRAINING

Research on occupational socialization during periods of formal training has concentrated mainly on occupations at the profession end of the nonprofession-profession continuum. Within this segment of the occupational structure, the socialization of medical students has received an inordinate amount of attention. While we are concerned with developing an understanding of socialization as a general occupational process, a good starting point is the research on the professions since it has in many ways identified the conceptual and methodological issues with which research on occupational socialization has dealt.

THE MERTON AND BECKER STUDIES: CONFLICTING INTERPRETATIONS OF PROCESS AND OUTCOME

The landmark studies of occupational socialization were conducted during the 1950s. Robert K. Merton initiated a series of studies at three medical schools (Western Reserve University, the University of Pennsylvania, and Cornell University) that resulted in the publication of *The Student-Physician*.[6] At the University of Kansas, Howard Becker conducted a study of medical students that culminated in the publication of *Boys in White*.[7] These two studies are of particular interest because they reached rather different conclusions about the nature of the socialization process and its outcomes. They also directly and indirectly set the agenda for subsequent research on the topic.

Merton's study covered a number of factors such as when the decision to study medicine occurred, the sources of influence on this decision, and the development of specialty interests within medicine. A good deal of attention was directed to the issue of how the medical student acquires a conception of self as a physician. The assumption is that passage through medical school involves a progressive and incremental change in the direction of thinking of oneself more as a physician and less as a student. The findings of the study support this assumption. While less than one-third of the first- and second-year students reported that they thought of themselves primarily as physicians, 59 percent of the third-year students did so, and this increased to 83 percent of the fourth-year students.[8] Interaction with faculty, nurses, other students, and patients all contributed to the development of a professional self-concept; this is consistent with the symbolic interaction theory of how the self develops. However, experiences with patients were especially important. As patients define the student as a doctor and seek and follow the student's advice, the student begins to act and feel more like a doctor. In other words, the self-concept begins to reflect the images and conceptions that others have of the student.

What emerges from this and other parts of the Merton study is a picture of occupational socialization as a process in which the student moves progressively from student to junior colleague to full-fledged professional. The process is seen as an orderly one in which the student acquires the skills that will be needed to perform the role of physician. Students are also portrayed as uncritically absorbing the values, norms, and attitudes of their mentors. The medical school faculty replicate the values and orientations of the profession in each new generation of students, and the students are portrayed as relatively passive actors in the process.

Becker's study of medical students at the University of Kansas presents a rather different picture of the socialization process. This study concluded that medical students do not take on a professional self-concept during their training because the social system of the medical school does not allow them to do so. During the training process they are denied responsibility and faculty make it clear that they are in a subordinate status. Becker points out that the students occasionally fantasize about being doctors but they know full well that they will not be doctors until they have graduated and are licensed.[9] Rather than developing in an incremental and smooth manner, the professional self is seen as suppressed and emerging only at the completion of training. The relationship between students and faculty is portrayed as one of tension, conflict, and manipulation. The faculty control access to the profession and only they can grant the certification students want. Student attention becomes focused on figuring out what they need to know to pass examinations and get through the process. While students enter medical school with a strong sense of idealism and dedication, their experiences are such that they become cynical and utilitarian. Idealism is simply not relevant to the problems they face in school. Idealistic concerns become suspended and reemerge at the end of the process as the student is about to leave school and as he or she begins to think about actually being a practitioner.

Clearly, these studies differ in terms of their conception of the student's status and how it is transformed. One sees the student as a junior colleague who gradually becomes an equal (i.e., a fellow physician). The other sees the student as a subordinate throughout the process with an abrupt transformation into a professional at the end. Another difference is between a process that is a smooth and gradual professional maturation versus one that is made up of cycles of conflict and dramatic change. A final difference revolves around the issue of how complete the socialization process is. Merton's study portrays the student as emerging from medical school adequately equipped to participate as a full-fledged member of the profession. Becker's study sees the medical school laying the groundwork for professional development by providing basic skills and competencies. But the product that emerges is by no means a finished or polished one. Indeed, it is portrayed as quite rough around the edges. The finishing touches presumably come later through membership and involvement in the life of the profession as a practitioner and through continued interaction with and socialization from colleagues.[10]

There are several possible explanations for the different findings of these studies. One possibility is that there are real differences in the organization of medical education in the schools studied that produce these different conclusions. Even within the same occupation there may be variation in the structure of training that results in differences in both outcomes and how the process is experienced by those going through it. Another possibility is the differences in methodology of the two studies. The Merton study was cross-sectional with findings based on comparisons between first-, second-, third-, and fourth-year students while the Becker study was longitudinal and followed the same students through their medical education. The Merton study is based on data collected from questionnaires and structured interviews while the Becker study used participant observation and relied more on informal interaction with students and faculty.

THE OUTCOME OF SOCIALIZATION:
HOMOGENEITY, DIVERSITY, AND THE PERMANENCE OF CHANGE

These classic studies of occupational socialization raised additional questions that have been pursued by other researchers. One is whether the changes that occur among students result in greater similarity in values and perspectives than existed when students entered training. There is some support for this "homogenization" hypothesis.[11] The issue of decreasing idealism and increasing cynicism raised by Becker has also been investigated by others with support for the notion that cynicism does increase. Students become less interested in helping others and dealing with the social and emotional problems of patients.[12] On the other hand, there is also support for Becker's contention that cynicism is a situational response to the demands of medical school, not a permanent value change. One study found that after leaving medical school cynicism decreased for all physicians as they entered practice and decreased most for those whose practices involved a great deal of direct patient contact.[13]

These and other issues were dealt with by Jane Leserman in a study of students at three North Carolina medical schools (Duke University, University of North Carolina, and Bowman Gray School of Medicine) from 1975 to 1978.[14] Her study was longitudinal, following the same students from their freshman to their senior year, and relied primarily on questionnaire data supplemented by interviews. Leserman focused on two major issues. The first was changes in the professional orientations of students during their training and the second was differences between men and women in the changes that occurred.

In general, her findings support the conclusion that students enter medical school with relatively liberal and idealistic attitudes, and leave more conservative and less concerned with patient needs. Although students do not come out of medical school with identical professional values, they do emerge with a perspective supporting traditional, conservative positions on a number of issues. Students maintained their commitment to general humanistic values but they became more realistic about the extent to which physicians can contribute to their realization. However, when it came to specific things involving their own conduct and careers, a different picture emerged. During their training there was a decrease in their support for government intervention in health care and compulsory physician service in deprived areas. They also showed less concern with reducing the profitability of medicine and decreased the amount of time they expected to devote to volunteer work. In addition, there was a decrease in their expectations of practicing primary care medicine (rather than a specialty), practicing in a rural area or inner city ghetto, or choosing a specialty or geographic area that needed more physicians. These changes may well reflect the acquisition of the traditional professional value of autonomy which reflects in career choices based on the physician's preferences rather than the needs of patients or the larger society.

Leserman was also interested in whether there were changes in student perspectives on women in the medical profession. These included such things as student awareness of public and professional prejudice against women physicians, pressure on women to choose certain specialties (e.g., pediatrics), whether students believed there was a need for more women physicians, and whether they felt that physicians treated women patients in patronizing and prejudicial ways. The study found no evidence that students became more sensitive to issues of sex discrimination during their training. These attitudes remained quite stable during their training except that there was actually a decrease in the proportion of students who felt that there should be more women in medicine.

In attempting to explain the changes that occurred, Leserman emphasizes that the medical school environment is very conservative. The faculty generally hold very traditional professional values. It is clear that some students resist taking on the professional views of their mentors. They may actually reject faculty as role models for patient care and for attitudes on political and economic issues relevant to the profession. But some students do not engage in such rejection and take on the conservative perspectives presented consciously and unconsciously by the faculty. Unfortunately, the study does not provide an explanation of why some students resist the pressure toward conservatism and traditionalism and others do not. It is also unclear whether a liberal perspective is the cause or consequence of rejecting faculty values. While the changes documented in this study shed light on some issues, new questions about the reasons for value change and the absence of change also are raised.

Leserman's findings on sex differences in professional orientations and changes during the course of training also raise some new issues. Compared to men, women students begin medical school more concerned with humanitarian patient care, and with bringing about liberal political and economic changes in the profession. They are also more concerned with the problems of women physicians and patients, and more committed to an inner-city ghetto practice. Like men students, the women become more traditional and conservative in their views; however, since they start medical school more liberal than their male counterparts, they are more liberal and less traditional than the men at the end. In addition, they retain their strong concern about women's issues. Apparently, the greater initial liberalism of female students does not insulate them against pressures to become more traditional in their views of medical practice and a medical career. Leserman suggests that in the long run the increased entry of women into the medical profession may result in a greater overall concern with issues of patient care. This of course would occur not because of anything in the professional socialization experiences of medical students but because women recruited to medicine are more liberal and less traditional than their male counterparts to begin with.

Another study of medical students conducted in the late 1960s by Robert H. Coombs dealt with similar issues.[15] This longitudinal study followed the entering class of 1967 at an anonymous "Eastern Medical School" through their medical training. Data on a number of issues were collected by means of questionnaires, interviews, and participant observation.

Coombs concluded that students do not become more cynical and less concerned with humanitarian issues in the course of their training. Yet, students are highly critical of the structure of their training and their teachers. There is a big discrepancy between their *expectations* of medical education and physicians and their *actual experiences*. They are basically disappointed with the way they are treated and the way patients are treated. While this disillusionment fosters a kind of generalized cynicism (perhaps "malaise" would be a better term), Coombs argues that students retain a fundamental commitment to quality patient care and a strong sense of pride in the work of the profession they are entering.

Student views on political issues affecting the medical profession are highly varied. On the issue of governmental involvement in health care, student opinions become more definite in the course of their four years in medical school. During the course of their training, there is an increase in the proportion of students who oppose and an increase in the proportion who approve of governmental intervention. By the time they are seniors, however, the students are about equally divided among those who oppose, approve, and are ambivalent about governmental intervention in health care. In other words, the study does not support the conclusion that student attitudes become necessarily more conservative or that they become more homogeneous.

SOCIALIZATION FOR UNCERTAINTY

One theme that runs through the literature on occupational socialization is the idea that training for much professional work involves preparation for *uncertainty*. This issue was first raised by Renee Fox who worked on the Merton study of medical students.[16] She pointed out that two traits acquired by medical students were the tendency to become *emotionally detached* from patients and their problems and the ability to *tolerate uncertainty*. Medical students experience uncertainty when they realize that they will not be able to learn everything they might about medicine and that there are limitations in medical knowledge and technique. An additional uncertainty results in the form of an inability to distinguish their personal ignorance and shortcomings from the limitations of medical knowledge available. These uncertainties are dealt with by developing a style that emphasizes careful, objective weighing of the available evidence when making a diagnosis. The result is a "detached concern" that reflects a balance between human concern for the patient and the scientific detachment required by the uncertainties of the situation.[17]

Increased detachment from patients and the development of impersonal attitudes toward patients have been reported in several other studies of medical students.[18] This may be due in part to the uncertainties involved. It may also be a way of masking what one does not know with a "cloak of competence."[19] It is also the result of a strong emphasis on learning about the functioning of the components of the human body, about illnesses, and about techniques rather than about patients. Donald Light's study of students in a psychiatric residency program reports a similar outcome.[20] He concluded that one major result of the socialization of psychiatric residents was that they placed less emphasis on being advocates for their patients and greater emphasis on technique. In other words, they came to focus their attention on the development of technical skills rather than grappling with the plight of the patient. They judged and evaluated their own performance in terms of their command of those skills rather than on the progress the patient was making. Light attributes this to the uncertainty that residents have about their knowledge, the anxiety that comes from being given responsibility for patients, and the necessity of having to make choices and decisions.

CONFLICT BETWEEN STUDENTS AND SCHOOLS: CHANGING ORIENTATIONS, EXPECTATIONS, AND GOALS

While medicine has been the focus of many studies of occupational socialization, additional questions and issues have been raised in studies of other occupational groups. One such issue is the way in which the orientations that students bring with them (which result from anticipatory socialization) conflict with the objectives of the training organization.

Occupational socialization involves changing people's attitudes, values, beliefs, and self-concepts as well as providing them with particular skills and knowledge. Every occupation has a readily identifiable, if not unique, idea of the attitudes and values its future members ought to be developing and what the end product of the process ought to look, think, and feel like. At the same time, there is always selectivity of some sort operating that affects the characteristics (skills, abilities, beliefs, etc.) of those who aspire to be members of the occupation. Students may bring with them a host of correct or incorrect assumptions about how easy it will be to complete the program, the rewards the occupation offers, and the demands it makes. They also bring varied conceptions of what the work involves, and interests and objectives that may or may not be compatible with the objectives of the program. These two factors—the *goals of the program* and the *orientations students bring with them*—combine to create a variety of problems and conflicts in the socialization process.

Nursing Schools

Several studies illustrate the potential for these kinds of problems and conflicts. One of these is a study of nursing students by Ida Harper Simpson.[21] Simpson suggests that occupational socialization involves a sequence with several phases. First, there is a shift from broad, societally derived goals that led to choice of the occupation, to proficiency and mastery of specific work tasks. Next, a reference group develops from among significant others in the work environment. Finally, the values of the occupational group are internalized and the newcomer takes on the attitudes, values, and behavior that the group prescribes. There is certainly variation in how rapidly students move through this sequence and the ease with which they accept the occupational group's standards. However, these phases seem to capture the experiences of the ninety-five students Simpson followed through their training at a collegiate school of nursing attached to a teaching hospital.

According to Simpson, the students were motivated to enter nursing primarily by the humanitarian desire to help sick and suffering people. However, the initial training period places great emphasis on learning a wide variety of technical skills of varying complexity and mastering the standardized procedures for performing a number of basic nursing tasks. Students are very disappointed that they are not able to immediately begin helping people. The result is a noticeable shift away from humanitarian and helping concerns to an emphasis on mastering the skills that distinguish the professional from the layperson. Thus, this initial phase of the socialization process forces students to at least temporarily suspend the goal they brought to the training program and redirects their attention to a new and quite different set of concerns.

The second phase involves the development of a new reference group. In the second year, training shifts from the classroom to a clinical (hospital) setting. Initially, students look mainly to patients for feedback about how they are performing their work. This focus on patients as a source of evaluation is replaced by a concern with the judgements of co-workers, both physicians and nurses. In effect, students begin to acquire the norms of the colleague group as standards for judging their own performance and competence. In addition, they begin to evaluate others (nurses, student nurses, doctors) in terms of universalistic, professional standards of competence rather than on the basis of idiosyncratic characteristics and particularistic criteria such as personal likes and dislikes.

The third phase in the process involves an extension and intensification of the second phase. Professional norms and values become internalized and replace nonprofessional standards as bases for judging both self and others. Simpson suggests that complete internalization of professional norms may depend on what happens after training. Internalization is more likely to occur where people work mainly with colleagues rather than outsiders and where one's work is insulated from pressure, control, and evaluation by outsiders. What is especially noteworthy about this process in nursing is how patients recede into the background. Evaluation of work ultimately comes down to the question of what colleagues think of it. There is evidence that this occurs in other fields, too. Teachers often criticize the use of student evaluations to judge their work on the grounds that colleagues, not clients, are the best judges of their competence.[22] A six-year study of residents at the famous Menninger School of Psychiatry also concluded that the evaluation of the work of psychiatrists relies almost exclusively on the judgements of colleagues. Rarely is the psychiatrist's performance judged in terms of how well his or her patients do.[23]

Another study of nursing students by Genevieve Rogge Meyer also deals with changes that occur during training and generally supports the findings of Simpson's study.[24] Nursing students were classified into types on the basis of the kinds of work situations they preferred. Beginning students overwhelmingly preferred work that involved dealing with patients on a one-to-one basis unaided by colleagues. The proportion of students of this type (Meyer calls them "ministering angels") decreases dramatically during the following years of training as students acquire a conception of nursing as work that involves much more than just attending to the care of patients by oneself. As training proceeds, students come to prefer work that involves technical and administrative tasks and work situations that involve teamwork (with other nurses, aides, practical nurses, and physicians) in dealing with patients. The fundamental shift that occurs is away from a direct orientation to patients to a preference for work that is colleague-oriented.

The studies just reviewed provide cases where socialization agents are successful in bringing about changes in those being socialized. This is not always the case, however. The orientations students bring with them may be so strongly held that they prove to be impervious to change, or students may be unable or unwilling to "buy" what their mentors have to offer. An example of this comes from a study of a collegiate nursing program committed to training not only well-qualified nurses but also to producing future leaders for the profession.[25] Fred Davis, Virginia L. Olesen, and Elvi Waik Whittaker report that young women entering this program were primarily oriented toward the traditional wife and mother role and did not see nursing as a dominant, lifelong, primary commitment. The nursing school faculty made numerous conscious efforts to develop in them a stronger commitment to a long-term nursing career and to assuming an active leadership role in the profession. These efforts proved to be remarkably unsuccessful. By the end of their training students were no more committed to a long-term career and the assumption of leadership roles than they were when they entered. Davis, Olesen, and Whittaker conclude that these conventionally oriented young women entered the program firmly committed to a traditional female role. This commitment was apparently so strong that it enabled them to resist a concerted effort to develop alternative commitments. Thus, while they may have experienced some changes as they passed through the program, they were unchanged with respect to this primary goal of the nursing school.

Graduate School

Conflict between the goals of students and those of the programs they enter can also result in failure to complete the program. A study of graduate students in sociology by Charles R. Wright illustrates this.[26] Wright studied first-year graduate students in sociology at a large, private, eastern university. Of the fifty students entering the program in the fall, thirty–five indicated a desire to become sociologists while the remainder planned to enter other occupations for which they apparently felt that sociological training would be useful. By the end of their first year, three of the fifteen students who had not planned to become sociologists had changed their minds. Nine of these fifteen continued to be uninterested in sociology as a career and had dropped out of the program. Eighteen of the thirty-five students initially committed to careers in sociology retained this commitment. The remaining seventeen either became uncertain about their future plans or had developed a desire to work in other occupations. None of these seventeen students returned for a second year of graduate work. Thus, the initial pattern was a high degree of self-selection out of the program and the development of very little commitment to the field among these initially uncommitted to it.

Focusing on the thirty-five students initially committed to a career in sociology, Wright tried to explain why some (eighteen) retained their commitment and others (seventeen) did not. He concluded that neither the motivation to succeed nor previous exposure to the field could account for the retention or loss of commitment. Rather, the crucial factor seemed to be the kinds of preconceptions of sociology the students brought with them and whether these were consistent or in conflict with what they actually encountered in their coursework. Wright identified three preconceptions or orientations to sociology among the students. The first was a *reformist orientation* where students felt that the main task of the sociologist was to attack social problems and evil conditions in society. The second was a *philosophical orientation* which emphasized humanistic aspects of sociology, the solution of conceptual and logical problems, and the integration of theoretical systems. A third orientation Wright called the *scientific orientation*. This included a view of sociology as an empirical science dealing with issues and problems of limited scope. The courses that first-year students were required to take strongly emphasized the "scientific" aspects of sociology. Courses in contemporary theory, research methodology, and statistics presented this definition of the field to students. Wright concluded that the retention (or loss) of commitment to the field depends upon the degree of congruence between the students' orientations and what they are actually presented with in their training. Those who enter with an image that does not fit the model they encounter are likely to resolve the conflict by losing interest in the field. In this case those with reformist or philosophical orientations lost their initial commitment while those with a compatible scientific orientation retained theirs.

Military and Police Academies

Conflicts between the characteristics of individuals and the demands of socializing organizations have been investigated in other settings. Irving Rootman studied the entering class at the U.S. Coast Guard Academy, 30 percent of whom withdrew from the academy by the end of their first year.[27] In attempting to explain why some recruits withdrew and others did not, he concluded that those whose personality, interests, and values are at variance with the expectations and demands of the academy represent a poor fit with the role for which they are being prepared. Thus, attrition results from discrepancy between individual qualities and the goals of the organization. As a result of this self-selection out of the training, those who remain tend to be those whose personal qualities are amenable to the socialization efforts of the organization.

Another study of cadets in the Austin (Texas) Police Academy by Marianne Hopper reports similar findings.[28] Some cadets entered the program with an idealistic concern for helping people. The realities of police work, as presented in the academy and on patrol, severely challenged this orientation and its viability as a primary motivation for a career as a police officer. Three of the eight cadets with this initial orientation left the academy, and the other five changed their perspective dramatically in the direction of a more practical and realistic view of police work consistent with the focus of their training.

Assuming that these findings from nursing schools, graduate school, and military and police academies can be generalized to other socialization settings, they suggest another function of occupational socialization. Socialization in the early phase of training may operate to encourage self-selection out of the occupation. This function may be just as (if not more) common than bringing about changes in students. These findings do suggest that incomplete or incorrect information about an occupation or a particular training program can result in a course of action that is costly (in terms of time, energy, and money) for those seeking training as well as those providing it.

DEVELOPING A PROFESSIONAL SELF-CONCEPT

Occupational socialization includes opportunities to engage in the activities that make up the work of the occupation. Typically, the neophyte has few opportunities to perform the role in a complete way. The trainee is usually moved through a sequence of stages which include assuming responsibilities, making decisions, and taking actions that increasingly resemble what full-fledged practitioners do. This aspect of the occupational socialization process is evident in Merton's study of medical students, Light's study of psychiatric residents, and the several studies of nurses discussed above. In addition to Huntington's analysis of the increase in the professional self-concept of medical students as they take on clinical responsibilities, several other studies have looked at how a professional self-concept is shaped by opportunities to *perform the actual work* of the occupation the way it is performed by its practitioners.

Charles Kadushin dealt with this issue in a study of students in two eminent music conservatories, the Manhattan School of Music and the

Julliard School of Music. [29] Kadushin reports that the schools themselves and the instruction that occurs within them contribute little to the development of a professional self-concept among the students. While faculty serve as role models and become an important reference group in setting standards by which technical competence is judged, they contribute little to the emergence of students' image of themselves as professionals. Rather, the schools are "facilitating mechanisms." They are intermediaries whose function is to develop musical skills in their students. The acquisition of these skills leads to successful and rewarded performances and it is through actual performance that the self-concept of professional musician is developed. In this case, the socialization function of the schools is not so much to change values and orientations as it is to transmit and develop technical skills that will lead to successful performance. A professional self-concept then develops as a result of opportunities to demonstrate one's competencies.

Similar conclusions were reached in a study of 364 graduate teaching assistants at Florida State University by Ronald M. Pavalko and John W. Holley.[30] The work that the teaching assistants actually did was quite varied. Some worked at grading tests and keeping records for a faculty member, or supervised laboratory sections and conducted quiz sections, activities *dissimilar* to those of the faculty. Others, however, had full responsibility for the teaching of introductory and (less frequently) even advanced courses, work activities *similar* to those of the faculty. Those whose work as teaching assistants was more similar to what faculty did were more likely to have a conception of themselves as "members of their discipline or profession" rather than primarily as students. The effect of doing faculty work on self-concept was especially strong when students were given autonomy in such things as determining the content of the course, deciding how they would evaluate their students, and having complete responsibility for final grade assignments.

WHAT'S IN AN OCCUPATIONAL TITLE?
VARIATION IN SOCIALIZATION EXPERIENCES AND OUTCOMES

Occupational groups vary in the degree to which they have developed standardized training programs. This is an important point to keep in mind when we attempt to assess the impact that occupational socialization has on the attitudes, values, and orientations that exist in an occupation at a given time. The absence of uniformity and agreement among members of an occupation may be due in part to the fact that training programs do not "homogenize" their students, a point already noted.

In general, standardization in the content and structure of training is greatest in those occupational groups where licensing is required by law and depends on passing licensing examinations. The licensing of practitioners on the basis of successful completion of an examination of some kind creates pressure to standardize the content of training to make sure that it covers those things with which the examination deals. In general, this kind of standardization has become evident in health care occupations, the legal profession, and in the apprenticeship programs of many skilled craft occupations. Yet many occupations have multiple routes by which they can be entered. This creates a situation in which people may share a common occupational label but they may differ in outlook, the way in which they practice the occupation, the meaning their work has for them, and the kinds of career opportunities they have.

One of the best examples of this kind of internal variation is graduate training in the arts and sciences disciplines in American universities. Programs at different universities that lead to masters and doctoral degrees in the same field may vary tremendously in terms of the particular specialty they emphasize, how courses are sequenced, the kinds of examinations students must complete, etc. For example, programs producing PhD psychologists may emphasize clinical psychology, experimental psychology, or developmental psychology. Biology graduate programs may similarly specialize in cell biology, ecology, or genetics. Graduate programs may also vary in terms of the amount and kind of "hands on" research experience they provide their students, and whether they see themselves as training researchers or practitioners. The enumeration and illustration of such variation in every field of study could go on for many pages. The point is that here we have a situation where a shared occupational label does not guarantee a shared sense of what the occupation is all about or a shared occupational identity that has the same meaning.

There has not been a great deal of careful study of how such variation comes about and what its consequences are. There has been enough, however, to suggest that this is a potentially important issue to pursue. Three studies, dealing with the socialization of U.S. Air Force officers, Protestant clergy, and psychiatrists, can illustrate the implications of such internal variation.

Gary L. Wamsley's study of two officer training programs presents a picture of great variation in both the structure and desired outcomes of socialization within the U.S. Air Force.[31] One program, the Aviation Cadet Pre-Flight Training School (Pre-Flight) began early in World War II and was phased out between 1961 and 1964. The six-month program took civilians and some enlisted men and prepared them for flight training and eventual commissioning as officers. Those who entered the program were motivated primarily by the desire to fly and only secondarily by the desire to become officers. Wamsley describes the training program as "harsh" in the sense that it involved hazing, rigid discipline, frequent punishment, insults and degradation, and a high level of stress created by continual questioning of the cadets' competencies, worth, and capabilities for completing the program. The goal of the program was to produce graduates with "heroic" qualities useful in combat such as group loyalty, obedience, toughness, and aggressive enthusiasm. The officers operating the program had this outcome as a conscious goal, and felt that they were producing not only future pilots but also fellow officers. They felt many of those entering the program were not officer material. Not surprisingly, about one-third failed to complete the program. Those who did complete it acquired the heroic qualities that the program sought to produce. They developed a strong sense of honor and loyalty to the air force, respect for military traditions and the chain of command, and pride in themselves and their capabilities.

The second program that Wamsley studied was the Officers Training School (OTS). OTS was a response to increasingly complex technology and the anticipation of the air force's role in space flight. Planning for the program began in the late 1950s and the three-month program graduated its first class in 1960. In sharp contrast to Pre-Flight, OTS had as its goal the training of managers who could perform complex and specialized managerial activities. Those recruited to the program were better educated than the Pre-Flight cadets, were mainly concerned with becoming officers, and had little interest in flying. Their training involved a gradual transition to military life. Unlike the Pre-Flight cadets, they were not subject to restrictions on where they could go and they were permitted to bring their families with them. There was no hazing, physical punishment, or ridicule, and their training was, by and large, "low-keyed," with an emphasis on developing technical and administrative skills. There was an emphasis on keeping OTS recruits in the program. OTS recruits who wanted to leave the program were viewed as a serious crisis, with the implication that the training was not accomplishing its purpose, in contrast to Pre-Flight which encouraged the departure of recruits unable to meet its demands. OTS did indeed accomplish its objectives, producing graduates skilled in managerial techniques. According to Wamsley, the air force views OTS as a great success, and by 1970 it had become the single largest source of commissioned officers. These two training programs illustrate rather sharply the differences that can exist in the socialization experiences of those entering what is ostensibly the same occupation. There is little doubt that those entering the officer ranks through these two routes will have very different conceptions of themselves and their roles as U.S. Air Force officers.

Another study illustrating internal variation in socialization deals with Protestant clergy. Jackson W. Carroll investigated how the theological orientation of 1,541 recent graduates of twenty-one Protestant seminaries was shaped by the goals of the seminaries they attended.[32] There are basically three types of seminaries, based on the kinds of goals they have. The "religious community" emphasizes mastery of the Christian tradition and development and deepening of the spiritual life and commitments of the seminarian. On the whole, such schools are rather traditional and conservative in their approach to seminary training. A second type of school is the "vocational school." Here the goal is the development of practical skills and competencies as well as the development of the spiritual life of the student. The third type Carroll calls the "graduate school." The emphasis here is achieving mastery of the Christian tradition but also developing a "secular awareness." The latter refers to becoming aware of and involved in the secular world in ways that express the Christian mission. Carroll found that graduates of the "religious community" type seminary had the most conservative theological orientation, those who completed their training in the "graduate school" type were the most liberal, and graduates of "vocational schools" were intermediate in their own theological orientations. The liberal-conservative orientation of clergy was more strongly related to the type of seminary they attended than to their denomination. Thus, the study illustrates how diversity among members of an occupation can be created by differences in the climate and goals of organizations responsible for their socialization.

A final example of variation within the same occupation comes from a study of psychiatric residents by Rue Bucher and Joan G. Stelling.[33] They compared residents in two different training programs. One was located in a private hospital with a teaching staff consisting of private practitioners committed to a psychoanalytic approach to therapy. Their goal was to train psychoanalytically oriented therapists for careers as private practitioners. The training of residents in this program consisted mainly of one-on-one therapy with outpatients. The other program was located in a state psychiatric hospital. The teaching staff was not committed to any particular approach to therapy but took an eclectic approach emphasizing diversity in both the kind of treatment that occurred in the hospital and in the orientations of their graduates. The past careers and career aspirations of the staff included some private practice but they were more committed to careers in hospitals, community mental health, and the state mental health system. The staff saw the training of new psychiatrists as important, but they were also committed to the broad goal of improving the overall quality of mental health care in the state. In this program the actual training of residents included an emphasis on creating a therapeutic milieu in collaboration with other psychiatrists, nurses, aides, psychologists, occupational therapists, and activity therapists, in addition to direct therapy with patients. As they approached the completion of their training, residents in these two programs differed considerably in their professional identities, their approach to psychiatry, and their anticipated careers. Residents in the private hospital developed strong identities as psychiatrists, were committed to a psychoanalytic approach, and used the language of psychiatry to explain their own behavior and events around them. They expected to pursue careers in private practice working with individual outpatients. Those completing their residency in the state hospital had a different orientation. While they thought of themselves as psychiatrists, they did not see the practice of psychiatry tied to any single approach. They also saw the language and concepts of their field as limited to their work but not the dominant perspective from which they explained everything. They also anticipated careers involving a diversity of activities with less than half of their total work time being devoted to private practice.

INFORMAL SOCIALIZATION AND SOCIALIZATION AFTER TRAINING: MECHANISMS OF SOCIAL CONTROL

The vast majority of research on occupational socialization has dealt with the effect of highly organized and formal training experiences on individuals. But occupational socialization does not end when people complete their training and begin to work at their occupation. Occupational socialization should be thought of as a continuing, ongoing process imbedded in the very nature of work. Not all occupations have a sharp distinction between preparation for work and the performance of work. In many cases there is a very short training period that transmits minimal skills and a rudimentary sense of what membership in the occupation means. Most of what goes into making a person a member of the occupation may be learned on the job. In other cases learning a job and doing it may be one and the same. Many occupations have very informal recruitment procedures. Training may amount to nothing more than a tacit and informal agreement that a person in the occupation will "show the ropes" to the newcomer. Many small business occupations, semiskilled and skilled craft occupations, and deviant or illegal occupations have this kind of entry and training process.

One key factor that makes socialization a continuing process is the tremendous *interdependence* that exists in modern work. In the occupational system of modern societies there are very few occupational activities in which people are not dependent in some way on others. In some cases there is dependence on co-workers for assistance, advice, help in covering up mistakes, referrals of clients and customers, and the like.

There is also dependence on members of other occupational groups for a variety of services. Garage mechanics are dependent on parts suppliers, and small business people are dependent on banks for short-term loans and on suppliers for credit. In hospitals, physicians are dependent on nurses, technicians, and others for information. The listing of such examples could go on and on. In many occupations people are dependent on organizations such as professional associations and unions for certification, information about new employment opportunities, or access to opportunities for advancement. Another rather obvious form that dependence takes is reliance on organizations for employment, economic security, and career advancement. The significance of all this is that dependence makes people vulnerable to the control of those individuals, groups, or organizations on which they may be dependent. Our next task is to illustrate these principles by examining a number of occupations and work contexts in which they occur.

SOCIALIZATION IN DEVIANT AND ILLEGAL OCCUPATIONS

When thinking about occupations it is easy to neglect or overlook the fact that some activities viewed as deviant behavior or social problems such as crime are in fact occupational roles. Illegal occupations refer to activities that are explicitly defined as criminal. Deviant occupations are not as easy to define. Following George Ritzer and Gale Miller's approach, we will regard deviant occupations as those in which (a) some central activity violates some norm or value that has not been incorporated into the criminal law and (b) the culture, lifestyle, or setting in which the occupation is performed is popularly viewed as involving conduct that violates norms.[34]

Prostitution

Socialization processes are evident in research that has been done on prostitution. James H. Bryan studied thirty-three Los Angeles call girls and documented the patterned and structured nature of their induction, training, and socialization.[35] All but one of the girls indicated that entry into the occupation resulted from personal contact with someone involved in prostitution (either a pimp or other call girls). The typical pattern for novices is to seek out a call girl for help directly or through a pimp. Once an established call girl agrees to help the beginner, she also assumes the responsibility of training her.

The apprenticeship period, usually two or three months, is spent with the established call girl, either by moving into her residence or commuting there on a daily basis. The content of training consists of the learning of two things: first, a value structure, and second, a set of "do's and don'ts" regarding relationships with customers, other call girls, and pimps.

The value structure transmitted to aspiring call girls emphasizes maximizing financial gains and minimizing effort. The values taught stress a cynical orientation in which people (especially men) are portrayed as corrupt and out to get whatever they can. All social relationships are seen as a "con" and prostitution is viewed as a more honest (or at least a no more dishonest) activity than that of "squares" as they go about ripping each other off in their everyday lives. Customers are defined as being out to exploit the call girl and therefore fair game for exploitation by her. Bryan sees these values as creating a sense of "in-group solidarity" that distances the would-be call girl from "square" society, giving the trainer greater control over the trainee, and equipping the newcomer to maximize her financial gain.

The "do's and don'ts" regarding interpersonal conduct cover several points. One point that is stressed is to keep the relationship with customers as brief and emotionally uninvolved as possible. Other tips deal with the use of alcohol and other drugs. Still other points deal with such things as how and when to obtain the fee, personal hygiene, and how to talk to a customer on the telephone. Bryan notes that specific instruction regarding sexual techniques is quite rare despite the fact that many novices have had little previous sexual experience. To facilitate the novice's development, it is not uncommon for the trainer to eavesdrop on her transactions with customers and immediately critique the way in which she handled herself. More common, however, is a pattern in which the novice learns mainly by observing the way in which the established call girl handles her customers.

The established call girl is also instrumental in helping the trainee build a clientele. The trainer arranges the first meeting between novice and customer and gets from 40 to 50 percent of the fee. After that the novice is on her own. If she can get the customer's name and phone number, she is free to negotiate future contracts without having to split the fee with her trainer. Bryan reports that the termination of training is usually abrupt, often resulting from interpersonal conflicts between trainer and trainee or from conflict over the trainee's theft of the trainer's list of customers, rather than because training has been in some sense completed. As this study indicates, the process of becoming a call girl has parallels with socialization into many more conventional occupations. There is a demarcated training period during which distinctive occupational values and role conceptions are transmitted.

Call girls represent an elite segment of the occupation of prostitution. They develop a regular clientele of relatively high-status customers and command high fees. Another member of the occupation is the street-walker who typically has single contacts with a large number of different customers over time and who solicits in bars, hotel lobbies, and on the street. Diana Gray's study of streetwalkers indicates both similarities and differences in socialization compared to call girls.[36] Most of the training is done by a pimp rather than by other prostitutes. Sexual techniques and social skills are largely learned on the job through trial and error. While pimps do teach such things as how to wash a customer, check for venereal disease, and persuade him to use a condom, only about one-third of the streetwalkers in Gray's sample were taught such things as avoiding detection by the police, birth control techniques, picking up customers, and how to locate "trick houses" (hotels or other safe places where the prostitute can take her customer). Thus, compared to call girls, the socialization of streetwalkers appears to be less complex and explicit, with greater reliance on learning skills on the job rather than during a period of apprenticeship.

Stripping

Stripping (or "exotic dancing" as it is sometimes called) is another occupation that illustrates informal on-the-job socialization and the social control exercised by others. Jacqueline Boles and A. P. Garbin point out that one of the main problems faced by strippers is harassment and heckling by members of the audience.[37] There is very little training prior to actually working as a stripper that provides the skills needed to handle an audience. A competitive relationship among strippers precludes the development of mentor-apprentice relationships. Newcomers, however, learn a repertoire of standard insults, "comebacks," and "put-downs" from experienced strippers through a process of informal socialization. Male troublemakers are put down with insults about their sexual prowess. Assuming that female hecklers are reacting to the fact that she is exposing her body, the stripper accentuates her physical movements and flaunts her body and nudity.

External controls vary depending on whether the stripper is a feature performer or "house girl." Feature performers are the elite of the occupation. Highly skilled and often formally trained as dancers, they travel a national and even international nightclub circuit. Consequently, they become identified with the occupation but not with any particular club. While both feature performers and "house girls" are dependent on club owners and managers, "house girls" work in one club on a full-time basis and are subject to many more controls. The club manager has control over hiring, firing, and the content of the stripper's performance.[38] "House girls" have no job security and can be fired at the whim of the club manager. Boles and Garbin report that strippers do not have a shared orientation toward management that would enable them to manipulate managers and gain control over the conditions and content of their work. Consequently, their individualized dependence exposes them to extensive control by club managers.

Career Criminals

Traditionally, the dominant sociological perspective on crime has dealt with such topics as the social characteristics of criminals, the criminal justice system, how official agencies enforce criminal laws, the functioning of the penal system, and the like. Although there have been a few studies of crime as a way of life,[39] an occupational perspective on crime has begun to develop only since the 1970s.

Two works, by Peter Letkemann[40] and Gale Miller,[41] have been especially important in developing an awareness of the fact that, for many habitual criminals, crime is work, and different types of crime can be viewed as occupational specialization. Once such a perspective is articulated, it is possible to ask many of the same kinds of questions about criminal occupations that we ask about conventional ones. Clearly, we can enrich our understanding of occupational socialization by including criminal work in our analysis.

An initial point that needs to be made is that the particular kinds of skills that need to be acquired vary from one type of criminal work to another. For example, safecrackers need technical and mechanical skills more than bank robbers who need skill in manipulating people and social settings as well as speed in doing their work. People who work at various kinds of "cons" involving deception and trickery, or what Miller has called "false pretense work"[42] need to develop sophisticated dramaturgical skills in order to entice, manipulate, and control their victims.

Letkemann's analysis, based on interviews with habitual bank robbers and safecrackers, focuses on their acquisition of technical skills and the meaning that their work has. Techniques are learned in prisons which, in effect, are the training grounds for criminal careers. Entry into a criminal career is not necessarily a conscious or deliberate choice. A typical scenario begins with involvement in juvenile delinquency that is not very skilled and is more of an adventure than a career choice. For those sent to reformatories an informal learning process, usually without explicit mentors, results in the acquisition of skills and distinctive values. Letkemann argues that in the reformatory the idea of a possible criminal career begins to crystallize. At this point people assess their skills and their relative chances in the criminal and noncriminal worlds. Those who conclude that crime is a viable way of making a living become involved with others who share that view and acquire additional skills. Getting caught for committing a crime and being sent to jail, from an occupational perspective, mean that one's skills are not yet sufficient for successful performance of the work and it is necessary to go back to school (i.e., jail) to refine them. According to Letkemann, apprenticeships or on-the-job training for bank robbers and safecrackers are uncommon. Rather, the socialization process is a matter of trial and error. Awkward, unskilled, and unsuccessful performances as a juvenile result in further training and sharpening of skills in prison. Informal, intermittent advice from those with more experience and skill gradually leads to greater competence and improved performances.

Miller's analysis of deviant as well as criminal work points out that socialization also includes the acquisition of a value system and rationales for the work. In other words, entry into criminal work includes the development of ideologies that deal with the goals, satisfactions, and disappointments that are part of the work. For example, people who engage in various forms of theft will claim that they have not committed a serious offense and that they are not any more dishonest than those in many kinds of conventional work. People who cheat or trick their victims out of money or other resources point out that their victims often willingly collaborate in their own victimization as in the case of the person eager to invest in a get-rich-quick scheme that turns out to be a fake.

In discussing Bryan's study of call girls earlier it was pointed out that prostitutes rationalize their exploitative orientation toward customers on the grounds that their customers are out to exploit them. Prostitutes also learn an ideology that defines their work as providing a variety of services. For example, they argue that they help prevent sex crimes by satisfying the needs of people who may have difficulty finding sexual partners because they are unattractive, deformed, or have unusual sexual preferences. The learned justifications for prostitution also include the notion that the work helps save marriages by satisfying sexual needs that, for whatever reason, cannot be met by wives.[43]

Although much more informal and loosely structured than in conventional occupations, socialization processes clearly exist in deviant and criminal occupations. Socialization results in the acquisition of skills and supporting attitudes and values as well as the development of shared conceptions of the work role and a conception of oneself as a member of the occupation.

COLLEAGUE GROUPS AS AGENTS OF SOCIAL CONTROL

Throughout the occupational structure, *colleague groups* operate as a continuing source of socialization and social control. Like socialization in deviant and illegal occupations, that done by colleague groups is rarely formal and organized. Rather, it tends to be more informal and not always easy to observe. It is part of the "private" life of occupational groups and is largely hidden from public view.

What colleague groups actually do may vary from one occupation to another but one thing that members of all occupational groups do is make judgements about one another's competencies. The content and form that such judgements take will obviously vary. Evaluations are typically not made public but remain within the group. They become part of the folklore of the occupational culture and a powerful mechanism of social control.

Sponsorship in Medicine

Advancement in many types of work at the professional end of the continuum is often dependent on acceptance and sponsorship by members of the profession who control access to a variety of rewards. Oswald Hall has pointed out that in the medical profession control over key hospital appointments is exercised informally by an "inner fraternity" of specialists who dominate major hospital posts.[44] General practitioners are dependent on the inner fraternity for referrals, and newcomers to the profession become dependent on them to the extent that they aspire to become members of this inner circle in the future. The inner core's power derives from its cohesiveness; shared educational experiences; similar socioeconomic backgrounds; and regular, ongoing working relationships. They control the medical market and their colleagues by controlling the referral of patients and hospital appointments.

Hall's study was done in the 1940s and one can appropriately ask whether its conclusions are valid today. There have not been very many recent studies of this kind of colleague control. However, two studies done in the 1970s are generally supportive of Hall's portrayal. Donald K. Freeborn and Benjamin J. Darsky found a similar power structure in a study of physicians in a Canadian community.[45] The only differences were that the inner circle was dominated by general practitioners rather than specialists and the fraternity was not quite as closed as in Hall's study. Otherwise, it operated in a similar manner, controlling younger colleagues and those on the fringe of the professional community. In a study of a national sample of physicians, Robert J. Marshall, Jr. concluded that an informal system of sponsorship controlled the career opportunities of physicians in ways similar to that described by Hall.[46]

Academicians

Colleague control can be expected to operate as a socialization mechanism in any occupation that develops a strong sense of community and comes to value the principle of autonomy and colleague evaluation. Joseph H. Fichter also has pointed out that money and income may not be viable indicators of success and achievement in occupational groups that emphasize service motives and minimize the importance of self-interest.[47] Success may be measured differently inside the occupation and outside of it. Outside, money may be a valid measure of success, but inside it may be less meaningful than positive evaluations by colleagues. To the extent that people are strongly identified with their occupational group, the seeking of colleague approval gives colleagues control over their behavior and legitimates both subtle and coercive efforts to further socialize them.

In the academic world the notion that university professors are expected to "publish or perish," or at least publish in order to be rewarded, continues to receive a good deal of attention and discussion both within and outside universities. The mandate to do research and write as a requirement for continued employment, salary increases, or tenure is often characterized as an unreasonable demand. From a socialization perspective, however, it illustrates the principle of colleague evaluation and control. The work of the contemporary university professor includes a variety of activities. Teaching skills, evaluated by students, require client rather than colleague evaluation. Service on committees is another activity that provides an occasion for evaluation by faculty colleagues and administrators, but this is less an evaluation of scholarly competence than problem-solving and decision-making abilities. However, publications reporting the results of the faculty member's scholarly activities are subject to exclusive evaluation by colleagues. Thus, the emphasis on publications represents a reliance on colleague control over the evaluation of the work of academics.

Skilled Craft and Industrial Workers

Colleague control is also a feature of work in many skilled craft occupations. The building trades have a long tradition of colleague control that can be traced back to the medieval guilds. Although the guilds were internally stratified (masters, journeymen, apprentices), they nevertheless maintained a high degree of equity with regard to pay, the amount of work required, and decision making. The guild usually specified the way in which work was to be done and the specific tools to be used. Since each guild had a virtual monopoly over its craft in a given geographic area, it was able to enforce its standards and control its members with the very powerful threat of expulsion.[48]

Although the guilds were replaced by the factory system as a way of organizing work, the traditions of workmanship and colleague control that were so important in the guilds have carried over to many skilled craft occupations. Many craft unions, especially in the building trades, maintain their own apprenticeship systems in which standards of quality, norms regulating the quantity of work that can be expected by employers, and the principle of colleague evaluation are transmitted to the apprentice. The building trades are somewhat of an anomaly in that the construction industry is a sector of the economy in which the introduction of standardized, assembly line methods of production has not been successful or far reaching. It remains an area in which separate craft groups go about their work in a relatively autonomous manner. Consequently, it has remained possible for occupations such as carpenters, cabinetmakers, bricklayers, plasterers, stonemasons, electricians, tile setters, painters, plumbers, etc., to maintain distinct occupational identities and a meaningful sense of membership in colleague groups. These circumstances have produced a situation in which colleague control over both the quality and quantity of work has remained strong relative to industrial workers, although it varies from one craft to another and may be affected by the characteristics of particular construction projects and sites.[49]

Evidence of the socializing impact of colleague groups among industrial workers comes largely from studies by industrial sociologists dealing with the "restriction of output" by workers. The well-known Hawthorne studies illustrated this.[50] The earnings of workers were tied to a system of incentives related to individual and group productivity. The assumption was that group pressure would maximize individual productivity since everyone would benefit if each worker produced more. This strategy, however, did not increase productivity. The work group developed an informal norm regarding what was considered to be a proper day's work. Those who exceeded it were called "rate busters" and those who fell short were regarded as "chiselers." The norm was enforced by name-calling, ridicule, and "binging" (a sharp and painful punch on the arm). In effect, the colleague group socialized its members to its norms and controlled the productivity of its members.

Donald Roy's studies of machine shop workers also document the fact that workers are socialized to group norms of productivity.[51] He found that informal norms emphasized the importance of "beating the system." When jobs were being timed for the purpose of setting pay rates for piecework, workers would intentionally stretch out the amount of time needed to do the job. Group norms stressed that production rates were not to be exceeded for fear that management would simply raise the minimum up to actual production levels. Workers learned that they had to cooperate with one another to restrict production by loafing, working slower, and collaborating with workers in other units of the plant.

In both this and the Hawthorne studies, socialization and control by the work group are clearly evident.

ORGANIZATIONS AS AGENTS OF SOCIALIZATION

Organizations are another source of socialization and control. In looking at their socialization effects, two types of organizations are of interest: occupational associations, and organizations in which people are employed.

Occupational Associations

Occupational associations are of various types, including learned societies and professional associations, labor unions, and trade associations; they perform various functions, including the setting of fees, wages, and prices. They may also articulate goals for the occupation which individuals are then encouraged to support and take as their own. As trade, labor, or occupational associations lobby for favorable legislation, they contribute to the creation of the public image of their respective occupations. In so doing they present their members with an image that may be accepted, resisted, or modified. In such cases, the socializing impact of the association on its members may be very subtle and indirect. Occupational associations perform a function that is of particular importance for our concern with post-training socialization. They serve as a source of identity and by so doing they exert a degree of control over their members.

Occupational associations function as a source of identity in a variety of ways. For example, despite their many differences, the monthly union meeting, the weekly luncheon meeting of the local Chamber of Commerce, and the annual meetings of professional associations and learned societies have one thing in common. They reinforce their members' sense of identity with and membership in the occupational group. They represent what anthropologists call "rites of intensification"—occasions on which feelings and sentiments of belonging to the group are nurtured, developed, and reinforced. Thus, people who in the normal course of their work may be competitors (business owners), or physically and spatially separated (academics in different universities, scientists in different laboratories, bricklayers at different construction sites) are brought together under the aegis of the occupational association in a way that minimizes their differences and maximizes their sense of common interest, concern, and destiny.

Occupational associations are an especially important source of conflict over occupational identity where members of an occupation typically work in large organizations. Employing organizations often strive to get their members to develop an identification with and loyalty to the organization. Where people have strongly developed occupational identities and ties, the result may be a competition for their identification and loyalty. A good example of this occurs in universities which consist of a variety of specialists with a highly developed sense of membership in scholarly disciplines or professional specialties. As an organization, the university would like the faculty to think of themselves as "members of _____ University" and develop a strong commitment to it. The faculty, however, are likely to think of themselves as primarily members of a particular discipline and to view the university as a convenient device that facilitates their work as historians, psychologists, physicists, etc. Involvement and participation in association activities help maintain disciplinary identities in the face of pressure for identification with the organization. Such competition and conflict are by no means limited to universities. They also occur in private businesses that employ highly trained specialists. The engineer in a manufacturing concern may be encouraged to develop an identity as a member of "the company" first and an engineer second. The research chemist for a pharmaceutical company may find it difficult to maintain an identity as a chemist in the face of pressure to see himself or herself as primarily a member of the organization. In very large organizations occupational associations may be particularly important to maintenance of one's self-conception as a member of a particular work tradition rather than simply a specialist in an organization.

Employing Organizations

Besides attempting to shape the identities and loyalties of their members, there are several other ways in which employing organizations socialize their new members. The socializing potential of organizations is really a special case of the more general principle that whenever people join a new group they are obliged to learn something about the group's sense of purpose, its ways of doing things, its traditions, etc. Just as societies have distinctive cultures, so do organizations. Newcomers to any group represent a potentially disruptive, change-producing force. Work organizations may attempt to minimize potential disruption by socializing new members to a wide range of things.

In effect, entry into an organization involves the learning of a formal as well as informal culture. While every organization has an official definition of how particular tasks are supposed to be done, there are also unofficial rules and understandings that may be as important (and in some cases more important) for successful functioning in the organization. Becoming familiar with official and unofficial authority and power structures and developing an understanding of who can help and who can hinder the attainment of one's goals are important outcomes of organizational socialization.

Organizations also present people with new reference groups. A study of pharmacists by Carol L. Kronus illustrates how the kind of organization in which members of the same occupation are employed affects their choice of reference group.[52] Those employed in neighborhood and chain-store pharmacies developed very different reference groups than those employed in hospitals and clinics. In hospitals, physicians become the dominant reference group because they control both the work flow and the evaluation of pharmacists. On the other hand, colleagues were the main reference group of those employed in neighborhood pharmacies. They work in a more autonomous situation and their occupation and colleagues become their most important source of status and identity.

As noted earlier, employing organizations also strive to develop among their members a sense of loyalty and commitment to the organization, whether or not this sense competes with occupational identities. Both formal and informal strategies may be used to try to accomplish this. For example, organizations may offer a variety of rewards such as the promise of permanent employment (as in the case of tenure in the academic world), bonuses, stock options, special privileges, and attractive retirement plans.

Entry into an organization also includes socialization to another important aspect of work: the hierarchical structure of organizations presents individuals with new career possibilities and aspirations. As Curt Tausky has pointed out, organizational hierarchies are an inducement to mobility and a way of controlling and motivating people.[53] During training for an occupation, individuals may develop career goals and a sense of what they would like their careers to look like. Organizations may open up new possibilities, reinforce previously acquired career goals, or force people to change their career plans. While it is important to recognize this as part of the socialization of individuals to organizations, careers are a whole separate topic of major interest and will be dealt with in chapter 5.

SUMMARY

Socialization is an important and ongoing process in the occupational world, as this chapter has attempted to demonstrate. It occurs during preparation for entry into occupations and in the routine conduct of work.

Research on socialization during training has documented a number of factors and raised a variety of issues. It is clear that socialization changes people's identities and their conceptions of their occupations. This is an extremely important outcome of the process. Socialization during training is not always smooth and often involves conflict between aspirants to the occupation and the people and institutions responsible for their training. Nor is it always successful in the sense that the changes desired by those doing the training do not necessarily occur. While shared subcultures and identities are transmitted, we cannot conclude that the process results in the production of occupational "clones." Some people resist accepting all aspects of the occupational subculture and role presented to them. Within a given occupation there may be differences in how members perceive themselves and their occupation due to the existence of multiple routes into the occupation that involve fundamentally different socialization. Still, it is appropriate to conclude that occupational socialization is more a conservative than a change-producing force. Although subcultures, roles, and identities undergo some modification, socialization strongly contributes to the replication of existing ways of doing things and the continuity of established beliefs and practices over time.

Clearly, not all occupations have elaborate, formal training and socialization processes, and in many occupations socialization occurs on the job. In deviant and illegal occupations there is strong evidence that socialization occurs although the process is relatively informal and loosely structured. What is most striking and important, however, are the similarities in the outcome of the process in deviant/illegal and conventional occupations. In both cases, occupational ideologies justifying the work and identities are developed, and a sense of membership in the occupation results.

As our examination of the exercise of power in the medical profession illustrated, informal control and socialization are exercised by colleagues in both subtle and overt ways. Although their efforts may be relatively more indirect, occupational associations of various kinds reinforce a sense of membership in and identification with the occupation. In both professional and many blue-collar occupations, work groups socialize members to group norms and place limits on what they can and cannot do in their work. Colleague-based social control is an ever-present reality in the work lives of people throughout the occupational structure.

Employing organizations also socialize their members, mainly by transmitting an understanding of the formal and informal culture of the organization and presenting new career possibilities. Conflicts that individuals have with employing organizations over their loyalties and occupational identities are more than just isolated, idiosyncratic events. They are the result of (and evidence of) a process of socialization that is continually occurring in many different kinds of organizations.

NOTES

1. Robert K. Merton et al., *The Student-Physician* (Cambridge, Mass.: Harvard University Press, 1957), 287.
2. Key works on which this perspective is based include Charles Horton Cooley, *Human Nature and the Social Order* (New York: Free Press, 1965); John Dewey, *Human Nature and Conduct* (New York: Modern Library, 1930); and George Herbert Mead, *Mind, Self, and Society* (Chicago: University of Chicago Press), 1934.
3. Herbert H. Hyman, *The Psychology of Status*, Archives of Psychology, No. 269 (June, 1942).
4. Harold H. Kelley, "Two Functions of Reference Groups," in Theodore Newcomb et al., *Readings in Social Psychology*, rev. ed. (New York: Holt, Rinehart, and Winston, 1952), 410–414.
5. Tamotsu Shibutani, "Reference Groups as Perspectives," *American Journal of Sociology* 61 (May 1955): 562–569.
6. Merton et al., *Student-Physician*, 287.
7. Howard Becker et al., *Boys in White* (Chicago: University of Chicago Press, 1961).
8. Mary Jean Huntington, "The Development of a Professional Self-Image," in Merton et al., *Student-Physician*, 180.
9. Becker et al., *Boys in White*, 420.
10. Samuel W. Bloom, "The Sociology of Medical Education: Some Comments on the State of a Field," *Milbank Memorial Fund Quarterly*, 43 (April 1965): 143–184.
11. Leonard Eron, "The Effect of Medical Education on Attitudes: A Follow-up Study," *Journal of Medical Education* 33, pt. 2 (October 1958): 25–33.
12. Leonard V. Gordon and Ivan N. Mensh, "Values of Medical School Students at Different Levels of Training," *Journal of Educational Psychology* 53 (1962): 48–51.
13. Robert M. Gray et al., "The Effect of Medical Specialization on Physicians' Attitudes," *Journal of Health and Human Behavior* 7 (Summer 1966): 128–132.
14. Jane Leserman, *Men and Women in Medical School: How They Change and How They Compare* (New York: Praeger, 1981).
15. Robert H. Coombs, *Mastering Medicine: Professional Socialization in Medical School* (New York: Free Press, 1978).
16. Renee C. Fox, "Training for Uncertainty," in Merton et al., *Student-Physician*, 207–241.
17. Renee C. Fox, "Is There A 'New' Medical Student? A Comparative View of Medical Socialization in the 1950s and 1970s," in *Ethics of Health Care*, ed. Laurence R. Tancredi (Washington, D.C.: National Academy of Sciences, 1974), 197–220.

18. Coombs, *Mastering Medicine*; Martin Shapiro, *Getting Doctored* (Kitchner, Ontario: Between the Lines, 1978); and Israel Adler and Judith T. Shuval, "Cross Pressures During Socialization for Medicine," *American Sociological Review* 43 (October 1978): 693–704.

19. Jack Haas and William Shaffir, "The Professionalization of Medical Students: Developing Competence and a Cloak of Competence," *Symbolic Interaction* 1 (1977): 71–78; and "Ritual Evaluation of Competence: The Hidden Curriculum of Professionalization in an Innovative Medical School Program," *Work and Occupations* 9 (May 1982): 131–154.

20. Donald Light, *Becoming Psychiatrists: The Professional Transformation of Self* (New York: W. W. Norton, 1980).

21. Ida Harper Simpson, "Patterns of Socialization into Professions: The Case of Student Nurses," *Sociological Inquiry* 37 (Winter 1967): 47–54.

22. Debate about the proper use of student evaluations of teaching has been going on for decades. For a recent discussion see Randi S. Ellis, "Ratings of Teachers by Their Students Should Be Used Wisely—or Not at All," *Chronicle of Higher Education* 31 (November 20, 1985): 88.

23. Robert R. Holt and Lester Luborsky, *Personality Patterns of Psychiatrists* (New York: Basic Books, 1958).

24. Genevieve Rogge Meyer, *Tenderness and Technique: Nursing Values in Transition* (Los Angeles: Institute of Industrial Relations, University of California at Los Angeles, 1960).

25. Fred Davis, Virginia L. Olesen, and Elvi Waik Whittaker, "Problems and Issues in Collegiate Nursing Education," in *The Nursing Profession: Five Sociological Essays*, ed. Fred Davis (New York: Wiley, 1966), 138–175.

26. Charles R. Wright, "Changes in the Occupational Commitment of Graduate Sociology Students," *Sociological Inquiry* 37 (Winter 1967): 55–62.

27. Irving Rootman, "Voluntary Withdrawal from a Total Adult Socializing Organization: A Model," *Sociology of Education* 45 (Summer 1972):258–270.

28. Marianne Hopper, "Becoming a Policeman: Socialization of Cadets in a Police Academy," *Urban Life* 6 (July 1977): 149–170.

29. Charles Kadushin, "The Professional Self-Concept of Music Students," *American Journal of Sociology* 75 (November 1969): 389–404.

30. Ronald M. Pavalko and John W. Holley, "Determinants of a Professional Self-Concept Among Graduate Students," *Social Science Quarterly* 55 (September 1974): 462–477.

31. Gary L. Wamsley, "Contrasting Institutions of Air Force Socialization: Happenstance or Bellwether?" *American Journal of Sociology* 78 (September 1972): 399–417.

32. Jackson W. Carroll, "Structural Effects of Professional Schools on Professional Socialization: The Case of Protestant Clergymen," *Social Forces* 50 (September 1971): 61–74.

33. Rue Bucher and Joan G. Stelling, *Becoming Professional* (Beverly Hills: Sage, 1977).

34. George Ritzer and Gale Miller, "Conflict in Deviant Occupations," in George Ritzer, *Working: Conflict and Change*, 2nd ed. (Englewood Cliffs, N.J.: Prentice-Hall, 1977), 299.

35. James H. Bryan, "Apprenticeships in Prostitution," *Social Problems* 12 (Winter 1965): 287–297.

36. Diana Gray, "Turning Out: A Study of Teenage Prostitution," *Urban Life and Culture* 1 (1973): 401–425.

37. Jacqueline Boles and A. P. Garbin, "Stripping for a Living: An Occupational Study of the Night Club Stripper," in *Deviant Behavior: Occupational and Organizational Bases*, ed. Clifton Bryant (Chicago: Rand McNally, 1974), 312–335.

38. Esther Newton, *Mother Camp* (Englewood Cliffs, N.J.: 1972), 122.

39. Edwin H. Sutherland, *The Professional Thief* (Chicago, University of Chicago Press, 1930); Clifford Shaw, *The Jack Roller* (Chicago, University of Chicago Press, 1930); and David Maurer, *The Big Con* (Indianapolis, Bobbs-Merrill, 1940).

40. Peter Letkemann, *Crime as Work* (Englewood Cliffs, N.J.: Prentice-Hall, 1973).

41. Gale Miller, *Odd Jobs: The World of Deviant Work* (Englewood Cliffs, N.J.: Prentice-Hall, 1978).

42. Ibid., chap. 3.

43. Alex Thio, *Deviant Behavior*, 2nd ed. (Boston: Houghton Mifflin, 1983), 199–200.

44. Oswald Hall, "The Stages of a Medical Career," *American Journal of Sociology* 53 (March 1948): 327–336.

45. Donald K. Freeborn and Benjamin J. Darsky, "A Study of the Power Structure of the Medical Community," *Medical Care* 12 (1974): 1–12.

46. Robert J. Marshall, Jr., et al., "Physician Career Outcomes and the Process of Medical Education," *Journal of Health and Social Behavior* 19 (1978): 124–138.

47. Joseph H. Fichter, *Religion as an Occupation* (South Bend, Ind.: University of Notre Dame Press, 1961), 176–180.

48. Wilbert E. Moore, *Industrial Relations and the Social Order*, rev. ed. (New York: Crowell, Collier, and Macmillan, 1951).

49. Marc L. Silver, "The Structure of Craft Work: The Construction Industry," in *Varieties of Work*, ed. Phyllis L. Stewart and Muriel G. Cantor (Beverly Hills: Sage, 1982), 235–252.

50. Fritz Roethlisberger and William J. Dickson, *Management and the Worker* (New York: Wiley, 1964). See also George C. Homans, "The Western Electric Researches," in *Readings on Modern Organizations* (Englewood Cliffs, N.J.: Prentice-Hall, 1969).

51. Donald Roy, "Quota Restriction and Goldbricking in a Machine Shop," *American Journal of Sociology* 57 (March 1952): 427–442; and "Efficiency and the Fix: Informal Intergroup Relations in a Piecework Machine Shop," *American Journal of Sociology* 60 (1954): 255–266.

52. Carol L. Kronus, "Occupational Versus Organizational Influences on Reference Group Identification: The Case of Pharmacy," *Sociology of Work and Occupations* 3 (August 1976): 303–330.

53. Curt Tausky, *Work Organizations: Major Theoretical Perspectives*, 2nd ed. (Itasca, Ill.: F. E. Peacock, 1978).

CHAPTER 5

Occupational Careers

T HE TOPIC of careers focuses our attention on changes that take place over time in the work people do. We first want to look at the way the term *career* is popularly used and the way it is used by sociologists. Several different perspectives can be taken. We can think of careers in a biographical sense, as something belonging to individuals, as something they "have." Careers can also be viewed as a characteristic or property of occupations. Within an occupation there may be a variety of activities that are in some way patterned and ordered; these activities can be viewed as a set of options or sequences through which individuals may move. Careers can also be regarded as a property of organizations. The positions or roles, often hierarchically arranged, that exist in employing organizations can constitute a career in the sense that individuals may move to different positions, some of which may offer greater rewards than others.

An additional goal of this chapter is to develop a scheme for mapping the career mobility of individuals. To accomplish this, various concepts and scales for measuring vertical (status) and horizontal (situs) mobility will be presented and research on the mobility process will be summarized.

There are a number of things that operate as contingencies or factors that make a difference in how people's careers progress. Especially important are changing environmental and organizational expectations and demands. In addition, changes in the status of entire occupations can have an effect on the careers of their members. We will deal also with the impact of such contingencies on people's careers.

POPULAR USAGES AND MEANINGS OF CAREER

Like the term "profession" the term "career" has a number of popular meanings and usages that differ from the way it is used by sociologists. The term "career" is often used popularly in an *evaluative* sense. Sometimes it is used without reference to an occupation when, for example, a woman is described as "making a career" of raising a family. The expression implies that she has forgone employment outside the home and done a good job of raising her children or performed the role of mother with a sense of dedication and commitment. A positive evaluation is also implied when the term is used to refer to attitudes toward work, especially in relatively low-status occupations: "He's only a garbage collector, but he views his work as a career" implies that the person referred to takes his work seriously and does it conscientiously. An evaluation also is implied when we say that one person has a "career" while another has "just a job." People also may be described as having "successful" or "unsuccessful" careers. Here there is an implication that the person has or has not achieved some unspecified amount of prestige, income, recognition, and the like. Negative evaluations can also be conveyed, for example, when we say that a person did something in order "to advance his or her own career" or that a person is more interested in career advancement than anything else. Such statements imply selfishness, surreptitiousness, and perhaps dishonesty.

"Career" is also popularly used to refer to nothing more than *full-time employment*. The expression "career woman" is an example of this. Here the term implies some kind of continuing commitment to work. It may also be used in this way when it refers to occupations or activities typically engaged in on a temporary basis. Thus, the term "career soldier" refers to a person with a long-term commitment to the military. In a similar way a person who has prolonged her or his education beyond the usual length of time may be described as "career student" or "making a career" out of going to school.

Such usages are valuable. They tell us a good deal about how people perceive work and work-related activities. However, to use the concept of career to analyze and compare work activities and experiences, we need a more precise definition of the concept and particularly one that minimizes the evaluative aspect noted above.

SOCIOLOGICAL MEANINGS OF CAREER

There are three main ways in which the concept of career is used in the sociological literature. Careers may be conceptualized as a property of individuals, of occupations, and of organizations. Each of these usages represents a different way of comprehending the changes that occur in the work of people over time.

CAREER AS A PROPERTY OF INDIVIDUALS

In this perspective on careers, individuals are the main unit of analysis. The data we look at are essentially biographical, as we trace the work lives of individuals over time. As a property or characteristic of individuals, careers have an objective and a subjective dimension.

Subjective career emphasizes the meaning that individuals give to their work and work-related experiences. Robert A. Stebbins has defined the subjective career as "the actor's recognition and interpretation of past and future events associated with a particular identity, and especially his interpretation of important contingencies as they were or will be encountered."[1] Thus, work activities and experiences may be interpreted in light of past experiences and anticipated future events. This opens up the possibility that people may "rewrite" their occupational biographies as time goes on. Although people's work experiences have an external reality, the meanings that people give to them can be quite varied. Two people with the same objective work experiences could have very different subjective careers.

There are a number of ways in which people may interpret and reinterpret their work experiences as they produce a subjective career. It is not unusual for people to make comparisons with various groups that essentially serve as comparative reference groups. They may compare themselves to others who are in the same employment or education cohort, such as others who entered the labor market or a particular organization at the same time. Similarly, people may compare their careers to those of others with whom they graduated from high school or college. In addition, they may compare themselves to others who entered an employing organization at the same time that they did.

There is also an *objective* dimension to the careers that individuals have. This consists of changes in work activities and changes in status that individuals experience. This aspect of careers is evident in Harold L. Wilensky's definition of career as "a succession of related jobs, arranged in a hierarchy of prestige, through which persons move in an ordered, predictable sequence."[2] Careers may not always be as orderly as this definition implies and prestige is not the only aspect of careers in which we are interested. However, this definition captures the idea that people do experience objective changes in their work that we can observe.

CAREER AS A PROPERTY OF OCCUPATIONS

While it is obvious that individuals "have" careers, it is also useful to think of careers as existing within occupations. Every occupation may be regarded as having distinctive *career lines,* that is, certain regularities in the sequences of jobs that people have over time. In some cases these sequences may be defined by employing organizations, but mainly they exist as part of the structure of the occupation.[3] If one looks at an entire occupational group, it becomes apparent that people who share an occupational title may do very different things. The occupational category "physician," for example, includes people who diagnose and treat illness, some who engage in research, others who teach, and still others who combine one or more of these activities in their work. Among carpenters, work activities may include work on new construction, the management of a construction business, repair of existing structures, supervision of other carpenters, etc. The point is that occupations include a diversity and variety of ways in which one can be a member of the occupation. That diversity, in turn, represents a set of career lines.

Occupational groups may also develop conceptions of what an "ideal career" should look like. These will typically include the idea that some kinds of work are better, more prestigious, more worthy, or more desirable than others. Many different criteria can go into a group's definition of the kinds of work that are superior and should be sought and the kinds that are inferior and should be avoided. The criteria used may include autonomy, security, income, client characteristics, safety, freedom from supervision, etc. The medical profession's model of an ideal career is the private practitioner operating on a fee-for-service basis. Consequently, being a salaried employee of a private industrial organization, a clinic, or a public health organization is seen as a less desirable career. In law, the most prestigious career is one that involves working for a law firm the represents prestigious and powerful corporations.[4] Lawyers view with disdain their colleagues who make a living representing accident victims and refer to them as "ambulance chasers."[5] The academic profession views research and graduate education as more prestigious than undergraduate teaching, and new faculty members are encouraged to seek research grants that will enable them to devote more of their time to research activities.[6] Illustrations of such differential evaluation of work activities within occupations are numerous.

The culture of occupational groups includes these kinds of understandings which are transmitted to new members through normal socialization processes. Once internalized, an occupation's definition of an ideal career can also serve as a "benchmark" for its members. As they create their subjective careers they may use their occupation's conception of desirable and undesirable work activities as a baseline for evaluating their careers.

CAREER AS A PROPERTY OF ORGANIZATIONS

An understanding of careers must include a consideration of organizations. The vast majority of people work in and for organizations of varying size and complexity. In 1983, for example, only 7.7 percent of the nonagricultural labor force was self-employed.[7] Barney G. Glaser regards an organizational career as a kind of "status passage," a movement from one type of status to another in an organization.[8] According to Glaser, organizations offer careers as an inducement to recruit people and obtain work from them.[9] In general, the hierarchy of positions that make up an organization can be viewed as a potential career. Of course, the particular kinds of careers that are presented will be different in different organizations. Organizations may offer people careers that involve advancement to different jobs with greater skill, responsibility, and authority. In other cases, the career may provide changes in income, authority, and privileges without a change in the work that the person actually performs. In either case the career only has meaning within the organization and in this sense it "belongs to" the organization.

Another aspect of organizations is important for understanding careers. This is the fact that they do not exist in a vacuum but are part of an *organizational set*.[10] An organizational set consists of organizations that produce similar goods or services, or perform similar activities. Automobile manufacturing companies, law firms, airline companies, universities, life insurance companies, constuction companies, hospitals, and computer manufacturers are examples of organizational sets. Regardless of the particular kinds of organizations that make up a set, the one thing that they have in common is that they consist of a hierarchy based on notions of prestige, quality, or something that orders them in terms of status.[11] What this means is that careers may also involve movement *between* organizations, especially those within the same set. Such movement may occur with no changes in the work that people actually do, as in the case of the professor of chemistry who moves from a university of lesser to one of greater prestige. However, movement between organizations also includes the possibility of changes in what people do. An example would be a vice-president for marketing in one insurance company becoming vice-president for finance in another. Movement between organizations can involve changes in organizational status, changes in individual status, changes in both, or changes in neither.

VERTICAL AND HORIZONTAL MOBILITY

As the discussion up to this point has indicated, studying people's careers requires that we focus attention on their mobility over time. Sociologists typically deal with mobility in intergenerational terms. In the study of social stratification, social mobility refers to movement up or down in the stratification system over one or more generations and usually involves comparing people's occupational status with that of their parents. In contrast to intergenerational mobility, we are interested in career mobility of which there are two basic types: *vertical career mobility* and *horizontal career mobility*.

VERTICAL CAREER MOBILITY

Vertical career mobility refers to movement up or down in some system of status or prestige that might be occupationally or organizationally based. Theodore Caplow has identified several ways in which this type of mobility can occur. An individual may move from one occupation to another of higher or lower status. Vertical mobility can also occur through promotion or demotion within the same occupation. In addition, the accumulation of seniority within an occupation may lead to a change in status.[12] We can add to this list movement up or down in an organization and changes in the status of an entire occupation. In the latter case individuals may experience a change in their status simply because of increases or decreases in the status of their occupation. Professionalization and deprofessionalization, discussed in chapter 2, would be examples of such occupational status changes.

Occupational *status* and *prestige* are important tools for measuring vertical career mobility. They have developed from different research traditions concerned with measuring differences in the relative position of occupations.

Occupational Status

One approach to the measurement of occupational status began with the development of a scale by Alba M. Edwards for the U.S. Bureau of the Census in the 1940s.[13] The scale was intended as a classification scheme that could "(1) fit all occupations reported in the census into (2) a relatively limited set of categories, that (3) would combine occupations together insofar as they connoted a common life style and social characteristics."[14] This scale grouped occupations into the following six broad categories, ranked from high to low:

1. Professional persons
2. Proprietors, managers, and officials
3. Clerks and kindred workers
4. Skilled workers and foremen
5. Semiskilled workers
6. Unskilled workers

Over the years researchers have used variants of this scale in particular research projects, sometimes distinguishing between professionals and semiprofessionals, small and large business owners and managers, or using separate categories for clerical and sales workers, and the like.[15] Within the U.S. Bureau of the Census this scale has been modified over time, and most recently developed into the scale presented in chapter 1 (see p. 11).

While this scale has proven to be a useful way of grouping occupations into broad status levels, questions can be raised about the underlying dimension of the scale. If skill is the basis for the ordering of occupational categories, in what ways can the skills of professionals and clerks be compared? While the skills of "skilled workers" are certainly *different* from those of managers, in what sense are the skills of managers *greater* than those of skilled workers? The categories may tell us more about the life-style of people at different levels of social status (Alba's original intention) than they tell us about occupation per se. A difficulty with these categories is that they do not form an interval scale, a fact that limits their utility in relating occupation to something else.

The desire for more refined scales for measuring occupational status has led to the creation of "indexes" that order occupations on the basis of the average educational attainment and income of people in those occupations, as reported in the national decennial censuses. The best known and most widely used scale of this kind was developed by Otis Dudley Duncan using 1950 census data[16] and has been updated with data from the 1970 census.[17] It is commonly referred to as the Duncan Socioeconomic Index (SEI). The scale includes nearly 500 occupations. The actual listing of occupations and their scores is quite long and since it is readily available in several sources, it will not be reproduced here.[18]

Using data from the 1950 and 1960 censuses, Charles B. Nam and Mary G. Powers constructed an occupational status scale also based on information on occupation and income.[19] They used the same occupations that Duncan used but scored them using a slightly different procedure. The Nam and Powers scale has also been updated for 1970 so comparisons over time as well as between scales are possible.[20] Like the

Duncan scale, its length prohibits reproduction here, but it too is readily available elsewhere.[21]

Occupational Prestige

While occupational status refers to the education and income associated with an occupation, occupational prestige refers to the evaluation of an occupation by people. Occupational status gets at an objective dimension of occupations; prestige captures a subjective (but no less measurable and meaningful) dimension. Prestige refers to the subjective evaluations and judgements that people hold about occupations. The measurement of occupational prestige involves asking people for their evaluation of the standing of particular occupations.

The first attempt to develop an occupational prestige scale was made by George S. Counts in 1925.[22] He had 450 college students and teachers rank some forty-five occupations. The 1930s and 1940s produced a number of studies similar to that of Counts.[23] In 1946, M. E. Deeg and D. G. Paterson replicated Counts' study (reducing the list of occupations to twenty-five). Like Counts, they had college students do the rankings. The correlation between the 1925 and 1946 studies was .97, indicating a high degree of agreement about occupational prestige over this period of time.[24]

The studies done up to this point all suffered from a variety of weaknesses including rating techniques of doubtful validity and lists of occupations that were unrepresentative of the total universe of occupations that exist in the labor force. Most serious, however, was the use of raters who were not representative of the general population. In fact, college students, undoubtedly because of their availability and accessibility to the researchers, seem to have been an especially popular group of subjects for performing occupational prestige ratings. To be really useful, occupational prestige ratings need to reflect the evaluations of the population in general.

The first picture of how a representative, national sample of Americans view occupations was obtained in 1947. In that year the National Opinion Research Center (NORC) questioned a national sample of 2,920 people, a cross section of the American population, regarding their views about the relative desirability of different occupations, occupational mobility, the importance of education, etc.[25] Included in the survey was the following question:

> For each job mentioned, please pick out the statement that best gives *your own personal opinion* of the *general standing* that such a job has:

1. *Excellent* standing
2. *Good* standing
3. *Average* standing
4. *Somewhat below average* standing
5. *Poor* standing
x. I don't know where to place that one

A total of ninety occupations were rated. The ratings of all respondents were averaged to arrive at a prestige score for each occupation. The scoring scheme used was such that the highest possible score was 100 and the lowest possible score was 20. For an occupation to get a score of 100, everyone in the sample would have had to rate it as excellent. The actual range of scores was from 96 to 33.

In 1963, researchers at NORC became interested in the question of stability and change in occupational prestige over time and replicated the original study on a national sample of 615 people.[26] Their main finding was a dramatically high degree of similarity in the scores obtained in 1963 compared to those from 1947. The correlation between the two sets of scores was .99, indicating virtually no change in the prestige accorded occupations. Table 5.1 presents the results of both the 1947 and 1963 studies.

The NORC occupational prestige studies have served as prototypes for the development of similar scales in Canada[27] and several European nations.[28] When the results of these two prestige studies are compared with the studies of occupational status (e.g., the Nam-Powers status scores for 1950 and 1970) it is apparent that occupational prestige is more stable over time than is occupational status. Despite changes in the relative income and educational attainment associated with occupations, public perceptions do not seem to reflect those changes. Rather, there appears to be a lag between changes in status and the perception of prestige.

Our main concern of course is with the use of these measures of status and prestige as tools for studying careers. The purpose of this discussion of occupational status and prestige is to point out the ways in which sociologists have addressed the *vertical* or hierarchical dimension of occupations. In other words, occupational status and prestige represent important ways of measuring, describing, and analyzing vertical career mobility.

The most common way of thinking about career mobility is in terms of the vertical dimension. Both sociological research and common sense thinking about careers emphasize differences and changes in status and prestige. Yet, it is important to recognize that there is also a *horizontal* dimension to careers. People experience changes in their occupations that cannot be interpreted solely in terms of status and prestige.

Table 5.1
Distributions of Prestige Ratings, United States, 1947 and 1963

Occupation	March, 1947 Percent								June, 1963 Percent							
	Excellent*	Good	Aver-age	Below Aver-age	Poor	Don't Know†	NORC Score	Rank	Excellent‡	Good	Aver-age	Below Aver-age	Poor	Don't Know§	NORC Score	Rank
U.S. Supreme Court justice	83	15	2	=	=	3	96	1	77	18	4	1	1	1	94	1
Physician	67	30	3	=	=	1	93	2.5	71	25	4	=	=	1	93	2
Nuclear physicist	48	39	11	1	1	51	86	18	70	23	5	1	1	10	92	3.5
Scientist	53	38	8	1	=	7	89	8	68	27	5	=	=	2	92	3.5
Government scientist	51	41	7	1	=	6	88	10.5	64	30	5	1	1	2	91	5.5
State governor	71	25	4	1	=	1	93	2.5	64	30	5	1	1	1	91	5.5
Cabinet member in the federal government	66	28	5	1	=	6	92	4.5	61	32	6	1	1	2	90	8
College professor	53	40	7	=	=	1	89	8	59	35	5	1	=	1	90	8
U.S. representative in Congress	57	35	6	1	=	4	89	8	58	33	6	2	=	2	90	8
Chemist	42	48	9	1	=	7	86	18	54	38	8	=	=	3	89	11
Lawyer	44	45	9	1	1	1	86	18	53	38	8	=	=	=	89	11
Diplomat in the U.S. foreign service	70	24	4	1	=	9	92	4.5	57	34	7	1	1	3	89	11
Dentist	42	48	9	1	=	=	86	18	47	47	6	=	=	=	88	14
Architect	42	48	9	1	=	6	86	18	47	45	6	=	=	2	88	14
County judge	47	43	9	1	=	1	87	13	50	40	8	1	=	1	88	14
Psychologist	38	49	12	1	=	15	85	22	49	41	8	1	=	6	87	17.5

Occupation																
Minister	52	35	11	1	1	1	87	13	53	33	13	1	1	1	87	17.5
Member of the board of directors of a large corporation	42	47	10	1	—	5	86	18	42	51	6	1	—	1	87	17.5
Mayor of a large city	57	36	6	1	—	1	90	6	46	44	9	1	1	—	87	17.5
Priest	51	34	11	2	2	6	86	18	52	33	12	2	1	6	86	21.5
Head of a department in a state government	47	44	8	—	1	3	87	13	44	48	6	1	1	1	86	21.5
Civil engineer	33	55	11	1	—	5	84	23	40	52	8	—	—	2	86	21.5
Airline pilot	35	48	15	1	1	3	83	24.5	41	48	11	1	—	1	86	21.5
Banker	49	43	8	—	—	1	88	10.5	39	51	10	1	—	—	85	24.5
Biologist	29	51	18	1	1	16	81	29	38	50	11	—	—	6	85	24.5
Sociologist	31	51	16	1	1	23	82	26.5	35	48	15	1	1	10	83	26
Instructor in public schools	28	45	24	2	1	1	79	34	30	53	16	1	—	—	82	27.5
Captain in the regular army	28	49	19	2	2	2	80	31.5	28	55	16	2	—	1	82	27.5
Accountant for a large business	25	57	17	1	—	3	81	29	27	55	17	1	—	1	81	29.5
Public school teacher	26	45	24	3	2	—	78	36	31	46	22	1	—	1	81	29.5
Owner of a factory that employs about 100 people	30	51	17	1	1	2	82	26.5	28	49	19	2	1	1	80	31.5
Building contractor	21	55	23	1	—	1	79	34	22	56	20	1	—	—	80	31.5
Artist who paints pictures that are exhibited in galleries	40	40	15	3	2	6	83	24.5	28	45	20	5	2	4	78	34.5
Musician in a symphony orchestra	31	46	19	3	1	5	81	29	25	45	25	3	1	3	78	34.5
Author of novels	32	44	19	3	2	9	80	31.5	26	46	22	4	2	5	78	34.5
Economist	25	48	24	2	1	22	79	34	20	53	24	2	1	12	78	34.5

Table 5.1 (Continued)

| Occupation | March, 1947 | | | | | | | | June, 1963 | | | | | | | |
| | Percent | | | | | | NORC | | Percent | | | | | | NORC | |
	Excellent*	Good	Average	Below Average	Poor	Don't Know†	Score	Rank	Excellent‡	Good	Average	Below Average	Poor	Don't Know§	Score	Rank
Official of an international labor union..	26	42	20	5	7	11	75	40.5	21	53	18	5	3	5	77	37
Railroad engineer......	22	45	30	3	=	1	77	37.5	19	47	30	3	1	1	76	39
Electrician.............	15	38	43	4	=	1	73	45	18	45	34	2	=	=	76	39
County agricultural agent.............	17	53	28	2	=	5	77	37.5	13	54	30	2	1	4	76	39
Owner-operator of a printing shop........	13	48	36	3	=	2	74	42.5	13	51	34	2	=	2	75	41.5
Trained machinist.....	14	43	38	5	=	2	73	45	15	50	32	4	=	=	75	41.5
Farm owner and operator.............	19	46	31	3	1	1	76	39	16	45	33	5	=	1	74	44
Undertaker..........	14	43	36	5	2	2	72	47	16	46	33	3	2	3	74	44
Welfare worker for a city government....	16	43	35	4	2	4	73	45	17	44	32	5	2	2	74	44
Newspaper columnist..	13	51	32	3	1	5	74	42.5	10	49	38	3	1	1	73	46
Policeman..........	11	30	46	11	2	1	67	55	16	38	37	6	2	=	72	47
Reporter on a daily newspaper.........	9	43	43	4	1	2	71	48	7	45	44	3	1	1	71	48
Radio announcer......	17	45	35	3	=	2	75	40.5	9	42	44	5	1	1	70	49.5
Bookkeeper..........	8	31	55	6	=	1	68	51.5	9	40	45	5	1	=	70	49.5

Occupation																
Tenant farmer—one who owns livestock and machinery and manages the farm	10	37	40	11	2	1	68	51.5	11	37	42	8	3	1	69	51.5
Insurance agent	7	34	53	4	2	2	68	51.5	6	40	47	5	2		69	51.5
Carpenter	5	28	56	10	1		65	58	7	36	49	8	1		68	53
Manager of a small store in a city	5	40	50	4	1	1	69	49	3	40	48	7	2		67	54.5
A local official of a labor union	7	29	41	14	9	11	62	62	8	36	42	9	5	4	67	54.5
Mail carrier	8	26	54	10	2		66	57	7	29	53	10	1		66	57
Railroad conductor	8	30	52	9	1	1	67	55	6	33	48	10	3		66	57
Traveling salesman for a wholesale concern	6	35	53	5	1	2	68	51.5	4	33	54	7	3	2	66	57
Plumber	5	24	55	14	2	1	63	59.5	6	29	54	9	2		65	59
Automobile repairman	5	21	58	14	2		63	59.5	5	25	56	12	2		64	60
Playground director	7	33	48	10	2	4	67	55	6	29	46	15	4	3	63	62.5
Barber	3	17	56	20	4	1	59	66	4	25	56	13	2	1	63	62.5
Machine operator in a factory	4	20	53	20	3	2	60	64.5	6	24	51	15	4	1	63	62.5
Owner-operator of a lunch stand	4	24	55	14	3	1	62	62	4	25	57	11	3	1	63	62.5
Corporal in the regular army	5	21	48	20	6	3	60	64.5	6	25	47	15	6	2	62	65.5
Garage mechanic	4	21	57	17	1		62	62	4	22	56	15	3		62	65.5
Truck driver	2	11	49	29	9		54	71	3	18	54	19	5		59	67
Fisherman who owns his own boat	3	20	48	21	8	7	58	68	3	19	51	19	8	4	58	68
Clerk in a store	2	14	61	20	3		58	68	1	14	56	22	6		56	70
Milk route man	2	10	52	29	7	1	54	71	3	12	55	23	7	1	56	70
Streetcar motorman	3	16	55	21	5	2	58	68	3	16	46	27	8	2	56	70

Table 5.1 (Continued)

Occupation	March, 1947								June, 1963							
	Percent						NORC Score	Rank	Percent						NORC Score	Rank
	Excel- lent*	Good	Aver- age	Below Aver- age	Poor	Don't Know†			Excel- lent‡	Good	Aver- age	Below Aver- age	Poor	Don't Know§		
Lumberjack...............	2	11	48	29	10	8	53	73	2	16	46	29	7	3	55	72.5
Restaurant cook.........	3	13	44	29	11	1	54	71	4	15	44	26	11	=	55	72.5
Singer in a nightclub..	3	13	43	23	18	6	52	74.5	3	16	43	24	14	3	54	74
Filling station attendant	1	9	48	34	8	1	52	74.5	2	11	41	34	11	=	51	75
Dockworker.............	2	7	34	37	20	8	47	81.5	2	9	43	33	14	3	50	77.5
Railroad section hand .	2	9	35	33	21	3	48	79.5	3	10	39	29	18	2	50	77.5
Night watchman........	3	8	33	35	21	1	47	81.5	3	10	39	32	17	1	50	77.5
Coal miner.............	4	11	33	31	21	2	49	77.5	3	13	34	31	19	2	50	77.5
Restaurant waiter......	2	8	37	36	17	1	48	79.5	3	8	42	32	16	=	49	80.5
Taxi driver............	2	8	38	35	17	1	49	77.5	2	8	39	31	18	1	49	80.5
Farm hand.............	3	12	35	31	19	1	50	76	3	12	31	32	22	=	48	83
Janitor................	1	7	30	37	25	1	44	85.5	1	9	35	35	19	1	48	83
Bartender.............	1	6	32	32	29	4	44	85.5	1	7	42	28	21	2	48	83
Clothes presser in a laundry...............	2	6	35	36	21	2	46	83	2	7	31	38	22	1	45	85
Soda fountain clerk.....	1	5	34	40	20	2	45	84	=	5	30	44	20	1	44	86
Sharecropper—one who owns no live stock or equipment and does not manage farm.....	1	6	24	28	41	3	40	87	1	8	26	28	37	2	42	87

Garbage collector......	1	4	16	26	53	2	35	88	2	5	21	32	41	1	39	88
Street sweeper........	1	3	14	29	53	1	34	89	1	4	17	31	46	1	36	89
Shoe shiner...........	1	2	13	28	56	2	33	90	‖	3	15	30	51	2	34	90
Average..............	22	31	30	11	7	4	70	....	22	32	29	11	6	2	71	....

* Bases for the 1947 occupational ratings are 2,920 less "don't know" and not answered for each occupational title.
† Base is 2,920 in all cases.
‡ Bases for the 1963 occupational ratings are 651 less "don't know" and not answered for each occupational title.
§ Base is 651 in all cases.
‖ Less than 0.5 percent.
Source of 1947 distributions: Albert J. Reiss, Jr., and others, *Occupations and Social Status* (New York: The Free Press 1963), Table ii-9.
Source: Robert W. Hodge, Paul M. Siegal, and Peter H. Rossi, "Occupational Prestige in the United States, 1925–63," *American Journal of Sociology,* 70 (November, 1964), pp. 290–92. Reprinted by permission of the University of Chicago Press.

HORIZONTAL CAREER MOBILITY

While there is a very substantial sociological literature on occupational status and prestige, much less thought and research have been devoted to looking at occupations in a nonevaluative, nonhierarchical manner. The concept of occupational *situs* is an exception to this statement. It is a useful alternative for thinking about occupations and describing and analyzing horizontal career mobility.

In 1944, Emile Benoit-Smullyan introduced the term "situs" into the sociological literature.[29] He used the term to refer to a category of individuals or positions placed on a level with other categories, all of which are given the same evaluation.

The first application of this nonhierarchical conception of social position of occupations was made by Paul K. Hatt, one of the initiators of the 1947 NORC prestige study.[30] Using data from the NORC study, he combined occupations into eight situs categories based on similarities in their prestige scores. The situs categories he came up with were:

1. Political
2. Professional
3. Business
4. Recreation and aesthetics

5. Agriculture
6. Manual work
7. Military
8. Service

While this is an interesting and potentially useful typology of occupations, careful examination clearly indicates that there are built-in status differences between the categories. "Professional" occupations, as a group, tend to have higher status and prestige than "manual work" or "agriculture," for example. Hatt's categories are quite different from what Benoit-Smullyan had in mind when he proposed the idea of situses as categories with the same evaluation.

In 1959, Richard T. Morris and Raymond J. Murphy developed a set of occupational situs categories that comes closer to the equal-evaluation criterion.[31] They developed a classification scheme consisting of ten situs categories defined as follows:

1. *Legal authority.* All occupations primarily concerned with the formulation, arbitration, interpretation, or enforcement of the law, including those primarily concerned with the custody of lawbreakers.
2. *Finance and records.* All occupations primarily concerned with the handling of monetary affairs or the processing of records, accounts, or correspondence.
3. *Manufacturing.* All occupations primarily concerned with the fabrication of articles or the processing of raw materials on a production-line basis.

4. *Transportation.* All occupations primarily concerned with the movement of persons or goods from one location to another.
5. *Extraction.* All occupations primarily concerned with the extraction, procurement, or production of raw materials.
6. *Building and maintenance.* All occupations primarily concerned with the construction of buildings or other non-mass-produced units, or the installation, maintenance, or repair of equipment, property, or facilities.
7. *Commerce.* All occupations primarily concerned with the buying, selling, exchange, or marketing of goods or persons.
8. *Aesthetics and entertainment.* All occupations primarily concerned with the creation of art forms or with the provision of entertainment, recreation, information, or aesthetic satisfaction for the public.
9. *Education and research.* All occupations primarily concerned with formal instruction or training or with the acquisition of knowledge as an end in itself.
10. *Health and welfare.* All occupations primarily concerned with the detection, prevention, or alleviation of illness, hazard, or distress.

The basic assumption behind this classification scheme is that the occupations in each situs contribute to the performance of an essential societal function. Societal function is the basic criterion on which the situs categories are distinguished. Each situs includes occupations *of different status and prestige* that contribute to the performance of a particular function.

Morris and Murphy were interested in the amount of agreement that exists regarding the situs in which specific occupations belong. They asked 200 college students to classify forty occupations according to situs and to give each occupation a prestige rating according to the same format used in the NORC studies of occupational prestige. The results are presented in diagram 5.1. The arrows in this diagram identify those occupations where over 25 percent of the students placed the occupation in a situs other than the one theoretically expected on the basis of the situs definitions. For example, over 25 percent of the student respondents placed "city manager" in the Legal authority rather than the theoretically appropriate Finance and records situs.

A question that can be raised about these situs categories is the extent to which they are in fact equally valued. To explore this issue, the author asked 322 college students to compare pairs of situs categories (with verbatim definitions provided) and indicate which one they thought was "most necessary and important for society." Respondents were given the option of indicating that they thought that the two situs categories

Diagram 5.1
Theoretical Situs Location of Selected Occupations and
Empirical Location Made by Sample of Student Raters

SITUSES

Prestige rank quartiles (Student Ratings) / STRATA	1 Legal Authority	2 Finance & Records	3 Manufacturing	4 Transportation	5 Extraction	6 Building & Maintenance	7 Commerce	8 Aesthetics & Entertainment	9 Education & Research	10 Health & Welfare
1	Supreme Court Justice Lawyer	City Manager	Owner of a large factory	President of a railroad				Conductor of a symphony orchestra	College president	Physician Minister
2		Banker	Biologist for a pharmaceutical company	Airline pilot	Geologist in an oil company	Architect	Advertising executive Commerical artist		Philosopher County agricultural agent	Welfare worker
3	Policeman	Book-keeper	Machinist		Farmer Forest ranger	Building contractor	Manager of a hardware store	Radio announcer Singer in a night club	Music teacher	Fireman
4	Prison guard	Cashier in a restaurant	Restaurant cook	Mail carrier Truck driver	Coal miner	Waiter in a restaurant Garbage collector	Milk route man	Barber		

Note: Arrows indicate that over 25 percent of the students placed the occupation in a situs other than that theoretically expected on the basis of situs definitions supplied.

Source: Richard T. Morris and Raymond J. Murphy, "The Situs Dimension in Occupational Structure," *American Sociological Review* 24 (April 1959), 237.

were "about the same in importance." The results of the study are presented in table 5.2. Clearly, the students attached more importance to some situses than others in these comparisons. To highlight some of the extremes, 82.9 percent rated Legal authority as more important than Aesthetics and entertainment, over 81 percent rated Education and research and Health and welfare as more important than Finance and records, 76.1 percent saw Education and research as more important than Transportation, and over 80 percent viewed both Education and research and Health and welfare as more important than Aesthetics and entertainment. However, there is some support for the equal-evaluation assumption. Of all the possible situs-pair comparisons, the least amount of equal evaluation occurs in the comparison of Legal authority with Aesthetics and entertainment. Only 12.4 percent of the students regarded these as the same in importance. The greatest equal evaluation occurs in the comparison of Manufacturing with Extraction where 64.3 percent felt that these situses were equal in importance. In only seven of the forty-five possible comparisons did at least 50 percent of the respondents regard the situses as equally important. When all possible comparisons of a particular situs with all others are considered, it is possible to average the percentage of respondents who rated the situs as more important than others. When this is done, the rank order of importance given to the situses, from most to least important is:

1. Education and research
2. Health and welfare
3. Legal authority
4. Manufacturing
5. Extraction
6. Commerce
7. Building and maintenance
8. Transportation
9. Finance and records
10. Aesthetics and entertainment

Despite the fact that some situses are perceived as being more important than others, the concept of situs and the scheme developed by Morris and Murphy remain a useful way of looking at the nonhierarchical dimension of the occupational structure. By themselves, situs categories can be used to chart and describe individual careers. Used in combination with status and prestige, the vertical and horizontal aspects of career mobility can be handled simultaneously.

Status/Prestige and Situs: A Two-Dimensional Model for Analyzing Career Mobility

While the vertical and horizontal dimensions of occupation are analytically distinct, actual mobility may involve combinations of both occurring in varying degrees. When the concepts of status (or prestige) and situs

Table 5.2
Percentage of Respondents Rating Each Situs Category as
More Important than the Others or the Same in Importance

Categories Compared			Percentage Rating Category More Important or Same			
A	With	B	A	B	Same	Total
Legal authority	Finance and records		72.4	3.4	24.2	100.0
	Manufacturing		55.9	14.9	29.2	100.0
	Transportation		69.3	10.2	20.5	100.0
	Extraction		69.6	12.7	17.7	100.0
	Building and maintenance		64.9	13.4	21.7	100.0
	Commerce		57.1	12.1	30.7	99.9
	Aesthetics and entertainment		82.9	4.7	12.4	100.0
	Education and research		14.3	32.6	53.1	100.0
	Health and welfare		17.1	35.4	47.5	100.0
Finance and records	Manufacturing		15.2	59.3	25.5	100.0
	Transportation		21.7	42.2	36.0	99.9
	Extraction		22.7	52.2	25.2	100.1
	Building and maintenance		18.9	43.8	37.3	100.0
	Commerce		7.1	41.3	51.6	100.0
	Aesthetics and entertainment		49.4	29.5	21.1	100.0
	Education and research		1.9	81.7	16.5	100.1
	Health and welfare		5.6	81.4	13.0	100.0
Manufacturing	Transportation		43.2	11.2	45.7	100.1
	Extraction		19.6	16.1	64.3	100.0
	Building and maintenance		34.2	9.3	56.5	100.0
	Commerce		23.0	13.4	63.7	100.1
	Aesthetics and entertainment		67.7	14.9	17.4	100.0
	Education and research		7.5	64.0	28.6	100.1
	Health and welfare		11.8	69.6	18.6	100.0

are combined, they produce three logical possibilities in terms of types of career mobility:

1. Status mobility without situs mobility (vertical movement).
2. Situs mobility without status mobility (horizontal movement).
3. Simultaneous status and situs mobility (diagonal movement).

Diagram 5.2 presents these three general types of mobility in schematic form. Status mobility of course can occur within any situs. Similarly, situs mobility can occur between any two (or more) situses. Status/situs mobility can occur in a variety of ways involving movement between adjacent or distant status levels and across one or more situses.

Within the framework of this typology a number of questions can be raised. For example, what are the rates of status mobility within each situs? If situses have different rates, why are they different? What kinds of intersitus mobility are most and least common? Are patterns and rates of intersitus mobility different at different status levels? Are some situses more stable than others in the sense that once in them people tend to

Table 5.2 (Continued)

Categories Compared			Percentage Rating Category More Important or Same			
A	With	B	A	B	Same	Total
Transportation	Extraction		22.0	31.4	46.6	100.0
	Building and maintenance		21.4	34.8	43.8	100.0
	Commerce		17.7	28.0	54.3	100.0
	Aesthetics and entertainment		54.3	21.4	24.2	99.9
	Education and research		4.0	76.1	19.9	100.0
	Health and welfare		9.3	72.7	18.0	100.0
Extraction	Building and maintenance		35.4	16.1	48.4	99.9
	Commerce		30.4	36.0	33.5	99.9
	Aesthetics and entertainment		67.7	19.6	12.7	100.0
	Education and research		7.8	75.2	17.1	100.1
	Health and welfare		9.6	68.6	21.7	99.9
Building and maintenance	Commerce		20.8	38.8	40.4	100.0
	Aesthetics and entertainment		66.5	17.1	16.5	100.1
	Education and research		5.3	73.6	21.1	100.0
	Health and welfare		5.9	71.1	23.0	100.0
Commerce	Aesthetics and entertainment		71.4	13.0	15.5	99.9
	Education and research		7.1	68.0	24.8	99.9
	Health and welfare		10.6	67.7	21.7	100.0
Aesthetics and entertainment	Education and research		0.9	85.4	13.7	100.0
	Health and welfare		2.5	82.6	14.9	100.0
Education and research	Health and welfare		22.7	18.3	59.0	100.0

stay there, and few people enter the situs late in their careers? Are some situses more transitory than others in that large numbers of people enter and leave them? Are some situs/status locations "dead ends" in the sense that future mobility is difficult?

These and similar questions are important for our understanding of the way in which career mobility occurs. Yet, there is not enough descriptive information about such patterns for any large number of individuals or occupations that would provide a basis for sound generalizations. However, preliminary and qualified answers to many of these questions can be derived from studies of specific occupations and from inferences drawn from the known characteristics of occupations.

CAREER PATTERNS

Research on occupational careers has involved a number of strategies. These include longitudinal studies of the process by which occupational

Diagram 5.2
Hypothetical Types of Career Mobility in Terms of Status and Situs

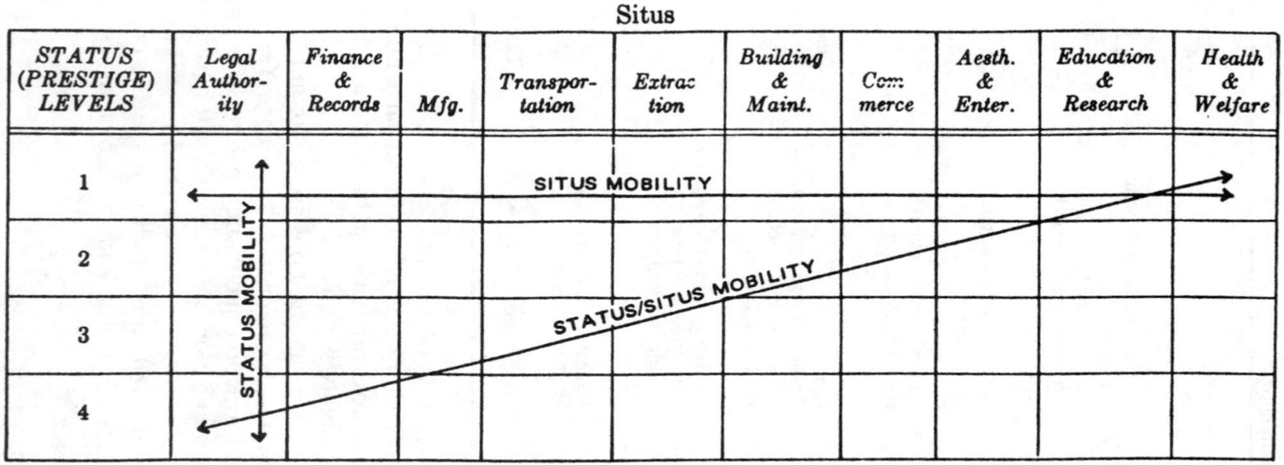

Situs

STATUS (PRESTIGE) LEVELS	Legal Author- ity	Finance & Records	Mfg.	Transpor- tation	Extrac- tion	Building & Maint.	Com- merce	Aesth. & Enter.	Education & Research	Health & Welfare
1										
2										
3										
4										

SITUS MOBILITY

STATUS/SITUS MOBILITY

STATUS MOBILITY

status is attained as well as research on the career mobility of large samples of people in many different occupations. In addition, there have been many studies that look intensively at the careers of people in specific occupations. This section will review this research and identify some of the main conclusions about careers that have emerged from it.

THE STATUS ATTAINMENT PROCESS

A major research program at the University of Wisconsin has focused on the educational and occupational attainment process. Over 10,000 graduates of Wisconsin's high schools in 1957 were followed up in 1964 and again in 1975. Information about their educational and occupational attainment has been examined in relation to a number of factors such as their parents' socioeconomic status; their academic ability and high school performance; their aspirations; and the influence of parents, teachers, and peers. The pattern of relationships between these variables and attainment has come to be known as "The Wisconsin Model."[32]

The model has sought to address several issues. One of these is the relative influence of ascribed characteristics, such as family background, and achieved characteristics, such as school performance, on eventual attainments. In addition, the study has dealt extensively with the role of academic ability in the attainment of educational and occupational status. A final issue has been the way in which aspirations and motivation affect attainment and how the school and family support the development of aspirations.[33]

The main outline of the status attainment process involves the following sequence: Family socioeconomic status and academic ability are correlated and each of them affects academic performance, although the effect of socioeconomic status on performance occurs through ability rather than directly. Socioeconomic status, academic performance, and ability affect the influence from significant others. Influence from significant others toward college attendance and the development of high occupational aspirations links the effect of family socioeconomic status, via these aspirations, on educational and occupational attainments. Academic ability directly affects high school performance and has direct and indirect effects on encouragement from significant others and on educational and occupational aspirations. Thus, the effect of ability on occupational attainment is mediated by these intervening steps.[34]

This model of the status attainment process has been replicated in other states, various regions of the United States, the nation as a whole, and several foreign countries. Remarkably, the basic pattern and sequence of effects presented in the original model have been supported in these replications. Where differences have been found, they appear to be the result of variations in question wording and differences in how particular variables were measured.[35]

CAREER MOBILITY: THE BLAU/DUNCAN STUDY

The well-known 1962 study by Peter M. Blau and Otis Dudley Duncan, based on a national sample of men age twenty-five to sixty-four, provides some information on career mobility in terms of movement between broad status levels.[36] While the main focus of this study was on intergenerational mobility, it is possible to look at career mobility by comparing the occupational status of men in 1962 with the status of their first job. We can also identify the kinds of movement that occurred from their first job to their 1962 occupation. There are several patterns that are of interest.

The majority (58.5 percent) of men who were self-employed professionals report that their first job was as either a self-employed or salaried professional.[37] Of all those whose first job was that of self-employed professional, 79 percent were self-employed or salaried professionals in 1962. This suggests that there are very few departures and little downward career mobility from this occupational level.

Of all the men who were managers, only 5 percent report that their first job was as a manager. This implies that managerial work is something into which people move over time, rather than a career starting point. Similarly, a very small proportion of retail salesmen (15.5 percent) indicate that their first job was in retail sales.

Craftsmen in manufacturing settings report a wide variety of first jobs. The most frequent first job for these men was operatives in manufacturing, which shows a pattern of very modest upward movement. The vast majority of men in this occupational category in 1962 report a first job as a semiskilled or unskilled manual worker. Craftsmen in construction are similarly diverse in terms of their first jobs. However, a little over one-fourth of the men who began as construction craftsmen were in the same type of work in 1962.

Of the men who were operatives in manufacturing, 28.3 percent report that their first job was also as an operative in manufacturing. Men who move into this category come primarily from other kinds of semiskilled and unskilled occupations. Laborers in manufacturing have a similar pattern except that 22.2 percent of them report operative in manufacturing as their first job, suggesting some downward career mobility into the laborer category.

Farmers and farm laborers present a picture of relative stability. Three-fourths of those who were farmers in 1962 reported that their first job was either farmer or farm laborer. Similarly, nearly 60 percent of the farm laborers indicated that their first job was also farm laborer.

These findings suggest a pattern of career mobility in which there is relatively little movement into and out of occupations at both the top and bottom of the occupational status hierarchy. At the same time, there is a relatively high degree of movement into occupations at intermediate status levels (e.g., salesmen and craftsmen).

THE OAKLAND MOBILITY STUDY

Although conducted some time ago (1949), the Oakland (California) Mobility Study includes some useful information about career mobility. The findings of this study, carried out under the direction of Seymour Martin Lipset and Reinhard Bendix, were based on work histories from 935 people who were the principal wage earners in their families.[38]

One finding of the study was that changes in jobs within the same occupation were much more common than changes to a totally new occupation. Dramatic moves to a new occupation were a relatively rare occurrence in people's careers. Looking at the proportion of each respondent's total work life spent in his or her present occupation, Lipset and Bendix concluded that there is more instability among unskilled than skilled workers and that professionals experience more stability than other white-collar workers. Professionals were the most stable group with 70 percent having spent more than 80 percent of their work lives in their present occupation. In contrast, only 18 percent of the unskilled workers had done so.

Another issue dealt with in this study was the extent to which people had worked in jobs at status levels different from their present occupation. This turned out to be a fairly common occurrence. For example, about one-third of the unskilled workers had held skilled manual or white-collar jobs at some point in their careers. One-fifth of those in professional and semiprofessional occupations had been employed, at some time in the past, in semiskilled manual work. The majority of those in sales occupations also had held semiskilled jobs at some time. Business owners and managers had the most diversity and variety in their past work. A little over one-third had worked at some time in a manual job and a little less than 30 percent had worked at some other type of nonmanual job. Only one-fifth had previously owned or managed another business.

Despite evidence of a good deal of variety in the work people do over the course of their careers, this study found that there was relatively little *permanent* movement from manual to nonmanual occupations and vice versa. Those whose careers were predominantly manual have brief work experiences in small business or sales jobs and those with predominantly nonmanual careers may work briefly and early in their careers in manual jobs. The work experiences of most people, however, tend to be homogeneous in the sense that they are either manual or nonmanual.

CAREER PATTERNS WITHIN THE PROFESSIONS AND SEMIPROFESSIONS

In professional and semiprofessional occupations a variety of factors have emerged as typical features of careers and as sources of career problems. These factors include informal recognition from colleagues, the internal stratification system of the occupation, and organizational pressures to move into administrative roles. In some cases the prestige of the organization in which the occupation is located is a crucial career concern. In others (teaching and nursing for example) factors that lead to remaining in the occupation or leaving it have been the focus of research attention.

Physicians: Informal Recognition from Colleagues

In medicine there is a fairly short career line. Once physicians complete residency programs a key next step in the career is to gain admitting privileges at a hospital with a good reputation. A major task faced by the new physician is building a clientele. Entering a group practice or buying into a physician-owned clinic is one way the physician may assure himself or herself clients through the referral system. In building and expanding a clientele, physicians are dependent on the informal colleague network that exists in the community in which they practice. Since building a practice depends so much on these informal relationships, medical careers typically involve geographic stability rather than mobility. Medicine is a good example of what has been called an "early-ceiling" career.[39] People rapidly move to a position which represents the achievement of what the occupation defines as full-fledged membership in the group. Honors and recognition come from the colleague group through a process of informal evaluation.

A sizable majority of physicians (about 67 percent) are engaged in patient care and work in an office-based practice. An additional 24 percent also provide patient care in hospitals; this includes residents as well as full-time hospital employees. Only about 9 percent of all physicians are full-time hospital employees. In addition, about 9 percent work as teachers, researchers, or administrators.[40] Thus, the internal structure of the occupation is one with little diversity and few opportunities for movement through organizationally defined careers.

Lawyers: Internal Stratification

In the case of lawyers, an important aspect of careers is the setting in which work is done. Several types of practice tend to predominate. These are solo practice, working in a law firm, and working for a governmental agency. These practice settings also constitute a kind of stratification system reflecting the characteristics of the clients one represents.[41] Solo practice is usually the least prestigious. Here clients tend to be people who are poor, relatively powerless, and not very influential. Law firms, especially those representing powerful corporations, offer a more prestigious and prized setting. The prestige of government employment varies a great deal. On the one hand, working in the public defender's office in a small city is a relatively low status position within the legal profession. However, lawyers employed by state and federal governmental agencies are in positions of power, influence, and high prestige.

The majority of lawyers (72 percent) are private practitioners. They are evenly divided between solo practitioners and those who are partners and associates in law firms. About 14 percent are in salaried positions in the private sector. An additional 10 percent are employed by governmental agencies at all levels, and about 4 percent work in the judicial system.[42]

Law is a profession in which one career path involves doing work other than practicing the law. For example, there is a strong connection between law and politics. At all governmental levels, elected officeholders come to politics from the practice of law more often than from any other occupation.[43] Michael Cohen has pointed out that law and politics share a common "subculture."[44] They are, in effect, part of the same occupational situs. Since lawyers can control the pace and volume of their work, law is an occupation that enables its members to be politically active. Combining a legal and political career is relatively easy and a pattern of movement between legal practice and politics is not uncommon.[45]

Lawyers also hold a large proportion of powerful positions in business organizations. T. B. Priest and Robert A. Rothman have looked at the backgrounds and careers of lawyers who have achieved top positions in the nation's largest and most influential business corporations.[46] In 1970, 22.2 percent of the 424 chief executives of the nation's leading corporations had legal backgrounds. For those executives with backgrounds in law, there was a strong pattern of having attended an Ivy League institution as a undergraduate (23.4 percent) and for one's legal training (33.0 percent). In terms of career mobility, the vast majority of these lawyer-chief executives began their careers in private practice (62.7 percent). An additional 23.4 percent started out in the employ of a business organization, and only 9.6 percent began their careers in government employment.

Priest and Rothman identify several distinct patterns in the careers of these executives. In the "organizational career," people are recruited to an organization early and move up within it. What little law they actually practice is almost entirely concerned with corporate issues. Another pattern they call the "professional career." Here, a fairly long period of time is spent in private practice and corporate positions are attained on the basis of having achieved distinction as a private practitioner. There is also a pattern that Priest and Rothman call the "interlocking career." This describes movement back and forth between business corporations and government agencies. Lawyers with government experience are valued for their knowledge of the functioning of government and for the personal contacts they have with government officials. They are recruited to corporate positions for this reason rather than because of their legal expertise.

Engineers: Pressures to Leave the Occupation

Like lawyers, engineers have a distinctive career pattern that involves essentially leaving the occupation. Engineering is an example of an occupation "created" by technological advances.[47] Valued for their technical expertise, engineers are recruited to organizations for work in production, research and development, and similar roles where their training and expertise are directly related to the work they do. Yet, the technical skills that engineers have make them also valuable in a variety of activities that have little to do directly with engineering, such as sales, advertising, public relations, and the like. In addition, engineers share the general professional value of colleague control which creates a demand for engineers to supervise, evaluate, and coordinate the work of other engineers.

The result of this is a good deal of pressure on engineers to move into supervisory and administrative work. A national survey of engineers by the Engineering Manpower Commission, for example, turned up some surprising results on how extensive this career pattern is. For example, by age sixty-five, 63 percent of all engineers in the United States are employed as managers. By the time they are in the forty-five to fifty age bracket, 73 percent have "significant" managerial duties, and during their first five years of employment, 37 percent have taken on more than "nominal" managerial responsibilities.[48] The shift from engineering to management work is often a difficult and stressful one. For example, a study based on interviews with 610 engineers at the National Aeronautics and Space Administration and the National Institutes of Health identified several problems associated with this career change. For one thing, there is a change in the activities for which people are rewarded. In particular, autonomy and independence are less likely to be rewarded in administrative roles than they were in engineering jobs. In moving to administration, engineers found that their technical skills had not prepared them for the kinds of interpersonal tasks they faced. Many had difficulty moving away from dealing with "things and data" and learning to deal effectively with other people.[49]

Academics: The Importance of Organizational Prestige

Although not completely standardized, universities and colleges have a fairly well defined structure of professorial ranks that constitute the typical academic career. New faculty who have not yet completed the terminal degree in their field (usually the PhD) are generally hired at the rank of instructor or lecturer. Those who have completed the terminal degree are hired as assistant professors. Promotion to associate professor and the awarding of tenure (a guarantee of continuing employment) usually occur after five to seven years at the assistant professor rank. Promotion to the highest rank (professor) is highly unstandardized and variable in terms of the amount of time one must be at the associate level, and some faculty may retire as associate professors. In 1984 about one-third of American university faculty held the rank of professor, one-fourth were associate professors, and one-fifth were assistant professors. The remainder held positions as instructor or lecturer.[50] Opportunities for administrative work in universities exist in the form of positions such as department chair, dean, vice-president, and president, but these are fairly small in number. For most faculty, teaching and research activities within the professorial rank system are the main components of the career.

   Institutions of higher education exist within an elaborate system of stratification based on institutional reputation and prestige. At the top of the hierarchy are the main campuses of public universities. Sometimes referred to as "flagship" campuses, the universities of the Big Ten and Pacific Coast schools are overrepresented here. They are joined in this elite status by a number of highly selective private universities, especially those of the Ivy League as well as schools like the University of Chicago, Stanford University, and Vanderbilt University. Public universities in the South, New England, and the Mountain States constitute a second tier along with the regional universities of states whose main campuses are in the top group of twenty or so schools with the greatest prestige. There is also a group of small, private, liberal arts colleges with a highly selective, nationally recruited student body that constitutes a separate prestige system. Next in the hierarchy are small, unselective, often church-sponsored schools that serve a local clientele. At the bottom of the stratification system are community colleges.

This stratification system is important because one dimension of the academic career is the prestige of the institution in which people are located. The careers of faculty are often charted as much by their movement through this stratification system as by their movement through the professorial rank structure. Movement between institutions is a central feature of the academic career. In 1985, a national survey of faculty conducted by the Carnegie Foundation for the Advancement of Teaching found that over half would seriously consider taking a job at another university or college if one were offered.[51]

In general, the careers of academics exhibit a pattern of movement from institutions of higher to lower or similar prestige but rarely from lower to higher prestige. This is especially true in the recruitment of new faculty fresh out of graduate school.

A good deal of research has examined this aspect of academic careers. Some years ago Logan Wilson noted that the prestige of the institution from which people receive their PhD's has consequences for their careers.[52] Similarly, Theodore Caplow and Reece McGee pointed out that decisions about the hiring of new faculty were based less on the actual evaluation of their work than on the prestige of their doctoral department and the reputation of their sponsors.[53] Robert K. Merton has argued that the social system of science is governed by the norm of universalism which stresses accomplishments.[54] Extending this principle to universities, one would expect that careers would be governed by *universalistic* criteria such as accomplishment and productivity rather than by such *particularistic* and subjective criteria as prestige and reputation. Research on academic careers has attempted to assess the relative importance of the prestige of a faculty member's PhD-granting department and his or her actual productivity in determining the prestige of the institution at which that faculty member is located. Jonathan R. Cole and Stephen Cole found that, among scientists, productivity and prestige of doctoral department were equally important.[55] Lowell L. Hargens and Warren O. Hagstrom also found that productivity and prestige were about equally important in determining the prestige of the current institution of faculty. However, the effect of doctoral origins was stronger among younger faculty, suggesting that as time goes on and faculty develop a "track record," their accomplishments become a more important determinant of their career mobility.[56] Diana Crane's study of faculty found that prestige of the doctoral department was more important than productivity in determining selection for a position at a prestigious university. She concluded that, in practice, universalistic criteria are not used as much as the rhetoric would lead one to believe.[57] Rachel A. Rosenfeld and Jo Ann Jones' study of academic psychologists also found that new faculty in this field took their first academic jobs at institutions similar in prestige to those from which they received their PhD's.[58] Despite some variation in the findings of these studies, it is clear that institutional prestige (especially the prestige of the PhD-granting department) plays an important role in the careers of academics.

Some research has also been done on careers in another occupation in universities and colleges: that of athletic coach. It has dealt with the relative importance to the coaching career of coaching successful teams versus the prestige of one's athletic and academic credentials. John W. Loy, Jr., and George H. Sage obtained career information from 624 head football and basketball coaches in universities and colleges affiliated with the National Collegiate Athletic Association (NCAA).[59] The prestige of athletic programs was measured using a scale based on the caliber of competition within athletic conferences, and the Associated Press and United Press International rankings for basketball and the Harmon Football Forecast for football. Loy and Sage concluded that the mobility of coaches is not dependent upon an open contest in which they compete for jobs on the basis of their coaching records. Rather, the (athletic) prestige of their undergraduate institutions shapes their careers in several ways. Coaches at high-prestige institutions are more likely to be alumni of high- rather than low-prestige undergraduate institutions. Also, coaches who got their first head coaching job at high-prestige schools were more likely to be employed at a high-prestige school than were those who got their first head coaching job at a low-prestige school. In addition, serving an apprenticeship as an assistant coach under a well-known head coach at a prestigious institution is extremely important in gaining access to a head coaching job at a high-prestige school. It appears that career mobility occurs within institutional prestige levels. Unless one starts out at a high-prestige school, it is extremely difficult to "break into" the top ranking schools later in a career, regardless of one's coaching record.

This portrait of the coaching career is generally supported by an analysis of coaching vacancies by D. Randall Smith and Andrew Abbott.[60] They examined the moves of 1,260 senior- and junior-college football coaches in the NCAA and the National Association for Intercollegiate Athletics (NAIA) over a two-year period. They used school size as well as the several divisions within these athletic associations as their measure of prestige. Smith and Abbott concluded that there is much less movement between these levels of athletic competition than within them.

Elementary and Secondary School Teachers: Departures from an Early-Ceiling Career

Elementary and secondary school teaching has long been recognized as an occupation with poor "holding power." Compared to students majoring in other fields, college students who major in education come to the field as a second choice after having been initially attracted to other areas,[61] and the professional socialization of teachers is less intense and produces less commitment to the occupation than is the case with other professions.[62] As a predominantly female occupation, departures from it result from marriage and the assumption of child-rearing responsibilities. It is also an occupation with an early-ceiling career. Once teachers achieve continuing contract status, there are severe limits to the kinds of positions through which they can move. Opportunities for movement into administrative positions such as a school principalship are few in number and are not a realistic option for very many teachers.

An important aspect of the teaching career is the kind of school to which one is assigned. In large school systems in particular, new teachers are typically assigned to the least desirable schools—those with deteriorating buildings and few resources. Often located in central city ghettos, they are the schools that serve the poor, minorities, and new immigrants to the city. They also tend to be schools with severe disciplinary problems and high rates of violence against both students and teachers. For many new teachers, the first step in their career involves working to get transferred to schools in more affluent neighborhoods.[63] Continuing in the occupation may well depend on obtaining a more attractive position.

Several studies have looked at actual and planned departures from the occupation. In Wisconsin, Ronald M. Pavalko followed the careers of female teachers who entered the occupation between 1959 and 1962.[64] By 1964, 40 percent were no longer teaching. Marital status was strongly related to attrition. Of those who were married, 54 percent had left teaching compared to only 10 percent of those who were not married. A North Carolina study by Phillip C. Schlechty and Victor S. Vance also reported high rates of attrition among teachers in that state.[65] Of the 3,950 teachers who began working in 1973, about 20 percent had left the occupation after one year. Within seven years (by 1980), only about 54 percent were still teaching, although this varied by sex and race. The percentage still teaching after seven years was 53 percent for white females, 58 percent for white males, 64 percent for black females, and 53 percent for black males. In a southwestern city (probably Houston, Texas), Anthony Gary Dworkin asked teachers about their plans to remain in or quit teaching.[66] Plans to quit varied by race and ethnicity with 27.8 percent of the white, 17.8 percent of the black, and 15.5 percent of the Chicano teachers saying that they were "seriously planning to quit teaching."

We have some information about the characteristics of teachers that are related to attrition. In Pavalko's and Dworkin's studies family socioeconomic origins were related to attrition. In both cases, teachers from higher socioeconomic origins were more likely to leave or say that they plan to leave the occupation. Both the Wisconsin and North Carolina studies looked at attrition in relation to ability. In the Wisconsin study, teachers of higher measured intelligence (based on scores of an intelligence test they took as juniors in high school) were more likely to leave the occupation than those of lower measured intelligence. The ability of the North Carolina teachers was measured by their scores on the National Teacher Examination which was required for certification. Again, those who left teaching had higher scores on the test than those who remained in the occupation. The implication of both these studies is that, over time, the aggregate ability level among elementary and secondary school teachers declines.

Nursing: Opportunities for Geographic Mobility

Like teaching, nursing is an occupation with an early-ceiling career. However, there is a greater variety of ways in which the occupation can be performed. Hospitals, clinics, physicians, offices, schools, industrial organizations, nursing homes, and public health departments represent a range of work settings that offer choice and variety. In addition, the opportunity to do special duty nursing offers the possibility of an entrepreneurial work style.

Ruth H. Pape has pointed out that nursing has for a long time been attractive to young women because of the opportunities it offers for travel.[67] In fact, she has characterized the occupation as a form of touristry. Nursing is a skill that is in high demand, it is comparatively easy to get licensed in a new location, and hospitals and other employers are continually advertising for nurses in professional journals, trade magazines, and the like. It is not clear how much this aspect of the nursing career enters into the decision to enter the occupation, but Pape suggests that once in the occupation, it is difficult to avoid awareness of the travel opportunities that it offers.

As a predominantly female occupation, nursing, like teaching, is one in which there is a potential for the disruption of careers because of marriage and child-rearing responsibilities. In a study of Wisconsin nurses, Ronald M. Pavalko followed the careers of women who completed high school in 1957, became nurses and completed their nursing training in 1960 and 1961.[68] By 1964, only 63.5 percent were still working as nurses. Marital status was strongly related to employment status. Of those who were married, 53.8 percent were working compared to 94.1 percent of those who were not married.

This study of recruitment to nursing was replicated by John E. Dunkelberger and Sophia C. Aadland using data from the National Longitudinal Study of the high school class of 1972.[69] Students from this high school senior cohort were followed up in 1979. Those who had become nurses completed their training about three years prior to the follow-up survey, putting them at the same career stage as those in Pavalko's Wisconsin study. Data from this national sample indicated that of those who had become nurses, 65 percent were still working as nurses, a figure virtually indentical to that reported by Pavalko for the Wisconsin nurses. However, Dunkelberger and Aadland found that marital status had a much weaker relationship with the current work status of the nurses in their sample. Of the nurses who were married, 61 percent were working as nurses while only 70.1 percent of those who were not married were working as nurses. The fifteen-year period between these two studies (early 1960s and mid-1970s for beginning work) was a time in which there were substantial changes in expectations about women's work and family roles. The differences in these two studies reflect some of these changes. For the more recent cohort of nurses, marriage appears to be less of a detriment to continuing with a career than it was earlier. In addition, nurses in the more recent cohort who had not married appear to have sought out other, perhaps less traditionally female, occupations than did their counterparts in the earlier study.

CAREER PATTERNS IN MANAGERIAL OCCUPATIONS

A variety of research has been done on the careers of managers and administrators. Careers in such occupations are, of course, played out in organizations. The pyramidlike structure of organizations means that as one moves up the hierarchy, the competition for higher ranking positions becomes more intense. While organizations often portray managers as having unlimited career opportunities, there is simply not enough "room at the top" for more than a very few of those in middle management positions. In addition, the culture of organizations includes timetables and schedules that define the times and ages at which people can expect to be moving upward if they are going to move at all. Such timetables are not always revealed to aspiring managers. This may result in considerable ambiguity about where people stand on the organizational career ladder.

The Meaning and Perception of Promotion Opportunities

Concern with career advancement and promotional opportunities is a dominant feature of life and work in many occupations, but it is especially strong in managerial occupations. Promotions may be valued because they result in an increase in salary, but other things may be involved too. In a study of British managers, Cyril Sofer has pointed out that promotions are valued for a variety of reasons. Promotion means more than just an increase in one's status in an organization. It also affects a person's status in the larger society. It increases people's self-esteem and validates their sense of worth to others as well as to themselves. Promotion also enables people to exercise power and influence, if they desire to do so.[70]

There is a good deal of evidence to indicate that people develop distorted and unrealistic images and expectations of their opportunities in organizations. Victor H. Vroom and K. R. MacCrimmon studied promotion patterns in a large corporation and found that employees in finance and marketing had greater opportunities for advancement than those in manufacturing and personnel.[71] Yet, lower level managers were unaware of these differences, believing instead that they all had virtually unlimited opportunities for promotion. Fred Goldner's study of middle-level managers in a manufacturing concern also illustrates this.[72] He asked managers about their expectations for promotion and then returned five years later to see what had actually happened to them. Although over three-fourths had *expected* promotions, only one-half of those who expected to be promoted actually were. Of those expecting promotions, 20 percent were in the same job, 15 percent experienced lateral moves, and 13 percent were actually demoted. Rosabeth Moss Kanter also reports that people at the lower rungs of the management ladder often have only a vague sense of their promotional opportunities, do not always realize when they have been earmarked for higher ranking positions, and may not acknowledge that they have become "stuck" at a lower level.[73]

Career Anchorage

One of the more useful concepts that has emerged from research on managerial careers is that of *career anchorage*. Curt Tausky and Robert Dubin have pointed out that people can evaluate their careers in one of two ways.[74] They can look backward to the point at which they began working (downward career anchorage) and focus on their past ac-complishments; or, they can look ahead toward some maximum goals and strive to achieve them (upward career anchorage). In a study of 380 middle managers, they found that only 10 percent were upwardly an-chored, assessing their careers against the top organizational positions. Some 47 percent were downwardly anchored, judging their careers in terms of the progress they had made. An additional 43 percent exhibited some characteristics of both the upwardly and downwardly anchored managers. These "ambivalents," as Tausky and Dubin called them, said they would be dissatisfied if they did not reach a top-level position, but, like the downwardly anchored, they looked to activities beyond the work-place for satisfaction and did not actively pursue the goal of success and organizational advancement.

Robert Presthus has characterized the mobility motivations of managers in a similar way.[75] He argues that "upwardly mobile" managers committed to a lifelong ascent up the organizational hierarchy are in the minority. The majority of managers are "indifferent" about upward mobility and use their work as a means of obtaining satisfaction else-where. According to Presthus, there are also many "ambivalent" man-agers who may find the idea of success and power appealing, but find it distasteful to play the game of self-promotion. Consequently, they do not develop the kinds of relationships with others on the job that they believe are necessary for moving ahead. Although not identical, Presthus' managerial types and Tausky and Dubin's typology defined in terms of "anchorage" are very similar. Both lead to the conclusion that, as Tausky has noted, many managers are dissatisfied *without* advancement but they are unwilling to devote themselves completely to the total pursuit of success.[76]

Tausky and Dubin also found that differences in career anchorage were strongly related to age. As managers increase in age, they become more downwardly anchored. Among those under age thirty, only about one-fourth are downwardly anchored (i.e., this group has the highest as-pirations for advancement upward). Between age thirty-one and forty-five the proportion downwardly anchored increases to about two-fifths. The mid-forties appear to be a dramatic turning point. By age forty-six the percentage downwardly anchored jumps to nearly 70 percent and remains at that level through age sixty. Among managers age sixty-one and over, 88 percent were downwardly anchored.[77]

Daniel R. Goldman has replicated the Tausky-Dubin study using a sample of 493 middle managers in seven business firms.[78] He found almost identical proportions of managers with these three types of mobil-ity orientations: 14 percent were upwardly anchored, 44 percent down-wardly anchored, and 43 percent were ambivalent. Goldman found a slightly different relationship between age and anchorage, although the overall pattern was similar. For the managers in this study, the big increase in downward anchorage occurred in the mid-thirties. Thirty-three percent of the group aged thirty-one through thirty-five were downwardly anchored, but this increased to 51 percent in the thirty-six through forty age group. From this point on, downward anchorage remained fairly constant, ranging from 47 percent to 55 percent. Goldman's study supports Tausky and Dubin's conclusion that the popular image of American business as consisting of organizations full of people striving endlessly to reach the top is largely a myth.

Although the concept of career anchorage has been developed in research on managers, the idea is clearly more generally applicable. The kind of career assessment that it involves can be engaged in by people in virtually any occupation. Above all, it illustrates how the *subjective* career may be described quite differently from what is *objectively* happening to people in organizations.

Organizational Mobility

There have been surprisingly few studies that have traced managerial career patterns in organizations over time. One of the most comprehensive analyses has been done by James E. Rosenbaum who examined the complete personnel records of a large corporation for the period 1962–1975.[79] Rosenbaum's particular interest was in looking at the effect of promotions (or nonpromotions) at one point in time on future promotion chances. He suggests that organizational careers can be viewed in terms of a *tournament mobility model*. In this model careers are seen as a sequence of competitions with winners and losers at each selection point. A winner at one point has no assurance of attaining higher levels, but does get the opportunity to continue the competition. Losers at any given point, however, do not get the opportunity to continue in the competition, and for them the competition is over.

Rosenbaum found a good deal of support for this tournament model. For example, the chances of ever attaining a management position over this thirteen-year period are greater if one was promoted during the first three years in the company. In addition, nonmanagerial employees promoted to foreman within their first three years with the company have a much better chance of being promoted to a lower management position than those whose first promotion to foreman took up to seven years (81 percent compared to 33 percent). Similarly, in order to attain a middle management position, promotion to foreman had to occur within the first three years. Of those promoted to foreman after their third year with the company, none had attained a middle management position.

Another study of managerial careers by John F. Veiga provides some additional insight into managerial career patterns.[80] Veiga collected biographical data on the careers of nearly 1,200 managers up to the level of vice-president in three major manufacturing firms. Each firm employed more than 100,000 people and had a combined total of more than forty plant locations in the United States. His conclusions about mobility patterns are based on 6,332 job changes that these managers experienced over the course of their careers.

Veiga found that managers have a distorted subjective perception of what their job changes mean in terms of mobility. While about 40 percent of all moves are upward, 9 percent are downward, and 51 percent are lateral (i.e., no change in status), managers' perceptions of the meaning of these changes are quite different. About 85 percent view their moves as upward, only 3 percent regard them as downward, and 12 percent interpret them as lateral.

Among this sample of managers, a job change, or move, occurred on the average of every 3.5 years. The typical pattern is for movement to be high at the beginning of the career and to decline consistently in frequency. Geographic mobility also declines with age. It is high early and then declines up to around age forty-two. Between forty-two and fifty-four geographic movement increases again, but after age fifty-four it drops off rapidly, reflecting the decreasing opportunities of older managers. Newcomers move around a great deal, but between the ages of twenty-nine and thirty-six movement declines as people develop skills and competencies that, in effect, make them too valuable to move. Around age thirty-seven managers begin to enter the "corporate mainstream" and again experience movement, much of it lateral, as a way of increasing the variety of their experience and skill. Few people enter the "mainstream" after age forty-six. Those who are not clearly headed for the top by this age face the prospect of a "plateaued" career or seeking advancement opportunities in another company. About 14 percent of the managers had been in their present position for at least seven years and were classified as plateaued.

Most of the career moves that managers in this study made were within rather than between companies. *Inter*organizational movement is more common before age thirty-two than later. From age thirty-two to thirty-nine movement between organizations decreases but increases again between thirty-nine and forty-eight. After age forty-eight interorganizational movement decreases sharply. By the time they enter their fifties, those who may be dissatisfied with what they have been able to achieve in their present organization may not look attractive to other organizations. For them, movement to another company may not be possible. Those who have become valuable to their organization and have experienced upward movement may find that attractive pension plans, stock options, and other perquisites have become "golden handcuffs" that make movement to another organization very costly. For them, opportunities to move elsewhere may exist, but they may decide that what they have is not worth giving up.

Veiga also attempted to identify those factors that distinguished movers (those who changed jobs every 3.9 years or less) from nonmovers. Those who moved more frequently tended to be in positions and working on projects that gave them and their work greater exposure to top management. Activities that require people to cross the boundaries between different organizational units provide that sort of exposure, as does being in a position where others come to one for advice and information. In addition, mobile managers get into positions from which their predecessors moved quickly. This suggests that there may be *positions* which have a high mobility potential, regardless of the characteristics of the people in those positions.

Top Corporate Leadership

Attaining top leadership positions in major business organizations is related to both educational attainment and social class background. Michael Useem and Jerome Karabel collected background information on 3,105 senior managers and directors of 208 large corporations.[81] They found that movement to the top ranks of corporate management was enhanced by having an undergraduate degree from a high-prestige college, a masters degree in business administration from a prominent program, or a law degree from a prestigious institution. However, among people with similar educational backgrounds, coming from an upper-class family background increased the chances of entering the top ranks of corporate leadership.

Besides individual qualifications and characteristics, managerial careers in which people make it to the top leadership positions of corporations can be affected by the relative power and importance of the activities they perform within large corporations. Neil Fligstein has studied the careers of people who became chief executive officers of the 100 largest firms in the United States between 1900 and 1979.[82] The origins of these officers from within different parts of their firms changed as the activities with which they were associated changed in importance. During the early part of the century, major corporations were controlled by entrepreneurs or people who came up through manufacturing. In the middle decades chief executives were drawn from sales and marketing. Since 1959, however, they have been drawn increasingly from backgrounds in finance. Thus, changes in the kind of experience deemed important as preparation for top leadership responsibilities can operate as an independent influence on career opportunities.

CLERICAL, TECHNICAL, AND BLUE-COLLAR WORK

With few exceptions, career patterns of the kind that have been studied in professional, semiprofessional, and managerial occupations are difficult to identify in other major segments of the occupational structure. People have careers to be sure, but career lines are shorter, and opportunities for engaging in different kinds of work and for working in different kinds of settings are fewer.

In technical, skilled craft, and clerical occupations, once people have acquired the skills for the occupation and been hired by an employer, they very quickly reach a ceiling beyond which it is extremely difficult to move. Concerns about job security, fringe benefits, and wages loom much larger in importance than do the kinds of issues discussed with respect to careers up to this point. In other words, career takes on a very different meaning.

Among clerical workers there are typically few gradations and ranks. In the large offices of organizations that employ clerks, bookkeepers, secretaries, receptionists, keypunch operators, and the like, the formal status that people occupy is similar. There may be differences in pay reflecting experience and length of service to the company, but not much more. The opportunities that do exist are largely for horizontal mobility—movement into different *kinds* of clerical jobs at the same status level of the organization. Clerical workers may change jobs in order to be in a more pleasant physical environment or to be with co-workers that they find more enjoyable. Secretaries may attempt to get assigned to the offices of powerful and influential executives in order to share in the recognition, attention, and prestige associated with the office. Such moves may enable them to claim greater informal status and power even though their formal position and even salary may be unchanged. Limited career opportunities among clerical workers are also a consequence of the fact that they are mainly women, an issue that will be dealt with in chapter 7 which will look at differences in men's and women's careers.

People in skilled craft and semiskilled factory or construction work experience comparable limits on their career opportunities. Among skilled craft workers, wages, working conditions, and job security are highly salient. After completion of an apprenticeship program, employment opportunities are limited, at least initially, to working for someone else. The reputation of a company or contractor as well as the demands it makes on its workers enter into the decision to take a job with a particular employer or to change jobs. Mobility may occur in order to find a less offensive and demanding foreman, or, like clerical workers, to work with other people who one finds more compatible. Consequently, much of the career mobility that occurs involves horizontal rather than vertical movement. One exception to this is the possibility of moving into self-employment. This is particularly important in the construction industry where mass production has not occurred. Here, the practice of subcontracting different kinds of work has made it possible for small-scale skilled craft entrepreneurs to operate. Obtaining a contractor's license and competing in this arena is a career option and opportunity that exists in this segment of the labor force.

CAREER CONTINGENCIES

A good deal of sociological and popular thinking about careers includes the idea that careers consist of orderly events that individuals can and do control. Yet, there are several kinds of uncertainties and unpredictable events over which individuals may have little or no control. The best laid career plans may be disrupted, set back, or changed (in a positive or negative direction) by a number of such *contingencies*.

CHANGING ENVIRONMENTS AND EXPECTATIONS

For a variety of reasons the kinds of career opportunities that people face and the kinds of alternatives and options open to them may be different from (if not in conflict with) their career plans. For example, people may be ignorant of or misinformed about the kinds of work activities that currently exist in the occupation they are entering and the kinds of options they may or may not face in the future. They also may be unable to anticipate future changes in the occupation. Technological changes, the development of new specialties, and the like, may create new choices that are difficult to anticipate, prepare for, and move into. People who develop a commitment and investment in a particular specialty or activity within an occupation may find themselves left behind and out of the mainstream as new techniques and specializations emerge.

While such internal changes within an occupation may disrupt careers, another contingency has to do with *changing organizational expectations*. Organizations may recruit people on the basis of one type of competency and later discover that they have other kinds of skills that are useful to the organization. This may be followed by an attempt to get them to redefine their role in the organization and to modify their career plans. The case of engineers who are moved into management positions, discussed earlier, is an example of this. From the individual's point of view such a redefinition may represent a substantial departure from the kind of career she or he had planned to pursue. Such changing expectations become a problem when people are reluctant or unwilling to accept a new definition of themselves and their careers. Such occasions become significant turning points in their careers. Those who resist such new definitions may find that they come to be seen as less valuable to the organization. Resources and privileges may become increasingly difficult to claim, their careers become sidetracked, and their future in the organization becomes problematic.

Career disruption of this kind occurs in a variety of different occupations and organizations. In universities and colleges individuals may be recruited on the basis of their teaching and research competencies but, like engineers in industrial organizations, they may be encouraged to move into administrative activities. If a shift of this kind is seen as an important organizational need, faculty who choose not to do so run the risk of being devalued in the eyes of others in the organization. Organizations may also experience a change in their goals and the kinds of activities they reward. Universities may, over time, go through changes in the relative priority they give to instruction, research, and public service. Faculty recruited on the basis of their ability to contribute to a particular goal (e.g., quality instruction) may find that new goals (e.g., being known as a leading research institution) have developed. Unwilling or unable to change their activities to make a contribution to the new goals, faculty may find themselves passed over for promotions and salary increases. Their views and opinions may be ignored and resources of many kinds may be channelled to those who are seen as contributing more to the new goals of the organization.

Government agencies are another example of organizations where changing goals may disrupt the careers of individuals. This happens most noticeably when a change in leadership results in a change in domestic or international policies and goals. Those recruited to government agencies under the ousted administration may find that their orientations and commitments are no longer appropriate and may actually be in conflict with the new policies and goals. This is one reason why the heads of government agencies typically offer their resignations when a new political administration comes into office.

In the private sector the careers of individuals are subject to a wide range of disruptions linked to organizational growth or the lack of it and to fundamental changes in the economy. Opportunities to move up in an organization may only be realized by "moving out" to a new branch, plant, subdivision, or subsidiary of the organization. Such opportunities may create conflicts with the nonwork aspects of people's life. People may be unwilling to disrupt personal friendships, recreational pursuits, or other locally based commitments and investments. On the other hand, people may enter organizations expecting that growth will create new opportunities for them. Should this fail to occur, they face the possibility of disappointment, stagnation, and a truncated career. By the time this is realized it may be too late to shift to an organization or occupation that offers opportunities and alternatives compatible with one's career expectations and aspirations.

DEMOTION

Another career contingency occurs in large organizations where demotions—reductions in status—may occur without those being demoted or others in the organization realizing what has happened. Individuals may find themselves in situations of extreme ambiguity with regard to how to interpret the implications of these events for their careers.

Organizations often attempt to conceal or mask the fact that a demotion has occurred. Rarely are such changes in status made explicit and public. Douglas M. More has identified several ways in which demotion can occur.[83] A person's status may be lowered through lower compensation. People may have their salaries cut or they may be passed over for raises or receive token increases in salary. Demotion can also occur by being passed over for promotion or being moved to a less desirable job. A person's status may also be reduced by having some or all subordinates moved, giving the person fewer people to control and direct. Another subtle form of demotion involves having steps added above one in the organizational hierarchy. Thus, although the individual's position does not change in an absolute sense, there is a relative decline in status. Lateral moves may also be a form of demotion, especially when one is moved out of a line of positions that have high promotion potential to one with fewer chances for future promotion. Melville Dalton also has pointed out that organizations often use "assistant to" positions as a way of setting aside people whose careers have come to an end for any number of reasons.[84] Being made someone else's assistant may be made to look like a promotion while in reality it is a demotion. In his study of industrial managers, Dalton also noted the existence of "sinecures" or positions that have no functional purpose. Individuals who occupy them are not expected to do anything in particular except keep quiet and out of the way of others. Movement into such positions may occur when a career is essentially over but this is rarely made explicit or publicly admitted.

COLLECTIVE MOBILITY:
CHANGES IN THE STATUS OF OCCUPATIONS

Changing expectations and demotion are contingencies that create problems and have negative effects on individuals and their careers. Our final contingency is one that is mostly positive. Changes in status over the course of a career may occur in ways that have nothing to do with the efforts and career plans of individuals. Efforts to make an occupation "professional," as discussed in chapter 2, may have effects on the careers of individuals by increasing the general status of their occupation and its public image. If an occupation is successful in increasing its status and power, the status, power, and opportunities of its members may also increase. Career mobility may occur without any change or special effort on the part of individual members. In a sense, this is an example of the old saying that "a rising tide lifts all ships." One is tempted to add that all ships rise regardless of their individual worth or merit. Of course, "deprofessionalization" of an occupation can produce the opposite effect. Downward mobility and a reduction of career opportunities may be experienced by the members of occupations that lose status or power.

In addition to the changes in status that occur through professionalization, efforts at status enhancement and the creation of career opportunities occur in less systematic, explicit, and formal ways. For example, changes can be made in the kinds of names and titles that people use to identify themselves and the work they do. Members of occupations that are stigmatized, suspect, or for whatever reason have a negative image or are low in status may use this device as a way of claiming status or enhancing the importance of their work and the significance and worth of their careers. Listed below are some examples of old occupational names and their newer, enhanced versions:

Old Name	Enhanced Version
Janitor	Custodian, environmental technician
Real estate salesperson	Realtor, developer
Undertaker	Mortician, funeral director
Used car salesperson	Transportation consultant, dealer representative
Schoolteacher	Learning facilitator
Librarian	Information retrieval specialist
Garbage collector	Sanitary engineer, waste management specialist
Bouncer	Crowd controller

In large organizations, complex and esoteric job titles may often convey much more substance, importance, power, and authority than actually is held by the position and the person who occupies it. In general, we find that the shorter the title, the higher the status of the position and person. For example, "president" is clearly a position of higher status than "deputy assistant to the associate vice president for domestic investments." While such occupational names and job titles may lack credulity, they reflect the desire of people to define their careers to themselves and others in ways that imply success, achievement, importance, and upward mobility. To the extent that such efforts are successful, they may produce the subjective image of a successful career regardless of its objective characteristics.

SUMMARY

As we have seen, the topic of careers deals with the kinds of changes that people experience in their work over time. Careers can be conceptualized as a property of individuals, of occupations, or of organizations. They also have a subjective and objective dimension. As our review of research on careers indicated, in addition to studying occupational changes that people experience, the study of careers also deals with the subjective meaning of those changes to individuals. Career anchorage is a good example of this, and research on the beliefs of managers about their promotion opportunities illustrates the idea that subjective and objective careers can be quite different.

The tracking of careers involves the use of concepts, scales, and models that can measure vertical and horizontal mobility. The concepts of status and prestige as well as situs are important tools for performing such analyses. Our ability to make generalizations about the careers of large numbers of people is limited by the kinds of data that have been collected. Both longitudinal research that follows people's careers over time and research that asks people to retrospectively reconstruct their careers is needed to provide information for making valid generalizations about career mobility.

Our review of research on career patterns included a large number of studies dealing with broad patterns of movement between occupational status levels as well as analyses of careers in particular occupations. Early ceilings are experienced in many occupations at very different status levels. The concept of career anchorage was introduced as a way of identifying the diversity of perspectives that individuals can and do take on their careers as they unfold. Careers in managerial occupations illustrate the way in which organizational hierarchies shape the careers of their members. Although the issue has not been directly dealt with, much of the research on careers suggests that the surprises people experience are not always positive ones. There is an implication that the dreams and goals that people have when they are starting their careers often go unrealized and that disappointing, plateaued careers are perhaps more common than exciting careers with expanding opportunities.

Finally, our discussion of career contingencies represents an exam ple of how changes beyond the control of individuals may alter their careers. Changes in the structure of occupations and in the expectations of organizations can have direct and immediate consequences for career opportunities. Changes in the general status and public image of occupations can have more subtle impacts on careers.

NOTES

1. Robert A. Stebbins, "Career: The Subjective Approach," *Sociological Quarterly* 11 (Winter 1970): 32–49; and "The Subjective Career as a Basis for Reducing Role Conflict," *Pacific Sociological Review* 14 (October 1971): 383–402.
2. Harold L. Wilensky, "Careers, Life Styles, and Social Integration," *International Social Science Journal* 12 (Fall 1960): 553–558.
3. Kenneth I. Spenner, Luther B. Otto, and Vaughn R. A. Call, *Career Lines and Careers* (Lexington, Mass.: D.C. Heath, 1982).
4. Erwin O. Smigel, *The Wall Street Lawyer* (New York: Free Press, 1964).
5. Kenneth J. Reichstein, "Ambulance Chasing: A Case Study of Deviation and Control within the Legal Profession," *Social Problems* 13 (Summer 1965): 3–17.
6. Theodore Caplow and Reece J. McGee, *The Academic Marketplace* (New York: Basic Books, 1958); Christopher Jencks and David Riesman, *The Academic Revolution* (Garden City, N.Y.: Doubleday, 1968); and Talcott Parsons and Gerald M. Platt, *The American University* (Cambridge, Mass.: Harvard University Press, 1973).
7. U.S. Bureau of the Census, *Statistical Abstract of the United States, 1985* (Washington, D.C.: U.S. Government Printing Office, 1984), 395, table 663.
8. Barney G. Glaser, "Toward a Theory of Organizational Careers," in *Organizational Careers: A Sourcebook for Theory*, ed. Barney G. Glaser (Chicago: Aldine, 1968), 13–16.
9. Glaser, *op. cit.*, "Introduction," in *Organizational Careers*, 1–12.
10. Theodore Caplow, *Principles of Organization* (New York: Harcourt, Brace, and World, 1964), 224.
11. Lowell G. Hargens, "Patterns of Mobility of New PhD's Among American Academic Institutions," *Sociology of Education* 42 (Winter 1969): 18–37.
12. Theodore Caplow, *The Sociology of Work* (Minneapolis: University of Minnesota Press, 1954), 59–60.
13. Alba M. Edwards, *Comparative Occupational Statistics for the United States, 1870–1940* (Washington, D.C.: U.S. Government Printing Office, 1943).
14. Leonard Reissman, *Class in American Society* (New York: Free Press, 1959), 145.
15. For illustrative examples see Richard Centers, *The Psychology of Social Classes: A Study of Class Consciousness* (Princeton, N.J.: Princeton University Press, 1949); and Ralph Turner, *The Social Context of Ambition* (San Francisco: Chandler, 1964).
16. Otis Dudley Duncan, "A Socioeconomic Index for All Occupations," in Albert J. Reiss, Jr., *Occupations and Social Status* (New York: Free Press, 1961), 263–275.

17. David L. Featherman and Gillian Stevens, "A Revised Socioeconomic Index of Occupational Status: Application in Analysis of Sex Differences in Attainment," in *Social Structure and Behavior*, ed. Robert M. Hauser et al. (New York: Academic Press, 1982). This paper has been reprinted in Mary G. Powers, ed., *Measures of Socioeconomic Status: Current Issues* (Washington, D.C.: American Association for the Advancement of Science, 1982), chap. 5.
18. Duncan's original scale can be found in the book cited in note 16. It is also reproduced in Richard H. Hall, *Occupations and the Social Structure* (Englewood Cliffs, N.J.: Prentice-Hall, 1969), 275–295. The most recent version, based on 1970 census data, appears in the two books cited in note 17.
19. Charles B. Nam and Mary G. Powers, "Changes in the Relative Status Level of Workers in the United States, 1950–60," *Social Forces* 47 (December 1968): 158–170.
20. Charles B. Nam et al., "Occupational Status Scores: Stability and Change," *Proceedings of the American Statistical Association*, 1975, 570–575.
21. The original Nam-Powers scale can be found in the article cited in note 19. It is also reproduced in Ronald M. Pavalko, *Sociology of Occupations and Professions* (Itasca, Ill.: F.E. Peacock, 1971), 115–128. The most recent version, based on 1970 census data, appears in the article cited in note 20. The Nam-Powers scale has an overall correlation of .97 with the Duncan SEI, and the 1950 and 1960 Nam-Powers scores have a correlation of .96. The revised (1970) Nam-Powers scale correlates .97 with the 1960–1970 comparison and .91 with the 1950–1970 comparison *for men* and .85 in the 1960–1970 comparison *for women*. What this means is that there is a great deal of stability in the relative status of occupations over time and that both of these scales can be used with confidence that they are reliable measures of occupational status.
22. George S. Counts, "The Social Status of Occupations," *The School Review* 33 (January 1925): 16–27.
23. H. C. Lehman and P. A. Witty, "Further Study of the Social Status of Occupations," *Journal of Educational Psychology* 5 (October 1931): 101–112; C. Menger, "The Social Status of Occupations for Women," *Teachers College Record* 33 (1932); W. A. Anderson, "The Occupational Attitudes of College Men," *Journal of Social Psychology* 5 (1934): 435–466; R. B. Stevens, "The Attitudes of College Women towards Women's Vocations," *Journal of Applied Psychology* 24 (1940): 615–627; Mapheus Smith, "An Empirical Scale of Prestige Status of Occupations," *American Sociological Review* 8 (April 1943); 185–192; and M. K. Welch, "The Ranking of Occupations on the Basis of Social Status," *Occupations* 26 (January 1949): 237–241.
24. M. E. Deeg and D. G. Paterson, "Changes in Social Status of Occupations," *Occupations* 25 (January 1947): 237–241.
25. The original report of this study is Cecil C. North and Paul K. Hatt, "Jobs and Occupations: A Popular Evaluation," *Opinion News* 9 (September 1, 1947): 3–13. It is reprinted in Reinhard Bendix and Seymour Martin Lipset, eds., *Class, Status, and Power* (New York: Free Press, 1953), 411–426.
26. Robert W. Hodge, Paul M. Siegel, and Peter H. Rossi, "Occupational Prestige in the United States, 1925–1963," *American Journal of Sociology* 70 (November 1964): 286–302.
27. Peter C. Pineo and John Porter, "Occupational Prestige in Canada," *Canadian Review of Sociology and Anthropology* 4 (1967): 24–40.
28. Donald J. Treiman, *Occupational Prestige in Comparative Perspective* (New

York: Academic Press, 1977).

29. Emile Benoit-Smullyan, "Status, Status Types, and Status Interrelations," *American Sociological Review* 9 (April 1944): 151–161.

30. Paul K. Hatt, "Occupation and Social Stratification," *American Journal of Sociology* 55 (May 1950): 533–543.

31. Richard T. Morris and Raymond J. Murphy, "The Situs Dimension in Occupational Structure," *American Sociological Review* 24 (April 1959): 231–239.

32. For an overview of the published research from this project as well as a summary of replications and critiques of the model, see William H. Sewell and Robert M. Hauser, "The Wisconsin Longitudinal Study of Social and Psychological Factors in Aspirations and Achievements," *Research in Sociology of Education and Socialization* 1 (1980): 59–99.

33. Richard T. Campbell, "Status Attainment Research: End of the Beginning or Beginning of the End?" *Sociology of Education* 56 (January 1983): 47–62.

34. Sewell and Hauser, "Wisconsin Longitudinal Study," 71–72; William H. Sewell, Archibald O. Haller, and Alejandro Portes, "The Educational and Early Occupational Attainment Process," *American Sociological Review* 34 (February 1969): 82–92; William H. Sewell, Archibald O. Haller, and George W. Ohlendorf, "The Educational and Early Occupational Attainment Process: Replication and Revision," *American Sociological Review* 35 (December 1970): 1014–1027; and Robert M. Hauser, Shu-Ling Tsai, and William H. Sewell, "A Model of Stratification with Response Error in Social and Psychological Variables," *Sociology of Education* 56 (January 1983): 20–46.

35. See Sewell and Hauser, "Wisconsin Longitudinal Study," for a review of these replications. For the most recent replication see Christopher Jencks, James Crouse, and Peter Mueser, "The Wisconsin Model of Status Attainment: A National Replication with Improved Measures of Ability and Aspiration," *Sociology of Education* 56 (January 1983): 3–19.

36. Peter M. Blau and Otis Dudley Duncan, *The American Occupational Structure* (New York: Wiley, 1967).

37. Percentages reported in this section are based on computations from Ibid., app. J, table J 2.3, 498.

38. Seymour Martin Lipset and Reinhard Bendix, *Social Mobility in Industrial Society* (Berkeley and Los Angeles: University of California Press, 1960).

39. James D. Thompson, Robert W. Avery, and Richard Carlson, *Occupations, Personnel, and Careers* (Pittsburgh: Administrative Science Center, University of Pittsburgh, 1962).

40. U.S. Bureau of the Census, *Statistical Abstract*, 103, table 158.

41. Howard S. Erlanger, "The Allocation of Status within Occupations: The Case of the Legal Profession," *Social Forces* 58 (March 1980): 882–903.

42. U.S. Bureau of the Census, *Statistical Abstract*, 177, table 300.

43. Michael Cohen, "Lawyers and Political Careers," *Law and Society Review* 3 (May 1969): 563–574; and Donald R. Matthews, *U.S. Senators and Their World* (Chapel Hill: University of North Carolina Press, 1960).

44. Cohen, "Lawyers and Political Careers," 563–574.

45. Seymour Martin Lipset, *Political Man* (New York: Doubleday, 1959).

46. T. B. Priest and Robert A. Rothman, "Lawyers in Corporate Chief Executive Positions: A Historical Analysis of Careers," *Work and Occupations* 12 (May 1985): 131–146.

47. Edwin Layton, "Science, Business, and the American Engineer," in *The En-*

gineers and the Social System, ed. Robert Perrucci and Joel E. Gerstl (New York: Wiley, 1969), 51–72.

48. M. K. Badaway, "How to Succeed as a Manager: Part 3," *Machine Design* 53 (1981): 91–95.

49. J. A. Bayton and R. L. Chapman, "Professional Development: Making Managers out of Scientists and Engineers," *The Bureaucrat* 1 (1977): 408–425.

50. "Who Faculty Members Are and What They Think," *Chronicle of Higher Education* 31 (December 18, 1985): 25.

51. "Nearly 40 Pct. of Faculty Members Said to Consider Leaving Academe," *Chronicle of Higher Education* 31 (October 23, 1985): 1, 22.

52. Logan Wilson, *The Academic Man* (New York: Oxford University Press, 1942).

53. Caplow and McGee, *Academic Marketplace.*

54. Robert K. Merton, *The Sociology of Science* (Chicago: University of Chicago Press, 1973).

55. Jonathan R. Cole and Stephen Cole, *Social Stratification in Science* (Chicago: University of Chicago Press, 1973).

56. Lowell L. Hargens and Warren O. Hagstrom, "Sponsored and Contest Mobility of American Scientists," *Sociology of Education* 40 (January 1967): 24–38.

57. Diana Crane, "The Academic Marketplace Revisited," *American Journal of Sociology* 75 (1970): 953–964.

58. Rachel A. Rosenfeld and Jo Ann Jones, "Institutional Mobility Among Academics: The Case of Psychologists," *Sociology of Education* 59 (October 1986): 212–226.

59. John W. Loy, Jr., and George H. Sage, "Athletic Personnel in the Academic Marketplace: A Study of the Interorganizational Mobility Patterns of College Coaches," *Sociology of Work and Occupations* 5 (November 1978): 446–469.

60. D. Randall Smith and Andrew Abbott, "A Labor Market Perspective on the Mobility of College Football Coaches," *Social Forces* 61 (June 1983): 1147–1167.

61. James A. Davis, *Undergraduate Career Decisions* (Chicago: Aldine, 1965).

62. Robert Dreeben, *The Nature of Teaching: Schools and the Work of Teachers* (Glenview, Ill.: Scott, Foresman, 1970).

63. Howard S. Becker, "The Career of the Chicago Public Schoolteacher," *American Journal of Sociology* 57 (March 1952): 470–477.

64. Ronald M. Pavalko, "Recruitment to Teaching: Patterns of Selection and Retention," *Sociology of Education* 43 (Summer 1970): 340–353.

65. Phillip C. Schlechty and Victor S. Vance, "Do Academically Able Teachers Leave Education? The North Carolina Case," *Phi Delta Kappan* (October 1981): 106–112.

66. Anthony Gary Dworkin, "The Changing Demography of Public School Teaching: Some Implications for Faculty Turnover in Urban Areas," *Sociology of Education* 53 (April 1980): 65–73.

67. Ruth H. Pape, "Touristry: A Type of Occupational Mobility," *Social Problems* 11 (Spring 1964): 336–344.

68. Ronald M. Pavalko, "Recruitment to Nursing: Some Research Findings," *Nursing Research* 18 (January-February 1969): 72–76.

69. John E. Dunkelberger and Sophia C. Aadland, "Expectations and Attainment of Nursing Careers," *Nursing Research* 33 (July-August 1984):235–240.

70. Cyril Sofer, *Men in Mid-Career: A Study of British Managers and Technical*

Specialists (London: Cambridge University Press, 1970).
71. Victor H. Vroom and K. R. MacCrimmon, "Toward a Stochastic Model of Managerial Careers," *Administrative Science Quarterly* 13 (1968): 26–46.
72. Fred Goldner, "Success vs. Failure: Prior Managerial Perspectives," *Industrial Relations* 9 (1970): 453–474.
73. Rosabeth Moss Kanter, *The Change Masters: Innovations for Productivity in the American Corporation* (New York: Simon and Schuster, 1973).
74. Curt Tausky and Robert Dubin, "Career Anchorage: Managerial Mobility Motivations," *American Sociological Review* 30 (October 1965): 725–735.
75. Robert Presthus, *The Organizational Society* (New York: Vintage Books, 1965).
76. Curt Tausky, *Work Organizations: Major Theoretical Perspectives*, 2nd ed. (Itasca, Ill.: F. E. Peacock, 1978).
77. Tausky and Dubin, "Career Anchorage," 731.
78. Daniel R. Goldman, "Career Anchorage: Managerial Mobility Motivations— A Replication," *Sociology of Work and Occupations* 5 (May 1978): 193–208.
79. James E. Rosenbaum, *Career Mobility in a Corporate Hierarchy* (Orlando, Fla.: Academic Press, 1984).
80. John F. Veiga, "Do Managers on the Move Get Anywhere?" *Harvard Business Review* 59 (March-April 1981): 20–38; and "Plateaued Versus Nonplateaued Managers: Career Patterns, Attitudes, and Path Potential," *Academy of Management Journal* 24 (September 1981): 566–578.
81. Michael Useem and Jerome Karabel, "Pathways to Top Corporate Management," *American Sociological Review* 51 (April 1986): 184–200.
82. Neil Fligstein, "The Intraorganizational Power Struggle: Rise of Finance Personnel to Top Leadership in Large Corporations, 1919–1979," *American Sociological Review* 52 (February 1987): 44–58.
83. Douglas M. More, "Demotion," *Social Problems* 9 (Winter 1962): 213–221.
84. Melville Dalton, *Men Who Manage* (New York: Wiley, 1959). See also Fred H. Goldner, "Demotion in Industrial Management," *American Sociological Review* 30 (October 1965): 714–724.

PART TWO

CHAPTER 6

The Work Setting

IT SHOULD BE apparent from the material presented in the chapters in part I that the settings and contexts in which work occurs are many and varied. Our discussion of occupational choice, socialization, and especially careers touched on these differences. Clearly, hospitals, factories, farms, schools, government agencies, construction sites, nonprofit agencies, etc., are settings that define and constrain work activities in different ways and to different degrees. For example, the work activities of a lawyer in private practice and an automobile assembly line worker differ tremendously in their pace, their repetitiveness, and the kinds of relationships the worker has with other persons, to mention only a few obvious differences.

We could begin by comparing occupations two or three at a time and noting differences in the settings in which they occur and the consequences of those differences for individuals. However, this would probably be a frustrating exercise and it is not clear what we would have when we were done. Even if it were possible to develop an exhaustive comparison of specific occupations and their settings, we would run the risk of "missing the forest for the trees." Our goal in this chapter is to make generalizations about the effects of work settings on people. In order to do this, we need to identify the key common features of different *types* of work settings that subsume or include a number of specific occupations. In creating such a typology we need to be guided by the principle of "parsimony." Our categories (types of work settings) should be as few

173

in number as it takes to identify the most salient differences in the settings in which occupations are performed. As we contrast different work settings we also need to identify the kinds of changes that have occurred in the context in which work takes place as the United States has moved from an agrarian to an industrial economy, and as we continue to develop a postindustrial economy.

As we look at contemporary work settings, it is clear that bureaucratic organizations have become the context in which most work occurs. Consequently, it is essential that we develop an understanding of organizations and how they affect people in their work. Professionals working in organizations face a variety of conflicts that are likely to be experienced by increasing numbers of workers as they become more and more dependent on organizational employment. Another major work problem—alienation and job dissatisfaction—also has an organizational basis. As our discussion of these topics will indicate, bureaucratic organizations create problems for both white-collar and blue-collar workers.

VARIETIES OF WORK SETTINGS

AGRICULTURE

Subsistence farming—growing crops and raising animals for one's own needs—has virtually disappeared in the United States. It has been replaced by commercial farming in which crops and animals are raised for their cash value in the marketplace. As a type of work setting, however, the self-sufficient farm represents a baseline for understanding the changes that have occurred in the organization of work. Throughout most of American history—certainly up to the beginning of the twentieth century—farming has been as much a way of life as an occupation. The farming subculture is one in which work and nonwork activities are fused together much more than they are in the case of industrial and postindustrial occupations.

The Self-Sufficient Farm

In its extreme form the work context of self-sufficient farming is characterized by a high degree of isolation. Great distances separate producing units and the units themselves tend to be small. The self-sufficient farm also is typically a family operation. When farming operations reach a size where members of the nuclear family cannot handle the work to be done, the work force may be expanded to include members of the extended family or younger members of neighboring families. Thus, the producing unit typically consists of people who have known one another intimately over long periods of time and who share common values and a common outlook on life. Work groups also tend to be highly stable over time and people are exposed to few external influences. The self-sufficient farm is marked by an absence of change. Work routines vary from one season to another, but there is little variation from year to year.

In addition to these distinctive characteristics of the self-sufficient farm, farm communities also have important characteristics that are part of the context of the work. The most important of these is homogeneity in terms of such things as ethnicity, religion, and a wide range of social, political, and economic values. In addition, as long as the units that make up a farm community are not producing for external markets, they have a low degree of interdependence with other segments of the society. Thus, in farm communities made up of self-sufficient farms, there tends to develop an all-inclusive subculture that is internally focused and that patterns social interaction, leisure activities, and religious and political perspectives as well as work behavior.

The self-sufficient farm has given way to commercial farming where one or a few crops are raised mainly to be sold in a market that has national and even international dimensions. As this change has occurred, many aspects of the context of farming have changed. Producing units and their work forces have become larger, and increasingly include people who are not members of the same nuclear or extended family. In addition, involvement with external markets has broken down the isolation and independence of the individual farmer as well as the farm community.

The changes that have occurred in farming can be described in a number of ways. For example, the total farm population decreased from 30,529,000 people in 1930 to 5,787,000 in 1983. Even more dramatic is the decline in the farm population as a proportion of the total United States population. In 1930, 24.9 percent of the population lived on farms compared to only 2.5 percent in 1983.[1] As recently as 1960 farm workers made up 6.6 percent of the total employed labor force but this figure had declined to 2.9 percent by 1982.[2] In 1983 farm operators (those who own or rent farms) and farm managers (those who direct the operations of a farm for a corporation or an absentee owner) made up only 1.4 percent of the labor force.[3]

Comparable changes can be seen if we look at the number of farms in the United States. In 1935 there were 6.8 million farms compared to 2.2 million in 1984.[4] However, the size of the average farm has been increasing. In 1950 the average farm was 213 acres compared to 437 in 1984.[5] In 1950 only 5.6 percent of all farms had 500 or more acres, but by 1982 this figure had increased to 16.3 percent.[6]

Agribusiness

Clearly, farming as we have known it historically in the United States is being replaced by agribusiness, a trend likely to continue in the future. While *direct* employment in farming has decreased, a variety of specialized "para-agricultural" work has developed. The application of scientific principles and procedues to farming, as well as mechanization and crop specialization have given rise to occupations that provide services to agribusiness. Educational specialists who disseminate information about new techniques and products have become increasingly important. Other service adjuncts to agribusiness include veterinary medicine, food and animal inspection, crop and livestock grading, and marketing information. Crop dusting, fertilizing, insect and fungus control, and farm building maintenance have emerged as specialized work roles as farming has become larger in scale and more internally specialized. Finally, the sale and servicing of farm machinery and the sale of feed, fertilizer, and seed have become major business activities in their own right.

Historically, technological changes have been important in the transformation from self-sufficient farming to agribusiness. Plows, combines, and harvesters reduced the need for farm labor and made large-scale farming operations possible. Fertilizers, fungicides, and insecticides have also contributed to the increased productivity of farming, making it possible to feed the population with only a small fraction of the farm labor force needed earlier.[7]

It is apparent that the work setting of the farmer has changed dramatically. The work has come to include planning, coordination, and management in a work setting that includes dependence on a number of other specialized occupations. No longer self-sufficient and inward looking, farming exists in a setting of increased complexity and external interdependence.

THE FACTORY

The decline of farming as an occupation in the United States has occurred hand in hand with an increase in industrial employment. As agriculture increased in productivity in the late 1800s and the early 1900s, surplus farm workers gravitated to urban areas to take advantage of expanding employment opportunities in factories. Data illustrating this change from an agrarian to an industrial and, more recently, a postindustrial labor force are presented in table 6.1

In table 6.1, *primary* occupations are those in farming, fishing, and lumbering; *secondary* refers to occupations in manufacturing, mining, and construction; and *tertiary* includes everything else, such as transpor-

Table 6.1
The United States Labor Force, by
Type of Work, 1850–1982 (in percent)

Year	Type of Work Primary	Secondary	Tertiary
1850	64.0%	17.5%	18.5%
1860	59.4	19.9	20.7
1870	53.5	22.7	23.8
1880	50.0	24.8	25.2
1890	42.8	28.1	29.1
1900	37.6	30.1	32.3
1910	31.6	31.5	36.9
1920	27.4	34.3	38.3
1930	22.0	31.1	46.9
1940	17.1	31.1	51.8
1950	12.5	33.7	53.8
1960	5.8	29.9	64.3
1970	4.2	31.6	64.2
1980	3.6	29.4	67.0
1982	3.6	27.2	69.2

Sources: For 1850–1940, U.S. Bureau of the Census, *Historical Statistics of the United States* (Washington, D.C.: U.S. Government Printing Office, 1960), 74; for 1950, *Statistical Abstract of the United States, 1956,* 199; for 1960, *Statistical Abstract of the United States, 1963,* 220 and 223; for 1970, *Statistical Abstract of the United States, 1972,* 225 and 230; for 1980, *Statistical Abstract of the United States, 1981* 390; for 1982, *Statistical Abstract of the United States, 1985,* 404.

tation, commerce, finance, communication, education, health care, etc. The tertiary category is often referred to as the "service" sector of the labor force.

Since 1850 the dramatic decline in primary occupations was accompanied by a gradual increase in both secondary and tertiary occupations up to 1900. Since 1900 the proportion of the labor force employed in secondary occupations has remained fairly stable while the tertiary labor force has continued to grow. The secondary category can appropriately be equated with industrial production. Although it is commonplace to refer to the United States as an industrial society, no more than one-third of the labor force has ever been directly employed in industrial production. In the decades ahead, the tertiary sector of the labor force is expected to continue to grow, with proportionate declines in secondary occupations.

If the self-sufficient farm epitomized the occupational world of eighteenth and early nineteenth century America, the factory is the late nineteenth and twentieth century counterpart. Although the production of manufactured goods is decreasing in importance in the economy of late twentieth century America and the production of services is increasing, the factory is still an important work context for a significant proportion of the labor force. As a work context, there are a number of characteristics that distinguish the factory and present a dramatic contrast to the self-sufficient farm.

An apparent but nevertheless important feature of industrial work is that it is differentiated from other areas of life. In both traditional and contemporary farming, workplace and home are the same. The factory, however, is a separate place with a particular function to which people go to perform work activities. While farm work tends to be integrated with family activities and routines, the factory establishes its own work routines, schedules, and cycles, independent of the nonwork lives of its workers.

Where homogeneity characterized the self-sufficient farm context, heterogeneity prevails in the factory. The factory brings together strangers who may differ in terms of ethnicity, religion, and the like. The intimacy, familiarity, and primary relationships of the self-sufficient farm are replaced by greater anonymity, impersonality, and secondary relationships in the industrial work context.

In addition, the factory has a complex division of labor with a great amount of routinization and specialization. Work processes and procedures are established on the basis of the demands of technology and the criterion of efficiency. Once established, the factory worker is expected to follow work routines as closely as possible. This is often referred to as *technological dominance*, a situation where technology is developed first and individuals are then required to adapt their behavior to the requirements of the technology. Little leeway, variation, discretion, or innovation is permitted in the way work activities are carried out. Work tasks are also specialized so that ideally each worker performs a limited, pre-established set of operations that are a small input into the production of some larger product that is produced by the inputs of numerous specialists.

Later in this chapter we will deal with bureaucratic organizations in some detail. At this point, however, it is important to point out that industrial work settings are typically organized along bureaucratic lines. They have a pre-established authority structure. The factory can be looked at as a hierarchy of positions with authority increasing as one moves from the bottom to the top of the structure. Production instructions are communicated through this authority structure and it represents a system of supervision in which responsibility for achieving production goals and maintaining discipline are located. Formal communication and interaction follow this authority structure and informal interaction is most likely to occur among peers at the same level of the structure.

Time also takes on a new meaning in the factory. In the case of farming, work is scheduled in terms of the seasons. In the factory, time is manipulated and work is organized in terms of much smaller units of time. Managers may set production goals in terms of the amount of a given product to be produced in a given amount of time. The productivity of workers may be measured in terms of temporal units and they may be paid on the basis of either the amount of time worked or the amount produced in a given time period.

In addition to time, *timing* becomes critical in the factory. Since large numbers of specialized workers are involved in the production of different parts of some larger product, it is essential that those parts appear at assembly points at the right time and in the right sequence. Consequently, specialization and an elaborate division of labor create the need for coordination and planning in which timing becomes a crucial consideration. A concern with time and timing produces a distinctive rhythm in the factory work context.

In thinking about the factory as a work context, the most frequent and appropriate image that comes to mind is the assembly line. Industrial sociologists have studied assembly line work extensively and it is virtually a prototype and symbol of the factory work context. According to William Foote Whyte, assembly line work is repetitive and its pace is mechanically controlled. A minimum of skill is needed and the highly specialized work to be done is predetermined. The simple and repetitive tasks to be performed make few mental demands on the worker. Yet, mistakes will occur unless workers give their work constant visual and mental attention.[8] Some of the personal consequences of factory work will be explored later in the chapter in the discussion of "Work Alienation and Job Satisfaction." At this point, suffice it to say that the basic features of the factory work setting are dramatically different from those of the self-sufficient farming context.

Finally, the factory is a unionized work setting. Although collective bargaining is not limited to industrial work, it is found more often in this work context than others. Unionization of the American labor force reached a peak in the 1940s. In 1946, for example, 34.5 percent of the nonagricultural labor force was unionized and during the 1950s about one-third of all nonagricultural workers were members of unions.[9] Union membership began to decrease in the 1960s and by 1980, 25.2 percent of the nonagricultural labor force was unionized.[10] However, in metropolitan areas of the United States in 1984, 51 percent of "production workers" were unionized compared to only 12 percent of "office workers." Among workers employed in manufacturing industries, union membership stood at 60 percent.[11]

THE OFFICE

As a work setting, the office includes a wide variety of specific occupations. It includes virtually all the occupations classified by the U.S. Bureau of the Census as "clerical" occupations. But even this category contains a great deal of variation. It includes such diverse occupations as bill collector, telephone operator, insurance agent, and typist. Specific census occupational categories cannot be equated with the office work context because such categories basically refer to the status of occupations. The concept of "the office" refers primarily to white-collar work that is nonmanagerial and nonprofessional.

The office work setting is found in both the public and private sector and in firms that manufacture tangible goods as well as those that provide services. The office is found in the administrative component of manufacturing concerns and throughout the business world including banks and other financial institutions, insurance companies, and the communications industry. It is also the basic form of work organization in governmental agencies and educational institutions both public and private.

The common characteristic of office work is that it takes place in organizations. Consequently, it is a bureaucratized work setting with a high degree of task specialization, routinization, and supervision. It is a world of rules and regulations in which procedures are externally specified. Work tasks in the office tend to be very repetitious over time with changes occurring when new technologies create new tasks and procedures which, in turn, become routine themselves. Jon M. Shepard has identified a sequence of changes in office work that illustrates this response to technology.[12] He calls early office work "craft accurate work." It included secretaries taking shorthand that required speed and accuracy, bookkeepers keeping accurate financial accounts by hand, and other clerks keeping precise records on all aspects of the enterprise's activities. The next stage, "early mechanization" occurred with the introduction of simple machines such as typewriters, adding machines, and dictating machines. Although operating such machines as these required skill, it did not result in the same sense of "craft" that existed earlier. "Punched card data processing" is the third stage identified by Shepard. As the IBM card became the dominant technology, the jobs of keypuncher and verifier developed along with jobs involving the operation of other business machines. The most recent phase is that of "electronic data processing" ushered in by the computerization of the office. Information, including words as well as numerical data, is electronically processed.

As a result of these changes identified by Shepard, office work has increasingly come to resemble factory work. Traditionally, office work has enjoyed the prestige generally accorded white-collar occupations. Perhaps because of the higher evaluation of "head work" in contrast to "hands work," office work has been seen as more desirable than semi-skilled factory jobs and even skilled manual work.[13] Early offices of the late nineteenth and early twentieth centuries tended to be relatively small and office work was more varied and diversified. Growth in size and scale has led to increased bureaucratization. Mechanization and computerization have contributed to standardization and routinization. The early generalist and craft worker have been replaced by the machine-tending specialist, and the similarity of office and factory work has increased.

Another important feature of office work is the fact that it is a highly feminized work setting. Despite the dramatic changes that have been occurring in the occupations of women (see chapter 7), the vast majority of office workers are women. About one-third of all employed women (compared to only about 6 percent of men) are in clerical occupations.[14] Table 6.2 presents the percentage of women in selected clerical occupations to illustrate the predominance of women in office work. The proportion of women in many of these occupations, especially bank tellers, has actually been increasing since the early 1960s.[15]

The introduction of office technology, especially the typewriter, contributed to the feminization of office work. Typing became "women's work" because it did not replace men since the occupation did not exist prior to the introduction of the technology. Other types of office work attracted women by offering higher pay and status than other jobs open to women.[16]

Clerical jobs offer few opportunities for upward mobility within organizations. In large measure this is a reflection of the predominance of women in these occupations. The banking and telecommunications industries in particular have excluded female clerical workers from opportunities for advancement.[17] The lack of opportunities for advance-

Table 6.2
Percentage of Women in Selected Clerical Occupations, 1982

Occupation	Percent Female
Secretary	99.2
Typist	96.6
Keypunch operator	94.5
Bank teller	92.0
Bookkeeper	92.0
Telephone operator	91.9
Cashier	86.8
Office machine operator	74.6

Source: U.S. Bureau of the Census, *Statistical Abstract of the United States, 1984* (Washington, D.C.: U.S. Government Printing Office, 1983), 419–420, table 696.

ment in office work is also a result of its location at the bottom of the administrative hierarchy. It is not part of the managerial, supervisory, and policy-making system that leads to advancement. The "better" office jobs into which people may aspire to move tend to be those that offer greater variety in work activities, greater freedom of movement, and more opportunities for informal interaction with co-workers. The formal status differences that exist within these office occupations are minimal. Since many of the routine work activities of the office are inherently uninteresting, informal interaction may become an important source of work satisfaction. Consequently, positions that offer opportunities for congenial informal relationships and interaction tend to become informally valued.[18]

A final feature of office work that contributes to its distinctiveness is its location on the boundary of organizations. Many occupations subsumed under the office work category provide the major link between an organization and its clients. Secretaries and receptionists are especially important boundary occupations in this sense. A client's first, and sometimes only, contact with an organization is typically with such organizational representatives. They perform a kind of public relations function and shape their organization's public image. Consequently, such things as physical attractiveness, grooming, pleasantness, tact, and helpfulness are frequently stressed as important attributes of those performing these types of office work.

ENTREPRENEURIAL AND MANAGERIAL WORK

The idea of going into business for oneself is linked in complex ways to the beliefs of Americans about economic opportunity and success. *Entrepreneurship* is connected with values such as individuality, self-responsibility, self-determination, and independence. Ely Chinoy has identified the desire to go into business for oneself as a central part of "the American dream."[19] Symbolically, it represents a way of escaping low status, dead-end jobs in factories and gaining a measure of autonomy and self-control.

Every year large numbers of people attempt to achieve the dream of becoming an entrepreneur. In 1983 some 600,000 new businesses were incorporated.[20] But in that same year, 31,300 businesses failed.[21] According to the Dun and Bradstreet Corporation, 39 percent of the businesses that fail annually are engaged in retail trade, the kind of business most likely to be pursued on a small scale by people seeking to become self-employed.[22] Small-scale entrepreneurship is extremely risky. People who try it and fail often lose the savings they have invested, end up in debt, and face the prospect of looking for a job as a new employee, having lost their seniority and possibly their pension rights in the job they left to pursue the American dream.

That the entrepreneurial work setting is characterized by economic marginality and the risk of failure is also illustrated in a study of ninety small businesses by Kurt B. Mayer and Sidney Goldstein.[23] They found that about half of these businesses (forty-four of them) had closed during their first two years of operation. Furthermore, 90 percent of those that make it through the first two years were evaluated as being "marginal survivors" or only "limited successes." According to Mayer and Goldstein, new small businesses fail for several reasons. They tend to be "undercapitalized" which means that they are started with very small amounts of money and little in reserve to fall back on, particularly during the first few months which tend to be a difficult period. People who start small businesses typically are inexperienced at running a business and this lack of familiarity with the business world contributes to failure. For example, of the forty-nine businesses started by blue-collar workers, 60 percent did not make it to their second anniversary and of those that did only two were judged to be clearly successful.

The entrepreneurial work setting is one in which there is high risk and a high probability of failure because of competitive pressures as well as the problems noted above. Some of these risks can be reduced through a relatively new form of quasi entrepreneurship. This is the franchise business, the best-known examples being establishments such as McDonald's, Burger King, Holiday Inn, and the like. Franchised retail establishments abound not only in the fast food industry but also in other areas such as dry cleaning, hardware, and computer sales and service. Franchising has grown in popularity in recent years. In 1970 there were 396,300 franchised businesses in the United States. This figure had increased to 461,800 by 1984. Total sales of franchised businesses increased even more rapidly, going from $120 million in 1970 to $457 million in 1984.[24] Gasoline service stations are the most common type of franchised business. They made up 28.2 percent of the total in 1984, with restaurants (including fast food businesses) in second place, comprising 16.2 percent of the total.[25]

Franchises are costly to acquire. In 1982 a Burger King franchise cost $500,000 and a McDonald's franchise ranged between $250,000 and $325,000.[26] Some franchises expire after a specified period of time and have to be repurchased and some require the payment of an annual fee in addition to the basic cost of the franchise. Despite such costs, there are many advantages to purchasing a franchise. Most importantly, the franchise holder gets the benefits of national advertising by the franchiser and a well-known product or service with a high degree of customer recognition. In most cases the franchise holder gets access to a ready-made clientele for a product or service that has a "track record" as a good seller. In addition, the purchase of the franchise includes guidelines for producing the product and running the business that are known to work. Managerial advice and assistance from the parent corporation, if needed, are also included as part of the franchise. However, franchise holders are subject to a great deal of supervision and regulation by the franchiser. Spot inspections, detailed rules to follow, and regular reports to be filed create a context in which independence and autonomy may be sacrificed in return for a reduction of risk and uncertainty. In an extreme sense, the franchisee is really an employee of the franchiser with a substantial investment at risk. At a minimum, the franchise business represents a compromise of the ideal of entrepreneurial independence.

The independent entrepreneur has of course given way to the salaried manager as the prototype occupation of the business world. The U.S. Bureau of the Census occupational category "executive, administrative, and managerial" comes closest to the kind of work we are dealing with here. In 1970, 7.5 percent of the labor force was classified this way and by 1980 this had increased to 10 percent.[27] In addition, the growth of government service organizations at all levels has created numerous managerial roles. For example, in 1980 there were 2,875,866 civilian federal government employees and 15.1 percent of them were classified as "administrators."[28] In 1981 state and local governments employed 4,665,000 people, 5.3 percent of whom were classified as "officials and administrators."[29] The work context of the manager is defined by the fact that the occupation is performed in a bureaucratic setting. Two related features of this context, power and conflict, are most salient.

Power is a key factor that defines the manager's responsibilities, places limits on what can and cannot be done, and specifies to whom the manager is responsible. Advancement within the organization is strongly affected by where managers stand in both the formal and informal power hierarchies of the organization.[30] Power has been defined in many ways but Robert Dahl has provided a very simple yet useful definition: "A has power over B to the extent that he can get B to do something B would not otherwise do."[31] While an emphasis on power calls our attention to the vertical dimension of organizations and their hierarchical structure, managers also are involved in struggles for power with other managers who are at the same horizontal level in the organization. Although individual managers derive power from the organizational positions they occupy, their actions and actual behavior may increase or decrease their official power. In addition, all organizations have an informal culture and system of social relationships which includes the unofficial distribution of power. Any given manager's formal power may be consistent or inconsistent with his or her informal power. Whether the manager is in a private or public organization, or one that manufactures goods or provides services, a continual concern with the acquisition and exercise of power dominates managerial work.[32]

Another major feature of the managerial work context is conflict. In a sense, conflict is a consequence of the unequal distribution of power and the quest for power.[33] Thus, managers are continually caught up in conflicts between individuals, groups, departments, and larger units within the organization as well as conflicts between the organization and other organizations. Although conflict can have many positive consequences and contribute to needed change in organizations, Theodore Caplow has suggested that excessive conflict and hostility can be detrimental to morale and productivity. He also emphasizes that the resolution of conflict is in fact one of the manager's major responsibilities.[34]

Another kind of conflict also pervades the context of managerial work. This is role conflict. In an attempt to describe what managers actually do, Henry Mintzberg has identified ten specific managerial roles that fall into three broad categories: interpersonal roles, informational roles, and decisional roles.[35] *Interpersonal* roles include such things as ceremonial activities, providing leadership through the recruitment and training of others, and serving as a liaison and go-between with others in the organization. In all of these activities the emphasis is on interpersonal relationships with other people. *Informational* roles include the collection and dissemination of information that others need to perform their jobs. Performing informational roles involves vertical communication (getting it from and passing it to those above and below one in the organization), horizontal communication (getting and passing information from and to those at the same level in the hierarchy), and external communication (communicating with significant individuals, groups, and publics outside the organization). *Decisional* roles include the taking of initiatives designed to enhance the status of the organization, reacting to external threats to the organization, allocating resources within the organization, and negotiating numerous decisions with a wide variety of individuals and groups.

In the performance of these roles, managers may experience role conflicts of various kinds. Conflict may arise from "role overload" where it is difficult if not impossible to meet all the expectations that descend upon the manager. Another type of role conflict is "inter-sender role conflict," a situation in which two or more people have conflicting expectations of the manager and it is not possible to satisfy them all. "Person-role conflict" occurs when role expectations are at odds with the manager's personal preferences, moral values, or needs. Another type of conflict is "inter-role conflict" where the expectations of the manager may conflict with another role (for example outside the organization) that she or he occupies. A final type of conflict is "intra-sender role conflict" where one other person has conflicting expectations of the manager. An example of this would be where the manager's organizational superior expects the manager to improve the quality of the department's output *and* simultaneously reduce production costs.[36] Clearly, not all managers will experience all of these types of conflict in the performance of all of their roles. However, the managerial work setting is one in which the potential for such conflicts is exceptionally high.

THE PROFESSIONAL WORK CONTEXT

Professional work has already been discussed at some length in chapter 2. However, there are several additional aspects of the professional work context that deserve consideration. A basic distinction needs to be made between the salaried and the self-employed professional. The former, usually located in a bureaucratic organization, is subject to a variety of contextual pressures and conflicts that will be treated in a later section of this chapter. The primary focus at this point is on the self-employed professional although some features to be discussed apply to both types.

An important feature of the professional work context comes from the fact that clients seek out and initiate contact with the professional. Professional services are sought when clients have a problem or need that they believe the professional can help to solve or meet. Consequently, the client is cast in a dependent relationship and the professional is able to maintain control over the amount, pace, and scheduling of his or her work. In other words, the professional has a great deal of autonomy in deciding what will be done, when and how it will be done, and how much will be done in a given period of time. In this respect, the professional and factory work contexts are at opposite poles of the autonomy-control dimension.[37] Independent professionals faced with clients who are in a position to "shop around"[38] or who serve a small and exclusive clientele[39] may lose some control over their work. When professionals are employed by organizations, their control does not necessarily diminish. Where organizations assign clients to the professional, the client's opportunity for choice and control is reduced and the professional's control over the client may actually be increased.[40]

Professional work has another distinctive feature: a complex, informal network of communication. Even among individuals who may be ostensibly in competition with each other, the professional colleague group represents a resource of advice and expertise upon which they may draw. Professional associations can and do serve this function. In addition, there exist informal networks that may be used in a wide variety of ways—from exchanging information on particular techniques to sharing information about career opportunities and the financial condition of potential clients. Professional networks also are a mechanism whereby professionals share with one another their judgements and evaluations of the strengths and weaknesses of their colleagues. While informal communication and evaluation systems often exist side by side with formal mechanisms, the distinctive feature of the professional work setting is that these networks transcend particular work organizations and communities, linking together individuals who are physically and spatially separated.

A closely related aspect of the professional work context can be best referred to as its "cosmopolitanism." Though employed by an organization (e.g., as a research scientist in a private company or government laboratory), the most important and compelling aspects of the professional's work life may occur outside of the organization in connection with the work of other members of the profession working in other organizations. The professional is linked through both formal associations and informal communication networks with colleagues on a regional, national, and often international basis. Drawn outward by these professional connections and away from an exclusive concern with the employing organization, the boundaries of the professional's work context are substantially broader than those of the farm, factory, office, or managerial setting.

A final feature of the professional work setting is the blurring of the distinction between work and nonwork life. Leisure time activities, for example, may involve many work elements. "Leisure" reading may amount to reading back issues of professional and technical journals that have piled up. "Vacations" may be planned around professional meetings and conferences. Given the unstandardized and nonroutine nature of professional work, it may become difficult to say when one is and is not working. While professional and managerial work may be similar insofar as they both involve "bringing the job home," this feature of the professional work context distinguishes it sharply from the factory and office contexts.

DEVIANT WORK SETTINGS

Deviant occupations have been discussed earlier under the topic of occupational socialization (chapter 4). While deviant work is in many ways similar to conventional forms of work, this section is concerned with highlighting some of its distinctive features.

Risks and hazards are a much more central and continuous part of work in deviant occupations as compared to conventional occupations. In the case of illegal occupations, the risks of detection and arrest are rather obvious. A good deal of the work may involve elaborate efforts to prevent an awareness of the fact that the work is occurring. Unlike people in conventional occupations, those engaged in illegal work do not have recourse to law enforcement agencies when they encounter risks. For example, the prostitute whose customer refuses to pay or who threatens or injures her cannot very easily seek the assistance of the police without running the risk of being arrested herself. Work that involves conning people out of their money or property poses a special risk in that the victim may detect the con before it is completed.

Consequently, deviant work requires the development of a great deal of skill in manipulating other people or what has been referred to as "dramaturgical" skill.[41] Thus, con artists must get their victims to trust them and maintain that trust until, and even after, the con has been completed. Fences may need to develop ways of concealing their illegal activities behind a legitimate front.[42] Prostitutes must develop ways of manipulating their customers so that they remain in control of the transaction. Such skills also become important in deviant occupations that are not illegal. Strippers, female impersonators, and other stage entertainers face the problem of dealing with audiences that are rowdy, boisterous, and even physically threatening. One of the recurring themes in studies of such occupations is the use of put-downs and insults to control and manipulate the audience.[43]

While occupational subcultures exist and perform a variety of functions throughout the occupational world, the deviant work setting is one in which dependence on the occupational subculture becomes pronounced. People in similar deviant occupations or in conventional occupations that serve them are turned to for protection, assistance, and advice in dealing with the special problems of deviant work noted above. Since conventional sources of support and assistance may be inaccessible, others in the occupation and related occupations become especially important. Thus, prostitutes become dependent on pimps, madames, lawyers, and bail bondsmen; and entertainers such as strippers become dependent on masters of ceremonies, bouncers, and other strippers. The sociological literature on crime provides numerous examples of such dependency networks and reciprocal involvements among criminals of all kinds.[44] Consequently, since those involved in deviant work are in conflict with conventional norms and values, the occupational subculture may become almost identical with the social world within which one's nonwork life is lived.

THE ORGANIZATIONAL CONTEXT OF WORK

Throughout this and preceding chapters there have been numerous references to organizations. Factories are organizations, both clerical and managerial work occur in organizations, and professionals are increasingly employed in organizations. Quite clearly, to talk about work in contemporary society is to talk about organizations. The study of organizations has become a full-fledged specialty in its own right, as was pointed out in chapter 1.[45] In this section, we will identify some of the major models and perspectives on organizations and examine some of their effects on individuals. In addition, we will deal with two issues that have received a good deal of research attention: the problems of professionals in organizations, and worker alienation and job satisfaction.

MODELS OF ORGANIZATIONS

Numerous models have been developed to analyze organizations.[46] W. Richard Scott has pointed out that all organizations have some common elements. These include a *social structure* (patterns of relationships among participants), *participants* (those who contribute to the organization), *goals* (the desired ends or objectives of organizational activity), *technology* (the processes by which work gets done), and an *environment* (from which the organization obtains resources and to which it must adapt).[47] Nevertheless, it is useful to distinguish between different models—rational system, natural system, and open system—since each calls our attention to different aspects of organizations and to different variables in the organizational work context that may affect individuals in different ways.

The Rational System Model

The *rational system model* of organizations is the one with which most people are familiar. It is epitomized by the work of the late nineteenth-early twentieth century German sociologist Max Weber.[48] Weber used the term "bureaucracy" to identify what he regarded to be the most efficient form of administrative organization. Subsequently, the term bureaucracy has been used almost interchangeably with or as a modifier of the term organization.

Perhaps the most important thing about this model is that organizations are seen as *goal-driven*. Organizations don't just "happen," evolving out of common interests and attractions among participants. They are explicitly created for the purpose of accomplishing some specified goal or goals. Different kinds of organizations have different kinds of goals: teaching people to read and write or to be doctors and lawyers (schools), waging wars (the military), making sick people well (hospitals), saving souls (churches), punishing criminals (courts and prisons), or making a profit (businesses).

Organizations also have explicit *rules and procedures*. The rules and procedures specify what is and is not to be done as well as when and how things should occur. They are the means by which goals are presumably achieved. They specify what is expected of people occupying positions in the organization.

A bureaucratic organization is a structure of *positions or offices*. The rules and procedures of an organization define how the offices in it are supposed to function regardless of the unique characteristics of the people who happen to be occupying those offices at a particular time. This frees the organization from dependence on the services of particular individuals and makes continuity over time simpler and easier. As individuals come and go, the office remains, and the expectations and functions associated with it give stability to the organization. This separation of person and office also contributes to heightened formality in organizations and to the development of impersonal relations since the office is the dominant reality and people are seen as only temporary incumbents or even sojourners moving through the organization's positions.

The structure of positions in organizations is based on task *specialization*. Specialization in the work people do is a major, long-term trend that has been going on since the beginnings of the industrial revolution. However, bureaucratic organizations independently foster, encourage, and nurture specialization. All kinds of tasks are broken down and subdivided into the smallest possible units. Specialization also limits the kinds of competencies required for various positions and the responsibilities that go along with them.

In this model of organizations, selection of personnel is supposed to occur on the basis of *technical qualifications* for the position and competence to perform the expectations of the office. Related to this is the idea that not only selection but also evaluation, the distribution of rewards, and promotion are supposed to occur on the basis of merit and universalistic standards. Tradition, inheritance, friendship, kinship, or personal likes and dislikes are supposed to make no difference. Filling jobs in public organizations on the basis of political patronage (in exchange for political favors) or in private organizations on the basis of nepotism (favoring relatives) would be a violation of the principles of competence and merit.

In the rational model, the *formalization* of relationships is an extremely important dimension of organizations.[49] The emphasis on the importance of the office rather than the person, set procedures, specialized tasks, and technical competence encourages formal, impersonal relationships among those who work in the organization and between the organization and its clients. People are supposed to interact with others on the basis of the responsibilities of their positions, not their personal feelings or opinions. They are supposed to keep their likes and dislikes out of their relationships with others in the organization.

The rational model emphasizes the importance of *hierarchy* in organizations. Hierarchy refers to the structure of ranked positions through which authority is exercised, and which determines the distribution of status, power, privileges, and rewards. In other words, bureaucratic organizations are small-scale stratification systems. As we go from the bottom to the top of organizations, the authority and responsibility vested in positions increase. Orders are passed down to successively lower levels until they reach the position where they are to be carried out. The subordinate's task is to carry out orders as precisely and efficiently as possible. To question the legitimacy or appropriateness of orders from organizational superiors would be a violation of the principle of hierarchy.

The Natural System Model

Where the rational system model presents a highly mechanistic and rational image of organizations, the *natural system* perspective downplays the importance of goals and the formal structure as the means for achieving those goals. The imagery of the natural system model involves a *biological analogy*. The overriding goal of organizations (like all living entities) becomes survival.[50] Organizations are seen as "continually changing in efforts to cope with environmental modifications."[51] Organizational change is less the result of rational planning than the consequence of the desire to survive.

The focus is on the *actual behavior of people*. According to Scott, "organizations are more than instruments for attaining narrowly defined goals; they are, fundamentally, social groups attempting to adapt to and survive in their particular circumstances."[52] With an emphasis on people rather than positions, personal preferences and affect become relevant. The development of the "human relations" school of organizational analysis reflects this focus.[53] The assumption is that the way in which the personal needs of people are met will make a difference in their behavior that is consequential for the organization.

Variables like *leadership* also become important. The rational model assumes that once people understand the expectations of their positions they will act in appropriate ways that contribute to the achievement of the organization's goals. However, the natural system model assumes that people need to be motivated to behave in appropriate ways. Thus, leadership style becomes a major consideration and concern. Such factors as how authoritarian or democratic leaders are is presumed to make a difference in the behavior of people and consequently in the performance of the organization.[54]

Another feature of the natural system model is an emphasis on the importance of *informal* ways of doing things that may at times conflict with, but at other times supplement, the formal structure. While the rational model sees the formal structure as the organizational reality, the natural system model sees two realities—the formal structure and the informal—and argues that the informal can be more important.[55] Informal authority, communications systems, procedures, and norms may be more important in determining what an organization accomplishes than is its formal structure. For example, groups develop informal norms regarding such basic things as how much work should be done in a given period of time. Level of productivity may be more a consequence of such informal norms than the result of how work is officially organized.[56] In addition, informal cliques may develop to initiate and promote or to block and undermine a wide variety of actions.[57]

The Open System Model

The *open system model* is yet a different way of thinking about organizations. Its most distinctive feature is a strong and primary emphasis on the *environment* within which organizations exist.[58] The rational model focuses entirely on the internal structure and inner workings of the organization. Consequently, it is often referred to as a "closed" system. Like natural systems, open systems are seen as changing in response to environmental changes and especially environmental threats.

The nature of the *equilibrium* that organizations are able to develop in relation to their environments is seen to be their crucial feature. Because of this, organizations develop specialized activities (and work roles) to deal with the environment. These are usually referred to as "boundary" and "adaptation" activities.[59] Organizations develop activities and roles that are concerned with *inputs* such as the raw materials and resources they need and the quality and quantity of the specialized labor skills and competencies they require. Other activities and roles may focus on increasing the environment's receptivity to the organization's *outputs* or whatever it produces. Thus, advertising and public relations would be examples of such activities. Above all, organizations are sensitive to potential changes in the environment that might affect either their inputs or outputs. From this perspective, organizations are not passive actors at the mercy of their environment. Rather they are continually involved in efforts to shape and change the environment and to adapt to what they cannot change.

The open system perspective also presents a different picture of the internal workings of organizations. The rational model presents a picture of highly integrated, hierarchically controlled organizations in which different parts are tightly linked and very responsive to each other. The open system image is nicely captured in the concept of "loose coupling."[60] This refers to the idea that different parts of an organization may be capable of fairly independent action, and that an organization may function satisfactorily without a great deal of internal integration and centralized control.[61] Loose coupling also suggests that discrepancies between official rules of an organization and the actual behavior of people may be quite normal and that there may be inconsistencies if not conflicts between the goals of individuals and groups and the goals of the organization. It also implies that the behavior of people may be only minimally related to their own goals.[62]

Where the rational system model sees organizations as a unitary entity, the open system model sees them as "a coalition of groups and interests" that have their own (sometimes different and sometimes competing) preferences and objectives.[63] Scott regards this feature of organizations as central to the open system model in his emphasis on organizations as "a coalition of shifting interest groups that develop goals by negotiation."[64] Thus, organizational goals (and by implication the procedures for attaining them) are "emergent" and continually changing rather than firm and invariably fixed. The idea of negotiation by diverse interest groups also suggests that organizational functioning may be largely a *political process* that relies heavily on the acquisition and use of power, lobbying activities, and a wide range of bargaining strategies that may not be recognized as part of the organization's formal decision-making apparatus.[65] Rather than being seen as an aberration, the model also suggests that organizational politics is an inherent and normal feature of organizations.

THE IMPACT OF ORGANIZATIONS ON INDIVIDUALS

In our discussion of work contexts the effects of organizations on their participants has been dealt with implicitly and tangentially. In this section our goal is to make these effects more explicit. Both negative and positive consequences need to be identified.

The organizational work context clearly can be an impersonal one. Where organizations do in fact operate according to the rational model, an emphasis on the office, formality in the relations between people, strict rules, standardized procedures, and explicit lines of communication can indeed create a very impersonal atmosphere. A good deal of the popular negative image of bureaucracy focuses on that aspect of organizations.[66]

Organizations also produce a tension between the needs and desires of individuals to be creative and innovative in their work and the organizational need for order, predictability, and conformity to established ways of doing things. The degree to which such tension is generated will vary from one organization to another. But, an emphasis on following the rules and performing narrow, specialized roles can create pressures that lead individuals to suppress their creativity and originality in favor of a "don't rock the boat" attitude. The irony is that organizations also need creativity and originality of thought and action if they are going to thrive. This tension is nicely illustrated in an analysis of some of America's most successful businesses by Thomas J. Peters and Robert H. Waterman, Jr. One characteristic of what they regard as the best-managed firms is a "simultaneous looseness and tightness" where people are allowed to be autonomous and innovative but at the same time disciplined and subject to fairly close supervision.[67]

The hierarchical structure of authority also produces important impacts on individuals. Decisions and policies that originate at the top of organizational hierarchies are not usually subject to questioning by those at lower levels. Such decisions and policies have a great deal of legitimacy or inherent rightness about them. Subordinates are supposed to do what needs to be done to accomplish the goals set by those above them. In many organizations an uncritical following of orders and directives from superiors is a large part of the definition of good, competent performance. To the extent that people are evaluated on and rewarded for their obedience, it is in their self-interest not to question what they are told to do. The Watergate break-in and subsequent cover-up during the administration of President Richard M. Nixon illustrate this orientation. In the Nuremberg war crimes trials following World War II, the defense offered by middle- and low-ranking military and civilian officials who ran the concentration camps of the Third Reich and carried out the execution of millions of Jews and other Eastern European minorities was essentially a bureaucratic one. Their defense was basically that they were "just following orders." The good bureaucrat in this case did not question the content of those orders.[68] While these are admittedly dramatic and extreme examples, the principle holds in more mundane situations. The nurse who questions a doctor's orders or fails to follow them in a hospital may jeopardize not only her job but her career. The foreman whose work unit fails to meet production goals regardless of the hazards involved may be in for a poor evaluation or worse.

Another negative consequence of organizations is the development of what Robert K. Merton has called the "bureaucratic personality."[69] Here the problem is that bureaucratic emphasis on discipline and conformity to the rules can lead to overconformity. People can come to value the rules so much that the rules replace the goals they were originally intended to achieve. The means become ends in themselves. In medicine there is a bit of "gallows humor" in the form of the statement "the patient died but the operation was a success." Never mind the outcome, the proper procedures were followed. Similar orientations may develop in education. As long as the lesson plan is followed, it may not matter that the students didn't learn anything. According to Merton, an extreme concern with procedures can lead to timidity (never do anything that isn't specified in the rules) and conservatism (never do anything that sets a precedent). As an orientation, the bureaucratic personality seems to be at the heart of much of the negative public image of bureaucracies. Inflexibility, an unwillingness to "bend" the rules a bit, and little concern with solving the client's problem if it doesn't fit the procedures are common criticisms of organizations.

Despite the negative consequences of organizations, there are some positive features that need to be noted. For example, standardization *simplifies life* in organizations. Once procedures become established, the amount of new learning that needs to occur is reduced. As people's careers take them to new organizations, they carry with them a repertoire of skills and understandings about how organizations function that reduces the amount of time needed to figure out how things are done in their new organization. Over time, following established practices reduces the need to "reinvent the wheel."

The organizational emphasis on positions and offices helps to maintain continuity over time. As individuals come and go, the organization persists. Combined with the general organizational emphasis on putting things in writing, this helps create a situation where proof that a particular policy was to be followed, a particular decision was made, or that a particular event occurred does not depend on the memories of individuals who may no longer be in the organization.

For all their negative consequences, some aspects of bureaucracy, such as formality, impersonality, and the emphasis on technical competence, offer individuals a degree of *protection* from arbitrary and capricious action and evaluation. Evaluation by organizational superiors is supposed to be done on the basis of universalistic standards and accomplishments rather than personal likes and dislikes. In a more general way, the limited, and often written, responsibilities of positions place constraints on what incumbents can legitimately be asked to do or prohibited from doing.

PROFESSIONALS IN ORGANIZATIONS

The distinctive problems of professionals in organizations as well as the problems encountered by organizations that employ them have received a great deal of attention from sociologists who study occupations and from managers who deal with professionals. Interest in this topic has been spurred by the fact that more and more professionals are becoming salaried employees of organizations as self-employment in the professions has decreased. In the decades ahead, the problems posed by the employment of professionals in organizations will become increasingly common.

The basic issue revolves around *conflict.* Conflict is implied by several diametrically opposed principles around which professions and organizations are structured. Professions place a premium on autonomy while organizations emphasize the importance of rules, regulations, and procedures. There are also differences in how work is controlled. In organizations, control is located in the responsibilities of the offices that make up the hierarchy. Professions emphasize peer control located in the judgements, evaluations, and decisions of the colleague group.

Joseph H. Fichter has pointed out several other differences.[70] In organizations, leadership is located in formally defined leadership positions while in the professions it is dependent upon the demonstration of competence and expertise. Organizations encourage the standardization of procedures to cover a range of different types of cases. Professions, on the other hand, emphasize the uniqueness of each case and the development of appropriate procedures to fit the case that reflect the professional's best judgement. In a sense, organizations mandate the application of existing procedures while professions see the development of procedures on a case by case basis as more appropriate. Another difference is that responsibility in organizations is corporate responsibility. It is located in the office, not the person. Professions, however, emphasize the responsibility of the individual practitioner. As has already been pointed out, organizations foster formal, impersonal relationships but the professions are organized around the principle of close colleague relations. The professional community discussed in chapter 2 implies a sense of involvement quite different from the atmosphere of bureaucratic organizations. Finally, while bureaucracies stress service and loyalty to the organization and the attainment of organizational goals, professions stress service to the client and loyalty to the colleague group.

W. Richard Scott has also identified potential areas of conflict between organizations and professionals that are similar to those noted by Fichter.[71] Professionals are fundamentally resistant to bureaucratic rules as a result of their socialization to the principle of autonomy. They also tend to reject bureaucratic standards in favor of professional standards, especially when the two are in conflict. Professionals also are resistant to bureaucratic supervision, again because of the professional emphasis on independence and individual responsibility. Scott argues that conflict also arises over the professional's "conditional loyalty" to the organization. Professionals often view the organization as a means for accomplishing their professional goals. Loyalty to the organization may depend on its ability to facilitate the professional's objectives.

A variety of research has been done on the problems and modes of adaptation of professionals in organizations. There are a variety of forms that conflict takes and a variety of adaptations. Leonard Reissman conducted one of the first studies in this area.[72] He distinguished between what he called the "professional" and "bureaucratic" orientations of forty middle-level civil service workers. The professionally oriented looked upon their jobs as only a temporary place in which to pursue their professional interests. Reissman developed a continuum with the "functional bureaucrat" at one end and the "job bureaucrat" at the other. The functional bureaucrat was oriented toward and sought recognition from outside professional groups. The job bureaucrat was completely oriented to the organization and totally immersed within it. Between these two extremes were the "specialist bureaucrat" who was similar to the functional bureaucrat but more identified with the organization, and the "service bureaucrat" who was identified with the organization but also sought recognition from groups outside of it.

A landmark study on this topic was done by Alvin W. Gouldner who was interested in the professional commitment and organizational loyalty of faculty members at a small liberal arts college.[73] He pointed out that there is a tension between the organization's need for professional expertise and its need for loyalty. Gouldner distinguished between two types of role orientations among faculty. The "cosmopolitan" has little loyalty to the college, a strong commitment to specialized skills, and a strong identification with outside reference groups representing a professional specialty. The "local" orientation involves strong loyalty to the college, a weak commitment to specialized skills, and a strong identification with reference groups located within the organization. Cosmopolitans were less likely than locals to accept organizational rules. They were mainly concerned with their own research and scholarly activities and with developments in their own disciplines. In contrast, the main involvements and concerns of locals were with the internal workings of the college. The distinction between cosmopolitans and locals is useful for looking at issues of organizational loyalty and identification in all kinds of organizations, not just colleges.

Harold L. Wilensky developed a different typology to describe the orientations of professional staff experts employed by labor unions.[74] He used the term "professional service" orientation to refer to those who had little loyalty to the union per se but were oriented to some colleague group outside the organization. Other professionals were described as "careerists." These were people who strongly identified with the union and planned a long term career in it. The "politico" was a person who also was strongly identified with the union but was mainly concerned with attaining power and influence in the organization as an end in itself. A final orientation was represented by the "missionary" who identified not so much with the organization as with an abstract concept of "the labor movement" as well as with external religious and political reference groups.

Another study by Peter M. Blau and W. Richard Scott found substantial differences in the behavior of social workers in a county welfare office that were related to their relative organizational and professional identification.[75] Those social workers who were more strongly identified with the social work profession were more likely to deviate from administrative procedures and violate organizational rules in order to provide the best possible services to the agency's clients. On the other hand, the less professionally oriented social workers tended to adhere more strictly to the organization's rules and procedures.

The studies reviewed thus far do not explain why these different orientations and identifications develop. However, a study of nurses by Ronald G. Corwin suggests that professional socialization may play a role in these differences.[76] The focus of Corwin's study was on contradictions between the highly professional conceptions of the nursing role developed in the course of training and the hospital's bureaucratic emphasis on strict adherence to rules and procedures. Nurses trained in hospitals (diploma programs) were more familiar with hospital rules and were less likely to question hospital routines and regulations. Following graduation, they retained a strong loyalty to the hospital while their professional allegiance declined. On the other hand, nurses trained in collegiate programs independent of the hospital were more likely to question organizational rules and regulations. They maintained strong professional role conceptions after graduation while simultaneously increasing their loyalty to and identification with the hospital once they were employed in it.

Research on a number of different professionals employed in organizations reveals frequent and sometimes dramatic cases of conflict. Industrial scientists are often in conflict with their employing organizations over a number of issues. These include such things as recruitment, where there may be conflict over appropriate credentials for new employees as well as disagreement about who should evaluate those credentials. For example, administrators may want to evaluate prospective scientists on the basis of their managerial potential, something the research scientists already in the organization may care little about. In addition, conflict may arise over whether planning groups should be made up exclusively of scientists or whether they should also include administrators. Qualifications for leadership often become another contentious issue. Scientists are likely to press for the person with the best scientific credentials, while administrators are likely to favor the person with the strongest managerial skills. Another area of conflict is control over the results of research. Occasions may arise where scientists want to share their findings with colleagues through publication, but the organization wants to get the maximum benefit from the research by keeping it secret as long as possible.[77]

Psychiatrists in the military provide another example of professional-organizational conflict. Arlene K. Daniels reports that military psychiatrists often find their professional judgement in conflict with military rules about separation from the service as well as military manpower needs.[78] They are frequently asked to make diagnoses to justify the decisions of commanding officers or military courts. The styles and preferences of commanding officers at a particular time and place also become relevant. Some may give psychiatrists considerable leeway, while others may place great constraints on them. In general, the military psychiatrist becomes a "captive professional."

Physicians employed by private businesses also experience conflict in a number of ways. In a study of Canadian "company doctors" Vivienne Walters found several areas in which there is pressure to compromise professional judgement in order to accomplish organizational ends.[79] For example, they are pressured to minimize absenteeism and adopt management's view that workers are malingering. When doing preemployment physicals, they are encouraged to err on the conservative side and weed out "bad risks" where there is any question about the applicant's health. In other cases management may simply ignore or reject the physician's diagnosis or advice. Bitter disputes arise over work-related illnesses and injuries that may qualify an employee for worker's compensation. It is obviously in management's interest to keep the diagnosis of problems and company responsibility as low as possible, and in the worker's interest to get as generous an evaluation as possible. Thus, the physician is caught in cross-pressures that can lead to the compromising of purely medical judgements. Another dispute where company doctors are caught in the middle involves health hazards in the workplace. The union creates pressures to make the workplace as risk-free as possible, while management seeks an "acceptable" level of risk. Again, the physician's medical judgements are subject to distortion and misuse in such a highly politicized context.

Is Professional-Organizational Conflict Inevitable?

The professional and organizational models suggest a high potential for conflict and there is ample evidence that it occurs, as the foregoing examples illustrate. However, there are a number of reasons for questioning the idea that professional-organizational conflict is inevitable or endemic in all organizations.

George Ritzer has pointed out that there are some professions that exist only within the structure of bureaucratic organizations.[80] Examples would be the military and the priesthood. In these cases professionalization and bureaucratization go hand-in-hand and it really does not make much sense to talk about professional-organizational conflict.

In addition, there are many different kinds of organizations that include professionals and they vary considerably in how professionals are incorporated into them. For example, Amitai Etzioni distinguishes between three different kinds of organizations in which professionals are located.[81] One type is the *professional organization* where at least half of the members are professionals and organizational goals are compatible if not identical with those of the professional employees. A second type are *service organizations* that provide facilities and services for but do not actually employ professionals. The prime example here would be hospitals with which physicians are "affiliated." Since they are not employees of the hospital they are subject to only minimal organizational controls. Presumably, the potential for conflict would be low in such cases. There are also *nonprofessional organizations* in which professional units may perform specialized staff functions of a service or advisory nature. The physician in industry discussed above would be an example as would be the legal department of a manufacturing concern. In such organizational arrangements, the potential for conflict would be greater than in the other two types.

W. Richard Scott also has pointed out that there can be considerable variation in the extent to which professionals have discretion to act within professional organizations. Accordingly, he makes a distinction between *autonomous* and *heteronomous* professional organizations.[82] In autonomous professional organizations a great deal of responsibility is delegated to professional employees for such things as setting goals and deciding how to achieve them, as well as establishing performance standards and seeing that they are maintained. In effect, the professionals are permitted to organize themselves. They are not permitted to run everything, however. Rather, clear boundaries are established that distinguish the areas over which professionals have jurisdiction from those that are under the control of administrators. Examples of such organizations would be general hospitals, psychiatric hospitals, elite colleges and universities, and scientific research organizations, particularly those involved in basic research. In heteronomous professional organizations the subordination of professionals to administrators is explicit. They are granted little autonomy and when they are it is only for a limited range of activities. Professional employees are subject to administrative controls and routine supervision. Examples would be public organizations such as libraries, elementary and secondary schools, and social service agencies, as well as private organizations such as small colleges sponsored by religious denominations, engineering companies, applied research companies, and accounting firms.

Richard H. Hall has taken Scott's typology an additional step by pointing out that the autonomous-heteronomous distinction may be made within organizations as well as between them. His study of eleven professional groups in a wide variety of organizations found that there is variation in professional attitudes as well as the degree of bureaucratization. Hall's research supported the validity of the autonomous-heteronomous distinction. He also found that there were professional departments in nonprofessional organizations that were less bureaucratized than some of the professional organizations.[83]

Other analyses of professionals in organizations also question the inevitability of conflict and suggest some ways in which it has been resolved. Eugene Litwak has argued that there are cases where elements of the professional and bureaucratic models have been synthesized and that it makes sense to talk about "professional bureaucracies."[84] Erwin O. Smigel's study of prestigious Wall Street law firms concluded that they fit the idea of a professional bureaucracy in many ways.[85] Similarly, research on accountants in major accounting firms indicates that they are given a good deal of autonomy and are freed from many routine administrative responsibilities.[86]

A final view of the issue makes the point that professionals often are able to negotiate and shape the organizational structures within which they work. Using hospitals as their example, Rue Bucher and Joan Stelling argue that organizations are a political arena in which professionals negotiate with others to create definitions of their roles and responsibilities. New structures and working units may be created by professionals on the basis of their judgement of what is needed rather than by having them imposed by administrators at the top of the organizational hierarchy. They emphasize that different groups of professionals within an organization may be in competition with one another and that setting goals and acquiring the resources to achieve them are routine, ongoing processes that more often than not involves conflict. However, it is through the process of political conflict that new realities are continually being negotiated.[87] A similar point has been made by J. Kenneth Benson who sees professional-organizational conflict as but one example of many contradictions that exist in organizations. The ongoing life of organizations involves continual change, compromise, and negotiations of all kinds, including the place of professionals within it.[88]

WORK ALIENATION AND JOB SATISFACTION

There are few topics that have captured the imagination and attention of sociologists who study work as much as alienation and job satisfaction have. Unfortunately, alienation and job dissatisfaction are often discussed as if they were the same thing. As we will see, alienation refers to structural characteristics of work and the workplace, while job satisfaction and dissatisfaction refer to the sentiments, feelings, and attitudes that workers have toward their jobs. To complicate things further, some research on alienation has focused on sentiments and feelings of alienation.

Alienation

The concept of alienation has a long history ranging from the writings of Karl Marx to the research of contemporary social scientists. Marx's ideas about alienation apply mainly to the conditions of factory labor under capitalism. According to Marx, there are several ways in which work is alienating. There is alienation from the work *process*, alienation from the *product* of work, alienation from *oneself*, and alienation from *others*. These several meanings are illustrated in the following quotation from Marx's *Economic and Philosophical Manuscripts*, originally published in 1844:

> What then do we mean by the alienation of labor? First, that the work he performs is extraneous to the worker, that is, it is not personal to him, it is not part of his nature; therefore he does not fulfill himself in work, but actually denies himself; feels miserable rather than content, cannot freely develop his physical and mental powers, but instead becomes physically exhausted and mentally debased... Its [work's] alien character therefore is revealed by the fact that when no physical or other compulsion exists, work is avoided like the plague... Finally, the alienated character of work for the worker is shown by the fact that the work he does is not his own, but another's and that at work he belongs not to himself, but to another.[89]

In Marx's view, human beings are made for work. It is the most natural activity in which they can engage. But the structure of capitalist society (which is in effect the cause of alienation) interposes an artificial barrier between workers and all aspects of their work. The key factor involved in the generation of alienation is loss of control by workers over the work they do.

Marx's view of the alienation of labor under capitalism was extended by Max Weber who regarded all forms of bureaucracy as alienating. While Marx emphasized the alienation of labor through the production process, Weber saw a potential for alienation in all bureaucratically organized work settings. In this sense, Marx's concern with alienation as something inherent in the worker's separation from the means of production is for Weber but a special case of a more general phenomenon. Hans H. Gerth and C. Wright Mills comment on Weber's perspective with the statement that:

> Marx's emphasis upon the wage worker as being "separated from the means of production" becomes, in Weber's perspective, merely one case of a universal trend. The modern soldier is equally separated from the means of violence, the scientist from the means of inquiry, and the civil servant from the means of administration.[90]

From this perspective, hierarchical control, separation of person and position, an emphasis on procedures, and other characteristics of bureaucracies are conditions of work that constitute an alienating work setting. In particular, specialization is a major factor since it focuses attention on only part of the work process and makes the connection between work activities and a finished product (or organizational goals) tenuous at best.

Melvin Seeman's now classic essay, "On the Meaning of Alienation," represented a turning point in the study of alienation by American sociologists.[91] Drawing on both Marx's and Weber's ideas, Seeman did two things. He transformed alienation from a structural property of work to an internal, social-psychological property of individuals.[92] In addition, he defined several types of alienation in ways that encouraged empirical research on the topic.[93]

Seeman identified five varieties of alienation. *Powerlessness* refers to a sense of having little control over events and being dominated by other people and events; *meaninglessness* is a situation where people are uncertain about what they should believe and their personal and social worlds become incomprehensible; *normlessness* is a belief that socially unapproved means are necessary to achieve goals; *isolation* involves giving low value to or rejecting goals and beliefs that are typically valued in the society; and *self-estrangement* refers to engaging in behavior for its extrinsic or future rewards rather than because it is intrinsically rewarding. Although they are all relevant to work in some degree, Seeman has argued that powerlessness and self-estrangement are *most* relevant to the study of alienation in the workplace.[94]

Several critics have taken issue with this "psychologizing" of the concept of alienation.[95] However, as Kai Erikson has pointed out, it is essential to deal with the reaction of workers to alienating work as well as with the nature of the work itself.[96] Furthermore, several analysts have argued that there is a subjective as well as objective dimension to Marx's original conception of alienation.[97]

Research on alienation has used a variety of strategies and methodologies ranging from case studies of particular industries and work organizations to surveys of workers in different industries. Given that the modern assembly line contains characteristics associated with alienating work (specialization, external control, and the like), it is not surprising that a good deal of research has focused on the assembly line worker, especially in the automobile industry.

Several early studies of automobile assembly line workers concluded that they experience a high level of alienation. Workers in Charles R. Walker and Robert H. Guest's study made the following comments:

> The bad thing about assembly lines is that the line keeps moving. If you have a little trouble with a job, you can't take the time to do it right. . . on the line you're geared to the line. You don't dare stop. If you get behind, you have a hard time catching up.[98]

In this case the workers' ability to control the content and pace of their work is clearly in the hands of others. Work is, in effect, controlled by the line. This study, as well as Ely Chinoy's study of automobile workers, suggests a high degree of powerlessness in this work setting.[99]

There is a strong implication in these studies that the repetitiousness of assembly line work produces sentiments very close to what has been called meaninglessness. A worker in the Walker and Guest study commented on this:

> There is nothing more discouraging than having a barrel beside you with 10,000 bolts in it and using them all up. Then you get a barrel with another 10,000 bolts and you know every one of those 10,000 bolts has to be picked up and put in exactly the same place as the last 10,000 bolts.[100]

Chinoy also concluded that work on the assembly line produces self-estrangement. Work activities are not engaged in for their own sake but in order to obtain some extrinsic goal. He indicated that automobile assembly line workers have few opportunities to engage in work that is intrinsically interesting and satisfying. Rather, work is done in order to obtain money, a clearly extrinsic reward. Other studies support this point and suggest that skill level may be an important source of variation in the degree to which alienation of this kind is experienced. Chris Argyris' study of workers of different skill levels illustrates this variation. Compared to those of high skill, low-skill workers in a manufacturing concern performing simpler, more routine jobs expressed a lower sense of self-worth and a greater emphasis on the importance of material rewards.[101]

Although assembly line work has been used as an appropriate symbol of modern industrial work, there are clearly differences in the organization of skilled and semiskilled work. An interset in the effect on alienation of variations in the level and kind of technology found in the work setting was the impetus for what has become perhaps the most influential study of work and alienation. This is Robert Blauner's study of workers in four different industries with very different technologies—

printing, textiles, automobile assembly, and chemical processing.[102] Blauner concluded that there is a great deal of variation in both the kind and degree of alienation that people experience as a result, apparently, of differences in technology, as well as differences in the division of labor, the organization of the industry, and the economic structure of the industry.

For example, printers experience little powerlessness. Working with a highly skilled craft technology, they have a great deal of freedom and discretion in terms of the pace of the work, movement about the workplace, and supervision. Meaninglessness is also low since the printer works with an unstandardized product and quickly sees results in the form of a finished product. According to Blauner, printers have a strong sense of community, and this makes for little isolation and self-estrangement since the occupational community fosters both pride and a sense of involvement in the work. On balance, Blauner concluded that alienation was low among printers.

Textile workers, however, experience a higher degree of powerlessness. Movement about the work area is restricted, the pace of work is dictated and controlled by the rhythm of the looms, and there is close supervision. Meaninglessness is not too great since there is variety in the work and specific work activities are closely tied to a finished product. Textile workers in this study experienced little isolation due to a great deal of homogeneity in their backgrounds and the location of the mill in a relatively small town. Self-estrangement was also minimal since the workers' low educational level and their rural backgrounds led them to place little emphasis on self-expression.

The auto workers, not surprisingly, were relatively high on all aspects of alienation. The continuous flow of work with little interruption, predetermined techniques and standards, as well as restrictions on physical movement contribute to a high level of powerlessness. The repetitiousness of their work and the fact that the workers make only a small contribution to the finished product result in a high degree of meaninglessness. Isolation is also high due to the heterogeneous backgrounds of the workers and the high level of anonymity in the work setting. Both monotony and the lack of challenge contribute to self-estrangement with the paycheck as the primary motivation to work.

The chemical plant workers are in a setting that has a continuous-process technology. They are required to maintain a high degree of mental and visual alertness as they move about checking on a variety of equipment. Blauner concludes that they experience few feelings of powerlessness because of their freedom of movement, their sense of control over the quality of the product, and their ability to control the pace of their work. Meaninglessness is also low since workers are able to see a connection between their work and the quality of the finished product. Supervision is minimal and flexible, and there are strong informal work groups that minimize feelings of isolation. Self-estrangement is also low due to a strong sense of involvement in the work and the opportunity for variety through movement to different jobs over time.

Blauner's work clearly demonstrates that differences in technology result in variation in the degree to which alienation is experienced. Alienation tends to be low at the two extremes of technological sophistication—a craft industry and a continuous-process industry—and highest at the intermediate technological level (the textile and auto plant). These findings have come to be known as the "inverted U" hypothesis.

There have been a large number of studies of alienation that have followed the lead provided by Blauner.[103] Of special interest are those that have attempted to replicate or extend his basic findings. Jon Shepard studied workers in craft, assembly line, and continuous-process industries.[104] He also found the same "inverted U" relationship between technology and alienation. That is, alienation was low in craft and continuous process industries, but high in assembly line work. Shepard also looked at the relationship between technology and alienation among white-collar workers and found a similar relationship. Alienation was lowest for those working with computers compared to business machine operators and those doing nonmechanical tasks.

Another study of 110 New Jersey factories representing a range of industries and technologies also tested the "inverted U" hypothesis. Using turnover rates as a proxy for alienation, general support was found for this technology-alienation relationship. The more advanced and sophisticated the technology, the lower the rate of turnover (and by implication the lower the alienation).[105] This study also contains an important analysis of printers. Printing has undergone some major changes in recent years as computerization has replaced the need for conventional typesetting skills. Frank M. Hull and his colleagues studied 245 New York City newspaper printers who had been retrained to use the new computerized technology. There appears to have been no real increase in alienation among these retrained printers. In fact, they report that the new equipment gives them more control over their output. They are still able to control the pace of their work and direct supervision remains low. In a sense, the new technology has created new skills to be mastered and used in a job that retains many of its craft qualities.

There has also been a replication of the study of alienation among textile workers. Blauner's study was based on data collected in the late 1940s. There have been many changes in the textile industry since then, including less local and more corporate ownership, greater heterogeneity in the labor force as black employment has increased, and technological changes. In 1980, Jeffrey Leiter surveyed workers in four spinning-weaving mills in a small North Carolina town. Comparing his findings to those of Blauner, Leiter concludes that there has been a modest increase in alienation. Workers were most alienated in terms of powerlessness, and the lack of control over their work seems to be a major concern.[106]

Job Satisfaction

At the beginning of this section the need to distinguish between alienation and job satisfaction was pointed out. Unfortunately, this distinction is not nearly as sharp and clear in the research literature as our presentation here would suggest. Job satisfaction has been measured with questions that sound very much as though they were intended to measure alienation, and studies purporting to deal with alienation simply have asked workers how satisfied and dissatisfied they are with their jobs.[107] Job dissatisfaction does not imply the kind of deep-seated malaise suggested by the concept of alienation. The imagery of degradation and dehumanization so central to the original concept of alienation has a much milder and more superficial counterpart in the concept of job dissatisfaction.

Just how satisfied people are with their jobs is a matter of some debate and uncertainty. How the concept is defined and how it is measured can lead to different conclusions. Kurt Tausky has pointed out that research on the topic has taken two approaches.[108] One is to assess global or overall satisfaction with a person's job. The other is to ask how satisfied people are with particular aspects of their jobs, such as earnings, or promotion opportunities. Tausky analyzed national survey data from the years 1958 through 1982 and found that overall (or global) satisfaction ranges from 80 to 90 percent. He found no differences between men and women in overall job satisfaction but discovered that black workers are less satisifed with their jobs than are whites. When it comes to reactions to specific aspects of their jobs, workers at all status levels express discontent with extrinsic things such as pay, fringe benefits, job security, and promotion opportunities. Blue-collar workers are more likely than others to also be dissatisfied with the intrinsic aspects of their jobs. They find their jobs less interesting and challenging, and offering little autonomy and few chances to develop their abilities.

One approach to assessing job satisfaction is to ask people if they would go into the same work if they could begin their work lives over. In one survey only 24 percent of blue-collar workers said they would take the same jobs again, compared to 43 percent of white-collar workers. Only 16 percent of the unskilled auto workers and 21 percent of the unskilled steel workers said they would choose the same jobs. Skilled blue-collar workers were somewhat more positive, with 52 percent of the printers and 41 percent of the skilled auto workers and steel workers choosing the same job. However, among professionals, including professors, lawyers, and scientists, 75 to 90 percent said they would go into the same work.[109] H. Roy Kaplan has questioned the validity of this strategy for measuring job satisfaction. He suggests that when workers are asked if they would want the same jobs if they could start over, they really respond in terms of their overall life aspirations, not just their present job satisfaction.[110]

Occupational status has generally been found to be directly related to job satisfaction as the findings reported above illustrate. Tausky's analysis of national survey data for 1982 also found higher levels of satisfaction among professionals (53 percent "very satisfied") and managers (63 percent "very satisfied") compared to semiskilled and unskilled workers (37 and 39 percent "very satisfied" respectively).[111] Edward J. Walsh has challenged this generalization and suggested that there may be aspects of relatively low-status, low-prestige jobs that provide work experiences and opportunities for activities that are in fact satisfying.[112] Walsh studied garbage collectors, city parks department workers, bartenders, barbers, mail carriers, high school teachers, and university professors. He also distinguished between intrinsic satisfaction (how much people enjoyed the work they did) and extrinsic satisfaction (whether or not they felt that they were receiving fair pay for their work). The professors reported the lowest intrinsic dissatisfaction but, surprisingly, the bartenders and barbers were also low on intrinsic dissatisfaction. Despite their status differences, garbage collectors, mail carriers, and high school teachers expressed very similar levels of intrinsic job dissatisfaction. On the measure of extrinsic satisfaction (pay), barbers were most likely to express dissatisfaction and garbage collectors were least likely to do so. Walsh suggests that opportunities for self-direction among barbers and bartenders contributes to their low intrinsic job dissatisfaction, and cautions against sweeping generalizations about occupational status and job satisfaction.

In addition to status and prestige, age has also been found to be related to job satisfaction. In general, younger workers tend to be more dissatisfied with their jobs than older workers.[113] One possibility is that younger workers actually have poorer jobs that improve with age as they experience career mobility. It is also possible that this relationship reflects a gap or discrepancy between expectations and the reality of work. Young people are socialized to expect a great deal from work, and actual work experiences early in their careers may be disappointing. As workers age, they may come to expect less from their work, resulting in a decrease in their reported job dissatisfaction.

Currently, there is a great deal of interest in the issue of the relative importance of intrinsic and extrinsic factors for job satisfaction, a distinction made by Walsh and noted above.[114] There is evidence to support the importance of both. People who are satisfied with their work mention things like variety, responsibility, and interesting tasks as things they like about their work while those who are dissatisfied mention extrinsic things like pay and fringe benefits among their dislikes.[115] The opportunity for "occupational self-direction," a distinctively intrinsic aspect of work also seems to be a crucial factor in job satisfaction.[116] Using data from the national 1977 "Quality of Employment Survey," Douglas M. Eichar and John L. P. Thompson found that worker autonomy, job complexity, and task variety were positively related to job satisfaction.[117] There is also no doubt that extrinsic features of work affect job satisfaction. Patricia Voydanoff found that both intrinsic and extrinsic aspects of work were important in her analysis of a national sample of workers in a wide variety of occupations. She reports that job satisfaction is most influenced by intrinsic job characteristics among professionals and those in skilled craft occupations and concludes that the relative importance of intrinsic and extrinsic factors may be different in different occupational groups.[118]

SUMMARY

Diversity and variety in the settings in which people work have been the themes of this chapter. Our discussion of agriculture, factory work, and office work identified some of the major changes that have occurred as American society has been transformed from an agricultural to a post-industrial society. Entrepreneurial, managerial, professional, and deviant work contexts further illustrate the variety that exists. In the decades ahead, growth in the service sector of the economy will mean that office, managerial, and professional work contexts will be those in which increasing numbers of people work.

Since organizations have become the setting in which more and more work occurs, a great deal of attention has been devoted to this dimension of work. As we have seen, different theories and models of organizations call attention to different aspects of organizational life and their effects on individuals who work in them. Organizations make unique demands on workers at all levels of the hierarchy and they constrain and control their opportunities. The increasing employment of professionals in organizations creates conflict over issues of loyalty, the internal division of labor, and the authority of professionals vis-a-vis managers, although there is debate about the inevitability of that conflict.

The issues of alienation and job satisfaction, a major interest of sociologists who study work, highlights the negative side of work and work settings in contemporary society. While new technologies offer the promise of making work more interesting and challenging, many work activities will remain boring, monotonous, and inherently uninteresting. Satisfaction with and enjoyment of work are coming to depend heavily on finding ways of giving workers discretion, choice, variety, opportunities for exercising their judgement, and above all control over the work they do. Accomplishing this will depend on reversing the processes of specialization and close organizational control that have dominated our thinking about how work should be organized.

NOTES

1. U.S. Bureau of the Census, *Statistical Abstract of the United States, 1985* (Washington, D.C.: U.S. Government Printing Office, 1984), 631, table 1105.
2. U.S. Bureau of the Census, *Statistical Abstract of the United States, 1984* (Washington, D.C.: U.S. Government Printing Office, 1983), 417, table 693.
3. U.S. Bureau of the Census, *Statistical Abstract,* 1985, 403, table 676.
4. Rex R. Campbell, "Crisis on the Farm," *American Demographics* 7 (October 1985): 30–33.
5. U.S. Bureau of the Census, *Statistical Abstract,* 1985, 632, table 1109.
6. U.S. Bureau of the Census, *Statistical Abstract,* 1984, 651, table 1140; and U.S. Bureau of the Census, *Statistical Abstract,* 1985, 634, table 1112.
7. Wayne D. Rasmussen, "The Mechanization of Agriculture," *Scientific American* 247 (1982): 48–61.
8. William F. Whyte, *Men at Work* (Homewood, Ill.: Dorsey Press, 1961), 179.
9. Robert J. Flanagan, Robert S. Smith, and Ronald G. Ehrenberg, *Labor Economics and Labor Relations* (Glenview, Ill.: Scott, Foresman, 1984), 334.
10. U.S. Bureau of the Census, *Statistical Abstract,* 1985, 424, table 709.
11. Philip M. Doyle, "Area Wage Surveys Shed Light on Declines in Unionization," *Monthly Labor Review* 108 (September 1985): 13–20.
12. Jon M. Shepard, *Automation and Alienation: A Study of Office and Factory Workers* (Cambridge, Mass.: MIT Press, 1971).
13. Theodore Caplow, *The Sociology of Work* (Minneapolis, Minn.: University of Minnesota Press, 1954), 42–49.
14. U.S. Bureau of the Census, *Statistical Abstract,* 1984, 417, table 693.
15. Stuart Garfinkle, "Occupations of Women and Black Workers, 1962–1974," *Monthly Labor Review* 98 (1975).
16. Mary Frank Fox and Sharlene Hesse-Biber, *Women at Work* (Palo Alto, Calif.: Mayfield, 1984); and Evelyn Glenn and Rosalyn Feldberg, "Clerical Work: The Female Occupation," in J. Freeman, *Women: A Feminist Perspective* (Palo Alto, Calif.: Mayfield, 1979).
17. Fox and Hesse-Biber, *Women at Work.*
18. See Edward Gross, "Cliques in Office Organizations," in Neil Smelser, *Readings on Economic Sociology* (Englewood Cliffs, N.J.: Prentice-Hall, 1965), 96–100; and Rosabeth Moss Kanter, "The Impact of Hierarchical Structures on the Work Behavior of Women and Men," *Social Problems* 23 (April 1976): 415–430.

19. Ely Chinoy, *Automobile Workers and the American Dream* (Boston: Beacon Press, 1955).
20. U.S. Bureau of the Census, *Statistical Abstract, 1985,* 519, table 876.
21. Ibid.
22. Ibid., 520, table 879.
23. Kurt B. Mayer and Sidney Goldstein, "Manual Workers as Small Businessmen," in *Blue Collar Worlds: Studies of the American Worker,* ed. Arthur Shostak and William Gomberg (Englewood Cliffs, N.J.: Prentice-Hall, 1964), 545–558.
24. U.S. Bureau of the Census, *Statistical Abstract, 1985,* 788, table 1408.
25. Ibid., 778, table 1409.
26. Peter G. Norback and Craig T. Norback, *The Dow Jones-Irwin Guide to Franchises,* rev. ed. (Homewood, Ill.: Dow Jones-Irwin, 1982).
27. U.S. Bureau of the Census, *Statistical Abstract, 1985,* 400, table 673.
28. Ibid., 325, tables 528 and 529.
29. Ibid., 294, table 476.
30. See Robert N. McMurray, "Power and the Ambitious Executive," *Harvard Business Review* 51 (November-December 1973), 140–145.
31. Robert Dahl, "The Concept of Power," *Behavioral Science* 2 (July 1957), 201–215.
32. A great deal has been written about power in organizations. For additional discussion of this topic see W. Richard Scott, *Organizations: Rational, Natural, and Open Systems* (Englewood Cliffs, N.J.: Prentice-Hall, 1981), 275–286; Richard H. Hall, *Organizations: Structure and Process,* 3rd ed. (Englewood Cliffs, N.J.: Prentice-Hall, 1982), chap. 7; and J. Eugene Haas and Thomas E. Drabek, *Complex Organizations: A Sociological Perspective* (New York: Macmillan, 1973), 53–60.
33. Lewis A. Coser, *The Functions of Social Conflict* (New York: Free Press, 1956); *Continuities in the Study of Social Conflict* (New York: Free Press, 1967); and Ralf Dahrendorf, *Class and Class Conflict in Industrial Society* (Stanford, Calif.: Standford University Press, 1959).
34. Theodore Caplow, *Managing an Organization,* 2nd ed. (New York: Holt, Rinehart, and Winston, 1983), 151–156.
35. Henry Mintzberg, "The Manager's Job: Folklore and Fact," *Harvard Business Review* 53 (July-August 1975): 49–61.
36. These five types of role conflict have been proposed by Robert L. Kahn et al., *Organizational Stress: Studies in Role Conflict and Ambiguity* (New York: Wiley, 1964).
37. For a review of the topic of control in the workplace, see Richard L. Simpson, "Social Control of Occupations and Work," in *Annual Review of Sociology,* ed. Ralph H. Turner and James F. Short, Jr., 11 (1985), 415–436.
38. Ibid., 425.
39. John P. Heinz and Edward O. Lauman, *Chicago Lawyers: The Social Structure of the Bar* (New York: Russell Sage Foundation–American Bar Foundation, 1983).
40. For an example of this among lawyers, see J. Katz, *Poor People's Lawyers in Transition* (New Brunswick, N.J.: Rutgers University Press, 1982).
41. Erving Goffman, *The Presentation of Self in Everyday Life* (Garden City, N.J.: Anchor Books, 1959).
42. Carl B. Klockars, *The Professional Fence* (New York: Free Press, 1974); and Marilyn Walsh, *The Fence* (Westport, Conn.: Greenwood Press, 1974).
43. See Jacqueline Boles and A.P. Garbin, "Stripping for a Living: An Occupa-

tional Study of the Night Club Stripper," in *Deviant Behavior: Occupational and Organizational Bases*, ed. Clifton Bryant (Chicago: Rand-McNally, 1974), 312–335; Marilyn Salutin, "The Impression Management Techniques of the Burlesque Comedian," *Sociological Inquiry* 43 (1973): 159–168; and David M. Peterson and Paula L. Dressel, "Equal Time for Women: Social Notes on the Male Strip Show," *Urban Life* 11 (1982): 185–208.

44. For a review of this literature as it applies to deviant work, see Peter Letkemann, *Crime as Work* (Englewood Cliffs, N.J.: Prentice-Hall, 1973); Gale Miller, *Odd Jobs: The World of Deviant Work* (Englewood Cliffs, N.J.: Prentice-Hall, 1978); and Alex Thio, *Deviant Behavior*, 2nd ed. (Boston: Houghton Mifflin, 1983), especially chaps. 8, 15, and 16.

45. Two major recent works that provide an overview of the field of organizational analysis are Scott, *Organizations*, and Hall, *Organizations*.

46. For a concise review of theoretical perspectives on organizations, see Haas and Drabek, *Complex Organizations*, chap. 2. See also Kurt Tausky, *Work Organizations: Major Theoretical Perspectives*, 2nd ed. (Itasca, Ill.: F.E. Peacock, 1978).

47. Scott, *Organizations*, 13–19.

48. Max Weber, *From Max Weber: Essays in Sociology*, ed. and trans. Hans H. Gerth and C. Wright Mills (New York: Oxford University Press, 1946), chap. 8.

49. Scott, *Organizations*, 20, argues that formalization and explicit goals are *the* key features of organizations in the rational model perspective.

50. Robert Michels, *Political Parties*, trans. Eden Paul and Ceder Paul (New York: Free Press, 1949); Talcott Parsons, *The Social System* (New York: Free Press, 1951); and Philip Selznick, *TVA and the Grass Roots* (Berkeley and Los Angeles: University of California Press, 1949).

51. Haas and Drabek, *Complex Organizations*, 49.

52. Scott, *Organizations*, 80–81.

53. Fritz J. Roethlisberger and William J. Dickson, *Management and the Worker* (Cambridge, Mass.: Harvard University Press, 1939); Elto Mayo, *The Human Problems of an Industrial Civilization* (New York: Macmillan, 1933); Tausky, *Work Organizations*, 41–61, and Haas and Drabek, *Complex Organizations*, 43–48.

54. For a review of the literature on leadership, see Hall, *Organizations*, chap. 8.

55. Emphasis on informal structure is also an outgrowth of the human relations school. See the references in note 50.

56. The classic study on this topic is Donald Roy, "Quota Restriction and Goldbricking in a Machine Shop," *American Journal of Sociology* 57 (March 1952): 427–442. See also Stanley Seashore, *Group Cohesiveness in the Industrial Work Group* (Ann Arbor, Mich.: Survey Research Center, University of Michigan, 1954); and Roethlisberger and Dickson, *Management and the Worker*.

57. Melville Dalton, *Men Who Manage* (New York: Wiley, 1959); and Gross, "Cliques in Office Organizations."

58. Ludwig von Bertalanffy, *General Systems Theory* (New York: George Braziller, 1968); and Walter Buckley, *Sociology and Modern Systems Theory* (Englewood Cliffs, N.J.: Prentice-Hall, 1967).

59. Mary Zey-Ferrell, *Dimensions of Organizations: Environment, Context, Structure, Process, and Performance* (Santa Monica, Calif.: Goodyear, 1979), 41–42.

60. Scott, *Organizations*, 107–108; Buckley, *Sociology and Modern Systems*

Theory, 82–83; and W. Ross Ashby, "Principles of Self-Organizing Systems," in *Modern Systems Research for the Behavioral Scientist,* ed. Walter Buckley (Chicago: Aldine, 1968), 108–118.

61. Ashby, *Principles of Self-Organizing Systems;* and Robert Glassman, "Persistence and Loose Coupling in Living Systems," *Behavioral Science* 18 (March 1973): 83–98.

62. James G. March and Johan P. Olsen, *Ambiguity and Choice in Organizations* (Bergen, Norway: Universitetsforlaget, 1976).

63. Jeffrey Pfeffer and Gerald R. Salancik, *The External Control of Organizations* (New York: Harper and Row, 1978), 36. See also Richard M. Cyert and James G. March, *A Behavioral Theory of the Firm* (Englewood Cliffs, N.J.: Prentice-Hall, 1963).

64. Scott, *Organizations,* 22–23.

65. For an example see Jeffrey Pfeffer and Gerald R. Salancik, "Organizational Decision Making as a Political Process: The Case of a University Budget," *Administrative Science Quarterly* 19 (June 1984): 135–151.

66. For a good summary of such criticisms, both popular and scholarly, see Ralph P. Hummel, *The Bureaucratic Experience* (New York: St. Martin's Press, 1977).

67. Thomas J. Peters and Robert H. Waterman, Jr., *In Search of Excellence: Lessons from America's Best-Run Companies* (New York: Harper and Row, 1982), especially chap. 12.

68. For an analysis that links the Holocaust to the bureaucratic structure of German society, see Richard L. Rubenstein, *The Cunning of History: The Holocaust and the American Future* (New York: Harper and Row, 1975).

69. Robert K. Merton, "Bureaucratic Structure and Personality," in Robert K. Merton, *Social Theory and Social Structure* (Glencoe, Ill.: Free Press, 1957).

70. Joseph H. Fichter, *Religion as an Occupation* (Notre Dame, Ind.: University of Notre Dame Press, 1961), 219–226.

71. W. Richard Scott, "Professionals in Bureaucracies—Areas of Conflict," in *Professionalization,* ed. Howard M. Vollmer and Donald L. Mills (Englewood Cliffs, N.J.: Prentice-Hall, 1966), 265–275.

72. Leonard Reissman, "A Study of Role Conceptions in Bureaucracy," *Social Forces* 22 (March 1949): 305–310.

73. Alvin W. Gouldner, "Cosmopolitans and Locals: Toward an Analysis of Latent Social Roles—I," *Administrative Science Quarterly* 2 (December 1957): 281–306; and "Cosmopolitans and Locals: Toward an Analysis of Latent Social Roles—II," *Administrative Science Quarterly* 2 (March 1958): 444–480.

74. Harold L. Wilensky, *Intellectuals in Labor Unions* (New York: Free Press, 1959).

75. Peter M. Blau and W. Richard Scott, *Formal Organizations: A Comparative Approach* (San Francisco: Chandler Publishing Company, 1962).

76. Ronald G. Corwin, "The Professional Employee: A Study of Conflict in Nursing Roles," *American Journal of Sociology* 66 (May 1961): 604–615.

77. William Kornhauser, *Scientists in Industry: Conflict and Accommodation* (Los Angeles: University of California Press, 1962).

78. Arlene K. Daniels, "The Captive Professional: Bureaucratic Limitations in the Practice of Military Psychiatry," *Journal of Health and Social Behavior* 10 (1969): 255–265; and "Military Psychiatry: The Emergence of a Subspecialty," in *Medical Men and Their Work,* ed. Eliot Friedson and Judith Lorber (Chicago: Aldine/Atherton, 1972), 145–162.

79. Vivienne Walters, "Company Doctors' Perceptions of and Responses to

Conflicting Pressures from Labor and Management," *Social Problems* 30 (1982): 1–12.

80. George Ritzer, "Professionalization, Bureaucratization, and Rationalization: The Views of Max Weber," *Social Forces* 53 (1975): 627–634; and *Working: Conflict and Change*, 3rd ed. (Englewood Cliffs, N.J.: Prentice-Hall, 1986), 204–205.

81. Amitai Etzioni, ed., *The Semi-Professions and Their Organization* (New York: Free Press, 1969), xii–xiii.

82. Scott, *Organizations*, 222–224; and "Reactions to Supervision in a Heteronomous Organization," *Administrative Science Quarterly* 10 (June 1965): 65–81.

83. Richard H. Hall, "Some Organizational Considerations in the Professional-Organizational Relationship," *Administrative Science Quarterly* 12 (December 1967): 461–478; and "Professionalization and Bureaucratization," *American Sociological Review* 33 (February 1968): 92–104.

84. Eugene Litwak, "Models of Bureaucracy Which Permit Conflict," *American Journal of Sociology* 67 (September 1961): 177–184.

85. Erwin O. Smigel, *The Wall Street Lawyer: Professional Organization Man?* (New York: Free Press, 1964).

86. Paul Montagna, "Professionalization and Bureaucratization in Large Professional Organizations," *American Journal of Sociology* 74 (1968): 138–145.

87. Rue Bucher and Joan Stelling, "Characteristics of Professional Organizations," *Journal of Health and Social Behavior* 10 (1969): 3–15.

88. J. Kenneth Benson, "The Analysis of Bureaucratic-Professional Conflict: Functional Versus Dialectical Approaches," *Sociological Quarterly* 14 (1973): 376–394.

89. Eric Josephson and Mary Josephson, eds., *Man Alone: Alienation in Modern Society* (New York: Dell Publishing Company, 1962), 97–98.

90. Weber, *From Max Weber*, 50.

91. Melvin Seeman, "On the Meaning of Alienation," *American Sociological Review* 24 (December 1959): 783–791.

92. Scott, *Organizations*, 295; and Ritzer, *Working: Conflict and Change*, 328.

93. Ritzer, Ibid., 329.

94. Seeman, "On the Meaning of Alienation," and "Alienation Studies," in *Annual Review of Sociology*, ed. Alex Inkeles, James Coleman, and Neil Smelser, 91–123.

95. Joachim Israel, *Alienation: From Marx to Modern Sociology* (Boston: Allyn and Bacon, 1971); and Ritzer, *Working: Conflict and Change*, 328–331.

96. Kai Erikson, "Work and Alienation," *American Sociological Review* 51 (February 1986): 1–8.

97. Peter B. Archibald, "Using Marx's Theory of Alienation Empirically," *Theory and Society* 6 (1978): 119–132; Adam Schaff, *Alienation as a Social Phenomenon* (New York: Pergamon Press, 1980); and Richard Schact, *Alienation* (New York: Doubleday, 1970).

98. Charles R. Walker and Robert H. Guest, "The Man on the Assembly Line," in *Organizations and Human Behavior*, ed. Gerald D. Bell (Englewood Cliffs, N.J.: Prentice-Hall, 1967), 230–245 (quotation from p. 237).

99. Chinoy, *Automobile Workers and the American Dream*.

100. Charles R. Walker and Robert H. Guest, *The Man on the Assembly Line* (Cambridge, Mass.: Harvard University Press, 1952), 53.

101. Chris Argyris, "Individual Actualization in Complex Organizations," *Mental Hygiene* 44 (April 1960): 226–337.

102. Robert Blauner, *Alienation and Freedom* (Chicago: University of Chicago Press, 1964).
103. See Seeman, "Alienation Studies," for a more complete review.
104. Shepard, *Automation and Alienation.*
105. Frank M. Hull, Nathalie S. Friedman, and Theresa F. Rogers, "The Effect of Technology on Alienation from Work," *Work and Occupations* 9 (February 1982): 31–57.
106. Jeffrey Leiter, "Work Alienation in the Textile Industry: Reassessing Blauner," *Work and Occupations* 12 (November 1985): 479–498.
107. Michael Aiken and Gerald Hage, "Organizational Alienation: A Comparative Analysis," *American Sociological Review* 31 (August 1966): 497–507.
108. Kurt Tausky, *Work and Society: An Introduction to Industrial Sociology* (Itasca, Ill.: F. E. Peacock, 1984), 97.
109. U.S. Department of Health, Education and Welfare, *Work in America: Report of a Special Task Force to the Secretary of Health, Education, and Welfare* (Cambridge, Mass.: MIT Press, 1973), 16.
110. H. Roy Kaplan, "How Do Workers View Their Work in America?" *Monthly Labor Review* (June 1973): 46–48.
111. Tausky, *Work and Society*, 99. See also Beth E. Vanfossen, *The Social Structure of Inequality* (Boston: Little, Brown, 1979); Charles E. Hurst, *The Anatomy of Social Inequality* (St. Louis: Mosby, 1979); and Arne L. Kalleberg and Larry J. Griffin, "Positional Sources of Inequality and Job Satisfaction," *Sociology of Work and Occupations* 5 (November 1978): 371–401.
112. Edward J. Walsh, "Prestige, Work Satisfaction, and Alienation: Comparisons Among Garbagemen, Professors, and Other Work Groups," *Work and Occupations* 9 (November 1982): 475–496. See also Edward J. Walsh, *Dirty Work, Race, and Self-Esteem* (Ann Arbor, Mich.: Institute for Labor and Industrial Relations, University of Michigan–Wayne State University, 1975).
113. James D. Wright and Richard F. Hamilton, "Work Satisfaction and Age: Some Evidence for the 'Job Change' Hypothesis," *Social Forces* 56 (June 1978): 1140–1158; and Robert P. Quinn and Margaret R. McCullough, *Job Satisfaction: Is There a Trend?* Manpower Research Monograph 30 (Washington, D.C.: U.S. Department of Labor, Manpower Administration, 1974); and Arne L. Kalleberg and Karyn A. Loscocco, "Aging, Values, and Rewards: Explaining Age Differences in Job Satisfaction," *American Sociological Review* 48 (February 1983): 78–90.
114. Jeylan T. Mortimer and Jon Lorence, "Work Experience and Occupational Value Socialization: A Longitudinal Study," *American Journal of Sociology* 84 (May 1979): 1361–1385.
115. Gerald Gurin, Joseph Veroff, and Sheila Feld, *Americans View Their Mental Health* (New York: Basic Books, 1960).
116. Melvin L. Kohn and Carmi Schooler, "Occupational Experience and Psychological Functioning: An Assessment of Reciprocal Effects," *American Sociological Review* 38 (February 1973): 97–118.
117. Douglas M. Eichar and John L. P. Thompson, "Alienation, Occupational Self-Direction, and Worker Consciousness: An Exploration," *Work and Occupations* 13 (February 1986): 47–65.
118. Patricia Voydanoff, "The Relationship Between Perceived Job Characteristics and Job Satisfaction Among Occupational Status Groups," *Sociology of Work and Occupations* 5 (May 1978): 179–192.

CHAPTER 7

Women and Work

RESEARCH ON WOMEN and work has increased dramatically since the early 1970s.[1] In part, this is due to a tremendous increase in paid employment among women since World War II. It also reflects a growing realization on the part of sociologists that our understanding of occupations and work will be enhanced if we deal with similarities and differences in the occupational experiences of men and women, a point that holds for all sociological analysis, not just the study of occupations.[2]

Several major topics will be dealt with in this chapter. The first is a description of and explanations for the phenomenal increase in women's labor force participation in recent years as noted above. Next, we will be concerned with occupational sex segregation, both its extent and explanations that have been offered for its existence and persistence over time. The entry of women into traditionally and predominantly male occupations is another topic to be covered. Although the topic of careers was discussed extensively in chapter 5, this chapter will examine some of the distinctive career problems of women. Finally, the topic of sex equity in the workplace will be examined including factors related to women's earnings and the issues of nondiscrimination, affirmative action, and comparable worth.

THE PARTICIPATION OF WOMEN
IN THE LABOR FORCE

Women have always worked in American society (as well as in other societies). However, their participation in the "official" labor force is rela-

216

tively new.[3] In part, this is a consequence of the fact that unpaid household labor has not been counted as work. The U.S. Department of Labor defines the *labor force* as all civilians in the noninstitutional population sixteen years of age and over who during a particular week (*a*) did any work for pay or profit or worked fifteen hours or more as unpaid workers in a family business, (*b*) were not working but who had jobs or businesses from which they were temporarily absent because of such things as illness, weather conditions, vacation, labor-management conflicts, etc., and (*c*) were unemployed but made efforts to find work during the previous four weeks and were available for work. Beginning in 1983, members of the armed forces stationed in the United States were also counted as part of the labor force. Those classified as *not in the labor force* include people who are doing their own housework, in school, retired, institutionalized (e.g., in jail) mentally or physically disabled, and voluntarily idle, as well as seasonal workers in the off-season and discouraged workers who have given up trying to find work.[4]

Table 7.1 shows a steady increase in the number of women participating in the labor force during the period 1880 to 1983. While the percentage of men in the labor force has remained quite stable, the percentage of women has increased by 38 percent over this period. Table 7.2 illustrates the increase in women's paid employment from a different perspective. When we look at women's employment by marital status it is apparent that, since 1940, the percent increase in employment among married women has been greater than the increase among single women, and widowed and divorced women have experienced the smallest increase.

There are also some important patterns and changes in the labor

Table 7.1
Labor Force Participation Rates, 1880–1983, in Percent

Year	Total Noninstitutional Population 16 Years or Older (in thousands)	Total Participation Rate	Men	Women
1880	36,762	47	79	15
1900	47,950	50	80	19
1920	82,739	50	78	21
1940	100,147	53	79	25
1960	119,106	60	84	38
1970	139,203	61	80	43
1980	169,349	64	78	52
1983	175,891	64	77	53

Sources: U.S. Bureau of the Census, *Historical Statistics of the United States, Colonial Times to 1970*, Bicentennial Edition (Washington, D.C.: U.S. Government Printing Office, 1975), pt. 2, 127–128; and U.S. Bureau of the Census, *Statistical Abstract of the United States, 1985* (Washington, D.C.: U.S. Government Printing Office, 1984), 390, table 653.

Table 7.2
Percentage of the Female Population
in the Labor Force, 1940–1982

	Percentage in the Labor Force			
Year	All Women	Single Women	Married Women	Widowed, Divorced Women
1940	27.4%	48.1%	16.7%	32.0%
1950	31.4	50.5	24.8	36.0
1960	34.8	44.1	31.7	37.1
1970	42.6	53.0	41.4	36.2
1980	51.1	61.5	50.7	41.0
1982	52.1	62.2	51.8	42.1

Source: U.S. Bureau of the Census, *Statistical Abstract of the United States, 1984* (Washington, D.C.: U.S. Government Printing Office, 1983), 413, table 683.

force participation of women by age groups. In 1983, just under 70 percent of women between the ages of twenty and forty-four were in the labor force.[5] If we compare the years 1983 and 1940, the biggest increase in employment has occurred among women in the forty-five through fifty-four age group (20.8 percent in 1940 and 61.9 percent in 1983).[6] During the first half of this century there was a clear pattern of young women working from their mid-teens through their mid-twenties with labor force participation dropping off after that point as they married and assumed child-rearing responsibilities. What we find in recent years is a marked persistence in employment as age increases. In 1983, the labor force participation rate was even 41.5 percent among women in the fifty-five through sixty-four age group. For those in the sixty-five and over age group the rate drops off considerably (as it does for men). It was 7.8 percent in 1983 and this is the only age group where it has not been increasing.[7] The U.S. Department of Labor estimates that if recent trends continue, by 1995 the overall participation rate for women will be 60.3 percent and that slightly more than 80 percent of women between the ages of twenty and forty-four will be in the labor force.[8]

Among married women, labor force participation is related to the age of their children. In 1982, 48.7 percent of married women with children under age six and 63.2 percent of those with children age six through seventeen were in the labor force.[9] The rate for women with children probably would be higher if child-care facilities were more readily available. In one study, about 20 percent of nonworking women with preschool-age children said they would look for work if affordable, good quality child-care services were available.[10] In the future, an increase in the availability of child-care services could lead to an even greater increase in the labor force participation of (especially younger) women.

EXPLAINING THE INCREASE IN WOMEN'S EMPLOYMENT

What factors account for this increase in women's employment? A number of things are involved and are interrelated in various ways. For convenience, they can be grouped as demographic, economic, and social-cultural factors.

The most important *demographic* factor is the declining fertility of American women. The crude birth rate in the United States (the number of births per year per 1,000 population) decreased from 30.1 in 1910 to 15.4 in 1983.[11] Basically, having fewer children makes it easier for women to participate in the labor force. However, it is unclear whether fertility affects employment or whether the reverse is true. Women may consciously and deliberately decide to postpone childbearing or have fewer children in order to maximize their employment opportunities. Once employed, having children may be seen as a potential cost in the form of income that would be lost were the woman to leave the labor force. Employment may also reduce fertility by giving women who contribute to family income greater influence over the decision to have children.[12] Several recent studies have attempted to unravel the fertility-employment relationship with inconclusive results.[13] The most appropriate conclusion is that these factors simply have reciprocal effects. James Cramer has suggested that is is useful to distinguish between short-term and long-term effects. He argues that fertility affects employment in the short-term (women may leave the labor force during the later stages of pregnancy and while their children are very young), but in the long-term, employment affects fertility (women may limit their fertility in order to take advantage of career opportunities or simply to continue working and earning income).[14]

Another demographic consideration is the fact that women are marrying at a later age than they did in the past. For example, the median age at first marriage for women increased from 20.3 in 1950 to 22.0 in 1981.[15] Entering the labor force delays marriage and the decision to delay marriage increases the likelihood of either initial or continued employment. As with the fertility-employment relationship, there is reciprocal causality. Marriage at a later age also reduces potential lifetime fertility. The later women marry, the smaller their families are likely to be and, consequently, the more likely they are to participate in the labor force.

A final demographic factor (with economic implications) that has led to increased employment among women is an increase in the number and proportion of female-headed families. Between 1960 and 1983, the proportion of all families headed by women increased from 8.7 to 12.2 percent among whites and 22.4 to 41.9 percent among blacks.[16] This increase is a consequence of both a rising divorce rate and the fact that death rates are higher among men than women. About one out of every nine women in the labor force is a divorced, separated, widowed, or never-married woman heading her own family.[17] These changes have in turn created motivations to work that are essentially economic, a set of factors to which we turn next.

There are several *economic* factors related to women's increased labor force participation. The need to work and earn money was noted above in connection with the increase in female-headed families. This is also the main reason why most women work. A recent national survey asked working women to identify the primary reason why they worked. Some 43 percent said "to bring in extra money," 27 percent said "to support myself," and 19 percent said "to support my family."[18] With high inflation in the 1970s and early 1980s, economic necessity has undoubtedly sent many women into the labor force. The rising cost of higher education could also be an important factor. Without the additional income provided by a wife's employment, many low- and even middle-income families might find it difficult if not impossible to provide the financial resources for their children's education. This may well be a contributing factor to the large increase in employment among women in the forty-five through fifty-four age group noted above.

Another economic factor is simply the fact that the kinds of jobs that have increased have been jobs that are heavy users of female labor. In chapter 6, we described the kinds of changes that have occurred over time in the occupational composition of the labor force. The increase in "tertiary" occupations has meant an increase in white-collar clerical and service jobs that traditionally have been regarded as appropriate work for women and, as we also saw in chapter 6, most clerical jobs have remained predominantly female. The growth of industries like banking, insurance, and real estate, as well as the increase in clerical jobs that has accompanied the growth of governmental agencies, has created an increase in the demand for women workers.

One important *social-cultural* factor that has increased women's employment is their increasing educational attainment. The educational attainment of men and women has been converging. By the mid-1980s, the median number of years of schooling completed by men and women had become virtually identical. Women are more likely than men to have completed high school but men are more likely than women to complete college and go on to graduate or professional education. Most importantly, the rate at which women go on to college has been increasing. Between 1960 and 1983, the percent of high school graduates enrolled in college increased from 30.3 to 35.0 percent for men but it went from 17.8 to 30.3 percent for women.[19] These changes are also reflected in the makeup of institutions of higher education. The sex composition of students in American colleges and universities changed from 58.6 percent male and 41.4 percent female in 1970 to 48.8 percent male and 51.2 percent female in 1982.[20]

Rising educational attainments increase the range of occupations and career options open to women. Education is a costly investment and working represents a way of realizing a return on that investment. Also, acquiring an education often leads to the postponement of marriage noted above. This sets in motion the decrease-in-fertility–increase-in-employment sequence already discussed.

A final social-cultural factor involves changing norms and values regarding women's and men's roles and family responsibilities. As employment outside the home has become more socially acceptable, more and more women have entered the labor force. Having a working wife no longer implies that a husband is unable to support his family. Indeed, husbands with working wives share in the economic benefits of a two-paycheck family income. In some cases, a working wife may reflect a husband's commitment to an equal-partner marriage that involves the sharing of family responsibilities and decision making and a rejection of the traditional male-dominated family structure with its sharp division of labor based on gender.[21]

THE SEX SEGREGATION OF OCCUPATIONS

Despite the dramatic entry of women into the labor force, the sex segregation of occupations has remained remarkably strong and stable. While the entry of women into previously male-dominated occupations has received a great deal of media attention in recent years, such reports present a distorted picture of the distribution of women in the labor force.

The majority of women still work in occupations that are predominantly female. In fact, there has been little change in the sex segregation of occupations since the beginning of the century. For example, in 1900, 38 percent of working women were employed in occupations that were at least 90 percent female. By 1980, that figure had decreased only slightly to 32 percent. Sixty percent of working women were in occupations that were at least half female in 1900 and by 1980 that figure had increased to 76 percent.[22] Some occupations (including a number discussed in chapter 6 under the office work setting) have become even more predominantly female since the early 1900s. These include the occupations of nurse, stenographer, typist, secretary, telephone operator, and bookkeeper.[23]

Several studies have looked at occupational sex segregation over time in some detail. Edward Gross concluded that between 1900 and 1960 very little desegregation occurred. Predominantly male occupations actually became more resistant to the entry of women, but predominantly female occupations had become more open to men.[24] Another analysis found a slight increase in sex segregation between 1950 and 1960. This was due to the rapid growth of clerical and service occupations that are heavy employers of women. Although there was a decrease in sex segregation between 1960 and 1970, this was due mainly to the entry of men into predominantly female occupations, a finding similar to that of Gross. During the entire period of the study (1950–1970), the movement of men into traditionally female occupations was greater than the movement of women into traditionally male occupations.[25]

In table 7.3, the concentration of women in clerical and service occupations is readily apparent as is their relative absence from skilled craft and major managerial and professional occupations. Ten predominantly female occupations—registered nurse, licensed practical nurse, elementary school teacher, librarian, cashier, secretary, typist, private household worker, bank teller, and waitress—actually accounted for 31 percent of all women in the labor force in 1983.[26]

Besides the segregation of women and men into different occupations there is also hierarchical or vertical segregation within the same occupations and occupational categories.[27] Within the professions, for example, women are concentrated in those with less prestige, poorer pay, and fewer career opportunities such as nursing, elementary school teaching, librarianship, and social work. This pattern represents a case of the *sex typing* of work within the professions. In sales occupations, women are more likely to be found in retail sales, which offers fewer opportunities for earning substantial commissions or moving into management positions compared to wholesale sales positions. In many organizations, managerial and supervisory jobs are more likely to be given to outsiders than to clerical workers (mainly women) already in the organization.[28] In general, as the level of skill, status, and responsibility within an occupation increases, the proportion of women employed in it decreases.[29]

EXPLANATIONS FOR OCCUPATIONAL SEX SEGREGATION

As with explanations for women's increasing labor force participation, there are a variety of explanations for the persistence of occupational sex segregation. They range from a focus on the structure of the economy to childhood socialization patterns.

One explanation emphasizes the *dual labor market*.[30] According to this argument there is a primary and a secondary sector to the labor market. In the *primary* sector, there are jobs with relatively high wages, good working conditions, opportunities for advancement, work rules emphasizing fair and equal treatment, and predictable, stable, and secure employment. An *upper tier* within the primary sector includes professional, technical, managerial, and administrative occupations, while a *lower tier* includes clerical, sales, and skilled craft occupations.

The *secondary* sector refers to relatively poor paying jobs with less attractive working conditions, few if any opportunities for career advancement, unstable, unpredictable, and insecure employment, and work rules that allow for capricious, unequal, and harsh treatment of employees by supervisors. Semiskilled and unskilled blue-collar jobs as well as many service occupations would be found here.[31] The concentration of women in some secondary (service) and lower-tier–primary-sector jobs (sales, clerical) in part may be the result of the interaction of employers' decisions with labor market characteristics. Employers may assume that women are less committed to their jobs and to a career than men, more likely than men to quit because of marriage or child-rearing responsibilities, and more likely to present problems of absenteeism because of family responsibilities. Consequently, they may be less inclined to hire women for jobs in the primary sector.

A variant on the dual labor market explanation makes a distinction between internal and external markets. Within employing organizations jobs vary in terms of pay, responsibility, and promotion opportunities. Employers may make the same kinds of assumptions about women's commitments and potential interruptions in employment as those identified above. Those decisions can result in the channeling of women into the secondary sector. Even within the primary sector, women may be hired for and retained in the poorer paying jobs with fewer opportunities for advancement. The labor market within organizations becomes, in effect, internally stratified and segregated by sex. Men are more likely to be hired for and promoted in the managerial career ladder while women are retained in the dead-end clerical market. Just as movement between the primary and secondary sectors of the external market is rare, movement of women between the components of the internal market is severely restricted.

While the dual labor market explanation of occupational sex segregation in effect places the blame on employers and employing organizations, another line of reasoning places responsibility on the occupational choices and decisions that women make. In chapter 3, which deals with occupational choice, it was pointed out that, traditionally, women have aspired to lower-status occupations and to a more limited number and range of occupations than men. While there is evidence of a pattern of convergence in men's and women's occupational choices, substantial differences still exist. These differences are reflected in the choice of ma-

Table 7.3
Percent Female in Selected Occupations, 1983

Occupation	Percent Female
Managerial and Professional	40.9
Executive, Administrative, and Managerial	32.4
Public officials and administrators	38.5
Administrators, protective services	14.0
Financial managers	38.6
Personnel and labor relations managers	43.9
Purchasing managers	23.6
Marketing, advertising, and public relations managers	21.8
Administrators, education	41.4
Managers, medicine and health	57.0
Managers, properties and real estate	42.8
Management-related occupations	40.3
Accountants and auditors	38.7
Professional	48.1
Architects	12.7
Engineers	5.8
Mathematical and computer scientists	29.6
Computer systems analysts	27.8
Natural scientists	20.5
Physicians	15.8
Dentists	6.7
Registered nurses	95.8
Therapists	76.3
Physicians' assistants	36.3
College and university teachers	36.3
Elementary school teachers	83.3
Secondary school teachers	51.8
Educational and vocational counselors	53.1
Librarians	87.3
Social scientists and urban planners	46.8
Social workers	64.3
Lawyers and judges	15.8
Technical, Sales, and Administrative Support	64.6
Technicians and Related Support	48.2
Health technologists and technicians	84.3
Licensed practical nurses	97.0
Engineering technologists and technicians	18.4
Science technicians	29.1
Computer programmers	32.5
Sales Occupations	47.5
Supervisors and proprietors	28.4
Insurance sales	25.1
Real estate sales	48.4
Sales representatives, except retail	15.1
Sales workers, retail	69.7

jor made by men and women college students who are, after all, the most likely candidates for entry into the upper tier of the primary sector of the labor market. Women are more likely to major in the humanities, education, and social sciences while men are more likely to major in the physical and natural sciences, engineering, and technical fields, although this pattern has become less marked in recent years. One sign of change

Table 7.3 (Continued)

Occupation	Percent Female
Cashiers	84.4
Administrative Support, Including Clerical	79.9
Supervisors	53.4
Computer operators	63.7
Secretaries	99.0
Typists	95.6
Receptionists	96.8
File clerks	83.5
Bookkeepers, accounting and auditing clerks	91.0
Duplicating, mail and other office machine operators	62.6
Telephone operators	90.4
Postal clerks	36.7
General office clerks	80.6
Bank tellers	91.0
Data entry keyers	93.6
Teachers' aides	93.7
Service Occupations	60.1
Private household, child care	96.9
Firefighters	1.0
Police officers	9.4
Guards	20.6
Food preparation and service	63.3
Waiters and waitresses	87.8
Cooks	50.8
Nursing aides, orderlies, and attendants	88.7
Janitors and cleaners	28.6
Hairdressers and cosmetologists	88.7
Child care, not private household	96.8
Precision Production, Craft, and Repair	8.1
Mechanics and repairers	3.0
Construction trades	1.8
Carpenters	1.4
Precision production occupations	21.5
Operators, Fabricators and Laborers	26.6
Machine operators, assemblers, and inspectors	42.1
Motor vehicle operators	9.2
Truck operators	3.1
Freight, stock, and material handlers	15.4
Laborers, except construction	19.4
Farming, Forestry, and Fishing	16.0
Farm operators and managers	12.1
Other agricultural and related occupations	19.9
Forestry and logging	1.4
Fishers, hunters, and trappers	4.5

Source: U.S. Bureau of the Census, *Statistical Abstract of the United States, 1985* (Washington, D.C.: U.S. Government Printing Office, 1984), 402–403, table 676.

is that in 1982 nearly equal proportions of men and women were majoring in business.[32] However, a study of recent college graduates found that three-quarters of the women said that at age thirty-five they wanted to be working in occupations that are usually sex typed as women's occupations.[33]

Soloman Polachek has argued that in making occupational decisions many women may opt for jobs that allow them flexibility, lower demands, and easy movement in and out of the labor force rather than those that offer greater status and advancement opportunities. The implication is that such decisions may be made by women who plan to devote substantial amounts of their lives to family responsibilities.[34] However, there is evidence that women end up working more during their lifetimes than they expected to as adolescents and young adults.[35] This suggests that they may make occupational and educational choices on the basis of erroneous assumptions and incomplete or distorted information.

Another distinctive explanation of occupational sex segregation emphasizes the *differential socialization* of males and females. Both families and schools are involved in socialization that has important occupational implications.

On the basis of their review of the research on family socialization, Fox and Hesse-Biber conclude that parents respond differently to their male and female children.[36] They view their female children as "softer, quieter, and more delicate" and their male children as "stronger, bolder, and more active."[37] Parents generally encourage their sons to develop qualities like independence, competitiveness, objectivity, self-confidence, and initiative-taking. Daughters on the other hand are socialized in ways that encourage the opposite characteristics: dependence, cooperativeness, subjectivity, empathy, sensitivity, and passivity.[38] The characteristics developed in girls are less likely to lead to aspiration to upper-tier–primary-sector occupations than those encouraged in boys. They are also less advantageous in the pursuit of organizational and other careers. In effect, the argument is that males are more likely than females to be socialized in ways that "pay off" in the occupational structure.

A more direct link with occupational outcomes has been identified by Lynn K. White and David B. Brinkerhoff in their study of family chores and paid employment among children ages two through seventeen. They found very marked differences in boy's and girl's work. In terms of household chores, girl's work included general housework, cleaning, washing dishes, cooking, and babysitting younger siblings. Boy's work was quite different and included yard and garden work, shoveling snow, and taking out the garbage. Paid employment outside the home also varied sharply by sex. Boy's work was more likely to include such things as mowing lawns and shoveling snow, farm work, manual labor of various kinds, and having a paper route. Girls were more likely to do babysitting, work in a restaurant, or do office work.[39] White and Brinkerhoff conclude that although the sex typing of children's work may be declining it nevertheless remains strong. Most importantly, the sex typing of work in childhood contributes to the continued sex typing of work in adulthood.

Schools also socialize male and female students differently. Fox and Hesse-Biber point out that there are a number of practices, perspectives, and assumptions in schools that reinforce the effects of family socialization and have implications for later occupational outcomes.[40] Male and female students are tracked and channeled into different academic programs, courses, and classes and into different extracurricular groups and activities. Textbooks and other teaching materials present men's and women's roles in stereotyped ways that reinforce the outcomes of family socialization. Teachers are more attentive to male students and provide them with more opportunities for participation. In addition, the pattern of female classroom teachers and male administrators in the schools provides students with a model of male dominance and female subordination.

Guidance personnel also reflect and reinforce traditional conceptions of male-female differences, particularly in terms of appropriate occupational pursuits and careers. Job search instruments and vocational interest tests used in career counseling tend to replicate the sex segregation of labor markets and channel young women into sex-typed, low wage, dead-end jobs.[41]

No single one of these explanations can account for all of the sex segregation that exists in the labor force. They all make a contribution and they clearly interact in important ways. Differential socialization in families and schools produces sex-typed identities and conceptions of adult (especially occupational) roles. These contribute to differences in occupational choices, aspirations, goals, and educational decisions. Those choices and decisions in turn intersect with labor market sectors and employer preferences which culminate in sex segregation. Despite the overall persistence of occupational sex segregation, changes have been occurring and continue to occur. Some of the most important ones are dealt with in the next section.

THE ENTRY OF WOMEN INTO TRADITIONALLY MALE OCCUPATIONS

The entry of women into traditionally male occupations has been occurring in very selective and uneven ways. The professions, managerial occupations, and blue-collar occupations offer some significant contrasts.

In 1983, women accounted for 15.8 percent of all physicians (see table 7.3, above). This represents an increase from 9.7 percent in 1970.[42] Clearly, women are underrepresented in medicine, but their growing entry into the field is reflected in the fact that they have been receiving an increasing share of all degrees conferred by medical schools. As table 7.4 indicates, the proportion of MD degrees awarded to women increased four and one-half times between 1960 and 1982. While the proportion

Table 7.4
Percentage of Degrees Awarded to Women in
Medicine, Dentistry, Law, and Engineering,
1960–1982

	Percent Received by Women	
Field and Degree	1960	1982
Medicine (MD)	5.5	25.0
Dentistry (DDS and DMD)	0.8	15.4
Law (LLB and JD)	2.5	33.4
Engineering (BS, MS, and PhD)	0.4	10.8

Source: U.S. Bureau of the Census, *Statistical Abstract of the United States, 1985* (Washington, D.C.: U.S. Government Printing Office, 1984), 159, table 267.

of dentists who are women is small (6.7 percent in 1983), women's share of DDS and DMD degrees increased from an insignificant 0.8 percent in 1960 to 15.4 percent in 1982 (see table 7.4).

Among the major professions, the entry of women into law has been substantial. In 1970, 5.9 percent of lawyers and judges were women[43] and this had increased to 15.8 percent in 1983 (see table 7.3). Between 1960 and 1982 the proportion of LLB and JD degrees awarded to women increased at an even higher rate than did the MD degrees received by women (see table 7.4). According to the American Bar Foundation, the number of men admitted to the practice of law each year has remained very stable while the number of women admitted to the bar has consistently increased. Of all the women lawyers in the United States in 1980, nearly two-thirds had been admitted to the bar since 1975.[44]

While there also has been growth in the proportion of women engineers, they remain a very small segment of this profession. Women increased from 1.7 percent to 5.8 percent of all engineers between 1970 and 1983.[45] However, the enrollment of women in engineering programs has been increasing and is reflected in the proportion of degrees awarded to women. At the bachelor's degree level, women's share of both bachelor's and graduate degrees increased from 0.4 percent in 1960 to 10.8 percent in 1982 (see table 7.4).

University and college teaching is another field where women have made gains. Between the 1969–1970 and 1983–1984 academic years, the proportion of women faculty at U.S. colleges and universities increased from twelve to twenty-seven percent.[46] A doctoral degree is a virtual necessity for entry into this field, and increases in the proportion of doctorates earned by women is related to their entry into the academic profession. Between 1950 and 1982, the percentage of doctorates earned by women increased from 9.1 to 32.1 percent.[47]

The entry of women into managerial positions has been increasing, but they are still underrepresented, especially at top management levels in the private sector. Between 1970 and 1983, the proportion of women in the broad category "executive, administrative, and managerial" increased from 18.5 to 32.4 percent.[48] However, women tend to be concentrated at lower status, less powerful managerial positions. In the private sector, only about 1 percent of the positions of vice-president and president are held by women, and they occupy only 6 percent of the middle-management positions. They tend to be concentrated at the lower end of the management ladder as first-line supervisors, office managers, and department heads.[49] As of 1984, no woman was being groomed for the chief executive's job in any of the *Fortune 500* companies.[50]

Skilled craft occupations have remained a strongly male segment of the occupational structure, especially those that are part of the construction industry. Less than 2 percent of carpenters, electricians, and plumbers are women. Between 1970 and 1983 the proportion of women in precision production, craft, and repair occupations increased insignificantly from 7.3 to 8.1 percent.[51] Women have been a significant part of the blue-collar segment of the U.S. labor force since the beginnings of industrial development. In New England, young women from farms and small towns were recruited to work in the early textile mills and women have always been actively employed in the garment and shoe manufacturing as well as food processing industries. In recent years the employment of women as operators, fabricators, and laborers has been fairly stable at about one-fourth of this occupational category.[52]

Despite their low rate of actual participation in traditionally male jobs, there is some evidence that younger women in particular are quite interested in such occupational pursuits. Jane H. Lillydahl asked men and women in two small towns in Colorado about their interest in such occupations as coal miner, construction worker, truck driver, carpenter, mechanic, electrician, heavy equipment operator, and oil shale worker.[53] Among women under age thirty-five, 49.9 percent had given at least some consideration to getting such jobs. Of those between the ages of thirty-five and sixty, 34.5 percent had done so. In addition, 26.1 percent of the younger women and 14.6 percent of those in the older age group said that they would be interested in getting training for these or similar traditionally male occupations. The main reason for women's interest in such jobs was their good wages and fringe benefits, a finding consistent with our earlier point about economic motivations being a major factor in women's increased labor force participation.

One recent analysis of young women's occupational choices has attempted to identify factors related to the choice of nontraditional occupations. Linda J. Waite and Sue E. Berryman studied a national sample of over 12,000 young women and men ages fourteen through twenty-one in 1979.[54] They defined a "traditionally female" occupation as one that is 75 percent or more female, and a "traditionally male" occupation as one that is 75 percent or more male. Occupations ranging from 26 to 74 percent female were defined as "mixed." Nearly half (47.2 percent) of the women in the sample chose traditionally female occupations and one-fifth (19.5 percent) chose traditionally male occupations. In contrast, three-quarters (75.7 percent) of the men chose traditionally male occupations and only 2.3 percent chose occupations that are traditionally female.

Waite and Berryman found that labor force commitment was strongly related to choice of a traditional or nontraditional occupation on the part of these young women. Those who preferred to marry earlier, preferred to be homemakers at age thirty-five, and did not believe that a wife working outside the home benefits the family, were more likely to select a traditionally female occupation. Expecting to spend less time in the labor force and to have an intermittent career, they opted for typically female occupations. Family socioeconomic status was not related to traditionality of occupational choice, but ability was. Women with higher verbal and quantitative skills were more likely to select traditionally male occupations, but having stronger clerical skills increased the chances of selecting a traditionally female occupation. There is also some evidence in this study that choice of a traditionally male occupation is influenced by the work and family responsibilities of the mothers of these young women. Those with mothers in blue-collar occupations were more likely to choose a traditionally male occupation, suggesting that their mothers may serve as role models that indirectly shape their occupational choice. In addition, those whose mothers were heads of the household were less likely to select traditionally female occupations. If female-headed households increase in the future, the implication is that this feature of family structure may contribute to a decrease in the traditionality of young women's occupational choices.

Another study of choice of college major lends support to some of Waite and Berryman's findings about ability and women's occupational choices. Using data from a national sample of college freshmen in 1972, Thomas A. Lyson compared men and women majoring in predominantly male and predominantly female fields.[55] Women pursuing predominantly male majors had higher scores on the Scholastic Aptitude Test (especially in terms of quantitative skills) than women or men majoring in predominantly female fields. Thus, it appears that young women with greater academic potential are more likely to pursue majors that may lead to nontraditional occupational opportunities. Lyson also found traditionality of major to be related to work values. Men in traditionally male majors placed greater value on *extrinsic* job characteristics such as high earnings, freedom from supervision, leadership opportunities, and prestige. Women in traditionally female majors placed greater value on *intrinsic* features of jobs such as opportunities to help others, originality and creativity, steady progress, and work with people rather than things. Both women and men who were in atypical majors for their sex had work values that fell in between these two extremes. Lyson also suggests that the greater emphasis of women on intrinsic features of work may put them at a competitive disadvantage relative to men in the pursuit of careers. Compared to men, they may be less likely to seek out opportunities for leadership and advancement. There is also the implication, however, that women pursuing careers in predominantly male fields may behave more like men in this respect.

CAREER PATTERNS AND PROBLEMS OF WOMEN

There are some major differences in men's and women's careers. This is apparent if we take a status attainment approach and look at the socioeconomic status or prestige of the occupations that men and women hold over time. Rachel A. Rosenfeld has pointed out that, in general, men remain in or "attached to" the labor force in the same general line of work and move up in status over the course of their working lives.[56] A good deal of research since the 1930s supports this conclusion[57] as does the mobility research of Blau and Duncan and the status attainment research of Sewell and Hauser discussed in chapter 5.[58] In effect, men's careers can be visualized as a rising trajectory over time. On the other hand, women have a flat career line and one in which decreases in occupational status are more common and typical.[59] Women's careers exhibit continuity in terms of the general types of occupations they hold, but there are breaks and interruptions in their careers that are a consequence of family roles and responsibilities.[60]

Efforts to explain these differences, especially women's career patterns, have taken different directions. One explanation focuses on the individual behavior of women and is sometimes referred to as a *human capital* perspective. The argument here is that such things as education, training, and time in the labor force represent investments that pay off in future rewards (in this case, gains in occupational status). According to this argument, interruptions and breaks in employment result in a "depreciation" of previously accumulated capital and reduce the likelihood of achieving gains in occupational status. Because of their more continuous employment pattern, men are better able to build on their educational and other capital in developing and advancing their careers. While there is research supporting this conclusion,[61] it does not seem reasonable to conclude that career interruptions alone can account for the entire difference in men's and women's career attainments. A second, more structural, explanation emphasizes the importance of labor markets and involves the distinction between primary and secondary sectors discussed earlier. The reasoning here is that, regardless of how or why women find themselves in the secondary sector, once in it the opportunity for careers that provide gains in occupational status is severely limited. Furthermore, even in the primary sector, they would be at a competitive disadvantage in advancing their careers relative to men.[62]

Much of the research that lies behind these interpretations has dealt with women in relatively early stages of their careers. A more comprehensive picture of the extent to which women experience disruptions in their work careers can be obtained by looking at mature women for whom the opportunity to work has existed longer. Lillian C. Chenoweth and Elizabeth Maret examined the work experiences of a national sample of approximately 5,000 women ages thirty through forty-four in the late 1960s.[63] They found that about 30 percent of these women had no significant labor force experience, another 30 percent had very substantial labor force experience, and the remaining 40 percent had mixed careers. Of special interest are the factors related to involvement in these three different types of careers. In addition to determining different levels of labor force participation, they also suggest some of the distinctive work dilemmas women face.

Chenoweth and Maret found that women with careers exclusively in the home were more likely than others to have a strong commitment to traditional family values and the wife and mother role. There is of course a problem in interpreting the direction of causality here. It is unclear whether traditional family values and role conceptions lead to a career in the home, or whether they develop as a result of women's actual labor force (or home work) experiences. Nevertheless, those with a low commitment to traditional roles and values were more likely to have labor force careers, but this factor did not differentiate those with mixed careers. Husband's income was only weakly related to career pattern. Only married women whose husbands were in the top income group were more likely to have careers in the home and less likely to have labor force careers. Educational attainment distinguished between these career patterns only at the extremes. Women with less than five years of education were overrepresented in the home career type and those with sixteen or more years of education were overrepresented in the labor force career type. Married women were also asked about their husband's attitude toward their working (or starting to work). Although it would have been preferable to have asked this question directly of husbands, perceived husband's attitude was a very strong predictor of women's career type. Among women who perceived their husbands as "disliking very much" their working, 63.2 percent had home careers and only 3.6 percent had labor force careers. On the other hand, of those who perceived their husbands as "liking very much" their working, 45.9 percent had labor force careers and only 9.5 percent had home careers. The attitudes of both women and men toward work and family roles are an important factor affecting women's careers. Some of the recent changes in these attitudes, as well as their implications for women's careers, are discussed in the next section.

CHANGING ATTITUDES TOWARD FAMILY AND WORK

Since the 1960s there have been a number of national surveys of men's and women's sex role attitudes, including attitudes toward women's participation in the labor force. When we look at the results of these studies over time, it is apparent that there has been significant movement away from the traditional conception of women's roles revolving around home and family responsibilities and men's roles anchored in the workplace. Studies during the 1960s and early 1970s documented a shift in attitudes among both men and women to a more favorable view of women's participation in the labor force and to their increased participation in decision making within the family.[64]

Andrew Cherlin and Pamela Barnhouse Walters examined data from five national surveys conducted by the National Opinion Research Center between 1972 and 1978 and concluded that the trend toward less traditional sex-role attitudes continued among both men and women.[65] The key question asked in these surveys was: "Do you approve or disapprove of a married woman earning money in business or industry if she has a husband capable of supporting her?" Between 1972 and 1978 the proportion of white men indicating approval (i.e., supporting a nontraditional role for women) increased from 62 percent to 73 percent. Among white women the comparable increase was from 67 percent to 75 percent. In other words, by 1978 approval by both white men and women of a married woman working was virtually the same. A different pattern was found among blacks, however. Support for a nontraditional sex-role for women actually decreased slightly among black men, from 68 percent approval of the above statement in 1972 to 64 percent approval in 1978. Among black women there was essentially no change. In 1978, 75 percent of the black women approved of women working compared to 76 percent in 1972. Thus, among blacks in 1978, men were less likely than women to support the idea of women pursuing careers in the labor force.

A rather unique study has collected longitudinal data from women over an eighteen-year period (1962–1980) and makes it possible to trace changes in women's sex-role attitudes over time. The women in the study were a sample of all women in Detroit who gave birth in July, 1961. They were first interviewed in 1962 and in 1980 they and their children (age eighteen by this time) were also interviewed. Thus, in 1980 it was possible to compare mothers' attitudes with those of their children. In their analysis of data from this study, Arland Thornton, Duane F. Alwin, and Donald Camburn found that women's attitudes had consistently become less traditional in many areas and dramatically more supportive of labor force participation and the idea of women having work careers.[66] Daughters were also considerably less traditional in their attitudes than their mothers, although sons were more traditional in their sex-role attitudes than daughters were.[67] Thornton, Alwin, and Camburn also attempted to identify factors related to sex-role attitudes and changes in attitudes. In general, younger women were less traditional in their attitudes and their attitudes changed more over the period of the study. Actual labor force experience was also related to attitudes. Those with substantial work experience since marriage were less traditional in their sex-role attitudes, and changed more over time, but mothers' work experience was not related to their daughters' attitudes. Identification with an involvement in fundamentalist Protestant religious denominations was also related to sex-role attitudes. Since such groups have actively encouraged and supported traditional family roles for women, it is not surprising that women identified with them actually became more traditional in their attitudes over time.

Mothers with more education had less traditional attitudes, changed more over time, and had daughters who were less traditional in their views. This finding regarding the relationship between education and sex-role attitudes is especially important. It suggests that if the educational levels of women continue to rise (which has been occurring consistently in recent decades), they and their children will continue to develop more liberal, less traditional attitudes regarding the appropriateness and legitimacy of women pursuing careers in the labor force. Thus, rising educational levels among women may contribute to their increased labor force participation and shape the attitudes of the next generation as well.

WOMEN'S CAREERS IN THE PROFESSIONS: THE PROTEGE SYSTEM AND THE CONSEQUENCES OF SPONSORSHIP

Careers in the professions are shaped by a *protege system* in which senior members of the profession sponsor younger colleagues. In many respects this protege system is similar to the master-apprentice relationship that was the central organizing feature of work in the guild system of the Middle Ages and that still exists in many contemporary skilled craft occupations.[68] The protege system is controlled by those who are key members of the informal inner circles that exist in professional communities.[69] It controls access to training for specialties that offer opportunities for economic rewards, prestige, and visibility. Access to internships, fellowships, and research opportunities in prestigious organizations (e.g., hospitals, universities, law firms, courts) and access to powerful and influential senior colleagues are also managed through the protege system. People receive different amounts and kinds of sponsorship and some may not be sponsored at all. Sponsors open doors, "grease wheels," and "wire" opportunities for those they have chosen for special treatment. The opportunities they have to offer are limited in number and vary in their attractiveness and long-term career value. The kinds and amounts of sponsorship people receive early in their careers are critical for their eventual career attainments.

While the protege system operates to distribute opportunities unequally among younger aspiring members of the professions, its functions for sponsors are also very important. For sponsors, the system is a means of accomplishing several things. It may be used to recruit potential partners for a private practice or firm, or collaborators in research programs. The sponsorship system includes the principle of reciprocity. It is assumed that proteges will repay their sponsors for their favorable treatment. There are many forms that such repayment may take. Where research collaboration is involved, the sponsor may simply expect that the protege will carry on the sponsor's research program in ways that contribute to and enhance the sponsor's continued professional visibility and reputation. The protege's obligations may take other forms. If the protege reaches a position of power and influence, the opportunity to do favors for the sponsor may result in sufficient and appropriate repayment. In effect, the system serves sponsors by enabling them to maintain and expand their spheres of influence and control and expand their circle of colleagues with varying kinds and degrees of obligations to them. The system also serves to recruit the next generation of leaders and members of the inner circle, thus perpetuating itself.

Cynthia Fuchs Epstein has argued persuasively that the protege system may work to the disadvantage of women's careers in the professions.[70] Since the vast majority of people in the professions have been men, men have dominated the positions of leadership and power (i.e., the inner circles) in which effective sponsorship can be exercised. Sponsors may be reluctant to select women as proteges, or to sponsor them for the best opportunities. Sponsors may be less able to see a woman as a potential successor in a private practice, a firm, or a research laboratory. In discussing the professions in chapter 2, the importance of commitment as part of the professional ideology was emphasized. In all likelihood, sponsors assume that the long-term commitments of women are weaker than those of available male proteges, and that women's careers are more likely to be interrupted by family responsibilities. In selecting proteges (be they men or women) there are no guarantees that the sponsor's investment will pay off; sponsors may favor men as proteges and as candidates for the most attractive opportunities as a way of keeping their risks and losses to a minimum. The "community" dimension of the professions may also work against the selection of women as proteges. Given the "clubiness" of the professions and especially their inner circles, the entry of women into positions of visibility and power may be seen as disruptive and detrimental to the intimacy, solidarity, and informality of the (predominantly male) colleague group. Rather than risk the ire and hostility of fellow members of the inner circle, sponsors who might want to sponsor female proteges may be very reluctant to do so. Epstein argues that sponsorship may be even more important to women than to men on the grounds that women's access to opportunities and a recognition of their accomplishments may only occur if they are the protege of an influential sponsor. Furthermore, she suggests that sponsors may need to make special efforts to advance the careers of female proteges because of the distinctive obstacles they face.

One recurring theme points to a "double bind" for women in the professions. If married, it is assumed that they are more committed to their families than to their careers. If single, it is assumed that their main priority is marriage and they are therefore viewed as less viable candidates for sponsorship.[71] If they express a nurturant, supportive, and conciliatory style, they are regarded as poor candidates for leadership roles, but if they adopt an assertive, initiative-taking style, they may be seen as a threat to the leadership positions of men.[72]

Judith Lorber's analysis of the careers of women physicians concluded that although their performance in medical school is comparable to that of men, their career attainments are substantially lower.[73] She used such indicators of career attainment as prestige of the hospital in which they took their internships and residencies, receipt of a fellowship or award during training, and whether or not they had achieved the position of chief resident. About one-third of the women had "low" attainment compared to 15 percent of the men, but 18 percent of the men compared to 10 percent of the women had "high" attainment. About two-thirds of the men and 56 percent of the women were described as having "moderate" attainment. She also found that men had experienced sustained progress in their careers, but the careers of women had a "stop and go" pattern to them.[74] Another important finding in Lorber's analysis was that women physicians with family responsibilities were at a disadvantage in participating in the professional networks that are important to career advancement. Family demands simply left little time to nurture these contacts through informal socializing.[75] Most importantly, such colleague networks seem to be essential for women to be productive and receive recognition for their accomplishments.[76]

The careers of women in law appear to have undergone some dramatic changes in recent years along with a continuation of traditional patterns. Although their representation in the field of law has been very low until quite recently, women in law have traditionally worked at less prestigious and sex-typed specialties such as family law, trusts and estates, and public interest law. They have been concentrated in government employment and the public defender's office, and underrepresented in private practice. Cynthia Fuchs Epstein reports that this is still the case.[77] Where women have been employed in private firms they were less likely than men to be involved in courtroom litigation and more likely to be given responsibility for background work, case preparation, and administrative tasks. During the 1970s, women's career opportunities in law became more diverse with their increased involvement in poverty and public interest law, and feminist law practices. The most striking change in career opportunities noted by Epstein is the entry of women into prestigious and powerful Wall Street law firms. Prior to the 1970s women were virtually absent from these firms. However, by the late 1970s about 12 percent of the legal staff of thirty-two of the largest Wall Street firms were women.[78] By the early 1980s, 3.5 percent of all "partners," as distinct from salaried "associates," were women.[79] Epstein attributes this change as well as the generally expanding opportunities of women in law to the Civil Rights Act of 1964, antidiscrimination lawsuits, the active intervention of law school personnel in the recruitment process, and changing conceptions of women's competencies both within and outside the legal profession. Another important change in women's career patterns is their increasing acceptance as law school faculty. By the late 1970s women constituted about 10 percent of law school faculty although there was a great deal of variation among law schools.[80] Despite these gains, it appears that the informal and legendary "clubiness" of the legal profession poses a serious obstacle to women's careers. In firms where they are found in sufficient numbers, women's networks have formed as a vehicle for the sharing of career-relevant professional information, but in the long run the career attainments of women are likely to depend on their ability to become part of the dominant informal system.[81]

WOMEN IN MANAGERIAL CAREERS: PROBLEMS OF POWER

It has already been pointed out that women are even more underrepresented in managerial and executive occupations than in the professions.

It is probably the case that women encounter more discrimination, stereotyping, and resistance in the managerial world than in the professions. A cult and culture of masculinity permeates managerial work.[82] Managerial work in many respects is associated with male role characteristics like independence, initiative, forcefulness, competitiveness, and tough-minded objectivity. Ironically, although the *image* of the manager is one that emphasizes masculine traits, the actual *tasks* that managers perform are not exclusively those associated with maleness. Compassion, understanding, and interpersonal warmth, traits associated with the female role, may be just as important to managerial success as the male qualities.[83] Moreover, women in supervisory positions represent a reversal of traditional conceptions of the "appropriate" relationship between sex and power.[84] The consequences of exclusion from this male culture in managerial occupations are similar to the results of exclusion from the inner circles of the professions: the lack of access to information, contacts, and informal participation represents a barrier to career advancement.

One of the most influential and useful perspectives on the careers of women managers, and particularly supervisors, is that provided by Rosabeth Moss Kanter.[85] There is a good deal of evidence indicating that many employers believe that women simply do not make good supervisors.[86] They are viewed as overbearing, domineering, capricious, and overly concerned with bureaucratic routines and details. In addition, subordinates are seen as a potential problem. While men are likely to resist the idea of working for a female supervisor, many women have a preference for a male supervisor. National polls in the 1970s found that women preferred a male to a female supervisor by a margin of eight to one[87] and a study of business students found that the qualities identified as those of a good manager by both male and female students were predominantly male characteristics.[88]

Kanter has argued that such negative evaluations of women in managerial/supervisory positions reflect sex differences in power and influence within organizations. In particular, performance ratings by supervisors are affected by the supervisor's power and influence, and more powerful supervisors generate higher morale, tend to be less rigid and authoritarian, and generally are better liked.[89] Powerless supervisors, on the other hand, are more likely to be very controlling in their relationships with subordinates, show favoritism, and generate lower morale. Since men are more likely to be in formal positions of power and influence and to be part of the informal networks of organizational influence, differences in the perception and behavior of female supervisors are a result of the unequal distribution of organizational power rather than a reflection of simply sex differences in managerial or personal style. Support for this reasoning was found in a study of employees in a federal bureaucracy. Men and women supervisors with similar levels of power were perceived in similar ways by their subordinates.[90] Greater empowerment of women in management would help to mitigate these obstacles to career development.

There are very few studies that have attempted to follow the managerial careers of men and women over time. An exception is a study of a sample of men and women who received their Master of Business Administration (MBA) degrees from the same university during the 1950s, 1960s, and 1970s. Sharon Tucker reports relatively little movement of the women MBAs toward management positions. In fact, she found fewer graduates in the seventies starting out in corporate career ladders than in the sixties.[91] Although male graduates during the fifties did not pursue corporate careers, those of the sixties and seventies did and, on the whole, have experienced substantial upward movement. When they were interviewed in 1980, women graduates lagged behind the men considerably in both salary and authority. Tucker found no evidence that family responsibilities were a major factor leading to the pursuit of careers outside of the corporate setting. She concluded that women MBAs in the fifties had low expectations regarding a career but those in the sixties had high expectations. For the latter, the jobs they acquired offered few opportunities for advancement, resulting in a decrease in their commitment to a corporate career.

CAREERS IN BLUE-COLLAR OCCUPATIONS

As indicated earlier, the participation of women in skilled craft occupations has not increased appreciably in recent years, although a substantial minority of women have been employed in semiskilled factory work. Relatively little research has been done on women's careers in blue-collar occupations. Recent work on women in blue-collar occupations has included the issue of sexual harassment, which is discussed in the next section.

There is some evidence, however, that educational, training, and apprenticeship systems systematically discourage and exclude women from pursuing careers in skilled craft occupations. Sally Hillsman Baker has pointed out that in the mid-1970s New York City's public high schools offered extensive vocational training but it was sharply segregated by sex.[92] Male students were enrolled in fifty-three trade programs but women were enrolled in only thirty-six. Forty-five of the courses had students of one sex only; fifteen were all female and thirty were all male. Most importantly, the kinds of work for which this vocational training was preparing people varied markedly by sex. Excluding the young women who were in the home economics curriculum, 91 percent were in courses preparing them for office work, cosmetology, health occupations, retailing, and clothing manufacture. Only about 3 percent of the male students were in these programs, but four-fifths were in programs that emphasized mechanical, technical, and repair skills. These included courses in computer technology, and television and radio broadcasting technology and repair, as well as traditional skilled crafts like carpentry, plumbing, and printing.[93] Baker suggests that teachers and counselors play a major role in directing female students into vocational programs that prepare them for poor paying, low-skill, dead-end blue-collar jobs that offer few if any opportunities for a meaningful career. Although Baker's research was done in New York City, the sharply segregated pattern of vocational training she found there is probably not atypical. In Wisconsin in the mid-1970s, only 1.5 percent of the high school students enrolled in industrial vocational training programs were female. Those not in college preparatory programs were receiving training in business subjects, an educational experience likely to lead to work in traditionally female clerical occupations.[94]

With little exposure to technical, mechanical, and craft training in high school, few women are prepared to enter apprenticeship programs that might lead to stable careers in skilled blue-collar work. Sharon L. Harlan and Brigid O'Farrell have pointed out that the dual labor market that operates within firms results in women (and racial and ethnic minorities) being hired for lower-skill jobs that have few career opportunities.[95] They argue that women have traditionally been hired for "jobs with short lines of progression, which prevent them from gaining access to training and skill development, promotion opportunities, higher wages, and authority in the organization."[96] Their study of a large manufacturing concern found these kinds of patterns. Although a few "pioneers" had managed to gain entry to traditionally male jobs, the majority of women employees had not. The company studied by Harlan and O'Farrell had reached an Affirmative Action Agreement with the U.S. Equal Opportunity Commission to desegregate its labor force and they were primarily interested in the extent to which this agreement had affected women's opportunities. The agreement called for an upgrading of predominantly female jobs and the hiring and transfer of women to predominantly male jobs. Harlan and O'Farrell concluded that some integration of predominantly male jobs has occurred and the participation of women in a three-year machinist apprentice program had also increased. Women were still overrepresented, however, in the least skilled jobs—many of them previously male jobs—with the fewest opportunities for advancement. In effect, new patterns of sex segregation appear to have been created. The results of their study do not provide a basis for much optimism about the development of career opportunities in blue-collar work for women comparable to those of men.

SEXUAL HARASSMENT ON THE JOB

The topic of sexual harassment in the workplace has received a great deal of attention in recent years. It represents a distinctive career problem for women as well as a feature of work that is basically a form of sex discrimination.

The U.S. Civil Rights Commission has defined sexual harassment as "unwelcome sexual advances, requests for sexual favors, and other verbal or physical conduct of a sexual nature" when submission to such conduct is implicitly or explicitly made a condition of employment or is used as a basis for decisions affecting an individual, or when such conduct unreasonably interferes with a person's work or creates an "intimidating, hostile, or offensive working environment."[97] Mary Bularzik has provided a somewhat less formal, but nevertheless useful, definition of sexual harassment as "any unwanted pressure for sexual activity" including "verbal innuendos and suggestive comments, luring gestures, unwanted physical contact (touching, pinching, and so on), rape, and attempted rape."[98] Despite efforts to define sexual harassment with some precision, vagueness remains. It is unclear what constitutes "unreasonable interference" with work, when a sexual advance is "unwelcome," and what an "offensive" working environment is. But such ambiguities are grist for the legal mill. Indeed, the courts have ruled that when it is reasonable to believe that these conditions exist, they constitute a form of discrimination on the basis of sex and that there are grounds for legal action under Title VII of the Civil Rights Act of 1964.

It is very difficult to say how much sexual harassment exists in different work settings. Fox and Hesse-Biber suggest that it is so common that many women, especially those in clerical occupations, have come to regard it as inevitable and as virtually a condition of employment.[99] Women may be reluctant to try to do anything about harassment out of fear of reprisals that might include being fired, demoted, passed over for promotion or a raise, transferred to an undesirable job, or given a poor recommendation for another job.

There has been some research on sexual harassment that provides a sense of the scope of the problem and the forms it takes. Of 155 women surveyed in the Ithaca, New York area, 70 percent said that they had experienced sexual harassment of some type at least once. Organizational superiors and supervisors were the most frequent source of harassment (40 percent reported harassment from a supervisor), but co-workers (22 percent) and customers, clients and others (29 percent) also contribute to the problem. Only 1 percent of the women reported harassment from a subordinate.[100] This, along with the high level of harassment from superiors, is an especially important finding because it underscores the importance of power in harassment. In effect, harassment can be seen as a reflection of the unequal distribution of power in the workplace and the use of power in inappropriate ways. Support for this interpretation also comes from a study of women assembly line workers in the automobile industry. James E. Gruber and Lars Bjorn conducted a study (using female interviewers) of 138 women regarding their experiences with harassment, their responses to it, and the consequences of harassment.[101] Some 36 percent of the women reported having experienced sexual harassment. Over half of the incidents reported took the form of sexual propositioning and abusive language. Other less frequent forms of harassment included physical attacks, verbal innuendo, sexual bribery, social derogation, body language, and other actions including whistling, stares, etc. Gruber and Bjorn found that women with lower status and/or power were the targets of more frequent harassment. Black women, younger women, those who were unmarried, and those with lower-status jobs were all more likely to be harassed. Again, relative powerlessness results in greater risk and frequency of harassment. Women's responses were surprisingly mild. The most common response was some mild verbal comment intended to make light of the incident or convey the point that the woman being harassed was not interested in pursuing the matter. However, about one-fourth of the women responded more assertively with very strong verbal responses, by physically attacking the harasser, or by reporting the incident to someone in authority. Harassed women also had lower self-esteem and greater general dissatisfaction with life, suggesting that sexual harassment on the job can have negative consequences for women that go beyond the workplace.

JOB SATISFACTION AMONG WOMEN

The research on job satisfaction discussed in chapter 6 dealt largely with men and their responses to their work. The entry of women into the labor force in large numbers, however, has led to increased interest in their job satisfaction and dissatisfaction.

A few comparisons of the job satisfaction of men and women are available. One study, based on national survey data, found only minor differences in how satisfied men and women were with intrinsic and extrinsic aspects of their jobs. However, when women were divided into those who were the primary breadwinner in their family and those who were not, the convenience of their jobs was an important factor in job satisfaction. Convenience refers to such things as ease of getting to and from work, the pleasantness of the physical aspects of the work setting, having good hours, an absence of conflicting demands, and the like. For women who were not primary breadwinners, these convenience aspects of their jobs had a much greater effect on job satisfaction than they did for women who were primary breadwinners. Jack K. Martin and Sandra L. Hanson, the authors of the study, suggest that where work is a secondary role, job convenience and flexibility are important sources of satisfaction because they enable women to perform more effectively in both work and family roles.[102]

Other kinds of sex differences are reported by Joanne Miller in her analysis of job satisfaction.[103] Men and women attached the same amount of importance to such things as pay, fringe benefits, how inherently interesting or exciting a job is, job security, pride in the job, and characteristics of supervisors and co-workers as sources of job satisfaction. They did differ, however, in some important ways. Men regarded the opportunity to exercise leadership, make decisions, and get ahead as more important than women did. Women, on the other hand, were more likely to emphasize working hours, how tiring a job is, its cleanliness, and job pressures. Men also gave greater importance to freedom, prestige, and the opportunity to use their abilities and help people.

Miller also found that educational attainment and rural-urban background were more strongly related to job satisfaction among women than among men. Women with more education and those from urban backgrounds were less satisfied with their jobs than less educated women and those from rural backgrounds. Educated urban women may have developed expectations about work that are more at odds with their actual work experiences than is the case for men from similar backgrounds. It is also possible that the "fit" between individual expectations and jobs is poorer for women than for men. One of the biggest differences in the job satisfaction of men and women involves their reaction to the complexity and autonomy of their jobs. Women's job satisfaction is directly related to job complexity, while for men autonomy is much more important. Although men also value complex work, they are more likely to be satisfied with it if the job also allows for autonomy. For women, complex work need not offer autonomy in order to be satisfying.

In addition to the survey research discussed above, an analysis of job satisfaction among clerical workers in a large federal agency has also been done. Although it focuses on different issues than the research discussed above and does not include male-female comparisons, it does suggest some factors related to job satisfaction in an occupation where women have predominated in the past as well as the present. Burke D. Grandjean and Patricia A. Taylor concluded that the clerical workers who were most satisfied with their jobs were those who felt that their skills were being fully utilized and that they were receiving adequate information about training programs that would improve their job performance. Those who perceived an absence of sex discrimination also had greater job satisfaction.[104] Grandjean and Taylor conclude that the perception of opportunities is a more important determinant of job satisfaction than the overall status of clerical work.

A final study of women's job satisfaction involves women in nontraditional, male-dominated, skilled and semiskilled occupations. Judith S. McIlwee interviewed eighty-six women who had recently entered or were training for entry into nontraditional blue-collar jobs.[105] Their concerns revolved largely around mastering the skills needed for their jobs, developing self-confidence, and getting along with male co-workers and supervisors. These were their main sources of satisfaction and dissatisfaction. A year later, the thirty-nine women who were still in these jobs were reinterviewed and there were some interesting changes in their attitudes toward their jobs. The majority (62 percent) said they were more satisfied with their jobs than a year ago, and 15 percent said they were less satisfied. The remainder (13 percent) said their satisfaction level was the same. Interviews with these women indicated that many problems that revolved around being women in traditionally male occupations were being resolved and diminishing as a source of dissatisfaction. At the same time, however, they were becoming increasingly aware of the problems of being in a blue-collar occupation. In many respects they were taking on the negative attitudes toward blue-collar work traditionally expressed by men in these occupations. Working conditions, relationships with management, and the nature of the work itself had begun to emerge as sources of dissatisfaction.

ISSUES OF EQUITY IN THE WORKPLACE

Our discussion of women and work has illustrated the dramatic sex segregation of the American labor force and major differences in men's and women's careers. In the 1970s and 1980s, issues of equity have come to the fore as women's participation in the labor force has increased. Involved here is more than just the issue of occupational sex segregation. The issues include concern about the persistent gap in men's and women's income and earnings as well as public policies to deal with workplace inequities such as equal opportunity, nondiscrimination, affirmative action, and comparable worth.

THE MALE-FEMALE INCOME GAP

Given the existence of occupational sex segregation and the concentration of women in clerical occupations at the lowest levels of the white-collar hierarchies of organizations and in service occupations, it is not surprising that they have consistently earned less than men. The simplest and most vivid way to illustrate this difference is to look at women's income as a proportion of men's income. On the average and across the occupational spectrum, women earn about 63 cents for every dollar earned by men. Chart 7.1 illustrates this difference in earnings. The top part of the chart indicates that both men's and women's earnings have been increasing since 1967, but the ratio of women's to men's earnings (see the bottom part of the chart) has remained remarkably constant.

There is some variation by broad occupational categories in the relative incomes of men and women. In 1982, the ratio of women's to men's earnings was highest (i.e., was most favorable for women) in professional specialty occupations (women earned 66 percent of men's earnings), in precision production, craft, and repair (65 percent of men's earnings), and among operators, fabricators, and laborers (64 percent of men's earnings). Earnings ratios were lowest (i.e., least favorable for women) in the "technical, sales, and administrative support" category, and service occupations with women's earnings at 59 percent of men's earnings in both cases. In executive, administrative, and managerial occupations, women earned 60 percent of what men earned.[106]

EXPLAINING MALE-FEMALE DIFFERENCES IN EARNINGS

A great deal of research has attempted to identify factors related to sex differences in earnings. Efforts to explain these differences in terms of the decisions of women to work in particular occupations have not been particularly successful. One argument is that women choose to work in occupations where their intermittent participation will not have a negative effect on their earnings. Another line of reasoning is that they choose to work in occupations that offer relatively high starting pay but few opportunities for improvements in pay. Paula England's research on this issue found no support for these arguments.[107] The higher turnover of women in the labor force (i.e., their intermittent work pattern) also does not seem to be a factor in explaining their unequal pay. When men and women with similar turnover rates are compared, men still receive higher pay.[108]

Occupational sex segregation of the kind identified throughout this chapter seems to be the most important factor involved in the disparity in men's and women's earnings and income. Women in the professions are in those of lower status and prestige which command lower salaries; in blue-collar occupations they are in those of lower skill and those with a poorer earnings potential; and their concentration in clerical occupations puts a substantial proportion in a low-paying occupational category.

Chart 7.1
Men's and Women's Earnings, 1967–1982

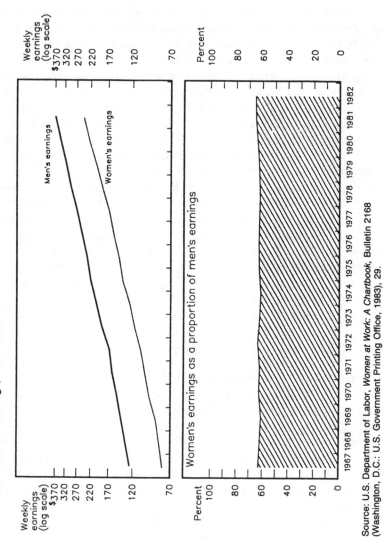

Source: U.S. Department of Labor, *Women at Work: A Chartbook*, Bulletin 2168
(Washington, D.C.: U.S. Government Printing Office, 1983), 29.

More than just *occupational* segregation is involved. The overrepresentation of women in the secondary sector of the *labor market* is a separate aspect of women's labor force participation that is also a factor in their lower earnings.

A distinction between labor markets that is useful for understanding sex differences in earnings has developed from analysis of the structure of the economy. This involves the distinction between core and periphery sectors of the economy. The *core* sector includes industries in durable goods manufacturing, mining, and construction. These are industries that have many monopolistic elements, high productivity, and high profits. They are capital intensive, unionized, have high job-skill requirements, and offer relatively high wages and fringe benefits as well as security of employment. Examples include the automobile, steel, rubber, aluminum, aerospace, and petroleum industries. Industries in the *periphery* sector tend to be smaller and more labor intensive. They have lower profit margins, lower productivity, and are in a more competitive market situation. They are relatively ununionized, wages and fringe benefits are low, and employment is less stable and predictable. The periphery includes industries concentrated in agriculture, nondurable goods manufacturing, and retail trade. Core industries have the advantage of size, assets, and political power. They are able to realize economies of scale, and they invest heavily in research and development. Periphery industries lack these resources and advantages.[109]

The importance of this distinction lies in the fact that women have been and continue to be disproportionately located in the periphery sector of the economy.[110] Thus, their relatively lower wages reflect the disadvantages of periphery employment and the earnings advantage that men have by virtue of their concentration in the core sector. Kathryn B. Ward and Charles W. Mueller have looked at the effect of economic sector and position in the authority hierarchy of organizations on the earnings of men and women.[111] They found that earnings were lower in the periphery sector and that earnings were directly related to position in the authority hierarchy for both men and women. Although men's incomes were slightly higher in the core sector, they received higher income benefits from being in positions of authority than women did. Since women are less likely to be in positions of authority and more likely to be concentrated in the periphery sector, they are at a double disadvantage with regard to earnings. Ward and Mueller report that education and work patterns also affect earnings in different ways in the core and periphery. A discontinuous work pattern had a greater negative effect on women's earnings in the periphery than in the core sector. Having a college degree had a more positive effect on their earnings in the core than in the periphery sector, however.

PAY EQUITY AND PUBLIC POLICY

Issues of equal treatment (especially regarding pay) in the labor market have become a major public policy concern in recent years. Since 1963, with the passage of the Equal Pay Act, federal law requires that people with similar qualifications doing the same work receive the same pay regardless of sex, although employers may take seniority and merit into account and pay may vary in those cases where people are being paid on the basis of piece work. However, the law applies only to those situations where people are doing the *same* work. As we have seen, women commonly work in highly sex-segregated occupations where they are doing work that is *different* from that being done by men.

Even where women and men in different jobs perform similar tasks (as defined by the U.S. Department of Labor's *Dictionary of Occupational Titles*), men receive higher pay than women do.[112] Such findings lend support to the conclusion that work done by women is systematically undervalued and pay is artificially depressed.[113] In effect, the principle of equal pay for equal work has not been achieved and discrimination in pay based solely on sex persists.[114]

Another pay equity concern deals more directly with the concentration of women in poorer paying, sex-typed occupations. This is the principle of *comparable worth*, which involves the idea that people should receive equal pay for work that is of equal value or worth. Determining the relative value or worth of jobs is a very difficult but not impossible task. It involves comparing jobs on the basis of skill, knowledge, formal training required, responsibility, number of people supervised, and the like.[115] Comparable worth has become and will continue to be a hotly debated emotional and legal issue.[116] It calls into question the validity of pay levels set in sex-segregated labor markets where the pool of potential employees is predominantly of one sex. If implemented, the principle of comparable worth would undoubtedly reduce the male-female earnings gap. However, it would not necessarily have a direct and immediate impact on the sex segregation of occupations per se.

SUMMARY

The entry of women into the labor force since World War II represents a significant change in basic conceptions of women's and men's roles as well as an important new dimension in the organization of work. A great deal of research in recent years has attempted to identify factors related to women's increased labor force participation. Demographic, economic, and cultural factors are all involved in interconnected ways.

Despite the increase in women's paid employment outside the home, the occupational structure remains sharply segregated on the basis of sex with few fundamental changes since the early part of the century. Women's socialization, their occupational choices, and the segmentation of the labor market all play a role in the continued sex segregation of occupations. The entry of women into traditionally male occupations is occurring, but at a relatively slow pace. Women's increasing educational attainment is likely to continue to create pressure for their entry into male-dominated occupations, especially in the professions.

Men's and women's careers differ in important ways. Where men's careers show continuous development and progression, women's careers lack the same degree of continuity and improvement. The discontinuous nature of women's labor force participation contributes to this difference. The attitudes of both men and women have been changing; they are becoming increasingly favorable toward women working outside the home and having significant careers. Nevertheless, women's careers are hampered by a variety of factors. In the professions, the protege system places limits on the kinds of opportunities women have for career mobility. In managerial work, their relative powerlessness compared to men remains a serious impediment to career advancement. In blue-collar occupations, career opportunities for women in skilled craft occupations are minimal, and in industrial settings, women are found in the lowest-skill job categories with the shortest career lines and the fewest opportunities for upward career movement.

Sexual harassment represents a serious problem for women in all types of work. Despite the pervasiveness of the problem, it has only recently become an issue of public policy and a policy concern of employing organizations. With women's large-scale entry into the labor force, new questions about job satisfaction have been investigated. Women appear to have similar as well as different sources of job satisfaction and dissatisfaction compared to men. Although the research to date has only begun to explore these differences, it appears that women's job satisfaction depends strongly on the inherent complexity and challenges that work presents, and less on autonomy and control.

Pay inequalities based on sex occur throughout the occupational structure. Although federal legislation prohibits discrimination in pay for men and women doing the same kind of work, sex segregation creates a situation where such policies simply do not come into play for many women. While discrimination in pay among women and men doing similar work persists, comparable worth, the principle of equal pay for work of comparable value, represents a way of addressing issues of pay equity in a sex-segregated occupational system.

NOTES

1. Richard H. Hall, "Theoretical Trends in the Sociology of Occupations," *Sociological Quarterly* 24 (Winter 1984):5–23.
2. Judith Stacey and Barrie Thorne, "The Missing Feminist Revolution in Sociology," *Social Problems* 32 (April 1985): 301–316.
3. See Joan Huber and Glenna Spitze, *Sex Stratification: Children, Housework, and Job* (New York: Academic Press, 1983) for an excellent history of women's work.
4. U.S. Bureau of the Census, *Statistical Abstract of the United States, 1985* (Washington, D.C.: U.S. Government Printing Office, 1984), 388.
5. Ibid., 392, table 655.
6. Ibid., and Linda J. Waite, *U.S. Women at Work*, Population Bulletin 36 (Washington, D.C.: Population Reference Bureau, 1981), 7, table 2.
7. U.S. Bureau of the Census, *Statistical Abstract, 1985*, 392, table 655.
8. Ibid.
9. Janet L. Norwood, *The Female-Male Earnings Gap: A Review of the Employment and Earnings Issue*, U.S. Department of Labor, Bureau of Labor Statistics, Report 673 (Washington, D.C.: 1982), 6.
10. Harriet B. Presser and Wendy Baldwin, "Child Care as a Constraint on Employment: Prevalence, Correlates, and Bearing on the Work and Fertility Nexus," *American Journal of Sociology* 85 (1980): 1202–1213.
11. U.S. Bureau of the Census, *Statistical Abstract, 1985*, 9 and 57, tables 7 and 80.
12. Robert H. Weller and Leon F. Bouvier, *Population: Demography and Policy* (New York: St. Martin's Press, 1981), 127–128; and Kenneth C. W. Kammeyer and Helen L. Ginn, *An Introduction to Population* (Chicago: Dorsey Press, 1986), 205–207.
13. Linda J. Waite and Ross M. Stolzenberg, "Intended Childbearing and Labor Force Participation of Young Women: Insights from Nonrecursive Models," *American Sociological Review* 41 (April 1976): 235–251; Ross M. Stolzenberg and Linda J. Waite, "Age, Fertility, and Expectations and Plans for Employment," *American Sociological Review* 42 (October 1977): 769–782; and Lynn Smith-Lovin and Ann R. Tickamyer, "Labor Force Participation, Fertility, Behavior, and Sex Role Attitudes," *American Sociological Review* 43 (August 1978): 541–556.
14. James Cramer, "Fertility and Female Employment: Problems of Causal Direction," *American Sociological Review* 45 (April 1980): 167–190.
15. U.S. Bureau of the Census, *Statistical Abstract of the United States, 1984* (Washington, D.C.: U.S. Government Printing Office, 1983), 84, table 120; and U.S Bureau of the Census, *Statistical Abstract, 1985*, 80, table 120.
16. Ibid., 41, table 55.
17. Waite, *U.S. Women at Work*, 5.
18. Cited in Mary Frank Fox and Sharlene Hesse-Biber, *Women at Work* (Palo Alto, Calif.: Mayfield, 1984), 30–31.
19. U.S. Bureau of the Census, *Statistical Abstract, 1985*, 149, table 145.
20. Ibid., 149, table 146; and U.S. Bureau of the Census, *Statistical Abstract, 1984*, 161, table 258.
21. John Scanzoni, *Sexual Bargaining: Power Politics in the American Family*, 2nd ed. (Chicago: University of Chicago Press, 1982).
22. Waite, *U.S. Women at Work*, 26, table 7.

23. Ibid., 26.
24. Edward Gross, "Plus Ca Change...? The Sexual Structure of Occupations Over Time," *Social Problems* 16 (Fall 1968): 198–208.
25. Francine D. Blau and Wallace E. Hendricks," *Journal of Human Resources* 24 (Spring 1979): 197–210.
26. Calculated from U.S. Bureau of the Census, *Statistical Abstract, 1985,* 402–403, table 676.
27. Fox and Hesse-Biber, *Women at Work,* 34–36; and Richard H. Hall, *Dimensions of Work* (Beverly Hills, Calif.: Sage, 1986), 209–214.
28. Ann Seidman, *Working Women: A Study of Women in Paid Jobs* (Boulder, Colo.: Westview Press, 1978), 77.
29. Gail W. Lapidus, "Occupational Segregation and Public Policy: A Comparative Analysis of American and Soviet Patterns," in *Women in the Workplace,* ed. Martha Blaxall and Barbara Reagan (Chicago: University of Chicago Press, 1976).
30. Peter B. Doeringer and Michael J. Piore, *Internal Labor Markets and Manpower Analysis* (Lexington, Mass.: D.C. Heath, 1971).
31. Michael J. Piore, *Notes for a Theory of Labor Market Stratification,* Department of Economics, Massachusetts Institute of Technology, Working Paper 95 (Cambridge, Mass., 1972).
32. U.S. Bureau of the Census, *Statistical Abstract, 1985,* 151, table 249.
33. Nancy S. Barrett, "Women in the Job Market: Occupations, Earnings, and Career Opportunities," in *The Subtle Revolution,* ed. Ralph E. Smith (Washington, D.C.: The Urban Institute, 1979), 31–61.
34. Soloman Polachek, "Occupational Segregation among Women: Theory, Evidence, and a Prognosis," in *Women in the Labor Market,* ed. Cynthia B. Lloyd, Emily S. Andrews, and Curtis L. Gilroy (New York: Columbia University Press, 1979), 29–31.
35. Barrett, "Women in the Job Market," 53.
36. Fox and Hesse-Biber, *Women at Work.*
37. Ibid., 67.
38. Elanor Emmons Maccoby and Carol Nagy Jacklin, *The Psychology of Sex Differences* (Stanford, Calif.: Stanford University Press, 1974), vol. 1; Janet G. Hunt, "Sex Stratification and Male Biography: From Deprivation to Ascendance," *Sociological Quarterly* 21 (Spring 1980): 143–156; and Claire Stasz Stoll, *Female and Male: Socialization, Social Roles, and Social Structure* (Dubuque, Iowa: William C. Brown, 1974).
39. Lynn K. White and David B. Brinkerhoff, "The Sexual Division of Labor: Evidence from Childhood," *Social Forces* 60 (September 1981): 170–181.
40. Fox and Hesse-Biber, *Women at Work,* 67–68.
41. Helen A. Moore and Jane C. Ollenburger, "What Sex is Your Parachute?: Interest Inventory/Counseling Models and the Perpetuation of the Sex/Wage Segregation of the Labor Market," *Work and Occupations* 13 (November 1986): 511–531.
42. U.S. Bureau of the Census, *Statistical Abstract, 1985,* 400, table 637.
43. Ibid.
44. "A Woman's Place is in the Bar," *American Demographics* 8 (March 1986): 14.
45. U.S. Bureau of the Census, *Statistical Abstract, 1985,* 400, table 673.
46. National Center for Education Statistics, *Digest of Educational Statistics, 1983–84* (Washington, D.C.: U.S. Government Printing Office, 1983), 101, table 88; and *Chronicle of Higher Education,* 31 (December 18, 1985): 25.

47. U.S. Bureau of the Census, *Statistical Abstract, 1985,* 157, table 265.
48. Ibid., 400 and 402, tables 673 and 676.
49. Fox and Hesse-Biber, *Women at Work,* 135.
50. Susan Fraker, "Why Women Aren't Getting to the Top," *Fortune* (April 16, 1984): 40–45.
51. U.S. Bureau of the Census, *Statistical Abstract, 1985,* 400 and 402, tables 673 and 676.
52. Ibid.
53. Jane H. Lillydahl, "Women and Traditionally Male Blue-Collar Jobs," *Work and Occupations* 13 (August 1986): 307–323.
54. Linda J. Waite and Sue E. Berryman, *Women in Nontraditional Occupations: Choice and Turnover* (Santa Monica, Calif.: The RAND Corporation, 1985).
55. Thomas A. Lyson, "Sex Differences in the Choice of a Male or Female Career Line: An Analysis of Background Characteristics and Work Values," *Work and Occupations* 11 (May 1984): 131–146.
56. Rachael A. Rosenfeld, "Women's Occupational Careers: Individual and Structural Explanations," *Sociology of Work and Occupations* 6 (August 1979): 283–311.
57. G.S. Palmer, *Labor Mobility in Six Cities: A Report on the Survey of Patterns and Factors in Labor Mobility, 1940–50* (New York: Social Science Research Council, 1954); and Herbert S. Parnes, *Research on Labor Mobility: An Appraisal of Research Findings in the United States* (New York, Social Science Research Council, 1954).
58. Peter M. Blau and Otis Dudley Duncan, *The American Occupational Structure* (New York: Wiley, 1967); and William H. Sewell and Robert M. Hauser, "The Wisconsin Longitudinal Study of Social and Psychological Factors in Aspirations and Achievements," *Research in Sociology of Education and Socialization* 1 (1980): 59–99.
59. William H. Sewell, Robert M. Hauser, and Wendy C. Wolf, "Occupational Achievement to Mid-Life of Male and Female High School Graduates," paper presented at the annual meeting of the American Sociological Association, Chicago, 1977; "Sex, Schooling, and Occupational Status," *American Journal of Sociology* 86 (1980): 551–583; and Rosenfeld, *op. cit.*
60. Rosenfeld, "Women's Occupational Careers."
61. Ibid.; and "Race and Sex Differences in Career Dynamics," *American Sociological Review* 45 (August 1980): 583–609; and Diane H. Felmlee, "The Dynamics of Women's Job Mobility," *Work and Occupations* 11 (August 1984): 259–281.
62. Robert Bibb and William H. Form, "The Effects of Industrial, Occupational, and Sex Stratification on Wages in Blue-Collar Markets," *Social Forces* 55 (1977): 974–996; Randy Hodgson and Robert L. Kaufman, "Economic Dualism: A Critical Review," *American Sociological Review* 47 (December 1982): 727–739; and E. M. Beck, Patrick M. Horan, and Charles M. Tolbert II, "Stratification in a Dual Economy: A Sectoral Model of Earnings Determination," *American Sociological Review* 43 (October 1978), 704–720.
63. Lillian C. Chenoweth and Elizabeth Maret, "The Career Patterns of Mature American Women," *Sociology of Work and Occupations* 7 (May 1980): 222–251.
64. Karen O. Mason, John L. Czajka, and Sara Arber, "Changes in U.S. Women's Sex Role Attitudes, 1964–1974," *American Sociological Review*

81 (August 1976): 573–596; and Arland Thornton and Deborah Freedman, "Change in the Sex-Role Attitudes of Women, 1962–1977," *American Sociological Review* 44 (1979): 832–842.

65. Andrew Cherlin and Pamela Barnhouse Walters, "Trends in United States Men's and Women's Sex-Role Attitudes: 1972–1978," *American Sociological Review* 46 (August 1981): 453–460.

66. Arland Thornton, Duane F. Alwin, and Donald Camburn, "Causes and Consequences of Sex-Role Attitudes and Attitude Change," *American Sociological Review* 48 (April 1983): 211–227.

67. This sex difference among young men and women is consistent with other research on the attitudes of young people toward family and work. For example, see Regula A. Herzog and Jerald G. Bachman, *Sex Role Attitudes Among High School Seniors: Views About Work and Family Roles* (Ann Arbor: Mich.: University of Michigan, Institute for Social Research, 1982).

68. For a discussion of the guild system see Wilbert E. Moore, *Industrial Relations and the Social Order* (New York: Macmillan, 1951).

69. Oswald Hall, "The Informal Organization of the Medical Profession," *Canadian Journal of Economics and Political Science* 12 (1946): 30–41; and "The Stages of a Medical Career," *American Journal of Sociology* 53 (1948): 327–336.

70. Cynthia Fuchs Epstein, "Encountering the Male Establishment: Sex-Status Limits on Women's Careers in the Professions," *American Journal of Sociology* 75 (May 1970): 965–982; and *Woman's Place: Options and Limits in Professional Careers* (Berkeley, Calif.: University of California Press, 1970).

71. Judith Lorber, "Trust, Loyalty, and the Place of Women in the Informal Organization of Work," in *Women: A Feminist Perspective*, ed. Jo Freeman (Palo Alto, Calif.: Mayfield, 1979); M. M. Osaka, "Dilemmas of Japanese Professional Women," *Social Problems* 26 (1978): 15–25; Patricia G. Bourne and Norma J. Wikler, "Commitment and the Cultural Mandate: Women in Medicine," *Social Problems* 25 (April 1978): 430–440; Debra R. Kaufman, "Associational Ties in Academe: Some Male and Female Differences," *Sex Roles* 4 (1978): 9–21; and Barbara F. Reskin, "Sex Differentiation and the Social Organization of Science," *Sociological Inquiry* 48 (1978): 3–37.

72. Patricia Y. Martin and Marie W. Osmond, "Gender and Exploitation: Resources, Structure, and Rewards in Cross-Sex Exchange." *Sociological Focus* 15 (1982): 403–416; and S. Brown and R. H. Klein, "Woman-Power in the Medical Hierarchy," *Journal of the American Medical Women's Association* 37 (1982): 155–164.

73. Judith Lorber, *Women Physicians: Careers, Status, and Power* (New York: Tavistock, 1984).

74. Ibid., 43.

75. Ibid., 97.

76. Ibid., 100.

77. Cynthia Fuchs Epstein, *Women in Law* (Garden City, N.Y.: Anchor Books, 1983), 97.

78. Ibid., 179.

79. Ibid.

80. Ibid., 219–220.

81. Ibid., 218.

82. Patricia Kosinar, "Socialization and Self-Esteem: Women and Management," in *Outsiders on the Inside: Women and Organizations*, ed. Barbara

L. Forisha and Barbara H. Goldman (Englewood Cliffs, N.J.: Prentice-Hall, 1981), 31–41.

83. Linda Keller Brown, *The Woman Manager in the United States* (Washington, D.C.: Business and Professional Women's Foundation, 1981).
84. Margaret Cussler, *The Woman Executive* (New York: Harcourt Brace, 1958).
85. Rosabeth Moss Kanter, *Men and Women of the Corporation* (New York: Basic Books, 1977).
86. K. M. Bartol, "Male versus Female Leaders: The Effect of Leader Need for Dominance on Follower Satisfaction," *Academy of Management Journal* 17 (1974): 225–233; Benson Rosen and Thomas H. Jerdee, "The Influence of Sex-Role Stereotypes on Evaluation of Male and Female Supervisory Behavior," *Journal of Applied Psychology* 57 (1973): 44–48; and Virginia Ellen Schein, "The Relationship Between Sex Stereotypes and Requisite Management Characteristics," *Journal of Applied Psychology* 57 (1973): 95–100.
87. George Ritzer and David Walczak, *Working: Conflict and Change*, 3rd ed. (Englewood Cliffs, N.J.: Prentice-Hall, 1986), 114.
88. Gary N. Powell and D. Anthony Butterfield, "The 'Good Manager': Masculine or Androgynous?" *Academy of Management Journal* 22 (1979): 395–403.
89. Kanter, *Men and Women of the Corporation*, 248.
90. Scott J. South, et al., "Sex and Power in the Federal Bureaucracy: A Comparative Analysis of Male and Female Supervisors," *Work and Occupations* 9 (May 1982): 233–254.
91. Sharon Tucker, "Careers of Men and Women MBAs: 1950–1980," *Work and Occupations* 12 (May 1985): 166–185.
92. Sally Hillsman Baker, "Women in Blue-Collar and Service Occupations," in *Women Working: Theories and Facts in Perspective*, ed. Ann H. Armstrong and Shirley Harkess (Palo Alto, Calif.: Mayfield, 1978), 339–376.
93. Ibid., 358–359.
94. Norma Briggs, *Women in Apprenticeship—Why Not?*, Manpower Research Monograph no. 33 (Washington, D.C.: U.S. Government Printing Office, 1974), 13.
95. Sharon L. Harlan and Brigid O'Farrell, "After the Pioneers: Prospects for Women in Nontraditional Blue-Collar Jobs," *Work and Occupations* 9 (August 1982): 363–386.
96. Ibid., 366.
97. Cited in Ritzer and Walczak, *Working*, 119–120.
98. Mary Bularzik, "Sexual Harassment at the Workplace: Historical Notes," *Radical America* 12 (July-August 1978): 25.
99. Fox and Hesse-Biber, *Women at Work*, 109.
100. Dierde Silverman, "Sexual Harassment: Working Women's Dilemma," *Quest: A Feminist Quarterly* 3 (1976–1977): 15–24.
101. James E. Gruber and Lars Bjorn, "Blue-Collar Blues: The Sexual Harassment of Women Autoworkers," *Work and Occupations* 9 (August 1982): 271–298.
102. Jack K. Martin and Sandra L. Hanson, "Sex, Family Wage-Earning Status, and Satisfaction with Work," *Work and Occupations* 12 (February 1985): 91–109.
103. Joanne Miller, "Individual and Occupational Determinants of Job Satisfaction: A Focus on Gender Differences," *Sociology of Work and Occupations* 7 (August 1980): 337–366.

104. Burke D. Grandjean and Patricia A. Taylor, "Job Satisfaction among Female Clerical Workers: Status Panic or the Opportunity Structure of Office Work?" *Sociology of Work and Occupations* 7 (February 1980): 33–53.
105. Judith S. McIlwee, "Work Satisfaction Among Women in Nontraditional Occupations," *Work and Occupations* 9 (August 1982): 299–335.
106. U.S. Bureau of the Census, *Statistical Abstract, 1985*, 419, table 699.
107. Paula England, "The Failure of Human Capital Theory to Explain Occupational Sex Segregation," *Journal of Human Resources* 17 (Summer 1982): 358–370; and "Wage Appreciation and Depreciation: A Test of Neoclassical Economic Explanations of Occupational Sex Segregation," *Social Forces* 62 (March 1984):726–749.
108. James R. Ragan, Jr., and Sharon Smith, "The Impact of Differences in Turnover on Male/Female Pay Differentials," *Journal of Human Resources* 16 (Summer 1981): 343–365.
109. Barry Bluestone, William M. Murphy, and Mary Stevenson, *Low Wages and the Working Poor* (Ann Arbor, Mich.: Institute of Labor and Industrial Relations, University of Michigan, 1973), 28–29. See also Glen G. Cain, "The Challenge of Segmented Labor Market Theories to Orthodox Theory," *Journal of Economic Literature* 14 (1976): 1215–1257.
110. Bibb and Form, "Effects of Industrial, Occupational, and Sex Stratification"; Beck, Horan, and Tolbert, "Stratification in a Dual Economy"; and Charles M. Tolbert II, Partrick M. Horan, and E. M. Beck, "The Structure of Economic Segmentation," *American Journal of Sociology* 85 (1980): 1095–1116.
111. Kathryn B. Ward and Charles W. Mueller, "Sex Differences in Earnings: The Influence of Industrial Sector, Authority Hierarchy, and Human Capital Variables," *Work and Occupations* 12 (November 1985): 437–463.
112. Paula England and Steven D. McLaughlin, "Sex Segregation of Jobs and Income Differentials," in *Discrimination in Organizations*, ed. Rudolfo Alvarez et al. (San Francisco: Jossey-Bass, 1979).
113. Ronnie Steinberg, "From Laissez-Faire to a Fair Wage for Women's Work: A Technical Fix to the Labor Market," *Contemporary Sociology* 13 (January 1984): 15–16.
114. Alice Abel Kemp and E. M. Beck, "Equal Work, Unequal Pay: Gender Discrimination Within Work-Similar Occupations," *Work and Occupations* 13 (August 1986): 324–347.
115. Ronnie Steinberg and Lois Haignere, "Separate but Equivalent: Equal Pay for Work of Comparable Worth," in *Gender at Work: Perspective on Occupational Segregation and Comparable Worth* (Washington, D.C.: Women's Research and Education Institute, 1984), 13–24.
116. Clarence Thomas, "Pay Equity and Comparable Worth," *Labor Law Journal* 34 (1983): 3–12; and Rachel Flick, "The New Feminism and the World of Work," *The Public Interest* 71 (Spring 1983): 33–44.

CHAPTER 8

Minorities and Work

FOR MEMBERS of racial and ethnic minority groups, occupational activities are an important indicator of participation and status in the society. Minorities are by definition groups that are disadvantaged economically (and in other ways), relatively powerless, and excluded from valued social positions, including occupational positions. The location of minorities in the occupational structure and their mobility patterns also can tell us a great deal about how the society is changing or not changing. The occupational opportunities of minorities are constrained by the existence of a dual labor market and the existence of core and periphery industries, issues identified in the discussion of women and work in chapter 7. While unemployment affects the entire society directly or indirectly, its effects on minorities are more dramatic, persistent, and tenacious.

In many ways, an understanding of minorities and work can contribute to our understanding of basic occupational processes, as well as social change and the broader experiences of minority groups. Throughout American history the experiences of immigrant groups have been shaped by the kinds of occupational opportunities available to them. The labor needs of the economy and the marketable skills of immigrants have played a crucial role in the fate of immigrant groups. In general, immigrants have entered the occupational structure at the bottom, taking the least skilled, lowest-status jobs. Over time, earlier arrivals have been pushed up the occupational hierarchy by those arriving later. Immigrants

256

from Eastern, Central, and Southern Europe who came to the United States between 1880 and 1920 overwhelmingly entered unskilled and, at best, semiskilled jobs in heavy industry, mining, and manufacturing. Their ethnicity served as a basis for discrimination in employment and served as a limitation on their mobility opportunities.

Indeed, we could look at the history of all immigrant groups to the United States as minorities attempting to improve their position in the occupational structure. Such an undertaking is beyond the scope of this chapter and others have in fact described these experiences for a wide range of racial and ethnic groups.[1] Our attention in this chapter will be limited to black Americans, Mexican-Americans, and Asian-Americans although we will compare their occupational experiences to those of other groups where appropriate.

BLACK AMERICANS

The present position of blacks in the occupational structure and the stratification system can only be understood in the context of their unique history in American society. While they were not the only group to be forcibly included in the society (Native Americans and Mexican-Americans were included through conquest), they were the only group to experience slavery.

SLAVERY AS AN OCCUPATIONAL SYSTEM

A great deal has been written about the American experience with slavery from a variety of perspectives. However else it might be described, it is clear that slavery was above all an economic and occupational system. The motive for importing African blacks was economic. Slavery represented a way of meeting the labor needs of the colonies. Slaves were used primarily as unskilled agricultural workers, although they were also used as domestic and personal servants and many were taught skilled crafts.

It is unlikely that slavery would have persisted and become institutionalized if it had not been extremely profitable. The plantation economy was both profitable and efficient. Virtually all slaves, from young children to the very old, were required to do work of some kind. With a monopoly on labor, plantation owners were able to control their markets, engage in price cutting, and force small independent farmers from highly productive land which then could be acquired cheaply. The supply and price of labor were predictable and subject to control by plantation owners. It has been estimated that Southern agriculture was about one-third more efficient than Northern agriculture and Southern farms using slave labor were about 28 percent more efficient than Southern farms operating with free labor. From an investment perspective slavery was a profitable investment. For example, when the annual rate of return on investment in Southern railroads was 8.5 percent, the return on slaves was 10 percent.[2]

For blacks, slavery represented a situation of total subordination. They were unable to accumulate property or wealth or to experience any kind of mobility. Those who did acquire nonagricultural skills were not free to compete with white workers but might be rented out by their owners.

THE OCCUPATIONAL CASTE SYSTEM

With the abolition of slavery at the end of the Civil War, it was expected that blacks might move in two occupational directions by becoming small, independent farmers, or industrial workers. Industrialists and former slaveowners encouraged competition and antagonism between black and white workers in order to discourage them from uniting and demanding higher wages. Out of fear of losing political power to the newly enfranchised ex-slaves, industrialists and planters supported the development of legal segregation that has come to be known as the caste system. This included the creation of an occupational caste system that excluded blacks from more skilled jobs. From the perspective of white workers this aspect of the caste system reduced the threat that black workers posed to their wages by giving them a monopoly on some types of work. In effect, planters, industrialists, and white workers reached an informal understanding that blacks could not hold better-paying, more skilled jobs.[3] The system also benefited employers. They gained tremendous control over the white labor force whose demands for higher wages and the like could always be countered with the threat of replacement with cheaper black labor. Employers could also set the price of black labor very low since it was not determined by market forces. The system enabled employers to retain a control over their labor markets that was nearly as strong as it was under slavery.

Most importantly, the system established a precedent for black employment in the least desirable, least rewarding jobs. By 1900, only 5 percent of all skilled workers in the South were black, compared to a little over 80 percent at the end of the Civil War.[4] Black workers dominated the construction and railroad industries of the South in the first few decades following the Civil War, but they had virtually disappeared from these industries by the end of the nineteenth century.[5] The vast majority were concentrated in unskilled laboring jobs (including farm labor), tenant farming, and domestic service. Tenant farming often involved working land rented from the former slaveowner. Black tenant farmers were kept continually in debt, and this work option amounted to little more than the substitution of peonage for slavery.[6] The caste system also affected later opportunities for occupational participation. Segregated education resulted in only a fraction of the money spent on the education of whites being spent for the education of blacks. It produced a tremendous educational gap between blacks and whites which in turn served as a major obstacle to access to higher-status jobs.

MIGRATION TO THE NORTH:
THE PULL OF ECONOMIC OPPORTUNITIES

While black migration to the North had occurred prior to the Civil War and in the second half of the nineteenth century, it amounted to little more than a trickle. In the late nineteenth century nine out of every ten blacks were living in the South. Black migration to the North was a response to the same forces that stimulated earlier migrations to the United States and that still operate today: a desire to escape political and economic oppression and the quest for economic opportunities.

Blacks began to move to Northern industrial cities in earnest during the decade 1910–1920. Southern agriculture experienced a serious depression that reduced the demand for farm labor and made tenant farming even less viable than it had been. World War I created a labor shortage and increased the demand for industrial labor. The war also exacerbated the shortage of industrial labor by reducing the flow of immigrants from Eastern, Central, and Southern Europe. By 1924 this source of new unskilled labor virtually disappeared with the passage of legislation drastically restricting immigration. Northern firms flooded the South with labor recruiters offering enticements to black workers such as free transportation, low-cost housing, and comparatively good wages. In this decade and the next (i.e., 1910–1930), over a million blacks left the South. They entered industrial employment at the bottom of the occupational hierarchy, taking unskilled and semiskilled jobs in steel mills, foundries, packing houses, and automobile factories. In this process, white workers were pushed up the occupational hierarchy into more skilled, technical, and supervisory positions. In a very real sense the separation of black and white workers into different occupational roles and levels that existed under the caste system of the South was perpetuated in Northern industry.

The Great Depression of the 1930s offered limited employment opportunities for whites as well as blacks, but its impact in the South was so severe that migration to the North continued. During the 1930s over 400,000 blacks left the South in search of increasingly scarce employment opportunities in Northern industrial centers. This decade also saw the transformation of black Americans from a rural to an urban minority group. In 1890 only 20 percent of the black population lived in cities, but by 1940 it was evenly divided between rural and urban areas.

World War II created industrial labor shortages just as World War I had done, and black migration continued in the 1940s. During this decade about 1,600,000 blacks left the South. Most went northward, but a sizable number headed to the West Coast where expanding defense industries offered employment opportunities. While the "pull" of industrial jobs contributed to black migration from the South, there were also important "push" factors. During the 1940s, the extensive mechanization of Southern agriculture drastically reduced the demand for unskilled black farm labor and made labor intensive tenant farming even less competitive and viable. The postwar economic boom of the 1950s and the continued mechanization of Southern agriculture resulted in another 1,500,000 blacks migrating from the South to the North and the West Coast in response to expanding industrial employment opportunities. By 1960, the occupations of blacks were beginning to show some significant changes. Only 12 percent were still employed in agriculture, another 26 percent were in semiskilled blue-collar occupations, and nearly 40 percent were service workers and unskilled laborers.[7]

CURRENT OCCUPATIONAL STATUS

The occupations of the black population continued to become more diversified during the 1970s and early 1980s. The occupational distribution of blacks and whites in 1980 is presented in table 8.1 for broad occupational status groups. Data are presented separately for males and females since, as we saw in chapter 7, the occupations of men and women differ greatly.

Black men are more likely to be in blue-collar rather than white-collar occupations, but equal proportions of black women are in these two types of occupations. Compared to whites of the same sex, blacks are underrepresented in professional, managerial, and sales occupations. Black women are also less likely than white women to be in clerical occupations, but almost equal proportions of white and black men are in clerical jobs. In blue-collar occupations, black men are overrepresented in the poorer paying, less secure operative, laborer, and service categories and underrepresented in skilled craft occupations. Compared to white women, black women are more likely to be employed as operatives, ser-

Table 8.1
Occupational Distribution of the Labor Force
by Race and Sex, 1980

	Male		Female	
Occupation	White	Black	White	Black
White Collar				
Professional	16.1%	10.4%	17.3%	14.5%
Managerial	15.1	7.1	7.1	3.3
Sales	6.7	2.7	7.5	3.0
Clerical	6.4	7.4	35.9	29.5
Total white collar	44.3	27.6	67.8	50.3
Blue Collar				
Skilled craft	21.7	17.5	1.9	1.1
Operatives	16.5	24.8	10.5	15.2
Laborers	6.0	11.7	1.3	1.7
Service	8.0	14.9	15.9	24.7
Private household	*	0.2	1.7	6.6
Total blue collar	52.2	69.1	31.3	49.3
Farmers and farm managers	2.3	0.6	0.3	0.1
Farm laborers	1.2	2.6	0.5	0.4
TOTAL	100.0%	99.9%	99.9%	100.1%

Source: U.S. Department of Labor, *Employment and Earnings, January, 1980* (Washington, D.C.: U.S. Government Printing Office, 1980), 38, table A-22.
*Less than 0.05 percent.
Note: Some totals do not equal 100.0 percent because of rounding error.

vice workers, and private household workers (mainly as maids, cooks, and baby-sitters).

Occupational Segregation

In addition to these differences in occupation, inequalities in occupation can also be seen by looking at the segregation of occupations by race, in much the same way that the sex segregation of occupations was identified in chapter 7. Table 8.2 presents the percentage of those in each occupational category who are black. In 1983, 9.3 percent of the labor force was black. Thus, occupations with less than that proportion of blacks reflect an underrepresentation of black workers and those with a larger percentage have an overrepresentation of blacks.

It is apparent from the data in table 8.2 that the segregation of occupations by race is not nearly as marked as the segregation of occupations by sex. That is, there are no occupations where the proportion black is in excess of 90 percent as is the case with the proportion female in many clerical occupations (see chapter 7). Still, it is also apparent that blacks are not evenly distributed in the occupational structure in proportion to their numbers in the labor force. There is substantial underrepresentation in executive, administrative, and managerial, sales, and

Table 8.2
Percentage of Persons in Major Occupational
Groups Who Are Black, 1983

Occupational Groups	Percent Black
Executive, administrative, and managerial	4.7
Professional	6.4
Technicians	8.2
Sales	4.7
Administrative support, including clerical	9.6
Private household	27.8
Protective service	13.6
Service (other than private household and protective service)	16.0
Mechanics and repairers	6.8
Construction trades	6.6
Extractive occupations	3.3
Precision production occupations	7.3
Machine operators, assemblers, and inspectors	14.0
Transportation occupations	13.0
Handlers, equipment cleaners, helpers, and laborers	15.1
Farming, forestry, and fishing	7.5

Source: U.S. Bureau of the Census, *Statistical Abstract of the United States,* 1985 (Washington, D.C.: U.S. Government Printing Office, 1984), 402–403, table 676.

extractive occupations. Blacks are overrepresented in the "private household, protective service, other services, machine operators . . . , transportation, and handlers . . ." categories.

These broad occupational categories mask some important absences and concentrations of blacks in more specific occupations. For example, only 1.6 percent of architects and 2.7 percent of engineers are black. They are also underrepresented among natural scientists (2.6 percent), physicians (3.2 percent), dentists (2.4 percent), and lawyers and judges (2.7 percent). Within the professions, blacks are overrepresented in lower paying, lower prestige fields such as social work (18.2 percent), educational and vocational counseling (13.9 percent), and elementary school teaching (11.1 percent). Within sales, blacks range from a low of 1.3 percent of real estate sales agents to 10.1 percent of all cashiers. Although the "administrative support" category averages out to reflect proportionate representation, there is a great deal of variation within this occupational grouping. Blacks are overrepresented among postal clerks (26.2 percent), data entry keyers (18.6 percent), teachers' aides (17.8 percent), and telephone operators (17.0 percent). However, they are underrepresented among secretaries (5.8 percent), bookkeepers (4.3 percent), and receptionists and bank tellers (both at 7.5 percent). Within the "service other than household and protective service" category, blacks make up 27.3 percent of all nurses aides, orderlies, and attendants, and 22.6 percent of all janitors and cleaners. Reflecting the decline in their participation in agriculture noted above, blacks make up only 1.3 percent of all farm operators and managers.[8]

To what extent have the occupational status differences between blacks and whites been changing? According to an analysis of the relative occupational status of blacks and whites by Mark A. Fossett, Omer R. Galle, and William R. Kelly, occupational inequality has been declining but there are important regional variations.[9] Focusing on the period 1940–1980, and controlling for age and education, they found that occupational inequality increased at the national level during the 1940s and decreased during the period 1960–1980. When the South and the rest of the nation are compared, the pattern over time in the non-South is similar to that in the nation as a whole. However, occupational inequality increased in the South in the 1940s and the 1950s. It began to decrease in the 1960s and continued to do so during the 1970s. Increases in occupational inequality in the South during the period 1940–1960 were so great that the absolute level of inequality in the South by 1970 had only decreased to what it was thirty years earlier in 1940. Fossett, Galle, and Kelly conclude that economic growth is less effective in promoting racial occupational equality than is intervention in the labor market and the educational system through public policies designed to eliminate discrimination and promote equality of opportunity.

EXPLANATIONS OF THE OCCUPATIONAL DISTRIBUTION OF BLACKS

There is no doubt that both overt and informal discrimination account for many of the differences in the occupations of blacks and whites. There are many parallels here with the experiences of women in the labor force discussed in chapter 7. The concentration of blacks in the secondary labor market and periphery industries locks them into dead-end jobs with few mobility opportunities. The internal labor markets of employing organizations similarly allocate blacks to low-skill jobs with truncated career lines.[10] As employing organizations look for low-cost labor, blacks and other minorities with few skills and job options are hired disproportionately for lower-skill and lower-paying jobs.

The discriminatory practices of craft unions have also severely limited the access of blacks to skilled craft occupations.[11] Around the turn of the century, immigrants from Eastern, Central, and Southern Europe were discriminated against and excluded from craft unions dominated by earlier immigrants from Northwest Europe and their descendants.[12] For black migrants during the following decades, the exclusion from membership in craft unions was even more severe. While the practices of craft unions limited the access of blacks to skilled craft jobs, industry-wide unions have included blacks, resulting in comparability of black and white earnings, fringe benefits, seniority rights, and promotional opportunities in jobs covered by such unions.[13]

Differences in educational attainment are also an important factor in explaining the different occupational distributions of blacks and whites. The median number of years of schooling completed by blacks has increased substantially since 1940, as table 8.3 shows. The discrepancy between blacks and whites in median number of years of schooling completed decreased from a full three years in 1940 to less than half a year in 1983. However, these averages mask some important differences that still remain and function as a handicap to access to better jobs. The proportion of blacks with four or more years of college is only half the proportion of whites with this amount of education. Seventeen percent more whites than blacks have completed four years of high school or more. And three times as many blacks as whites have less than five years of education.

While blacks have improved their overall educational attainment relative to whites, much of this improvement is recent and its main impact is on younger blacks. More recent educational opportunities do little for older black workers who terminated their education earlier than whites and who in many cases bear the additional handicap of an inferior segregated education. For example, among people age fifty-five and over in 1983, 19.6 percent of blacks had less than five years of education

Table 8.3
Educational Attainment of the White and Black Population
Age 25 and Over, 1940–1983

	Percentage of Population with:							
	Less than 5 Years Education		4 Years High School or More		4 Years College or More		Median Years of School Completed	
Year	White	Black	White	Black	White	Black	White	Black
1940	10.9	41.8	26.1	7.7	4.9	1.3	8.7	5.7
1950	8.7	31.4	35.5	13.4	6.4	2.2	9.7	6.9
1960	6.7	23.5	43.2	21.7	8.1	3.5	10.8	8.2
1970	4.2	14.7	57.4	36.1	11.6	6.1	12.2	10.1
1980	2.6	9.2	70.5	51.2	17.8	7.9	12.5	12.0
1983	2.4	7.1	73.8	56.8	19.5	9.5	12.6	12.2

Sources: National Center for Education Statistics, *Digest of Educational Statistics* (Washington, D.C.: U.S. Government Printing Office, 1980), 16, table 11; U.S. Bureau of the Census, *Statistical Abstract of the United States, 1982–83* (Washington, D.C.: U.S. Government Printing Office, 1982), 143, table 225; and U.S. Bureau of the Census, *Statistical Abstract of the United States, 1985* (Washington, D.C.: U.S. Government Printing Office, 1984), 134, table 214.

compared to 5.8 percent of the general population. In addition, over half
(53.1 percent) of blacks age fifty-five and over had eight years of schooling or less compared to 29.6 percent of the general population.[14] Such
differences mean that blacks are more likely than whites to lack the educational credentials that make it possible to gain access to anything other
than low-skill, poor-paying, dead-end jobs in the secondary labor market.

BLACK INCOME

Black-white disparities in education and occupation are reflected in the
lower incomes of blacks. Since the late 1950s the incomes of black families
have averaged between 50 and 60 percent of the incomes of whites. Between 1959 and 1969, for example, black income rose from 51.7 percent
to 61.2 percent of white income but by 1973 it had declined to 57.7 percent.[15] By 1983 the median income of black families ($14,506) was only
56.3 percent of that for white families ($25,757)[16] and 32.4 percent of
blacks (compared to 9.7 percent of the white population) had incomes
below the official poverty line.[17]

Human capital and labor markets interact to produce these income
differences. Blacks with low educational attainments are relegated to jobs
in the secondary labor market and peripheral industrial employment. The
quality of education makes a difference too. Dennis P. Hogan and
Michele Pazul compared black men who migrated from the South to
the North as adults with those who were reared in the North or who
migrated as children. Comparing those with similar amounts of education, they found that the Southern educated adult migrants had lower
earnings. In effect they had lower "returns" on their education compared
to those educated in the North.[18] Still, the discriminatory exclusion of
blacks from higher paying jobs is responsible for some of these earnings
differences. Eric A. Hanushek has argued that if individual human capital
characteristics (like amount of education and work experience) and region
were held constant and blacks were paid the same as whites for similar
jobs, about 80 percent of the difference in black-white earnings would
disappear.[19] In other words, a substantial part of the gap results from
discrimination in access to occupations and in pay. James R. Kluegel has
also pointed out that blacks are excluded from positions of authority and
that such exclusion contributes to lower earnings. He has estimated that
if blacks and whites were in positions of comparable authority, about
one-third of the black-white income gap would be eliminated.[20]

UNEMPLOYMENT

Unemployment also contributes to the income differences of blacks and
whites. When we compare black and white families where the head of

the household is employed full-time on a year-round basis, black income is 59 percent of white income; and when such families have two earners, black income rises to 85 percent of white income. However, a smaller proportion of black families (41.8 percent) compared to white families (56.7 percent) had a household head employed full-time, year-round in 1982.[21]

Unemployment is a serious problem among blacks. Since the mid-1960s black unemployment has been between two and two and one-half times the rate for whites. In January 1987 the unemployment rate for blacks was 14.3 percent compared to 5.9 percent for whites.[22] Unemployment is higher for blacks than whites in every age group, but it is most serious among black male teenagers. For the group ages sixteen through nineteen, in January 1987, unemployment among black men was 36.5 percent compared to 16.1 percent for white men.[23] When the overall unemployment rate increases, it increases more for blacks than for whites, reflecting the greater vulnerability of secondary labor market jobs to fluctuations in the economy.

The decline of employment opportunities in central cities also has affected black unemployment rates. In 1980, blacks made up between 17 percent (Los Angeles–Long Beach) and 70 percent (Washington, D.C.) of the population of the nation's seven largest Standard Metropolitan Statistical Areas.[24] In the Northeastern states, 75 percent of blacks are residents of central cities, and in the North Central region 66 percent of blacks live in central cities.[25] In recent years, however, central cities have been losing unskilled and semiskilled jobs as manufacturing industries have employed proportionately fewer people (see chapter 6), and cities try to attract cleaner light industries, many of which locate in suburban industrial parks. Many production activities previously located in cities also have been lost to foreign countries as industries seek cheaper labor supplies.[26] John D. Kasarda has emphasized that urban areas have changed from centers of production and distribution of manufactured goods to centers of administration, information exchange, trade, finance, and government services. This change has drastically replaced semiskilled and unskilled jobs for which blacks might qualify with professional, technical, and managerial jobs for which they lack the education, training, credentials, and experience.[27] In a sense, the better jobs for which they might be qualified have left the places where black workers are concentrated. The shift to a postindustrial service economy has actually resulted in a "polarization" of urban labor markets. While professional, technical, and administrative jobs are created in the primary labor market, poorly paid, unstable, low-skill, dead-end jobs typical of the secondary labor market are also created.[28] Lacking the credentials for the former, central-city blacks increasingly find their employment opportunities limited to the latter.

DIFFERENCES WITHIN THE BLACK LABOR FORCE

Prior to World War II blacks were overwhelmingly concentrated in the least-skilled blue-collar, agricultural labor, and domestic service jobs. In recent years, substantial differences in educational resources, job opportunities, and earnings have developed among blacks. According to William Julius Wilson, who focused attention on this change in his book *The Declining Significance of Race,* two distinct labor markets have developed:

> On the one hand, poorly trained and educationally limited blacks of the inner city...see their job prospects increasingly restricted to the low-wage sector, their unemployment rates soaring to record levels...their movement out of poverty slowing, and their welfare roles increasing. On the other hand, talented and educated blacks are experiencing unprecedented job opportunities in the growing government and corporate sectors, opportunities that are at least comparable to those of whites with equivalent qualifications.[29]

Wilson argues that class has replaced race as the main determinant of economic opportunities for blacks. A small, well-educated segment of the black population has been able to take advantage of expanding professional, technical, and managerial opportunities. But at the same time there is a poorly educated black "underclass" which, when employed, is locked into unstable, low-wage, secondary labor market jobs. Reynolds Farley and Suzanne M. Bianchi also have pointed out that unemployment and dropping out of the labor force entirely are conditions experienced by those with low educational attainment, while better educated blacks are experiencing more stable and continuous employment. In addition, the gap in black-white occupational attainment, as measured by occupational prestige, has also been widening for both men and women.[30]

In his analysis of the career mobility patterns of black men, Michael Hout concludes that economic class factors are more important than race in explaining occupational mobility.[31] Hout also points out that the growth of public sector employment has had an impact on both the mobility and employment patterns of blacks largely because discriminatory employment and promotion practices decreased sooner and more extensively in the public than in the private sector. This conclusion is also supported by the research of Marshall I. Pomer who examined the career mobility of black and white workers between 1962 and 1973. Pomer found that upward movement among blacks was only about one-third as likely as it was among whites, and when blacks did experience upward mobility they did not move as far up the occupational hierarchy as whites did. However, opportunities for upward movement for blacks were much better in the public than in the private sector. Upward movement within the public sector was even greater for blacks than for whites.[32]

BLACKS IN THE MILITARY

The armed forces of the United States include about 2.1 million men and women serving on active duty. Approximately 19 percent are black.[33] Analyses of both the careers of blacks in the military and the effect of military service on the civilian occupational experiences of blacks suggest that the military offers many blacks career opportunities not available in civilian life. However, evidence of the effect of military service on civilian occupational attainments is not entirely consistent.

In the military, blacks are concentrated in the army and in the enlisted ranks. In 1985, 30 percent of the enlisted personnel in the army were black compared to 20 percent in the marine corps, 17 percent in the air force, and 13 percent in the navy. Blacks made up 10 percent of the officer corps of the army, a figure that is twice that of the air force and three times that of the navy.[34]

Charles C. Moskos has argued that the army in particular represents a "success story" for blacks. If officers are viewed as analogous to "management," there are few civilian organizations that can claim a comparable proportion of blacks in positions involving managerial responsibilities.[35]

Military service has been especially attractice to young blacks for a number of reasons. The lack of civilian job opportunities offering decent pay and stability of employment has made the military an attractive option, and the relative absence of discrimination in the military has also been important. When the draft ended in 1973, about 17 percent of the army's enlisted personnel were black, but by the early 1980s this figure nearly doubled.[36] In the early 1980s, some 42 percent of all black youths who met military entrance standards actually enlisted compared to only 14 percent of comparably qualified whites.[37] Blacks re-enlist at one and one-half times the rate for whites. Consequently, they have come to make up a substantial proportion of noncommissioned officers. According to Moskos, approximately one-third of buck sergeants and staff sergeants and one-quarter of first sergeants, master sergeants, and sergeants major are black. Promotion to the top three enlisted ranks is lower than average for blacks, apparently because they are underrepresented in combat specialties where promotion comes more rapidly.[38] Nevertheless, there is evidence that blacks are promoted more slowly than whites even when education and scores on the Armed Forces Qualifications Test (an aptitude-ability test) are controlled.[39]

As indicated earlier, research on the effect of military service on later civilian employment presents a mixed picture. A study of former draftees found that their earnings in civilian occupations were equal to or lower than those of nonveterans. White veterans had lower earnings due to the two years of military service during which they did not participate in the civilian labor force. Among blacks, there was essentially no difference in earnings.[40] However, draftees may be different from a population of veterans that includes volunteers as well as draftees. Another analysis concluded that, in general, veterans have an earnings advantage over nonveterans when their civilian occupation is controlled. However, the earnings advantage is greater for blacks and Mexican-Americans than it is for Anglos.[41] The findings of both studies are based on earnings data from the early 1960s and may not reflect the current relative earnings capabilities of black and white veterans and nonveterans.

MEXICAN-AMERICANS

Like black Americans, the occupational experiences of Mexican-Americans have been shaped by a distinctive history. Unlike other immigrant groups, Mexican-Americans were initially brought into the United States through military conquest. After Mexico gained its independence from Spain in 1821, settlement of its northern border (what is now Texas, Arizona, and California) by Anglos was encouraged. Conflict between Mexico and the settlers led to the formation of the Texas Republic in 1836 and eventually to the Mexican-American War of 1846-1848. The war ended with Mexico losing half of its national territory. Mexicans living north of the new border were given the choice of moving back to what remained of Mexico or remaining and becoming U.S. citizens. The treaty ending the war granted American citizenship to those Mexicans who chose to remain. It is estimated that between 86,000 and 116,000 chose to do so.[42] The treaty also guaranteed their religious freedom, property rights, and the right to continue Mexican cultural traditions and the use of the Spanish language. These guarantees, especially those concerning property rights, proved to be rather empty promises.

The Making of a Laboring Class

During the remainder of the nineteenth century, Mexican-Americans were progressively dispossessed of their land through legal manipulation and the suppression of political rights. They were also displaced from higher-status occupations and commercial pursuits and limited to participation in lower-status occupations. The end result was economic sub-ordination on a large scale. With the westward expansion of the frontier, cattle and sheep raising, farming, and mining were financed by Anglo capital and depended heavily on Mexican-American labor and expertise. Mexican-Americans effectively became outsiders in what had been their own land. The conditions that developed have been described as a situation of *internal colonialism* in which Mexican-Americans became economically and politically subordinate to and exploited by the Anglo settlers.[43] The concept of internal colonialism suggests an analogy with the way Western European nations exploited their colonies in Africa and Asia during the nineteenth and the first half of the twentieth centuries.

What happened to Mexican-Americans in the second half of the nineteenth century varied from one area to another. Even before the Mexican-American War, Mexicans in these areas differed considerably in their economic position and their occupational activities. They included affluent ranchers, landowners, and merchants, as well as traders, skilled miners, and poor peasants. Following the war, Mexican-Americans throughout the conquered territory were systematically relegated to the bottom of the stratification system and to the bottom of the occupational hierarchy.

In Texas, they were employed mainly as laborers in cattle and sheep ranching and in cotton farming. In New Mexico, new taxes were imposed on land and small-scale farmers and ranchers were forced into debt to pay the taxes. More commonly, they sold some or all of their land at depressed prices, or it was purchased by Anglos for the price of the delinquent taxes. The federal government also declared communal grazing lands and privately owned farm and ranch land to be federal land, placed it under the control of the National Forest Service, and paid little or nothing to the owners. In Arizona, where copper and silver mining were important industries, Mexican-Americans provided a cheap pool of both skilled and unskilled labor. California presented a different situation, but the consequences were similar. Legal challenges to the land titles of Mexican-Americans, including both wealthy landowners and small-scale farmers and ranchers, were upheld in the courts. The cost of court battles forced many to sell their land so that they could respond to challenges to their ownership. Force and violence were also used to drive many Mexican-Americans from their land.[44]

By the turn of the century, Mexican-Americans had become largely a class of landless laborers. They were not excluded from the economy totally, however. Their agricultural and mining knowledge and skills were exploitable resources, but they were allowed to apply them only in the role of laborers. One analyst of this period, Joseph Hraba, suggests that Mexican-Americans were not herded into reservations as American

Indians were because their skills were needed in the Anglo-dominated economy.[45]

THE BEGINNINGS OF DIVERSITY

The Mexican-American population has continued to grow through immigration as well as natural increase. As was the case with black immigration to the North, the impetus for migration from Mexico has been a lack of economic opportunities in Mexico and a comparative abundance of them in the United States. Labor shortages during World War I led to active recruitment of Mexicans to work on railroads, in mining, and in agriculture in the Southwest. By 1930, about 15 percent of Mexican-Americans were living outside the Southwest, with notable concentrations in Chicago and Detroit and in the states of Ohio, Pennsylvania, and Kansas. Employment opportunities in these areas were largely industrial, limited to unskilled and semiskilled jobs in the meat-packing, steel, and automobile industries.

The Great Depression of the 1930s resulted in high rates of unemployment among Mexican-Americans whose marginal position in the labor force made them especially vulnerable. In the Southwest, agriculture (and to a lesser extent mining) became mechanized, reducing the demand for unskilled labor. Anglo migrants from the Dust Bowl also became a source of cheap labor with which Mexican-Americans had to compete. Substantial numbers found it necessary to turn to public welfare and pressure mounted for their deportation. From 1929 to 1934 over 400,000 Mexican-Americans (about half of them United States citizens) were deported to Mexico.[46]

World War II and the postwar economic boom created new labor shortages in the United States. The *bracero program,* an agreement between the governments of the United States and Mexico, brought about five million Mexicans to the United States between 1942 and 1964. The objective of the program was to provide a regulated, predictable, and cheap labor supply for agriculture, especially in California and the Southwest.

Since this program for importing workers ended in 1964, there has been considerable legal as well as illegal or undocumented immigration from Mexico. Many of these immigrants have come as "sojourners," intending to work for a time in the United States and then return to Mexico. Mexico's severely depressed economy with high inflation and chronic unemployment (about half the labor force has been unemployed or underemployed in recent years) has led many Mexicans to see employment in the United States as a very attractive option.

The 1980 census counted about eight million Mexican-Americans in the United States. About half live in the five southwestern states of Texas, Arizona, New Mexico, California, and Colorado. Movement out of the Southwest has been accompanied by movement to urban areas and a shift from agricultural and mining work to industrial blue-collar and white-collar work. Between 1950 and 1970 the percentage of Spanish-surname people (about 60 percent of whom are Mexican-Americans) employed as farm workers declined from 24.7 to 4.6 percent, while the percentage employed in white-collar occupations increased from 20.5 to 31.3 percent.[47]

CURRENT OCCUPATIONAL STATUS

Recent and continued immigration from Mexico makes it difficult to identify with precision what has happened to the occupational participation of Mexican-Americans over time. Immigrants generally have fewer occupational skills, less education, and lower earnings than Mexican-Americans born in the United States. The median family income of Spanish-surname families in the Southwest with a native-born head is much higher than that of families headed by a person born in Mexico, for example. Over half the Mexican-American population is native-born of native parentage, and this group is much more likely to be in white-collar occupations.[48]

Occupationally, Mexican-Americans are heavily concentrated in low-skill manual and service jobs. As of 1981, only about 7.5 percent of Mexican-American men worked as farm laborers, and 20.9 percent were in skilled craft occupations. Another 25 percent were in service and nonfarm laboring occupations, and one-fifth were in semiskilled jobs. Only 5.7 percent were in the professions and another 14 percent were in managerial, clerical, and sales occupations. The proportion of women in clerical occupations (about one-third) was approximately the same as for white and black women. However, they were underrepresented in all other white-collar occupations. Only 8 percent were in the professions, 4.3 percent in managerial, and 5.2 percent were in sales occupations. A little over one-fifth were in semiskilled manual occupations and another fifth worked in service occupations.[49] While occupational diversity is beginning to develop among Mexican-Americans, much as it is among black Americans, they are clearly overrepresented at the lower-status and skill levels of the occupational structure. Despite recent gains, Mexican-Americans represent an example of the occupational disadvantages associated with participation in the secondary labor market, a condition that still persists for virtually all new and recent immigrants from Mexico.[50]

The educational attainment of Mexican-Americans is low compared to the general population. In some respects they are more educationally disadvantaged than blacks. In 1983, for example, nearly one-fifth (19.1 percent) of Mexican-Americans age twenty-five and older had less than five years of formal education. This is two and one-half times the proportion of blacks with this low level of educational attainment. About two-fifths (41.1 percent) had four years of high school or more, a figure some 15 percent lower than for blacks. As was the case for blacks, educational opportunities have improved for younger Mexican-Americans. In 1983, 53.2 percent of those between the ages of twenty-five and thirty-four had completed four years of high school education or more compared to only 35.8 percent of those in the thirty-five through sixty-four age group.[51]

Not surprisingly, Mexican-Americans do not fare well in terms of income. Median family income is only 72 percent of that of the general population, which is somewhat better than the income of blacks compared to that of whites. Among all people of Spanish origin (of which Mexican-Americans constitute about 60 percent), about one in five families had annual incomes below the official poverty level in 1983.[52] Nearly 30 percent of all Spanish-origin families had incomes below $10,000 in 1982 compared to only 14 percent of white families. At the other extreme, only 4 percent of Spanish-origin families had incomes over $50,000 compared to 12 percent of white families.[53]

Given the continuing immigration of Mexicans to the United States, it is important to distinguish between immigrants and native-born Mexican-Americans when assessing their occupational status. Using data from a 1979 national sample of men ages twenty through sixty-four, Lisa J. Neidert and Reynolds Farley carried out an analysis of the attainments of ethnic groups that permits a three-generation comparison of Mexican-Americans.[54] While first generation (foreign-born) men had occupational status scores averaging 18, the scores for second generation (native-born of foreign or mixed parentage) and third generation (native-born of native-born parents) men averaged 30 and 32, respectively.[55] These gains reflect substantial improvement in occupational status for second and third generation Mexican-Americans. They are paralleled by improvements in educational attainment, especially for second and third generation men compared to the immigrant generation. From the first to the third generation, median years of school completed increased from 6.9 to 10.1 and 11.7 years, respectively. The percentage of Mexican-American men with at least some college also increased from 9 percent for the first generation to 21 and 29 percent for the second and third generations. These occupational and educational differences are also reflected in income. Average annual per capita income was $2,700 for the first generation but increased to $5,000 for the second generation and $5,200 for the third generation. Despite these gains on the part of second and third generation Mexican-Americans, they remain substantially below other ancestry groups on occupational, educational, and income attainment. For example, second generation Mexican-Americans had the lowest average occupational status score of all the seventeen ancestry groups that were compared. Third generation Mexican-American men fared only slightly better in comparison to other ancestry groups. They had the third lowest average occupational status score of the twenty-one ancestry groups used in this comparison.[56]

ASIAN-AMERICANS

According to the 1980 census, there were 3.5 million Asian-Americans in the United States, about 1.5 percent of the total U.S. population. While the U.S. population as a whole grew by 11 percent between 1970 and 1980, the Asian-American population grew by 141 percent.[57] Asian-Americans are a rapidly growing minority group. In 1985, they were estimated to number 5.1 million, or 2.1 percent of the population. It is estimated that by the year 2000 they will number 9.9 million and make up nearly 4 percent of the population.[58]

The category "Asian-Americans" subsumes a diversity of specific ethnic groups. We will deal with five of these groups: Japanese, Chinese, Filipinos, Koreans, and Asian Indians. The history of these groups in the United States is directly tied to their occupational participation and exclusion. Asian-American history really began with the immigration of Chinese to work in California following the beginning of the gold rush in the late 1840s and on transcontinental railroad construction in the 1860s. The historical role of these groups in the labor force as well as their current occupational status suggest a variety of different patterns in the interaction of ethnicity and occupation.

The attainments of Asian-Americans are especially intriguing because of the racism, prejudice, discrimination, harassment, exclusion, and segregation they have experienced. This especially has been the case with Chinese-Americans and Japanese-Americans. They have been the targets of violence, punitive legislation, and taxation explicitly designed to discourage specific business and occupational pursuits. Japanese-Americans were even put into concentration camps during World War II. Despite these experiences, their occupational (and educational) attainments have exceeded those of minority groups such as blacks and Mexican-Americans and in some instances even those of the caucasian majority.

JAPANESE-AMERICANS[59]

Japanese immigration to the United States occurred mainly between 1870 and 1924. In 1886 contract laborers were brought to Hawaii (which was not annexed as a U.S. territory until 1898). They came from relatively impoverished areas of Japan and worked mainly as laborers on sugar plantations. During the next eight years, nearly 29,000 Japanese came to Hawaii.[60] Immigration to the mainland United States, both from Hawaii and directly from Japan, occurred mostly after 1890. Japanese on the mainland numbered nearly 86,000 by 1900.[61] Most immigrants to the mainland were from agricultural backgrounds and, predictably, entered agricultural work, although significant numbers found employment as laborers on the railroads, in canneries, lumbering, the mining and meatpacking industries, and as personal servants, cooks, and butlers.

The success of Japanese-Americans in agriculture was remarkable. By 1909 approximately 30,000 were employed in agriculture, mainly as farm laborers.[62] Their hard work and thrift enabled many to begin working their own land either as owners or tenant farmers. In many cases they worked and developed some of the most marginal, undesirable land. By 1920, in California, there were 5,152 Japanese farmers working in excess of 361,000 acres and producing crops valued at $67 million.[63]

The success of Japanese-Americans in agriculture was viewed with alarm by non-Asian agriculturalists and others in California. In 1913, the California legislature passed the Alien Land Bill (also known as the Webb-Heney Bill) which provided that a Japanese alien could lease agricultural land for a maximum of three years and that land already owned or leased could not be bequeathed. The bill was blatantly intended to curtail Japanese competition in agriculture and to discourage further immigration. The short-term effect of the bill was as intended. By 1930 the number of Japanese farmers dropped to 3,956 and the number of acres farmed decreased to 191,427. However, the number of farmers had gone back up to 5,135 and acreage increased to 220,094 by 1940[64] as land was put in the names of caucasian friends and native-born children.[65] Despite this legal obstacle and the disadvantages of tenant farming, success in agriculture continued to grow. By 1941 Japanese-American farmers were growing 42 percent of California's truck crops and 90 percent of such crops as snap beans, spring and summer celery, peppers, and strawberries.[66]

Despite the popularity of farming among early Japanese-American immigrants, clearly not all opted for agricultural work. In urban areas on the West Coast, small businesses rivaled agriculture as the second most common occupation of Japanese-Americans. By the mid-1920s restaurants, small shops and stores, laundries, and barber shops were common. The success of small business enterprises was due in part to the expanding economy of the West but more important was cooperation, assistance, and interdependence within the Japanese-American community. Newly started businesses could always count on clients from within the ethnic group. There was also extensive pooling of resources to finance new businesses. Jobs would be filled by word of mouth within the community and many businesses operated in a highly paternalistic fashion exploiting fellow Japanese-Americans while simultaneously offering them security and relative comfort in a situation where there were few other options available. Many small businesses maintained a competitive advantage by employing extended family members and friends of family members, who worked long hours for low wages. While small businesses created employment opportunities within the Japanese-American community, they also reflected the cohesion of the community.[67]

A special form of small business enterprise was gardening. This involved watering and cutting lawns, trimming hedges, caring for plants and flowers, fertilizing, and disposing of trimmings at the homes and estates of upper- and upper-middle-class people. Although some Japanese-Americans were employed as caretakers on large estates, most contracted with the homeowner for a monthly fee and were self-employed. The work involved little investment of capital and offered stable, predictable employment. According to Kitano, gardening was an important urban occupation for Japanese-Americans, especially after World War II. Even by 1940 there were some 1,650 gardeners listed in the Japanese Southern California Telephone and Business Directory.

In many respects Japanese-Americans represented an example of a *middleman minority*. These are ethnic groups that come to occupy an intermediate rather than a low-status position. Discrimination and exclusion place limits on how high they can rise relative to dominant groups in the society. However, internal cohesion can provide the competitive advantage that enables them to rise above other racial and ethnic minority groups. Excluded from some occupations, they are forced to make their living in marginal lines of work and by carving out a special niche in the occupational structure.[68]

The incarceration of Japanese-Americans in concentration camps during World War II was a national tragedy that reflected the culmination of racism, discrimination, and prejudice toward them. Between the Japanese attack on Pearl Harbor (December 7, 1941) and August 7, 1942 more than 110,000 Japanese on the West Coast (about half of them U.S. citizens) were removed from their homes and relocated in ten camps located in California, Arizona, Idaho, Wyoming, Colorado, Utah, and Arkansas.

Relocation in the concentration camps meant financial ruin for many Japanese-Americans whose property and land were stolen, sold at depressed prices, lost, or confiscated. In 1942 the Federal Reserve Bank in San Francisco estimated the value of property lost by the evacuees to be $400 million.[69] The camps had an important effect on the postwar occupational activities of Japanese-Americans, especially the American-born second generation of Nisei. It was policy in the camps to use only American-born Japanese in positions of responsibility. The consequence of this was to reverse the traditional pattern of power, authority, and dominance between the Nisei and the immigrant generation Issei. Consequently, after the war younger Japanese-Americans were more likely to question and challenge parental pressure to follow in the family's small business. Work in the camps also exposed Nisei to a broader range of occupations, gave them experience in work that might not otherwise have been accessible, and gave them confidence in their capabilities. In a very paradoxical way, despite all of its negative aspects, the camp experience freed many second generation Japanese-Americans from some of the confining perspectives and controls of the ethnic community.[70]

The postwar period accelerated the occupational diversity that had begun to develop prior to the war. Well-founded concern about hostile anti-Japanese sentiments on the West Coast, especially in California, led many Japanese-Americans to move east upon their release from the camps. In this process, they became a more urban group and farming declined dramatically as an occupation. Among those who did return to the West Coast, small business employment was reestablished as an important occupational activity but with a greater diversity of businesses being pursued than before the war. Kitano estimates that by 1958 about 15 percent of the Japanese-American population of Los Angeles were operating their own businesses. The majority of these were self-employed gardeners, an occupation which became even more important than it was before the war.[71]

Present Occupational Status

Since the 1950s the Issei goal of owning and running a farm or small business has been transformed into the goal of attaining a high-status, clean, secure, white-collar or professional occupation among the Nisei and especially on the part of the third generation or Sansei. As shown in table 8.4, as of 1980 a little over 40 percent of Japanese-Americans are in managerial, professional, technical, and sales occupations with nearly another 20 percent in clerical occupations. Farming and skilled craft occupations are held by only a very small proportion of Japanese-Americans while a little more than 20 percent work in service occupations or as machine operators, fabricators, and laborers. In 1980 a comparatively high 8 percent of Japanese-Americans in the labor force were self-employed and unemployment was a very low 3.0 percent.[72]

Japanese-American women have high rates of labor force participation (exceeded only by Filipino women among Asian-American ethnic groups). In 1980, 72.5 percent of those who were heads of households and 55.9 percent of those who were married were in the labor force. There were important generational differences, however. Only 42.7 percent of the foreign-born women were in the labor force compared to 68.3 percent of those who were native-born,[73] indicating that the work patterns of more recent generations have become more similar to those of female members of the dominant majority group.

Since the 1950s education has played a key role in the occupational attainments of Japanese-Americans.[74] In 1980, 88.1 percent of Japanese men ages forty-five through fifty-four had at least completed high school compared to 68.7 percent of the caucasian men of the same age. People in this age group would have ranged in age from about five to fifteen years during World War II and would be mostly Nisei who completed their education after release from the camps. For Japanese-American men ages twenty-five through twenty-nine in 1980 (most of whom would be Sansei and Yonsei or fourth generation), 96.4 percent had completed at least a high school education compared to 87.0 percent of caucasian men in the same age group. Although Japanese-American women in the older age group trail their male counterparts (82.5 percent of women having completed high school), there is no difference in the high school completion rate for men and women in the younger age group (96.3 percent of women having completed high school). However, a larger percentage in both age groups have at least completed high school than is the case among caucasian women.[75] The commitment of Japanese-Americans to education can be seen in other ways. High school dropout rates are very low and college attendance rates are very high. In 1980, 96.2 percent of Japanese-American sixteen- and seventeen-year-olds were in school (compared to 89.0 percent of sixteen- and seventeen-year-old caucasians). In the twenty through twenty-four age group, 48.0 percent of Japanese-Americans, compared to only 23.9 percent of caucasians, were in school.[76]

Generational ties have played a role in upward mobility. One study of first and second generation Japanese-Americans in the early 1970s found that the higher the educational level of Issei, the higher the educational and occupational attainments of their Nisei children.[77] The three-generational study by Neidert and Farley referred to earlier in our discussion of Mexican-Americans did not identify Japanese-Americans separately. Only Filipinos are identified separately from all other Asians (who would be mainly of Japanese and Chinese ancestry). Nevertheless, the mean occupational status scores of first and second generation Asian men were 44 while those for the third generation were 51, a score exceeded only by men of Russian ancestry (many of whom are in all likelihood Jewish). The percentage of men with some college education was 64 percent for the first generation, 56 percent for the second (a decrease), and 69 percent for native-born sons of native-born parents, a figure again exceeded only by those of Russian ancestry. Average per capita income also increases across generations from $5,200 to $8,400 to $11,800, the highest figure of any ancestry group.[78]

CHINESE-AMERICANS

As noted in the introduction to this section, Chinese-Americans were the first Asian group to enter the United States. Like the Japanese, they came to Hawaii as agricultural workers. By 1884 they made up over 20 percent of the population of Hawaii. Chinese immigration to mainland United States began in the late 1840s and by 1852 there were 25,000 in California. Their numbers increased to 50,000 by 1862, and during the period 1850 to 1880 Chinese-Americans accounted for about 10 percent of the population of California.[79]

During the mid-1800s many areas of California, and mining districts in particular, were populated largely by men. The shortage of women created an occupational niche for many Chinese immigrants. They did "woman's work" such as cooking, cleaning, laundering, and general domestic service.[80] Many found their way to the gold fields, working mines that had been abandoned by caucasian miners. In the 1860s they were recruited to work on the construction of the transcontinental railroads. Chinese-Americans also worked in other kinds of mining, in fisheries and canneries, and in the manufacture of shoes, boots, and clothing. They also worked on land reclamation projects and as agricultural laborers.[81]

From the outset Chinese immigrants were the focus of racist attacks, frequently including violence, and legislation aimed at discouraging further immigration and restricting their occupational activities. In California they were forcibly expelled from mining and agricultural districts. A special Foreign Miner's Tax was directed specifically at Chinese miners, and in 1862 a California law (later declared unconstitutional) required that all "Mongolians" over age eighteen who had not paid the Foreign Miner's Tax and were engaged in the production of anything other than rice, sugar, tea, or coffee had to pay a special tax of $2.50 per month.[82] In San Francisco, where anti-Chinese sentiment was exceptionally strong, a variety of harassing ordinances were passed that were explicitly intended to drive the Chinese out of the state and discourage particular business activities. For example, Chinese laundries delivered their laundry in bundles hung on poles, so a tax was placed on laundries that did not deliver by horse and wagon. Even the pigtails worn by Chinese men were taxed.[83]

The anti-Chinese mood and its attendant harassing legislation in part reflected very real competition that Chinese-American workers offered caucasians. In California they dominated the laundry business and were extensively employed as domestic servants. After the railroads were completed they also entered certain manufacturing industries in large numbers. In San Francisco they made up 80 percent of those employed in shoe manufacture, 91 percent of workers in cigar manufacturing, and 64 percent of textile workers.[84] Within Chinese-American communities rotating credit associations, or *hui*, pooled small amounts of money from many individuals to make loans to start or expand businesses. Small businesses, many of them catering to the Chinese-American population, had become an important part of the local economy of many communities. A depression during the 1870s resulted in unemployment and lower wages, problems for which the Chinese were blamed. Labor unions also excluded Chinese-Americans from membership and lobbied for legislation restricting immigration and the kinds of work they could do. In 1882 Congress passed the Chinese Exclusion Act prohibiting Chinese immigration for ten years. In 1892 the law was renewed for another ten years and made permanent in 1902.[85] Ironically, hostility toward the Chinese led to support for the immigration of Japanese workers. By the turn of the century those who had not left the country retreated into the ethnic ghettos that are today's Chinatowns. The pressure of labor unions and local ordinances restricted them to occupations and businesses in which they would not compete with caucasians. They continued to operate laundries that served the needs of caucasians and to manufacture textiles. But by and large they withdrew from economic competition and engaged in businesses serving other Chinese-Americans or those serving tourists such as restaurants and shops selling exotic foods and imported oriental goods.[86]

The 1940s marked the beginning of occupational change among Chinese-Americans. In another ironic turn of events, the hostility toward Japanese-Americans that followed the outbreak of World War II was accompanied by more positive attitudes toward Chinese-Americans. Japan's invasion of China resulted in a great deal of sympathy for the Chinese which spilled over into attitudes toward Chinese-Americans. The 1930s and 1940s also saw the maturation of large numbers of the second generation which had been delayed because of the unbalanced sex ratio and the shortage of Chinese women in the United States during the period of restricted immigration in the nineteenth century.[87]

Native born Chinese-Americans have made extensive use of higher education to gain access to professional occupations. Within the professions, however, they have pursued careers in a very selective manner. This is illustrated in a study of 198 men and women who had completed at least four years of college by 1940. By 1947, 81.6 percent were in some type of professional work. The vast majority, however, were concentrated in engineering, chemistry, medicine, optometry, dentistry, pharmacy, and architecture and many were employed by state and federal government agencies.[88] These tend to be occupations that offer relative security, independence, and freedom from discrimination.[89]

The legal profession has not attracted many Chinese-Americans. Disputes within Chinese-American communities have been settled more often by clan organizations, mutual-aid societies, or secret societies than by the use of the courts. When legal services have been needed, Chinese-Americans have preferred to be represented by caucasian lawyers on the assumption that they will be more effective than a lawyer from their own ethnic group. Those Chinese-Americans who have entered the practice of law tend to be employed in the public sector.[90]

Several trends and patterns in the occupational distribution of Chinese-Americans evident by 1960 have continued into the present. In 1960 about half were in white-collar occupations. About 20 percent were in professional and technical occupations, 17 percent were proprietors, managers, or officials, and 14 percent were in clerical and sales work. Only a very small proportion were skilled craft workers (5 percent), but about 25 percent were in service occupations and an additional 14 percent were semiskilled workers. Very few (1.5 percent) were employed as unskilled laborers.[91] Overall, a "bipolar distribution" had developed with concentrations of workers in professional and technical occupations on the one hand and in low-skill manual and service occupations on the other. The concentration of Chinese-American professionals in a limited range of work has also continued.[92] In 1960, 54 percent of all professionals were in the natural sciences, accounting, engineering, drafting, and college teaching with the latter concentrated in the physical and natural sciences. By 1970, nearly 29 percent of all Chinese-Americans were in professional and technical occupations, but one-fourth were also employed as service workers and another 14 percent were in semiskilled and unskilled laboring jobs.[93] This suggests a further polarization in their occupational distribution.

Present Occupational Status

In 1980 over 60 percent of Chinese-Americans were in executive, professional, technical, sales, and administrative support occupations with nearly 26 percent in professional and technical work (see table 8.4). Some 41.1 percent of those in professional occupations were engineers and natural scientists, a continuation of the pattern of concentration within the professions noted earlier. At the other extreme, 30.3 percent were in the service and "machine operators, fabricators, and laborers" categories. The service category includes food service occupations and in 1980, 14.1 percent of all Chinese-Americans in the labor force were food service workers employed as waiters and waitresses, cooks, dishwashers, and busboys mostly in Chinese restaurants.[94] As in the preceding decades, there were very few Chinese-Americans in skilled craft occupations in 1980. The continuation of the "bipolar" pattern suggests that there are both opportunities for younger, well-educated Chinese-Americans and real limits on the mobility and attainment of those concentrated in low-skill service and laboring jobs. Unemployment among Chinese-Americans is exceptionally low. In 1980 their unemployment rate was 3.6 percent, only slightly higher than that of Japanese-Americans.[95]

Chinese-American women have rates of labor force participation that are comparable to those of Japanese-American women. In 1980, 70.3 percent of those who were heads of households were employed, as were 61.2 percent of married women. Generational differences are reflected in the fact that 65 percent of the native-born compared to 56 percent of the foreign-born women were in the labor force.[96]

The key role that education has played in the occupational attainments of Chinese-Americans can be documented in a number of ways. In 1970 the Chinese-American population included a sizable segment that had not gone beyond elementary school (23 percent) and the largest proportion of college graduates (25 percent) of any racial-ethnic group in the United States.[97] In 1980, 90 percent of men and 87.4 percent of women ages twenty-five through twenty-nine had at least completed high school, figures quite close to those for the caucasian population. Among Chinese-American men ages forty-five through fifty-four, 68.7 percent had at least completed high school, a figure identical to that of the caucasian population. However, only 57.7 percent of Chinese-American women in this age group had done so, a figure 12.4 percent below that for caucasian women.[98] High school dropout rates are extremely low among Chinese-Americans. In 1980, 96 percent of all sixteen- and seventeen-year-olds were enrolled in school. College enrollment is exceptionally high. In 1980, a phenomenal 59.8 percent of those ages twenty through twenty-four were in school. This figure is 11.8 percent greater than that for Japanese-Americans and 35.9 percent greater than the proportion of caucasians in this age group enrolled in school.[99]

FILIPINO-AMERICANS

The immigration of Filipinos to the United States followed that of the Japanese and Chinese by several decades. A few had been recruited to work in the Hawaiian sugar plantations in 1906 but immigration to the mainland did not occur in a significant way until the early 1920s. Restric-

Table 8.4
Occupational Distribution of Five Major Asian-American Ethnic
Groups, Employed Persons Age 16 and over, 1980, in Percent

	Ethnic Group				
Occupation	Japanese	Chinese	Filipino	Korean	Asian Indian
Executive, admin.,					
and managerial	12.8%	12.9%	7.7%	9.9%	11.9%
Professional	15.6	19.6	17.3	15.9	36.6
Technicians	4.3	6.3	6.0	3.7	7.6
Sales	10.3	8.6	5.8	13.4	7.0
Admin. support,					
incl. clerical	19.6	15.2	21.5	10.2	13.4
Service	12.8	17.6	15.0	16.5	7.8
Mechanics and					
repairers	3.4	1.6	2.3	2.9	1.4
Construction trades	2.7	0.9	1.9	1.8	0.8
Precision Produc-					
tion occupations	3.8	3.0	4.0	5.1	3.0
Machine operators,					
fabricators, and					
laborers	10.1	12.7	14.0	20.4	9.6
Farming, forestry,					
and fishing	4.4	0.5	2.8	0.9	0.9
TOTAL*	99.8	99.9	99.8	99.8	100.0
Total number					
in labor force	382,534	399,964	361,469	140,748	170,855
Total population	716,331	812,178	781,894	357,393	387,223

Source: U.S. Bureau of the Census, *1980 Census of Population*, vol. 1, *Characteristics of the Population*, chap. C, *General Social and Economic Characteristics*, pt. 1, U.S. Summary, PC 80-1-C1 (Washington, D.C.: U.S. Government Printing Office, 1981), 160, table 163.
*Totals do not add to 100.0 percent because of rounding error.

tive immigration legislation that became a reality in 1924 threatened the supply of Mexican field laborers. Hostility toward Japanese-Americans and the fact that they were becoming self-employed farmers also led California fruit and vegetable growers to look elsewhere for a source of cheap labor. Consequently, immigration from the Philippines was encouraged.

Early Filipino-American history was affected by American colonialism. The Philippines were annexed in 1898 and became a United States possession. Filipinos were not eligible for citizenship but they were considered U.S. "nationals" and could travel freely on U.S. passports and enter the United States without any restrictions. The census of 1910 counted only 2,767 Filipino-Americans, but by 1930 they numbered 108,424.[100]

Early immigrants worked mainly in agriculture as fruit and vegetable pickers and field hands, mostly in California but also in Washington. Sizable numbers found their way to the cities in search of educational and employment opportunities. Lacking education and job skills, they found work in relatively low-paying service jobs as domestic servants, drivers, and "houseboys." Some found employment in hotels and restaurants as bellboys, waiters, cooks, busboys, janitors, and elevator operators, while still others worked in hospitals as janitors, attendants, and orderlies.[101] By 1940, 90 percent of Filipinos in the labor force in California were in these kinds of service jobs.[102] Unlike the Chinese, Filipinos formed few associations that served the purpose of accumulating money and making loans to erstwhile entrepreneurs. Consequently, very little small business ownership developed among Filipino-Americans. However, at the beginning of World War II, some agricultural land was sold to Filipinos by Japanese-Americans being sent to concentration camps, especially in the San Fernando and San Joaquin Valleys and the Torrance-Gardena area of Southern California.

Like the earlier Chinese immigration, Filipino immigrants were mainly men. Of those coming to California between 1920 and 1929, 93 percent were male and 80 percent were single.[103] Racist hostility toward Filipinos discouraged intermarriage with caucasians, and in California the miscegenation law was extended to include Filipinos. As with the Chinese, the appearance of the second generation was delayed.

During the depression of the 1930s anti-Filipino sentiment in California led to riots, bombings, and killings. In 1935 Congress passed the Tydings-McDuffie Act which granted the Philippines "deferred independence" and set a quota of fifty immigrants per year from the Philippines. The result was to effectively halt Filipino immigration until 1965.

After World War II a number of Filipinos who had served in the U.S. Armed Forces against Japan in the Pacific immigrated, with their families, to California (mainly to San Francisco). According to Kitano, they possessed a commitment to hard work and a strong sense of discipline, but few occupational skills, and they found work in relatively unskilled jobs.[104] Still others circumvented immigration restrictions by enlisting in the U.S. Navy and working as mess stewards and officers' attendants.

The Immigration Act of 1965 lifted the restrictions of 1935 and encouraged the immigration of higher-status white-collar workers from many countries. Since 1960 more immigrants have come to the United States from the Philippines than from any other country except Mexico.[105] Between 1970 and 1980 the Filipino-American population more than doubled.[106]

The more recent arrivals from the Philippines have been relatively well-educated and of much higher occupational status than the immigrants of the 1920s. Physician, lawyer, engineer, educator, and nurse have been typical occupations of Filipino immigrants since the mid-1960s. Consequently, it is extremely difficult to assess the degree to which occupational mobility has occurred across generations since recent immigrants may often be of higher occupational status than members of the second and even some of the third generation.

Thus, the occupational distribution of Filipino-Americans presented in table 8.4 must be interpreted cautiously. While some of the 23.3 percent in professional and technical occupations are second and third generation people who have been upwardly mobile compared to their parents and grandparents, the majority are probably first generation immigrants. Like other Asian-Americans, very few are in skilled craft occupations. Some 29 percent are in service and low-skill manual occupations (machine operators, fabricators, and laborers).

The Neidert and Farley study referred to earlier provides some data on first generation men although there was an insufficient number of second and third generation men to make generational comparisons. They had a mean occupational status score of 38, four points below the "Asian" group and 12 points below those of English ancestry. Seventy-six percent of them, however, had at least some college. This was the highest percentage of all ancestry groups and 12 percent more than the next highest ancestry group (those of Russian-East European ancestry).[107] Part of this discrepancy between education and occupation is due to the fact that many well-educated recent immigrants find it difficult to find work commensurate with their qualifications and experience, a distinctive kind of underemployment. As Fred Cordova has pointed out, lawyers may have to work as clerks, dentists as medical aides, engineers as mechanics, teachers as secretaries, etc.[108]

Filipino-American women who are heads of households or who are married have the highest rates of labor force participation of all Asian-Americans. Seventy-nine percent of the former and 71.9 percent of the latter are in the labor force. Unlike their Japanese and Chinese counterparts, foreign born Filipino-American women are a little more likely to be in the labor force (68.8 percent) than those who are native born (64.5 percent).[109] This also reflects the greater education, credentials, and occupational skills of recent Filipino immigrants.

The educational attainment of Filipino-Americans is nearly as impressive as that of other Asian groups. In 1980, 88.8 percent of males and 85.0 percent of females ages twenty-five through twenty-nine had at least completed high school.[110] A very high (92.8) percent of all sixteen- and seventeen-year-olds were in school, reflecting low high school dropout rates. However, only 27.1 percent of the twenty through twenty-four age group were in school. This was the lowest of all Asian-American groups but still slightly higher than the figure for caucasians (23.9 percent).[111] This lower rate of college enrollment suggests that, in the future, the occupational attainment of the next generation of Filipino-Americans may not be as high as that of Japanese-Americans and Chinese-Americans.

KOREAN-AMERICANS

Korean immigration to the United States occurred briefly very early in this century and following the end of the Korean War in 1953. Between 1903 and 1905, 7,226 Koreans (only 637 of them women) immigrated to Hawaii to work in the sugar plantations.[112] Plantation owners, concerned about the growing power of large numbers of Chinese and Japanese coming to work in Hawaii, encouraged Korean immigration. Of this group of early immigrants, approximately 2,000 came to the mainland United States.[113] Emigration from Korea ended in 1905 when Japan established colonial control over the country, which it maintained until the end of World War II.

In 1910, the national census counted only 5,008 Korean-Americans and in 1940 they numbered only 8,568.[114] There is a scarcity of good data about the occupational characteristics of this group from the period of initial immigration through the end of World War II. They appear to have worked at relatively low-status service jobs and as agricultural laborers. Small in absolute number and more geographically dispersed than the Chinese and Japanese, they did not form communities large enough to support small businesses that served as a point of economic stability for other Asian groups.

Following the end of the Korean War and the passage of the Refugee Relief Act in 1953, Korean immigration to the United States increased dramatically. By 1970 they numbered 69,150 and by 1980 they had increased to over 350,000.[115] Immigration legislation of 1965 favored better-educated and occupationally skilled immigrants. Those comng from Korea had worked predominantly as professionals, technicians, and managers in their home country.[116]

Interpreting the data in table 8.4 on Korean-Americans presents the same problems encountered with Filipino-Americans. It is virtually impossible to determine generational changes in occupational status since most first generation persons are very recent immigrants. Disregarding generational differences, it appears that they exhibit a "bipolar" distribution similar to that of other Asian groups. That is, there is a concentration in professional and technical occupations (19.6 percent), very few in the skilled trades, and a concentration in service and low-skill manual occupations (36.9 percent).

With increased numbers, some Korean-American communities have reached a sufficiently large "critical mass" to support small businesses. A case in point is Los Angeles, which has the largest concentration of

Korean-Americans in the United States and where small businesses are becoming common.[117] Underemployment has been a serious problem for recent Korean immigrants just as it has been for those from the Philippines. According to David S. Kim and Charles C. Wong, in Los Angeles in the mid-1970s, half of those with professional degrees in fields like medicine, pharmacy, and nursing were working as skilled craft workers, semiskilled machine operators, and in sales. Among those educated in the liberal arts, only 7 percent were working at jobs consistent with their training.[118]

Korean-American women have labor force participation rates comparable to those of other Asian-American groups. Among those who are heads of households, 71.1 percent are employed, as are 56.2 percent of married women. Native-born women are only slightly more likely to be employed (59.1 percent) compared to the foreign-born (54.8 percent).[119]

While Korean-Americans, like other Asian groups, have high levels of educational attainment, they exhibit greater male-female differences than do other Asian groups. For example, in 1980, among those in the twenty-five through twenty-nine age group, 93.5 percent of the men had at least completed high school compared to only 79.0 percent of the women. The gap was even greater among those in the forty-five through fifty-four age group where 90.4 percent of the men compared to only 68.5 percent of the women had at least completed high school.[120] The school enrollment rates of younger Korean-Americans are also quite high. In 1980, 94.9 percent of the sixteen- and seventeen-year-olds were in school as were 40.1 percent of those in the twenty through twenty-four age group.[121] This high rate of college enrollment suggests the likelihood of high occupational attainments in the future.

AMERICANS OF ASIAN INDIAN ANCESTRY

Immigration from India was minimal prior to 1965. While historical immigration records note the arrival of one person from India in 1820, only a few hundred came before the twentieth century. Between 1899 and 1920 about 7,300 Asian Indians came to the United States. Many came from British Columbia, Canada, where they had been employed as contract laborers. They settled mainly in California where they worked as laborers in agriculture.[122] Much of the hostility directed toward the Japanese and Chinese in California was also experienced by Asian Indians. Between 1920 and 1940 some 3,000 returned to India.[123] Census data on Asian Indians are scarce prior to 1980. In order to estimate the number of Asian Indians in the Unites States for earlier time periods, it is necessary to rely on data from the U.S. Immigration and Naturalization Service that report the number of persons arriving from different countries. Between 1901 and 1960 nearly 13,000 persons entered the United States from India.[124] Of course, not all of them remained here.

According to Gary R. Hess, about one-half of all Asian Indians in the labor force in 1940 were farm laborers and another 15 percent were farm owners and managers. Another fifth were nonfarm laborers, and less than 5 percent were in professional occupations. This highly skewed occupational distribution was accompanied by a very low level of educational attainment. The median education of the Asian Indian population over age twenty-five was only 3.7 years.[125]

The Immigration Act of 1965, discussed earlier in conjunction with immigration from the Philippines and Korea, dramatically changed the number and occupational characteristics of immigrants from India since it gave priority to those with professional and technical skills. In the decade 1960–1970, over 27,000 Asian Indians came to the United States and in the five-year period 1971–1975, over 66,000 arrived.[126] Immigration from India continues to be high and the vast majority of Asian Indians are first generation immigrants.

It is clear from the data in table 8.4 that Asian Indians are concentrated in high-status occupations. Well over one-half are in managerial, professional, or technical work and another fifth are in sales and clerical occupations. This exceptionally high occupational status reflects the occupational training, skills, and experience immigrants brought with them rather than career mobility achieved since arriving in the United States. For example, of all persons arriving from India between 1965 and 1977 who had an occupation in India, between 59 percent and 90 percent were in professional and technical occupations.[127] Of those who arrived from June, 1974 to June, 1975, 77 percent had worked in professional and technical occupations in India.[128] Those admitted in 1978 were of comparably high occupational status. Nearly 58 percent were in professional and technical occupations and over 83 percent had worked in white-collar jobs in India.[129]

Despite their high occupational status and educational credentials, Asian Indians appear to have problems finding employment in occupations comparable to those held in India and experience the sort of underemployment (at least temporarily) encountered by recent Filipino and Korean immigrants.[130] Physicians, accountants, and engineers appear to have the fewest problems replicating their occupational status while scientists, managers, and administrators have been less likely to enter jobs comparable to those they held in India.[131]

Not surprisingly, the educational attainment of Asian Indians is exceptionally high. A study of those living in the New York metropolitan area in 1977–1978 found that 54 percent had graduate or professional training, 84 percent had at least graduated from college, and 90 percent had at least some college education.[132] In 1980, 93.5 percent of men and 87.9 percent of women of Asian Indian ethnicity had at least graduated from high school.[133] Americans of Asian Indian ancestry are comparable to other Asian-Americans in terms of the commitment of young people to education. Among those ages sixteen and seventeen, 92.2 percent were enrolled in school in 1980, as were 44.5 percent of those ages twenty through twenty-four.[134] With high rates of college attendance, it seems likely that second generation Asian Indians will replicate if not surpass the occupational status of the immigrant generation.

Asian Indian women are less likely than women of Japanese, Chinese, Filipino, or Korean ancestry to be in the labor force. In 1980, only 58.2 percent of the heads of households and 51.9 percent of married Asian Indian women were employed. Those who were foreign-born were much more likely than those who were native-born to be in the labor force (53.6 percent compared to 36.0 percent) reflecting the effect of greater amounts of education and work experience among more recent immigrants on labor force participation.[135]

SUMMARY

Our analysis of minorities and work has emphasized the importance of historical events and experiences in creating obstacles, limits, and opportunities affecting the kinds of work engaged in by members of racial and ethnic minority groups. Exploitation, exclusion, and discrimination have been typical experiences of minority group members. Exclusion from some occupations has led to the development of specialized occupational "niches," some of which have been turned into opportunities.

The legacy of slavery and the occupational caste system severely limited the occupational opportunities of blacks while conquest and subordination affected those of Mexican-Americans. During the first half of the 20th century the occupations of blacks began to shift from agriculture to the factory, as they responded to the labor needs of northern industry. In recent years greater access to education as well as nondiscrimination and affirmative action policies have led to increased diversity in the kinds of work black Americans do.

Once overwhelmingly concentrated in unskilled laboring jobs, Mexican-Americans are also beginning to exhibit increased occupational diversity. Like blacks, they also severely experience the problem of unemployment and a substantial proportion are stuck in dead-end and insecure jobs in the secondary labor market.

The early occupational experiences of Asian-Americans, especially those from Japan and China, were shaped by the labor needs of Hawaii and California agriculture. Starting at the bottom of the occupational hierarchy and subjected to many forms of exclusion, discrimination, and harassment, Asian-Americans have been unusually successful in achieving high occupational status. Small business enterprise and utilization of the higher education system have played an important role in this transformation. Nevertheless, some groups, especially the Japanese and Chinese, exhibit a bipolar occupational distribution with substantial concentrations of workers in service and low-skill jobs typical of the secondary labor market.

Recent Asian immigrants, particularly those from the Philippines, Korea, and India, have been affected by immigration policies enacted in the mid-1960s. Their concentration in high-status occupations is largely an artifact of those policies, especially in the case of Asian Indians. Labor force needs and preferences have resulted in the selective recruitment of professionals, technicians, and managers from these countries, just as immigration policies and labor needs resulted in the recruitment of unskilled laborers in the second half of the nineteenth and the early decades of the twentieth centuries.

NOTES

1. See Stanley Lieberson, A *Piece of the Pie: Blacks and White Immigrants Since 1880* (Berkeley: University of California Press, 1980); and Vincent N. Parrillo, *Strangers to These Shores: Race and Ethnic Relations in the United States*, 2nd ed. (New York: Wiley, 1985).
2. Robert William Fogel and Stanley L. Engerman, *Time on the Cross: The Economics of American Negro Slavery* (Boston: Little, Brown, 1974); and Edna Bonacich, "Abolition, the Extension of Slavery, and the Position of Free Blacks: A Study of Split Labor Markets in the United States, 1830–1863, *American Journal of Sociology* 81 (November 1975): 601–628.
3. Edna Bonacich, "Theory of Ethnic Antagonism," *American Sociological Review* 37 (October 1972): 547–559.
4. Bart Landry, "The Economic Position of Black Americans," in *American Minorities and Economic Opportunity*, ed. H. Roy Kaplan (Itasca, Ill.: F. E. Peacock, 1977), 53.
5. Thomas Sowell, "Three Black Histories," in *American Ethnic Groups*, ed. Thomas Sowell (Washington, D.C.: The Urban Institute, 1978), 7–64.
6. Sowell, "Three Black Histories."
7. The preceding summary of black migration draws extensively on Sowell, "Three Black Histories"; William Julius Wilson, *The Declining Significance of Race: Blacks and Changing American Institutions* (Chicago: University of Chicago Press, 1978); and Spencer R. Crew, "The Great Migration of Afro-Americans, 1015–1940," *Monthly Labor Review* 110 (March 1987): 34–36.

8. U.S. Bureau of the Census, *Statistical Abstract of the United States, 1985* (Washington, D.C.: U.S. Government Printing Office, 1984), 402–403, table 676.
9. Mark A. Fossett, Omer R. Galle, and William R. Kelly, "Racial Occupational Inequality, 1940–1980: National and Regional Trends," *American Sociological Review* 51 (June 1986): 421–429.
10. Edna Bonacich, "Advanced Capitalism and Black/White Race Relations in the United States: A Split Labor Market Interpretation," *American Sociological Review* (February 1976): 34–51.
11. Duane E. Leigh, "Racial Discrimination and Labor Unions: Evidence from the NLS Sample of Middle-Aged Men," *Journal of Human Resources* 13 (Fall 1978): 568–577.
12. Stanley Lieberson, *A Piece of the Pie.*
13. Leigh, "Racial Discrimination and Labor Unions"; and Richard Child Hill, "Unionization and Racial Income Inequality in the Metropolis," *American Sociological Review* 39 (August 1974): 507–522.
14. U.S. Bureau of the Census, *Statistical Abstract, 1985*, 136, table 216.
15. Andrew F. Brimmer, "The Labor Market and the Distribution of Income," in U.S. Bureau of the Census, *Reflections of America* (Washington, D.C.: U.S. Government Printing Office, 1980), 101, table 2.
16. U.S. Bureau of the Census, *Statistical Abstract, 1985*, 446, table 743.
17. Ibid., 456, table 762.
18. Dennis P. Hogan and Michele Pazul, "The Occupational and Earnings Returns to Education among Black Men in the North," *American Journal of Sociology* 87 (January 1982): 905–920.
19. Eric A. Hanushek, "Sources of Black-White Earnings Differences," *Social Science Research* 11 (June 1982): 103–126.
20. James R. Kluegel, "The Causes and Cost of Racial Exclusion from Job Authority," *American Sociological Review* 43 (June 1978): 285–301.
21. U.S. Bureau of the Census, *Statistical Abstract, 1985*, 449, table 749.
22. "Selected Unemployment Indicators, Monthly Data Seasonally Adjusted," *Monthly Labor Review* 110 (March 1987): 65, table 7.
23. Ibid.
24. U.S. Bureau of the Census, *Statistical Abstract, 1985*, 394, table 658.
25. U.S. Bureau of the Census, *Statistical Abstract of the United States, 1981* (Washington, D.C.: U.S. Government Printing Office, 1980), 18–23, tables 23 and 24.
26. Herrington J. Bryce, "Mobilizing the Black Unemployed," *American Demographics* 5 (July 1983): 19–21, 42–43.
27. John D. Kasarda, "The Implications of Contemporary Redistribution Trends for National Urban Policy," *Social Science Quarterly* 61 (1980): 373–400; and "Caught in the Web of Change," *Society* 21 (1983): 41–47.
28. Thomas M. Stanback and Theirry J. Noyelle, *Cities in Transition* (Totowa, N.J.: Allanheld, Osmun, 1982).
29. Wilson, *The Declining Significance of Race*, 151.
30. Reynolds Farley and Suzanne M. Bianchi, "The Growing Gap between Blacks," *American Demographics* 5 (July 1983): 15–18.
31. Michael Hout, "Occupational Mobility of Black Men," *American Sociological Review* 49 (June 1984): 308–322.
32. Marshall I. Pomer, "Labor Market Structure, Intragenerational Mobility,

and Discrimination: Black Male Advancement Out of Low-Paying Occupations, 1962–1973," *American Sociological Review* 51 (October 1986): 650–659.
33. U.S. Bureau of the Census, *Statistical Abstract, 1985,* 341, table 561.
34. Charles C. Moskos, "Success Story: Blacks in the Army," *The Atlantic Monthly* 257 (May 1986): 64–72.
35. Ibid.
36. Ibid., 67.
37. Based on a 1982 study by Martin Binkin and Mark J. Eitelberg of the Brookings Institution and cited in Moskos, "Success Story," 67.
38. Moskos, "Success Story," 68.
39. John Sibley Butler, "Inequality in the Military: An Examination of Promotion Time," *American Sociological Review* 41 (October 1976): 807–818; and Peter G. Nordlie, "Promotion Time of Black and White Army Officers in Command Positions," in *Discrimination in Organizations,* ed. Rudolfo Alvarez, et al. (San Francisco: Jossey-Bass, 1979).
40. Phillips Cutright, "The Civilian Earnings of White and Black Draftees and Nonveterans," *American Sociological Review* 39 (June 1974): 317–327.
41. Harley L. Browning, Sally L. Lopreato, and Dudley L. Poston, Jr., "Income and Veteran Status: Variations Among Mexican Americans, Blacks, and Anglos," *American Sociological Review* 38 (February 1973): 74–85.
42. Oscar J. Martinez, "On the Size of the Chicano Population: New Estimates, 1850–1900," *Aztlan* 6 (Spring 1975): 43–67.
43. Joan W. Moore, "Colonialism: The Case of the Mexican-Americans," *Social Problems* 17 (Spring 1970): 463–472; and Joan W. Moore with Harry Pachon, *Mexican Americans,* 2nd ed. (Englewood Cliffs, N.J.: Prentice-Hall, 1976).
44. Leobardo F. Estrada et al., "Chicanos in the United States: A History of Exploitation and Resistance," *Daedalus* 110 (Spring 1981): 103–131.
45. Joseph Hraba, *American Ethnicity* (Itasca, Ill.: F. E. Peacock, 1979).
46. Estrada et al., "Chicanos in the United States," 113.
47. Hraba, *American Ethnicity,* 248–249.
48. Hilda H. Golden and Curt Tausky, "Minority Groups in the World of Work," in Kaplan, *American Minorities and Economic Opportunity,* 20–21; and Lionel A. Maldonado, "Altered States: Chicanos in the Labor Force," in *Ethnicity and the Labor Force,* ed. Winston Van Horne (Milwaukee: University of Wisconsin System, Ethnic Studies Coordinating Committee/Urban Corridor Consortium, 1985), 143–166.
49. Dennis M. Roth, "Hispanics in the U.S. Labor Force," in Cary Davis, Carl Haub, and JoAnne Willette, *U.S. Hispanics: Changing the Face of America,* Population Bulletin 38 (Washington, D.C.: Population Reference Bureau, 1983).
50. Maldonado, "Altered States"; and Harry P. Pachon and Joan W. Moore, "Mexican Americans," *The Annals* 454 (March 1981): 111–124.
51. U.S. Bureau of the Census, *Statistical Abstract, 1985,* 136, table 217.
52. Ibid., 456, table 762.
53. Ibid., 447, table 744.
54. Lisa J. Neidert and Reynolds Farley, "Assimilation in the United States: An Analysis of Ethnic and Generational Differences in Status and Achievement," *American Sociological Review* 50 (December 1985): 840–850.
55. Occupational status scores were based on the Duncan Socioeconomic Index as developed by Otis Dudley Duncan, "A Socioeconomic Index for all Occupations," in Albert J. Reiss, Jr., *Occupations and Social Status* (New York: Free Press, 1961), 109–138.

56. Neidert and Farley, "Assimilation in the United States," tables 2 and 3.
57. Robert W. Gardner, Bryant Robey, and Peter C. Smith, *Asian Americans: Growth, Change, and Diversity*, Population Bulletin 40 (Washington, D.C.: Population Reference Bureau, 1985), 7.
58. Ibid., 3.
59. For a general discussion of Asian-Americans including more details of annual immigration, see Harry H. L. Kitano, *Race-Relations*, 2nd ed. (Englewood Cliffs, N.J.: Prentice-Hall, 1980), chap. 13; *Japanese Americans: The Evolution of a Subculture*, 2nd ed. (Englewood Cliffs, N.J.: Prentice-Hall, 1976), and William Petersen, *Japanese Americans: Oppression and Success* (New York: Random House, 1971).
60. Petersen, *Japanese Americans*, 11.
61. Gardner, Robey, and Smith, *Asian Americans*, 8.
62. Masakazu Iwata, "The Japanese Immigrants in California Agriculture," *Agricultural History* 36 (1962): 25–37.
63. Kitano, *Japanese Americans*, 19.
64. Ibid.
65. Since Japanese immigrants were prohibited from becoming U.S. citizens, it is clear that the Alien Land Bill was aimed at them. Their children born in the U.S. were of course citizens.
66. Iwata, "Japanese Immigrants in California Agriculture."
67. Ivan Light, *Ethnic Enterprise in America* (Berkeley and Los Angeles: University of California Press, 1972).
68. Edna Bonacich, "A Theory of Middleman Minorities," *American Sociological Review* 38 (October 1973): 583–594; and Harry H. L. Kitano, "Japanese Americans: The Development of a Middleman Minority," *Pacific Historical Review* 43 (November 1974): 500–519.
69. Kitano, *Japanese Americans*, 89. In 1964 the federal government paid $38 million to 26,560 claimants for property confiscated during World War II. Considering inflation between 1942 and 1964 and eighteen years of lost interest, only a small fraction of the Federal Reserve Board's estimated $400 million of lost property was ever recovered.
70. Kitano, *Japanese Americans*, 91; and William Petersen, "Chinese Americans and Japanese Americans," in Sowell, ed., *American Ethnic Groups*, 65–106.
71. Kitano, *Japanese Americans*, 95–96.
72. U.S. Bureau of the Census, *1980 Census of Population* (Washington, D.C.: U.S. Government Printing Office, 1981), vol. 1, *Characteristics of the Population*, chap. C, *General Social and Economic Characteristics*, pt. 1, U.S. Summary, PC 80-1-C1, p. 159, table 162.
73. Gardner, Robey, and Smith, *Asian Americans*, 28.
74. See Charles Hirschman and Morrison G. Wong, "The Extraordinary Educational Attainment of Asian-Americans: A Search for Historical Evidence and Explanations," *Social Forces* 65 (September 1986), 1–27, for an analysis of the role of education in the occupational attainments of many Asian-American groups.
75. Gardner, Robey, and Smith, *Asian Americans*, 25.
76. Ibid., 27.
77. Gene Levine and Darrel M. Montero, "Socioeconomic Mobility among Three Generations of Japanese Americans," *Journal of Social Issues* 29 (1972): 33–48.
78. Neidert and Farley, "Assimilation in the United States."
79. Kitano, *Race Relations*, 234.

80. Ibid.
81. Stanford M. Lyman, *Chinese Americans* (New York: Random House, 1974), 73.
82. Ibid., 72.
83. Kitano, *Race Relations*, 237.
84. Ibid., 236.
85. It was not until 1943 that foreign-born Chinese were permitted to become citizens. This change reflected the positive attitudes toward them that developed during World War II.
86. Petersen, "Chinese Americans and Japanese Americans," 77.
87. During the period of unrestricted immigration (i.e., up to 1882) slightly more than 100,000 Chinese men came to the United States, but only 8,848 Chinese women did so. Not all of these people remained in the country. The census of 1890 counted only 3,868 Chinese women compared to 102,620 Chinese men. By 1920 the sex ratio (number of males per 100 females) was 695, 395 by 1930, and 285 in 1940. Immigration restrictions were relaxed following World War II, births increased, and by 1950 the sex ratio was 190. Thus, despite the fact that Chinese immigration to the United States began nearly 150 years ago, many Chinese-Americans are not all that far removed from their immigrant origins if one thinks of that distance in generational terms. These data on sex ratios are from Lyman, *Chinese Americans*, 87–88.
88. Beula Ong Kwoh, "The Occupational Status of American-Born Chinese Male College Graduates," *American Journal of Sociology* 53 (November 1947): 192–200.
89. Lyman, *Chinese Americans*, 133.
90. Ibid., 135–136.
91. Calvin F. Schmid and Charles E. Nobbe, "Socioeconomic Differentials among Nonwhite Races," *American Sociological Review* 30 (December 1965): 909–922.
92. Mely Giok-Lan Tan, *The Chinese in the United States: Social Mobility and Assimilation*, Asian Folklore and Social Life Monographs, vol. 21 (Taipei: The Orient Cultural Service, 1971); and Shien Woo Kung, *Chinese in American Life* (Seattle: University of Washington Press, 1962).
93. Petersen, "Chinese Americans and Japanese Americans," 86–87.
94. U.S. Bureau of the Census, *1980 Census of Population*, vol. 1, chap. C, pt. 1, p. 160, table 163.
95. Ibid., p. 159, table 162.
96. Gardner, Robey, and Smith, *Asian Americans*, 28.
97. Kitano, *Race Relations*, 243.
98. Gardner, Robey, and Smith, *Asian Americans*, 25.
99. Ibid., 27.
100. Ibid., 8.
101. Parrillo, *Strangers to These Shores*.
102. Davis McEntire, *The Labor Force in California: A Study of Characteristics and Trends in Labor Force, Employment, and Occupations in California, 1900–1950* (Berkeley: University of California Press, 1952), 62.
103. Parrillo, *Strangers to These Shores*, 261.
104. Kitano, *Race Relations*, 222.
105. Gardner, Robey, and Smith, *Asian Americans*, 8.
106. Parrillo, *Strangers to These Shores*, 263.

107. Neidert and Farley, *"Assimilation in the United States,"* 844.
108. Fred Cordova, "The Filipino-American: There's Always an Identity Crisis," in *Asian Americans*, ed. Stanley Sue and Nathaniel N. Wagner (Palo Alto, Calif.: Science and Behavior Books, 1973), 136–139.
109. Gardner, Robey, and Smith, *Asian Americans*, 28.
110. Ibid., 25.
111. Ibid., 27.
112. Parrillo, *Strangers to These Shores*, 263.
113. Kitano, *Race Relations*, 210.
114. Gardner, Robey, and Smith, *Asian Americans*, 8.
115. Ibid., 8.
116. Kitano, *Race Relations*, 214.
117. David S. Kim and Charles C. Wong, "Business Development in Koreatown, Los Angeles," in *The Korean Diaspora*, ed. Hyung-Chan Kim (Santa Barbara, Calif.: Clio Press, 1977), 229–245.
118. Ibid., 231.
119. Gardner, Robey, and Smith, *Asian Americans*, 28.
120. Ibid., 25.
121. Ibid., 27.
122. Gary R. Hess, "The Asian Indian Immigrants in the United States: The Early Phase, 1900–65," in *From India to America*, ed. S. Chandrasekhar (La Jolla, Calif.: Population Review, 1982), 29–34.
123. Ibid., 31.
124. U.S. Department of Justice, Immigration and Naturalization Service, *Statistical Yearbook of the Immigration and Naturalization Service, 1978* (Washington, D.C.: U.S. Government Printing Office, 1979).
125. Hess, "The Asian Indian Immigrants in the United States," 31–32.
126. U.S. Department of Justice, Immigration and Naturalization Service, *Statistical Yearbook, 1978*.
127. Philip J. Leonhard-Spark and Parmatma Saran, with the assistance of Karen Ginsberg, "The Indian Immigrant in America: A Demographic Profile," in Parmatma Saran and Edwin Eames, *The New Ethnics: Asian Indians in the United States* (New York: Praeger, 1980), 136–162.
128. Bruce LaBrack, "Immigration Law and the Revitalization Process: The Case of the California Sikhs," in Chandrasekhar (ed.), *From India to America*, 59–66.
129. S. Chandrasekhar, "Some Statistics on Asian Indian Immigration to the United States of America," in Chandrasekhar (ed.), *From India to America*, 87–92.
130. Pelia A. Thottathil and Parmatma Saran, "An Economic Profile of Asian Indians," in Saran and Eames, *The New Ethnics*, 233–246.
131. Leonhard-Spark, Saran, and Ginsberg, "The Indian Immigrant in America," 153.
132. Ibid., 151.
133. Gardner, Robey, and Smith, *Asian Americans*, 25.
134. Ibid., 27.
135. Ibid., 28.

CHAPTER 9

Occupational Correlates, Leisure, and Retirement

AT VARIOUS POINTS in the preceding chapters it has been apparent that occupation affects many aspects of people's nonwork lives. This chapter will explore these effects more fully. First, our interest will be in the link between occupational status and a variety of risks that people experience, including the likelihood of death, illness, disability, suicide, and divorce. Political identification and attitudes on a number of political, economic, and social issues are also correlated with occupational status. Second, we will explore the concept of "occupational encapsulation" in order to examine the way in which occupational subcultures shape their members' nonwork lives. Next, we will deal with the relationship between work and leisure. Finally, we will examine the topic of retirement and how the retirement experience varies among occupational groups.

OCCUPATIONAL CORRELATES

There is a long tradition of sociological research on the relationship of occupational status to a great variety of behaviors, attitudes, and beliefs. Identifying and explaining such relationships have led to the conclusion that occupation indeed makes a difference in the experiences people have off the job. As we will see, some of these differences are directly and

296

immediately linked to occupation. Others, however, are more indirect and suggest that occupational subcultures may subtly shape the perspectives people carry over to their nonwork lives.

DEATH, DISABILITY, AND ILLNESS

One of the most striking and dramatic effects of occupation can be seen in its relationship to mortality. The probabilities of dying are linked to occupational status. While there is debate about the relative amount of stress involved in white-collar and blue-collar occupations, it is clear that blue-collar occupations (especially those in mining, construction, lumbering, and oil drilling) are more dangerous and that accidents *on the job* produce higher death rates in such work.[1]

The general conclusion of numerous studies is that mortality is inversely related to occupational status.[2] One of the earliest studies was conducted in 1930 using data from death certificates in ten states. The overall death rate for employed males was 9.1 per 1,000 workers. However, the rate was 6.7 for men in professional occupations and 14.5 for those in unskilled laboring jobs.[3] Another study using 1950 data reported similar findings, but as age increased the gap between professionals and laborers increased. For example, among those ages twenty-five through twenty-nine, professionals had a death rate of 1.2 per 1,000, while the rate for laborers was 2.8. However, for those in the forty-five through fifty-four age group the death rate was 9.4 for professionals and 14.5 for laborers, suggesting that the effects of occupational status on mortality become more pronounced with increasing age. This study also found that at all ages the death rates for people in professional, managerial, and clerical occupations were virtually identical.[4]

Differential death rates by occupation reflect a number of factors, including differences in access to medical care, diet, exposure to hazards, and accidents. According to the Metropolitan Life Insurance Company, occupations connected with lumbering, coal mining, and metal extraction are among the most hazardous. Lumbermen, raftsmen, and wood-choppers have death rates one and one-half times those of all workers.[5] Disabling work injuries also vary greatly by industry. Based on 1967 data, oil and natural gas drilling work was the most hazardous, with 69.1 disabling injuries per million employee-hours worked. The next highest rate was 63.9 for occupations requiring the handling of marine cargo (longshoremen, dock workers, etc.).[6]

In addition to being related to occupational status, death and disability also vary by industry. Data on death rates and disabling injuries in 1983 are presented in table 9.1. These death rates are based on the number of workers killed on the job. A disabling injury is one which "results in death, some degree of physical impairment, or renders the person unable to perform regular activities for a full day beyond the day of the injury."[7] As the data in table 9.1 indicate, members of the American labor force suffer nearly two million disabling injuries per year, and for every 100,000 workers there are eleven on-the-job deaths per year. It is also clear that there are very great differences in the likelihood of dying on the job in different industries. According to this measure, occupations in agriculture, forestry, fishing, and mining are the most hazardous; the least hazardous occupations are found in manufacturing, trade, and service industries.

Every year, nearly 11.5 million people are injured on the job to the extent that they require medical attention and/or must restrict their normal activities to some degree. The injury rate (per 100 workers) for men is 4.4 times the rate for women, a reflection of the different kinds of work men and women do.[8] The data in table 9.2 represent another way of illustrating occupational differences in exposure to health risks. In this case, the number of occupational injuries and illnesses and the total number of lost workdays (per 100 full-time employees) are the units of measure. Using the number of *cases* of injury and illness, construction appears to be the most hazardous work, but in terms of the number of *workdays lost,* mining is more hazardous. While mining and manufacturing have a very similar injury and illness rate, the number of lost workdays per 100 workers is much higher in mining. This suggests that the injuries and illnesses that occur in mining are more severe and debilitating. Occupations in trade, finance, insurance, real estate, and other service industries clearly present fewer risks.

The data in tables 9.1 and 9.2 illustrate the consequences of risks and hazards that are immediately and directly linked to work. However,

Table 9.1
Death Rate and Number of Disabling Injuries by Industry Group, 1983

Industry Group	Death Rate Per 100,000 Workers	Number of Disabling Injuries
Agriculture, forestry, and fishing	55	200,000
Mining and quarrying	50	40,000
Construction	37	200,000
Manufacturing	6	340,000
Transportation and utilities	25	140,000
Wholesale and retail trade	5	330,000
Service*	6	370,000
Government	10	280,000
Total	11	1,900,000

Source: U.S. Bureau of the Census, *Statistical Abstract of the United States, 1985* (Washington, D.C.: U.S. Government Printing Office, 1984), 425, table 712.
*Includes finance, insurance, and real estate.

Table 9.2
Occupational Injury and Illness Rates (per 100
full-time employees) for Selected Industries, 1982

Industry	Number of Cases	Number of Lost Workdays
Agriculture, forestry, and fishing	11.8	86.0
Mining	10.5	137.3
Construction	14.6	115.7
Manufacturing	10.2	75.0
Transportation and public utilities	8.5	96.7
Wholesale and retail trade	7.2	45.5
Finance, insurance, and real estate	2.0	13.2
Other services	4.9	35.8
Total	7.7	58.7

Source: U.S. Bureau of the Census, *Statistical Abstract of the United States,*
1985 (Washington, D.C.: U.S. Government Printing Office, 1984), 426, table
713.

occupations may expose people to long-term hazards that have a delayed effect on illness and mortality. Coal miners and textile mill workers (especially those working with cotton fibers) develop long-term respiratory problems that result in higher death rates. Working with asbestos, lead, radioactive materials, and a number of petrochemicals can also have harmful effects on health that may not become evident until a good deal of time has elapsed.[9]

MENTAL ILLNESS

Occupational status (along with educational attainment and income) has also been found to be related to mental illness. Two widely cited classics in the field of mental illness illustrate this relationshp. In 1950, August B. Hollingshead, a sociologist, and Frederick C. Redlich, a psychiatrist, obtained detailed information on 1,891 patients being treated by clinics, hospitals, and private practitioners in New Haven, Connecticut, for various types of mental illness.[10] They used data on occupation and education in the patients' records to create five social-class levels, and a sample of the general population of New Haven was used as a basis for comparison. They found that the prevalence of all types of mental illness (neuroses and psychoses combined) was three times higher at the lowest-class level than at the highest. However, they found that neuroses, the milder forms of mental illness, were *directly* related to occupational and educational status. The rate for neuroses was three and one-half times greater among people at the highest-status level compared to those at the lowest-status level. On the other hand, psychoses, the more severe and debilitating forms of mental illness, were *inversely* related to occupational and educational status. The rate for psychoses was eight times greater at the lowest- compared to the highest-status level. Thus, the more severe forms of mental illness were more likely to occur among people at the bottom of the occupational and educational status hierarchies.

The kinds of treatment being received by the patients studied by Hollingshead and Redlich also varied by occupational and educational status. At higher-status levels they were more likely to be treated as out-patients and to be receiving individualized treatment from a psychiatrist, psychoanalyst, or psychotherapist in a clinic or private practice setting. Patients at the lowest-status level were more likely to be receiving elec-tric shock or drug treatment (which was highly experimental at that time), if they were not simply hospitalized and receiving no treatment of any kind. A follow-up study of these patients a decade later found little change. Those from lower-status levels were still more likely to be hospitalized and those from higher-status levels were more likely to be receiving treatment from private practitioners and as outpatients.[11]

A second classic study of mental illness is the "Midtown Manhat-tan Study" conducted under the direction of Leo Srole.[12] This study in-volved a sample of 1,660 people in New York City and also used occupation and education to measure social status. Mental illness was found to be inversely related to status. For example, while 30 percent of those at the highest occupational and educational status level were judged to be "well," only 4.6 percent of those at the lowest level were evaluated this way. "Impaired psychological functioning" was found among 12.5 percent of those at the highest-status level compared to 47.3 percent of those at the lowest level. None of the highest-status people interviewed were judged to be "incapacitated" (the most severe illness category used in the study), but 9.3 percent of those at the lowest-status level were evaluated this way. Another striking finding was that at the highest-status level about 20 percent of those evaluated as "impaired" were receiving some kind of psychiatric treatment compared to only 1 percent of those at the lowest-status level.

SUICIDE

Occupational status has also been found to be related to suicide, but the exact nature of the relationship is not entirely clear. Elwin H. Powell's study of suicides by white males in Tulsa County, Oklahoma, from 1937 to 1956 found that the suicide rate was highest at the top and bottom of the occupational hierarchy and lower (and more stable over time) in the middle-status levels.[13] For example, the rate (expressed as the average annual number of suicides per 100,000 population) was 35.1 for men in professional and managerial occupations and 38.7 for unskilled workers. Between those extremes, however, the rates were lower: 11.6 for those in clerical and sales occupations, 14.3 for skilled craft workers, and 20.5 for semiskilled workers. Overall, the suicide rate was higher for white-collar workers than for blue-collar workers (24.6 compared to 19.6). Among those in specific white-collar occupations, the highest rates of suicide occurred among pharmacists and physicians and the lowest rates were among engineers and accountants. Similar variations occurred among blue-collar workers where the highest suicide rate was found among cab drivers and the lowest occurred among carpenters.

Suicide also appears to be related to downward career mobility and downward intergenerational mobility. Warren Breed's study of suicide among white males in New Orleans from 1954 to 1959 concluded that downward mobility of both types was involved in suicide.[14] At the time they committed suicide some 53 percent of the men were in occupations of lower prestige than those of their fathers. About one-third of those working full-time when they committed suicide had been downwardly mobile over the course of their own careers. However, only about half were employed full-time when the suicide occurred. About one-third were either unemployed or working part-time. Breed concluded that the sense of failure that may develop as a result of downward occupational mobility is a contributing factor in suicide. His conclusions are supported by research that has found that economic downturns, layoffs, and unemployment (especially among older persons) are related to suicide.[15]

DIVORCE

Occupational status is also involved in another major area of nonwork life—the family. Family disruption through divorce increases as we descend the occupational status hierarchy. This relationship is illustrated in studies dealing with a single city as well as the nation as a whole.

William M. Kephart found that divorces in Philadelphia between 1937 and 1950 were inversely related to occupational status.[16] Using a sample of 1,434 randomly selected divorces, he found that men in professional and business ownership occupations accounted for the smallest proportions of divorces (4.3 percent and 5.0 percent, respectively). Those in clerical and sales, and skilled manual occupations made up a much larger proportion of divorce (19.6 percent and 20.4 percent, respectively). Semiskilled workers accounted for 35.4 percent of the divorces and those in the "labor/service" category accounted for 15.3 percent. After comparing the occupations of men who were divorced with the occupational composition of the Philadelphia labor force, Kephart concluded that professionals and business proprietors were underrepresented in cases of divorce, while semiskilled workers and those in the labor/service category were overrepresented. Those in the middle-status occupational categories—clerical and sales, and skilled workers—were proportionately represented among divorce cases.

In another study using national census data for 1970, William J. Goode examined the relationship of occupational status to "proneness to marital instability" which included both separation and divorce.[17] He concluded that marital instability increased consistently as occupational status decreased. For example, his "index" of proneness to marital instability was 72 for men in professional and technical occupations, 103 for those in skilled manual occupations, and 135 for those in service occupations. Thus, those at the bottom of the occupational hierarchy were nearly twice as prone to separation and divorce as those at the top.

National data during the 1970s and in 1980 indicate a less dramatic but still noticeable relationship between occupational status and divorce. For example, among men, the percentage ever divorced or legally separated was lower among white-collar workers (21.2 percent for professionals, 19.7 percent for managers and administrators, 15.4 percent for those in sales occupations, and 19.5 percent for clerical workers) than among blue-collar workers (24.5 percent for skilled craft workers, 23.6 percent for operatives, and 29.8 percent for nonfarm laborers). The proportion divorced or separated was lowest among farmers and farm laborers (9.4 percent) and highest among those in service occupations (31.8 percent).[18] Data from the 1980 census support this pattern. In 1980, 18.5 percent of men in professional occupations had been divorced or separated at some time compared to 27.4 percent of those in "transportation and material moving occupations."[19]

POLITICAL IDENTIFICATION, BEHAVIOR, AND ATTITUDES

Occupational status has long been recognized as a strong predictor of political party preference, voting behavior, and a variety of political attitudes. Since 1936, blue-collar workers have tended to identify with and vote for the Democratic Party and its candidates while people in white-collar occupations have been predisposed to identify with the Republican Party and vote for its candidates.[20]

There are many examples that illustrate this relationship. In the 1964 presidential election, the strongest support for Barry Goldwater, the Republican candidate, came from people in sales occupations, 54 percent of whom voted for him. Other white-collar workers also supported him, including 45 percent of those in professional occupations and 49 percent of the managers, proprietors, and officials. Only 26 percent of blue-collar workers voted for him, however. This ranged from 29 percent of those in skilled craft occupations to 8 percent of laborers.[21] In 1986 the Gallup Poll asked a national sample of nearly 1,200 people whether they would like to see the Democratic or Republican Party win their Congressional district if an election were currently being held. Overall, 50 percent said Democratic and 43 percent said Republican (the remainder were undecided or preferred some other party). However, those in professional and business occupations preferred the Republican Party (52 percent) to the Democratic Party (43 percent). On the other hand, 55 percent of those in manual, blue-collar occupations said Democratic compared to 38 percent who preferred a Republican victory.[22]

The political identification of Americans also varies quite a bit by occupational status. In a Gallup Poll late in 1985 a national sample of nearly 4,000 people were asked to indicate their political affiliation. Thirty-three percent identified as Republican, 40 percent as Democrat, and 27 percent as independent. Identification as Republican decreased sharply as occupational status decreased: 40 percent of those in professional and business occupations, 35 percent of the clerical workers, 32 percent of skilled manual workers, and 27 percent of unskilled manual workers identified as Republican. Identification as a Democrat increased as occupational status decreased. Identification as independent differed little by occupation, ranging from 32 percent of skilled manual workers to 27 percent of unskilled manual workers. Twenty-eight percent of all white-collar workers identified themselves as independent.[23]

The perception of political figures and parties is also related to occupational status. National public opinion polls periodically measure the President's popularity by asking people to indicate their approval or disapproval of how the job is being handled. In January, 1986, 64 percent of a national sample of nearly 1,600 people approved of the way President Ronald Reagan was handling the job, 27 percent disapproved, and 9 percent had no opinion. However, 70 percent of the professional and business and clerical and sales workers said they approved compared to 59 percent of the unskilled workers.[24] Not surprisingly, people in business and professional occupations are more likely to see the Republican Party as probusiness. In a 1984 survey, 84 percent of those in business and professional occupations felt that the Republican Party served the interests of business and professional people best but only 62 percent of manual workers held this view.[25]

Surveys of this kind also indicate that occupational status is related to attitudes on a wide range of political and social issues. In January, 1986 a sample of nearly 1,600 people were asked to indicate their approval or disapproval of various strategies for reducing the federal deficit. Those in business and professional occupations were more likely to approve of cutting the defense budget (64 percent) than those in clerical and sales (58 percent) or manual occupations (57 percent).[26] Compared to blue-collar workers, those in white-collar jobs were more likely to approve of cutting government spending for social programs as a way of reducing the deficit.[27] Those in professional and business occupations were more likely than workers in all other occupations to approve of raising income taxes and cutting programs like social security and medicare to achieve a deficit reduction.[28]

Attitudes toward use of the death penalty in the case of people found guilty of murder vary by occupational status, but the relationship is not a consistent one. In a 1986 survey, the strongest support for the death penalty came from skilled blue-collar workers, 79 percent of whom favored the death penalty. However, the least support came from unskilled blue-collar workers, with 61 percent in favor. Those in professional and business (72 percent in favor) and clerical and sales occupations (78 percent in favor) fell in between the extremes represented by the two blue-collar groups.[29]

The control of handguns is another crime-related issue that has received a great deal of attention and debate in recent years. The attitudes people hold on this issue also vary by occupation. Unskilled workers express the strongest support for handgun registration (74 percent in favor) and people in professional and business occupations are least supportive (66 percent in favor). Seventy percent of clerical and sales and skilled workers support registration. When it comes to the stronger measure of banning the sale of handguns, unskilled workers are again the most supportive (44 percent in favor) but skilled workers are the least supportive (33 percent in favor). On this issue people in professional and business, and clerical and sales occupations are between the extremes of the two blue-collar groups with 37 percent and 39 percent, respectively, in favor of a ban on handgun sales.[30]

A final illustration of the relationship of occupation to attitudes on matters of public policy involves the issue of abortion. In 1986 a national sample of nearly 1,600 people were asked if they favored or opposed the U.S. Supreme Court ruling that a woman can go to a doctor for an abortion any time during the first three months of pregnancy. The sample as a whole was rather evenly divided on the issue. Forty-five percent favored and 45 percent opposed the ruling while 10 percent had no opinion. However, those in professional and business, and clerical and sales occupations expressed the greatest support for the ruling (53 percent and 51 percent, respectively), while blue-collar workers were more likely to be opposed. Only 46 percent of the skilled workers and 39 percent of the unskilled workers favored the Supreme Court ruling.[31]

Occupational Situs

In addition to occupational status, occupational situs (see chapter 5) also has been found to be related to political party affiliation. Raymond J.

Murphy and Richard T. Morris reasoned that occupations related to the performance of the same societal function may evolve distinctive subcultures that include shared political orientations that are independent of status. Using data collected in San Francisco, they were able to compare the political affiliation of people in four situs categories (commerce, finance and records, manufacturing, and building and maintenance). Substantial differences in party affiliation emerged. The percentages identifying as Republican were: commerce, 69 percent, finance and records, 60 percent, manufacturing, 36 percent, and building and maintenance, 26 percent. In order to rule out the possibility that these situs differences might be the result of average status differences between the situses, they controlled for the income and educational level of their respondents. Situs differences in party affiliation persisted at all income and educational levels except among those with a college education who tended to be similar in their party affiliation (predominantly Republican) regardless of the situs in which their occupation was located. These results suggest that occupational situs as well as status exerts an influence on political party affiliation.[32]

Political Attitudes of Professionals

A great deal of research has dealt with the political attitudes of professionals and particularly with differences within this occupational group. In a major review of this research, Steven Brint has pointed out that professionals tend to be relatively conservative on issues of economic policy and in their commitment to basic core values. However, they are relatively liberal on welfare state issues and issues of personal morality.[33]

On the conservative side, professionals are very similar to business elites in their hostility toward government policies that would redistribute income from the affluent to the poor. They are also much more likely than blue-collar workers to express support for and confidence in corporate business leaders.[34] Like people in business occupations, they also disapprove of labor unions and express a lack of confidence in and distrust of labor leaders.[35] Like well-educated members of other high-status occupations, professionals express a strong commitment to the principle of private property, a belief in progress, and a belief in the possibility of material success through individual effort and hard work.[36]

There are a number of issues on which professionals are particularly liberal. For example, they tend to have very liberal attitudes on civil rights issues. Brint found that professionals, along with those in managerial and business occupations, were twice as likely as people in blue-collar occupations to support racial integration, and they were more likely than business owners and executives to support "welfare state" social legislation and programs. Professionals, as well as managers, are more liberal than blue-collar workers on issues of personal morality such as sexual conduct, abortion, and divorce.[37] These attitudinal characteristics of professionals reflect their greater cosmopolitanism and tolerance that is probably a result of their high level of education.

Within the professions, the liberal attitudes of social and cultural specialists such as artists, writers, academics, and social scientists are especially strong. The greater conservatism is found among people in human service professions such as nursing, teaching, and social work, and among engineers and scientists employed in the private sector. Physicians and lawyers are more liberal than their public image would suggest, falling a little below social and cultural specialists in liberalism, although lawyers tend to be more politically conservative than physicians.[38]

Among professionals, academics have been the focus of much research dealing with their political attitudes and behavior.[39] In general, professors are politically more liberal than the general population. Given their relatively high incomes and high occupational prestige, they are also surprisingly more liberal than people in other high-status occupations such as managers and other professionals. For example, between 1944 and 1972, a larger proportion of American academics than the general population voted for the Democratic presidential candidate. In 1972, when only 39 percent of all voters, 31 percent of professionals, and 36 percent of people in managerial occupations voted Democratic, 57 percent of academics did so.[40] However, there is a great deal of variation among academics in terms of their political orientations. Those in the social and behavioral sciences tend to be more liberal than those in other disciplines[41] and those whose religious identification is Jewish are more liberal than those who identify as Protestant or Catholic.[42]

RELIGIOUS BEHAVIOR AND RELIGIOSITY

The relationship between religion and occupational status (as well as income and educational status) has been recognized for a long time. In general, religious denominations vary in their socioeconomic composition. The major Protestant denominations such as the Episcopal, Congregational, and Presbyterian churches have the highest-status congregations, followed by the Jewish faith, and the Methodist and Lutheran churches. The Roman Catholic church, as well as the Baptist and other evangelical Protestant churches tend to have congregations of relatively lower socioeconomic status backgrounds.[43]

In addition to religious affiliation, frequency of church attendance also varies by occupational status. This indicator of religiosity shows that church attendance decreases as occupational status decreases. A study by Richard F. Hamilton found that 64 percent of clerical and sales workers compared to 55 percent of skilled craft workers and foremen, and 53 percent of those in semiskilled occupations attended church at least once a month. While Catholics reported more frequent church attendance than Protestants, variation by occupation exists also within these groups. For example, among Catholics, 86 percent of those in clerical and sales occupations attended church at least once a month compared to 73 percent of those in the operative category. Similarly, 59 percent of the Protestants in clerical and sales occupations reported attending at least once a month while 49 percent of the Protestants in operative occupations did so.[44]

While there have been few analyses of the religiosity and religious behavior of people in specific occupations, the religiosity of university and college faculty has received some attention. Interest in the religiosity of this occupational group reflects a long-standing debate about the degree to which science and religion represent incompatible if not conflicting sets of assumptions and perspectives.[45] Yet not all academics are scientists in terms of either the content or methodology of their subject matter. Consequently, the effect of any scientific-religious conflict on their religious behavior is likely to vary by their discipline or field of specialization as well as by other characteristics.

One study of faculty religious behavior was carried out by Fred Thalheimer who surveyed 741 members of the faculty of a large West Coast state university.[46] While 97 percent of the general population claim some religious affiliation, only 54 percent of the faculty surveyed did so. Although 86 percent of the general population regard the Bible as the revealed word of God, faculty appear to be much more skeptical. Only 20 percent of them regard the Bible this way. Similarly, only 47 percent of the faculty said they believed in God compared to 96 percent of the general public.[47]

Thalheimer found a great deal of variation in religious behavior and beliefs by academic field. In general, religiosity was highest among those in the fine and applied arts (art, music, theater arts, journalism, home economics, physical education, and military science), followed by those in professional schools (education, engineering, law, library service, social welfare, and business administration). Next came faculty in the medical sciences, followed by those in the natural sciences and the humanities. Faculty in the social sciences were the lowest in religiosity. For example, 72 percent of the faculty in medical science fields reported some religious affiliation compared to only 35 percent of the social scientists. While only 27 percent of the faculty in professional schools reported that they never attend church, 48 percent of the social scientists responded this way. Furthermore, 29 percent of the faculty in fine and applied arts fields said that they prayed at least once a day, compared to only 11 percent of the social scientists.

In addition to these differences in religious behavior, religious beliefs also varied. While 32 percent of those in fine and applied arts and professional schools reported a belief that the Bible is the revealed word of God, only 7 percent of the social scientists held this view. Only 7 percent of the faculty in fine and applied arts said that they do not believe in God compared to 41 percent of the social scientists.[48]

Thalheimer concluded that the generally low religiosity of faculty and the variation between different fields is not a consequence of conflict between religious beliefs and the actual work that academics do. Rather, it is mainly the result of a process of secularization begun in late adolescence and a consequence of selective recruitment into particular fields of study. In some cases, secularization is reinforced by professional socialization experiences. For example, faculty in fine and applied arts and professional fields (who were the most religious) were high in religiosity as high school students. Their professional training did not especially challenge their religious beliefs and their stronger religiosity was retained. Natural scientists represent another sequence. Faculty in these fields were markedly nonreligious in high school and remained that way. They did not become less religious as a result of their training or their work. Faculty in the humanities experienced a different pattern. Their low religiosity is more a consequence of secularization occurring during their education, particularly during their graduate training. Finally, the low religiosity of social scientists reflects the fact that these fields recruited people who were low in religiosity as adolescents and who continued to abandon traditional religious beliefs and practices during their college education.[49]

OCCUPATIONAL ENCAPSULATION

The research on political identification and attitudes discussed above reflects the fact that occupational groups are subcultures or communities that act as agents of socialization and social control. They develop distinctive ideologies and value systems that shape the orientations and perspectives of their members and influence their lives well beyond the workplace.

While all occupational groups can be viewed as having some elements of a community or subculture, there are some cases where the impact of the occupational group is so strong, so dominant in the lives of its members, and so all-encompassing that they deserve special attention. The concept of *occupational encapsulation* captures such special circumstances. It refers to those cases where occupational group membership is the dominant factor that determines a person's self-concept, how one is perceived by others, the "social space" within which life is lived, and the kinds of norms and values one holds. Occupational encapsulation refers to those extreme circumstances where the occupational group becomes the most important community and reference group in the lives of its members.

There are a number of occupational groups that are good examples of encapsulated occupations. Some of the clearer cases would include career military officers, merchant seamen, the police, academics in university and college-dominated towns, long-haul truck drivers, members of the clergy, and the superstars of sports and entertainment. The sheer diversity of this list suggests the need to identify the underlying characteristics of such occupations. The main questions that need to be asked about occupational encapsulation are: what produces it and what are its consequences?

CONDITIONS GIVING RISE TO OCCUPATIONAL ENCAPSULATION

There are a number of conditions that can give rise to occupational encapsulation. In effect, occupational encapsulation can be thought of as a response to these conditions.

One such condition is *geographic mobility*. This is important because a high level of mobility, as a routine aspect of the occupation, may preclude or at least make difficult the development of ties and social relationships outside the occupational group. The frequent, expected, and predictable change in assignment of military personnel is a good illustration of this. Knowing that reassignment and movement will occur, military families may find it more attractive to limit their relationships to other military families than to develop relationships with nonmilitary people since the latter will inevitably have to be disrupted, perhaps permanently. In the long run, the probability of encountering military families that one has known in the past and reestablishing ties may be greater than the chances of ever being able to reestablish ties with civilians that one may get to know on a particular assignment. In addition, low-cost, subsidized housing on military bases encourages associating with others in the occupation, thereby reducing contact with outsiders. Since others in the occupation experience similar mobility, the disruption of relationships is seen as a normal part of the job, while outsiders are likely to see it as deviant. In effect, mobile military personnel can find "instant community" among others who have similar experiences. This, in turn, is likely to lead to the further development of shared norms, values, and attitudes.

The geographic mobility of long-haul truck drivers produces a different result, namely a good deal of disruption that heightens encapsulation. Although they may be residentially stable, their work requires long absences from their families and the communities in which they reside. This lowers the opportunity for developing relationships outside the work group and makes continuity of relationships and community participation difficult. British "lorry" drivers, for example, have lower rates of participation in such groups as political organizations, religious and social groups, and trade unions compared to workers in other blue-collar occupations.[50] Since so much time working is spent away from home, nonwork time is spent with their families, or simply resting and catching up on lost sleep. Time at home becomes especially valuable because of its scarcity and is more likely to be spent with family members than with others. Under such circumstances there is a greater opportunity for the occupational group to become dominant.

Merchant seamen also experience regular mobility and long periods at sea as a routine feature of their work.[51] Their work makes participation in land-based communities extremely difficult if not impossible. When not at sea, they interact with other seamen much more frequently than with people in other occupations. Bars, hotels, and churches that cater to seamen have created a kind of "institutional completeness" that enables them to live their lives almost entirely within the occupational community.

Isolation is another condition that gives rise to occupational encapsulation, particularly isolation from people in other occupations. Long-haul truckers and merchant seamen again represent excellent examples of this. On the road, the trucker typically works alone, or with another trucker. Rest breaks at truck stops typically result in contact with other truckers. It is not uncommon for service centers on American interstate highways to have dining areas and lounges reserved for truckers. The advent of the CB radio has made it possible for them to communicate with others while working, but that communication occurs most often with other truckers. Pick-up and delivery points provide opportunities for contact with other people, but again it is most likely to be with other truckers or with people in closely related work roles in the trucking industry. In his study of lorry drivers, Hollowell found that they interact with few people outside the occupation, but they have regular contact with one another in hotels, pubs, and cafes.[52] Similarly, once at sea the physical and social isolation of merchant seamen becomes extreme and the importance of the occupational community increases.

The *public image* of an occupation can also contribute to occupational encapsulation in a number of ways. Both negative and positive images can be important. A negative, hostile, or ambivalent public image can result in members of an occupation "closing ranks" in self defense and reaffirming to each other a shared sense of their worth. The result of a negative public image, especially when combined with a high level of public accountability and criticism, may be increased commitment to the occupational group. As colleagues sense that they are seen by outsiders in negative and critical ways, they may turn to each other as the only people who can be trusted or who understand their problems. Such developments are likely to increase the degree of occupational encapsulation.

The police are a good example of this. While there certainly is variation in public perception of the police, a recurring theme in discussions of police work is a concern with their public image.[53] The police also are an occupation in which the work role spills over to nonwork activities. On or off duty, the occupational role affects how police officers are perceived by others. Consequently, colleagues are likely to become the main people with whom leisure time activities are pursued.[54]

Similar processes may operate among military personnel. While the public image of the military careerist may wax and wane over time, periodic public concern over wasteful military spending and procurement practices, attractive retirement options, and subsidized living expenses suggest at least ambivalence toward this occupational group. As with the police, negative public attitudes may contribute to the development of internal cohesion, protective responses to external criticism, and an accentuation of occupational encapsulation.

Academics offer another case in point. While they are accorded considerable prestige, the "egg-head" image, tinged with a suspicion of elitism and a bit of anti-intellectualism, is also present. In particular communities the autonomy, opportunities for travel, and cosmopolitan life-style that academics enjoy may be admired. These conditions of work, however, often contrast sharply with those of people in industrial organizations and administrative bureaucracies and can be a source of envy and resentment. To the extent that such ambivalence produces a real or perceived hostile environment, it too may encourage encapsulation.

The examples used thus far have emphasized the effect of negative and ambivalent public images. However, positive and favorable images may also contribute to encapsulation. The clergy offer an example of this. Here, a positive public image is combined with the expectation that clergy should and will be exemplars of moral and ethical conduct in their personal as well as their occupational lives. The result is that their congregations probably subject their nonwork conduct to far greater scrutiny and evaluation than do the clients or customers of people in most other occupations. The result may be a lack of privacy that can only be achieved by turning to others in the same kinds of work who are experiencing similar strains. Again, the result of this distinctive combination of public image and role expectation is the encouragement of occupational encapsulation.

Positive public image may also facilitate encapsulation in another group of occupations—those represented by the superstars and celebrities of the entertainment industry (movies, television, and recorded music) and commercial sports. Stardom can cut both ways. While recognition may be highly prized and sought after, once achieved it can result in an extreme loss of privacy. Anything and everything that the celebrity does is potential news. An effort to live one's life within the confines of the occupational group is a possible response to such extreme occupational visibility. One consequence of such a response is the creation of occupationally segregated residential communities and "life-style enclaves" such as Malibu and sections of Beverly Hills and the Hollywood Hills in Southern California inhabited by the superstars of the entertainment industry.

Another condition that can contribute to occupational encapsulation is the presence of *hazards, stresses, and risks* as part of the work people do. Again, the military and the police offer the best examples. Police work routinely involves hazardous activities and the taking of risks. While the hazards facing military personnel are most obvious during wartime, peacetime training maneuvers can also be dangerous. Those in the occupation are continually aware of the hazards and risks involved, but outsiders may become aware of them only when actual crises and newsworthy events occur. The stresses that people in hazardous occupations live with may be difficult to explain to outsiders and outsiders may have difficulty comprehending them. Such circumstances create a situation in which only others in the occupation are seen as really understanding what goes on. The result is likely to be an enhancement of the importance of the occupational group in the lives of its members, a condition likely to contribute to the development of encapsulation.

SOME CONSEQUENCES OF OCCUPATIONAL ENCAPSULATION

Occupational encapsulation may contribute to the *development of ideologies* that enhance members' occupational self-concept and stress the importance of the occupational group and loyalty to it. Such ideologies result in the occupational group becoming the dominant reference group for its members. The occupational socialization literature stresses the development of the occupational group as a key reference group in a variety of training situations (see chapter 4). The implication here is that this socialization outcome will be extreme in encapsulated occupations.

Working in an encapsulated occupation also has potential *impacts on family life.* One question that can be asked about the families of people in encapsulated occupations is whether they are more or less stable (in terms of divorce and desertion rates) than other families. The instability of family life among celebrities in the entertainment industry is exceptionally high and widely publicized. The potential for stress in family relations created by long periods at sea results in low rates of marriage among merchant seamen and a variety of marital problems among those who attempt to combine marriage with a maritime career.[55] The social isolation that accompanies encapsulation generally would be expected to produce stress in families that would result in higher than average levels of instability. On the other hand, the high level of identification, intimacy, and involvement with colleagues (and by implication their families) in encapsulated occupations might well produce the opposite effect. Families in encapsulated occupations may more readily turn to others in the group that are experiencing similar stresses and find not only understanding but genuine comprehension of shared problems. Families in encapsulated occupations may represent unique resources with problem-solving skills that reduce marital instability in the long run.

Occupational encapsulation may also result in distinctive differences in the *socialization of children.* Are there identifiable impacts on children that are attributable to growing up in the context of an encapsulated occupation? It seems reasonable to assume that in such cases parental occupation is more salient and pervasive in the lives of children than other kinds of occupations would be. What are the consequences of extensive and intensive parental involvement with others in the same occupation? Do children in such families develop distinctive images and understandings of the occupational world that affect their own occupational choices and career plans? The research on the occupational origins of members of particular occupations discussed in chapter 3 presents a mixed picture (see table 3.1). Direct occupational inheritance is high (25 percent) among military officers, low (7 percent) among police officers, and intermediate (13 percent) among Protestant clergymen. Kurt Lang has characterized the high rate of occupational inheritance among military officers as a case of "occupational endogamy" that reflects not only the effects of social isolation but also the carrying on of family traditions.[56] The implication is that such traditions may develop more readily and become more intense in encapsulated occupations than in others.

The concept of occupational encapsulation also has implications for the issue of *work satisfaction* which was discussed in chapter 6. Encapsulation may have the effect of increasing or decreasing work satisfaction. If an encapsulated occupation is successful in developing an ideology stressing its importance that comes to be shared and believed by its members, the result may be increased work satisfaction. If the ideology succeeds in increasing pride, commitment, and the like, greater satisfaction with the work may follow. In addition, group membership, intensified in encapsulated occupations, may take on a special meaning of its own. A distinctive kind of satisfaction may derive from a sense of being part of an embattled group in a hostile environment, or being able to do a job that others cannot or will not do. On the other hand, life in an encapsulated occupation may include stresses that lead to dissatisfaction with the occupation. This might occur in cases where the occupational group was unsuccessful in developing an ideology to counteract a negative public image. It might also occur when members of the occupational group believe that the risks and hazards of the job are not appreciated by outsiders or those who benefit from their work. In the case of the clergy, the inability to escape from or reduce the salience of the occupational role and have a private life could be a distinctive source of work dissatisfaction. In any event, the concept of occupational encapsulation suggests some new dimensions and sources of work satisfaction and dissatisfaction.

WORK AND LEISURE

Sociologists and other social scientists have long been interested in the topic of leisure; the *sociology of leisure* has developed into a specialty in its own right. Our interest here will be mainly in one major area within the sociology of leisure—the relationship between work and leisure.[57]

One difficulty in dealing with the topic of leisure is that no universally agreed upon definition has been reached. B. G. Gunter and Nancy Gunter have pointed out that leisure has been defined as a type of *time* (nonwork time), a special type of *activity* (nonwork, nonremunerated activity), a *state of mind* (enjoyment, self-improvement), an opportunity for the exercise of *freedom of choice*, a state of *passivity*, and various combinations of these variables. They also point out that leisure should not be equated with free time, that it is a continuous rather than a discrete phenomenon, and that different kinds of life experiences (including work experiences) can produce different kinds of leisure behavior.[58]

In American society, attitudes toward work have been shaped by what is commonly referred to as the Protestant Ethic.[59] The Protestant Reformation, and particularly the views of Luther, Calvin, and Wesley, extolled the virtues of hard work, self-denial, and thrift as the means to salvation. In effect, the results of one's work were seen as signs of moral worth and value. Thus, the drive to work, excel, and accumulate were given divine sanction. Clearly, within the perspective of this work ethic, leisure or nonwork has traditionally been viewed negatively and equated with idleness, frivolity, and immorality. One consequence of this attitude has been a sense of guilt and anxiety about time spent in "unproductive" ways.[60]

While the Protestant work ethic in its literal form is no longer operative, it has become a secularized part of American culture and continues to shape our orientations toward leisure. Although there is evidence that Americans would like more leisure time, [61] no leisure ethic has developed to counterbalance or complement the work ethic.

The amount of time potentially available to people for leisure has increased over the years. In large measure this is a result of consistent and dramatic declines in the length of the workweek, an outcome for which organized labor fought long and hard. The length of the average workweek was 70 hours in 1850 and 60 hours in 1900. By 1950 it had dropped to 40 hours after which it began to decline at a much slower rate. The length of the average workweek was 38.5 hours in 1960 and had dropped to 34.9 in 1985.[62] This does not necessarily mean that in recent years people have had more free time in the sense of time free of all obligations that may be imposed by oneself or others. Time not spent at work should not be regarded as the same thing as free time or potential leisure time. In fact, one study by J. Robinson and P. Converse concluded that the average amount of free time available to Americans actually *declined* by two hours per day between 1930 and 1970.[63] Much of the decrease in the amount of time spent at jobs apparently is invested in quasi-work activities of an obligatory nature such as shopping, caring for homes, cars, and other material possessions, and in child care.[64]

How much free time do people actually have, and how do they spend it? One national survey by J. Robinson concluded that the average American has four hours of free time on a typical weekday, six hours on Saturdays, and almost eight hours on Sundays.[65] This survey also found that the amount of free time available is related to age (people under age 30 have more free time) and to marital status (single people have more free time than those who are married). Efforts to describe how people spend their free time have frequently made a distinction between active and passive leisure-time pursuits. Only about one in four Americans regularly engages in what might be considered active, outdoor, leisure pursuits and it has been estimated that such activities have declined since the 1930s.[66] Among passive activities, watching television stands out as a major way in which people spend their time. On average, about one and one-half hours of the average American's four hours of free time are spent watching television.[67]

There are significant occupational differences in the amount of time people spend at work and, by implication, the amount of free time they have. Farmers have the longest workdays and workweeks of any major occupational group. Among nonagricultural workers, managers, officials, proprietors, and professionals work more hours than people in other occupations.[68] Decreases in the length of the average workweek have occurred unevenly in the occupational structure. Professionals, executives, managers, and self-employed people have not reduced the amount of their working time as much as blue-collar workers have.[69]

OCCUPATION AND LEISURE

In dealing with the relationship of work and leisure, sociologists have assumed that such characteristics as occupation and income are primary, in a temporal sense, and that they determine such secondary activities as leisure. Two different perspectives on how work may affect leisure have come to be known as the *spillover* and *compensatory* models.

The main idea in the spillover model is that there are similarities in work and leisure and that leisure becomes an extension of work.[70] For example, a person whose work offered few opportunities for interaction with others might be expected to engage in leisure activities that do not involve sociability. In other words, leisure parallels work. There is some research evidence to support this interpretation of the work-leisure relationship. Melvin L. Kohn and Carmi Schooler have found that mentally demanding work is associated with mentally demanding nonwork activities.[71] Research on blue-collar workers indicates that those whose work involves greater autonomy are more likely to engage in leisure activities that require taking initiative, planning, decision making, and coordination. Similarly, social isolation on the job is associated with a greater likelihood of engaging in leisure activities that are limited to interaction with family members and a few close friends.[72]

In the compensatory model the assumption is that there will be differences between work and leisure as people use leisure to compensate for things that their work does not provide. Leisure is seen as an activity that is not used to replicate work experiences but to make up for something that is missing in work. For example, a person whose work was monotonous and uninteresting would presumably engage in leisure activities that were exciting and offered variety and involvement.[73] There is less research supporting this model and most of it has been done on blue-collar assembly line workers who are likely to use leisure in ways that compensate for the repetitive and routine nature of their work.[74] It also appears that people who derive few satisfactions from their work rely on leisure as a source of personal identity.[75] One study of employees of a small pharmaceutical firm found that nonwork activities are used to compensate for positive as well as negative aspects of work. Workers whose jobs lacked variety, creativity, and challenge used nonwork activities to obtain these experiences. However, those who had these experiences at work engaged in nonwork pursuits that contained less of them.[76] This suggests that whether work experiences are positive or negative, people may use leisure to experience something different from what their work provides.

Occupational status and prestige have for some time been associated with differences in the kinds of leisure-time activities in which people engage. In the 1950s Alfred C. Clarke found occupational prestige to be related to use of leisure time. Men in lower-prestige occupations were more likely to engage in spectator activities of a passive nature and in craftsmanlike activities (model building, painting, woodworking). When asked what they might do with an extra two hours per day, the most common response was that it would be used to relax, rest, loaf, or sleep. However, those in the lowest-prestige occupations were more likely to respond this way than those in highest-prestige occupations. Using this hypothetical extra time for reading or studying increased as occupational prestige increased. Those in higher-prestige occupations were more likely to say that they would spend it working at their jobs while those in lower-prestige occupations were more likely to say that they would use the extra time "working around the house."[77]

Even at the same broad status level there can be differences in the leisure pursuits of people in specific occupations. Joel E. Gerstl has pointed out that differences in the organization of work can lead to differences in leisure. He studied the leisure-time activities of men in occupations of comparable status but very different work environments. These were dentists, advertisers, and college professors. Gerstl asked men in these occupations a question similar to that asked by Clarke regarding what they would do with two extra hours per day. There were substantial differences in their responses to this question. Professors (50.0 percent) were most likely to say that they would use the extra time for "work or work-related reading," compared to 18.2 percent of the admen and only 8.8 percent of the dentists. They were also more likely to indicate "recreational reading" (28.1 percent compared to 12.1 percent of the admen and 14.7 percent of the dentists). The dentists and admen were more likely than the college professors to say that they would use this extra time on a "hobby or recreation." "Relaxation" was favored by 29.4 percent of the dentists and 12.1 percent of the admen, but *none* of the professors said they would spend the extra time this way.

The way members of these occupations actually spent their time also varied a good deal. Admen were nearly three times as active in sports as the professors, with the dentists intermediate between the other two groups. Admen reported the heaviest participation in golf (often connected with the conduct of business). They were also more likely to engage in occupationally related activities like painting or writing and to spend time visiting with friends. Organizational membership and participation also varied among the three groups with dentists belonging to the most organizations but participating the least. The college professors were relatively low on both organizational membership and participation, beyond minimal involvement in their professional organizations and societies. For admen, participation in local civic and fraternal organizations is an important mechanism for nurturing and maintaining business contacts as well as developing an image of the concerned and conscientious citizen.[78]

Gerstl concludes that the striking variation that exists between these occupations is a consequence of variations in work routines, work strains, occupational images, and the kinds of specialized skills used in them. He suggests that occupational groups may develop relatively clear norms about appropriate leisure-time activity. Membership in country clubs and yacht clubs is expected of people in many business occupations and leads to involvement in golf, tennis, and yachting as leisure-time pursuits.[79] While the number of specific occupations that have been studied regarding the leisure-time activities of their members is small, it is clear that leisure pursuits can vary within as well as between occupational status levels.

RETIREMENT

As a phase of the life cycle experienced by large numbers of people, retirement is a relatively recent phenomenon. Detailed national data on retirees are not particularly good. It is possible, however, to estimate the size of the retired population. In 1955, 6.3 percent of the population of the United States was over age sixty-five and "not in the labor force." By 1983, the comparable figure had increased to 9.7 percent.[80] Of course, not everyone over age sixty-five and not working had worked before turning sixty-five and many people leave the labor force before age sixty-five. Nevertheless, this comparison reflects the increasing proportion of the population experiencing retirement. Data on social security recipients also can be used to identify the increase in the retired population that has been occurring. In 1950, 1.7 million people (representing only 1.2 percent of the population) were receiving social security retirement benefits. By 1982 the number of retirees receiving social security benefits had increased to a little over twenty-four million and they made up 10.4 percent of the population.[81] In 1982 there were an additional 621,000 persons who were retired from the federal civil service, the armed forces, and railroad employment.[82]

The decision to retire can be affected by a wide variety of personal considerations including health, postretirement income, spouse's employment, and the like. The point in time at which people retire, however, is systematically related to occupational status. In general, retirement occurs earlier in lower-status occupations and later in higher-status occupations. In particular, those in professional and managerial occupations work to later ages than those in blue-collar occupations.[83] This pattern may be the result of corporate policies and collective bargaining agreements requiring mandatory retirement at a particular age (e.g., sixty-five among blue-collar workers covered by employer pension plans). Later retirement among professionals and other white-collar workers may reflect their greater intrinsic satisfaction with their work and the fact that their higher earnings make retirement more costly.[84] In addition to this relationship of occupational status to retirement, self-employed people tend to retire later than wage and salary employees. They are also more likely to go through a period of partial retirement in which they gradually reduce the number of hours they work before retiring completely.[85]

Professionals may also be in a position of greater control over when and how to initiate retirement than other workers. For example, physicians, dentists, and lawyers have at their disposal a variety of mechanisms that allow them to phase out their work activities and move into retirement more gradually. They may decide to work fewer hours per day or fewer days per week, decline to take on new clients, or even refer long-time clients to other practitioners. Another mechanism available to professionals involves taking on a younger colleague who then gradually takes over the practice while the retiring practitioner gradually eases out of the picture. Among academic scientists, the later work years may involve a gradual decline in active research and writing endeavors. Senior faculty may take on the roles of mentor and sponsor for junior colleagues who gradually assume the primary responsibility for the research program. The greater autonomy that is inherent in professional work allows for options and flexibility that make it possible for the change from full employment to retirement to be a gradual transition rather than an abrupt event.

The transition from work to retirement has received a good deal of attention from social gerontologists. They have stressed the point that it is more useful to think about it as a *process* rather than a discrete event. In addition, retirement involves the relinquishment of an occupational role and the assumption of the social role of a "retired person."[86] Since occupational roles become a central part of the personal identities of workers, it follows that the process of retirement and the shift to a new role can be disruptive and create problems of adjustment and adaptation.

Gerontologists have in fact stressed the importance of adjustment to a new role and identity as a problem of retired people.[87] However, there may be a good deal of variation among occupational groups in the degree to which this is a problem. Occupational identification and involvement may persist well beyond the point of formal retirement in many professional fields. Retired professionals may continue to play an active role in their professional associations or serve in consulting or advisory roles to hospitals, courts, regulatory commissions, and the like. It is also common practice for universities and colleges to award retired faculty the status of "emeritus professor." Retired faculty may continue to teach a course occasionally, serve on committees, and otherwise remain involved with students and their colleagues. In such cases, retirement does not result in a complete cessation of professional activities and work role involvements. In occupations where such mechanisms are absent there may be few if any opportunities to maintain continuity and identification with the work role and a work group. This would seem to be the case with most blue-collar occupations and many lower-status white-collar jobs (e.g., clerical and sales) where structural mechanisms that might create continuity are absent.

There is a good deal of variation in how and when people retire. There is some evidence that the phenomenon of *early retirement* (before age 65) is fairly common and actually has been increasing in recent years. In the early 1980s, about 60 percent of workers eligible to receive early social security benefits at age sixty-two actually did so.[88] In one study, 3,500 men between the ages of forty-five and fifty-nine in 1966 were followed over a ten-year period. Of those ages forty-five through forty-nine, 12 percent had retired by the end of the ten-year period. When the study began in 1966, only 28 percent of those ages forty-five through forty-nine were retired or said they expected to be retired by the time they reached age sixty-five. In 1971, however, by the time they were in their early fifties, 39 percent were already retired or said they expected to be retired by the time they were sixty-five. When the study was completed in 1976, half of these men (who were fifty-five through fifty-nine by this time) had already retired or said they planned to retire before age sixty-five.[89]

Early retirement appears to be increasing in popularity. For example, between 1970 and 1984 the proportion of men ages fifty-five through fifty-nine *in the labor force* declined from 89.5 percent to 80.2 percent. Among men in the sixty through sixty-four age group the decline was even more dramatic, going from 75.0 percent to 56.1 percent. Men age sixty-five and over also are retiring at an increasing rate. Their labor force participation rate fell from 26.8 percent in 1970 to 16.3 percent in 1984.[90] This trend toward early retirement among men has not been occurring among women. The labor force participation rate of women ages fifty-five through fifty-nine was almost identical in 1970 (49.0 percent) and in 1984 (49.8 percent). Among those ages sixty through sixty-four there was a modest decline in labor force participation from 36.1 percent to 33.4 percent. There was also a very small drop in the proportion of women sixty-five and over in the labor force between 1970 (9.7 percent) and 1984 (7.5 percent).[91]

Malcom H. Morrison has pointed out that American work organizations have been developing a variety of alternatives to conventional retirement that may bring about significant changes in how and when people retire in the future. One pattern he notes is that of *phased retirement* which involves reduced work time with a prorated salary. Workers may begin drawing a portion of their retirement annuity to supplement their reduced salary. Another strategy is to use *annuitant pools* for part-time or full-time employment on a short-term basis. Under this arrangement an organization's retirees (annuitants) join a pool of people whose skills and expertise may be utilized as the need arises in the organization. *Contract work* represents another alternative to complete disaffiliation. Here employers may contract with retirees for particular services for a specified period of time. Still another option involves *retraining* employees near retirement for jobs where the recruitment of new people is especially difficult or costly and encouraging them to remain with the organization after the training. Where older workers have long-standing clients (e.g., in financial, insurance, real estate, or law firms), jobs may be *redesigned* so that the workers service those clients exclusively prior to and following retirement.[92] To the extent that such alternatives grow in popularity, they will blur the distinction between working and being retired. They may also have the effect of reducing the identity and role-change problems brought on by retirement and increase and prolong the productivity of older workers.

SUMMARY

This chapter has emphasized the importance of occupation in several aspects of people's nonwork lives. While occupational specialization results in a diversity of work experiences on the job, the kinds of work people do also have far-reaching effects in creating diversity beyond the workplace.

Occupations differentially expose people to risks and hazards that result in differences in death and disability rates, mental illness, suicide, and divorce. The differences in political identification, behavior, and attitudes that were summarized have implications for the political system as well as for individuals. They suggest that occupational subcultures develop in ways that shape the political allegiances of people and their perceptions of a range of political, economic, and social issues.

The concept of occupational encapsulation was introduced to identify those extreme cases in which occupation becomes an all-encompassing, dominant force in people's lives. Our discussion of the sources and consequences of encapsulation is preliminary and suggestive rather than conclusive and definitive. It suggests the need for empirical research to investigate the extent of encapsulation and particularly its consequences for both individuals and families.

Both leisure and retirement are topics that are usually considered to be the opposite of work and the end of work, respectively. Yet, even here it is apparent that leisure orientations and behavior are shaped by occupational activities, and both the timing and adjustment problems associated with retirement are related to the characteristics of occupations.

NOTES

1. Frank Goldsmith and Lori E. Kerr, *Occupational Safety and Health: The Control and Prevention of Work-Related Hazards* (New York: Human Sciences Press, 1982).
2. Kenneth C. W. Kammeyer and Helen L. Ginn, *An Introduction to Population* (Chicago: Dorsey Press, 1986), 165–168.
3. Jessamine S. Whitney, *Death Rates by Occupation, Based on Data of the U.S. Census Bureau* (New York: National Tuberculosis Association, 1934), cited in Aaron Antonovsky, "Social Class, Life Expectancy, and Overall Mortality," *Milbank Memorial Fund Quarterly* 45 (April 1967): 31–73.
4. Lillian Guralnick, "Mortality by Occupation and Industry Among Men 20 to 64 Years of Age," *Vital Statistics, Special Reports* (September 1962), cited in Antonovsky, "Social Class, Life Expectancy, and Overall Mortality."
5. Metropolitan Life Insurance Company, "Hazardous Occupations," *Statistical Bulletin* 50 (March 1969): 3–4.
6. Metropolitan Life Insurance Company, "Trend in Work Injuries," *Statistical Bulletin* 51 (July 1970): 7–9.
7. U.S. Bureau of the Census, *Statistical Abstract of the United States, 1985* (Washington, D.C.: U.S. Government Printing Office, 1984), 425, table 712, note 2.
8. Ibid., 113, table 179.
9. Kammeyer and Ginn, *An Introduction to Population*, 166.
10. August B. Hollingshead and Frederick C. Redlich, *Social Class and Mental Illness* (New York: Wiley, 1958).
11. Jerome K. Meyers, Lee L. Bean, and Max P. Pepper, "Social Class and Psychiatric Disorders: A Ten Year Follow-Up," *Journal of Health and Human Behavior* 6 (Summer 1965): 74–79.
12. Leo Srole et al., *Mental Health in the Metropolis: The Midtown Manhattan Study*, rev. ed. (New York: New York University Press, 1978).
13. Elwin H. Powell, "Occupational Status and Suicide: Toward a Redefinition of Anomie," *American Sociological Review* 23 (April 1958): 131–138.

14. Warren Breed, "Occupational Mobility and Suicide Among White Males," *American Sociological Review* 28 (April 1963): 179–188.
15. D. S. Hamermesh and N. M. Soss, "Economic Theory of Suicide," *Journal of Political Economy* 82 (1974): 83–98.
16. William M. Kephart, "Occupational Level and Marital Disruption," *American Sociological Review* 20 (August 1955): 456–465.
17. William J. Goode, "Family Disorganization," in *Contemporary Social Problems*, ed. Robert K. Merton and Robert Nishet, 4th ed. (New York: Harcourt, Brace, Jovanovich, 1976), 513–554.
18. Norval D. Glenn and Michael Supancic, "The Social and Demographic Correlates of Divorce and Separation in the United States: An Update and Reconsideration," *Journal of Marriage and the Family* 46 (August 1984): 563–575.
19. U.S. Bureau of the Census, *1980 Census of Population* (Washington, D.C.: U.S. Government Printing Office, 1985), vol. 2, *Subject Reports, Marital Characteristics*, PC80-2-4C, p. 57.
20. For example, see Hazel Gaudet, *The People's Choice* (New York: Duell, Sloan, and Pearce, 1944); and Seymour Martin Lipset, *Political Man* (New York: Doubleday, 1964).
21. Gertrude Jaeger Selznick and Stephen Steinberg, "Social Class, Ideology, and Voting Preference," in *Structural Social Inequality*, ed. Celia S. Heller (New York: Crowell, Collier, and Macmillan, 1969), 216–226.
22. *The Gallup Report*, no. 246 (March 1986): 32.
23. *The Gallup Report*, nos. 244–245 (January-February 1986): 43.
24. Ibid., 22.
25. *The Gallup Report*, nos. 232–233 (January-February 1985): 23.
26. *The Gallup Report*, nos. 244–245 (January-February 1986): 30.
27. Ibid., 31.
28. Ibid., 32–33.
29. *The Gallup Report*, nos. 244–245 (January-February 1986): 12.
30. *The Gallup Report*, no. 237 (June 1985): 16–17.
31. *The Gallup Report*, nos. 244–245 (January-February 1986): 18.
32. Raymond J. Murphy and Richard T. Morris, "Occupational Situs, Subjective Class Identification, and Political Affiliation," *American Sociological Review* 26 (June 1961): 383–392.
33. Steven Brint, "The Political Attitudes of Professionals," *Annual Review of Sociology* 11 (1985): 389–414.
34. Steven G. Brint, " 'New Class' and Cumulative Trend Explanations of the Liberal Political Attitudes of Professionals," *American Journal of Sociology* 90 (1984): 30–71.
35. Brint, "The Political Attitudes of Professionals," 394–395; and Seymour Martin Lipset and W. Schneider, "Organized Labor and the Public: A Troubled Union," *Public Opinion* 3 (1981): 52–56.
36. Brint, "The Political Attitudes of Professionals," 395–396.
37. Brint, " 'New Class' and Cumulative Trend Explanations of the Liberal Political Attitudes of Professionals."
38. Brint, "The Political Attitudes of Professionals," 402–403.
39. For a review of the research on this topic see Michael A. Fava, "The Myth of the Liberal Professor," *Sociology of Education* 47 (Spring 1974): 171–202; and Seymour Martin Lipset and Everett C. Ladd, Jr., "The Myth of the 'Conservative' Professor," *Sociology of Education* 47 (Spring 1974): 203–213.
40. Lipset and Ladd, "The Myth of the 'Conservative' Professor," 206.

41. D. Stanley Eitzen and Gary M. Maranell, "The Political Party Affiliation of College Professors," *Social Forces* 47 (December 1968): 145–153.
42. Seymour M. Lipset and Everett C. Ladd, Jr., "Jewish Academics in the United States: Their Achievements, Culture and Politics," in *American Jewish Yearbook* (Hartford, Conn.: Prayer Book, 1971), 89–128.
43. For example see N. J. Demerath III, *Social Class in American Protestantism* (Chicago: Rand McNally, 1965); and Gerhard Lenski, *The Religious Factor* (New York: Doubleday, 1961).
44. Richard F. Hamilton, "The Behavior and Values of Skilled Workers," in *Blue Collar World: Studies of the American Worker*, ed. Arthur H. Shostak and William Gomberg (Englewood Cliffs, N.J.: Prentice-Hall, 1964), 42–57. Similar findings have been reported in Great Britain. For example, see Erich Goode, "Social Class and Church Participation," *American Journal of Sociology* 72 (July 1966): 102–111.
45. Rodney Stark, "On the Incompatibility of Religion and Science: A Survey of American Graduate Students," *Journal for the Scientific Study of Religion* 3 (Fall 1963): 3–20; Andrew M. Greeley, "Religion and the Intellectuals," *Partisan Review* 3 (1950); A. D. White, *A History of the Warfare of Science with Theology* (New York: Dover Press, 1960), and Ian G. Barbour, *Issues in Science and Religion* (Englewood Cliffs, N.J.: Prentice-Hall, 1966).
46. Fred Thalheimer, "Continuity and Change in Religiosity: A Study of Academicians," *Pacific Sociological Review* 8 (Fall 1965), 101–108; and "Religiosity and Secularization in the Academic Professions," *Sociology of Education* 46 (Spring 1973): 183–202.
47. Thalheimer, "Continuity and Change in Religiosity."
48. Thalheimer, "Religiosity and Secularization in the Academic Professions."
49. Ibid., 194–195.
50. Peter G. Hollowell, *The Lorry Driver* (London: Routledge and Kegan Paul, 1968).
51. Mariam G. Sherar, *Shipping Out: A Sociological Study of American Merchant Seamen* (Cambridge, Md.: Cornell Maritime Press, 1973); and Peter H. Fricke, ed., *Seafarer and Community* (London: Croom Helm, 1973).
52. Hollowell, *The Lorry Driver*.
53. Nicholas Alex, *Black in Blue: A Study of the Negro Policeman* (New York: Appleton-Century-Crofts, 1969); Arthur Niederhoffer, *Behind the Shield: The Police in Urban Society* (Garden City, N.Y.: Anchor Books, 1967); and James Q. Wilson, *Varieties of Police Behavior* (New York: Antheneum, 1970).
54. Richard N. Harris, *The Police Academy: An Inside View* (New York: Wiley, 1973).
55. Sherar, *Shipping Out*.
56. Kurt Lang, *Military Institutions and the Sociology of War* (Beverly Hills, Calif.: Sage, 1972).
57. For an overview and summary of the field of the sociology of leisure, see B. G. Gunter and Nancy C. Gunter, "Leisure Styles: A Conceptual Framework for Modern Leisure," *Sociological Quarterly* 21 (Summer 1980): 361–374; John Wilson, "Sociology of Leisure," *Annual Review of Sociology* 6 (1980): 21–40; Robert N. Wilson, "The Courage to be Leisured," *Social Forces* 60 (December 1981): 282–303; John R. Kelly, "Leisure Interaction and the Social Dialectic," *Social Forces* 60 (December 1981): 304–322; and Stanley Parker, "Change, Flexibility, Spontaneity, and Self-Determination in Leisure," *Social Forces* 60 (December 1981): 323–331.

58. Gunter and Gunter, "Leisure Styles."
59. Max Weber, *The Protestant Ethic and the Spirit of Capitalism* (New York: Charles Scribner's Sons, 1930).
60. Robert N. Wilson, "The Courage to be Leisured," 293–296.
61. F. Best, "Preference for Worklife Scheduling and Work/Leisure Trade-Offs," *Monthly Labor Review* 101 (1978): 31–37.
62. Figures from 1850 to 1960 are from Sebastian DeGrazia, *Of Time, Work, and Leisure* (New York: Doubleday, 1964), 419. Data for 1985 are from "Current Labor Statistics," *Monthly Labor Review* 109 (August 1986): 64.
63. J. Robinson and P. Converse, "Social Changes Reflected in the Use of Time," in *The Human Meaning of Social Change*, ed. A. Campbell and P. Converse (New York: Russell Sage, 1972).
64. S. Linder, *The Harried Leisure Class* (New York: Columbia University Press, 1970).
65. J. Robinson, *How Americans Use Their Time: A Social-Psychological Analysis of Everyday Behavior* (New York: Praeger, 1977).
66. Neil H. Cheek, Jr., and William R. Burch, Jr., *The Social Organization of Leisure in Human Society* (New York: Harper and Row, 1976).
67. John Wilson, "Sociology of Leisure," 24.
68. G. Moore and J. Hedges, "Trends in Labor and Leisure," *Monthly Labor Review* 94 (1971): 3–11.
69. Ibid.; and Harold L. Wilensky, "The Uneven Distribution of Leisure: The Impact of Economic Growth on 'Free Time,' " in *Work and Leisure*, ed. Erwin O. Smigel (New Haven, Conn.: College and University Press, 1963), 107–145.
70. Stanley Parker and Michael Smith, "Work and Leisure," in *Handbook of Work Organization and Society*, ed. Robert Dubin (Chicago: Rand McNally, 1976), 37–64; and Stanley Parker, *The Future of Work and Leisure* (London: MacGibbon and Kee, 1971).
71. Melvin L. Kohn and Carmi Schooler, "Occupational Experience and Psychological Functioning: An Assessment of Reciprocal Effects," *American Sociological Review* 38 (February 1973): 97–118.
72. M. Meissner, "The Long Arm of the Job: A Study of Work and Leisure," *Industrial Relations* 10 (1971): 239–260.
73. William A. Faunce and Robert Dubin, "Individual Investment in Working and Living," in *The Quality of Working Life*, ed. L. E. Davis and A. B. Cherns (New York: Free Press, 1975).
74. Ibid.
75. E. Spreitzer and E. Snyder, "Work Orientation, Meaning of Leisure, and Mental Health," *Journal of Leisure Research* 6 (1974): 207–219.
76. Joseph E. Champoux, "Perceptions of Work and Non-Work: A Reexamination of the Compensatory and Spillover Models," *Sociology of Work and Occupations* 5 (November 1978): 402–422.
77. Alfred C. Clarke, "The Use of Leisure and its Relation to Levels of Occupational Prestige," *American Sociological Review* 21 (June 1956): 301–307.
78. Joel E. Gerstl, "Leisure, Taste, and Occupational Milieu, in *Work and Leisure*, ed. Smigel, 146–167.
79. R. Burdge, "Level of Occupational Prestige and Leisure Activity," *Journal of Leisure Research* 1 (1969): 262–274.
80. Calculated from data in U.S. Bureau of the Census, *Statistical Abstract, 1985*, 11, table 11; and U.S. Bureau of the Census, *Statistical Abstract of the United*

States, 1968 (Washington, D.C.: U.S. Government Printing Office, 1968), 288, table 408.
81. Calculated from data in U.S. Bureau of the Census, *Statistical Abstract, 1985,* 11, table 11, and 359, table 596; and *Statistical Abstract, 1968,* 5, table 1, and 293, table 415.
82. *Statistical Abstract, 1985,* 359, table 596.
83. U.S. Department of Labor, *The Older American Worker* (Washington, D.C.: U.S. Government Printing Office, 1965), 74; L. Bixby, "Retirement Patterns in the United States: Research and Policy Interaction," *Social Security Bulletin* 39 (1976): 3–9; and John C. Henretta and Angela M. O'Rand, "Joint Retirement in the Dual Worker Family," *Social Forces* 62 (December 1983): 504–520.
84. Henretta and O'Rand, "Joint Retirement in the Dual Worker Family," 506.
85. Joseph F. Quinn, "Labor Force Patterns of Older Self-Employed Workers," *Social Security Bulletin* 43 (April 1980): 17–28, "The Extent and Correlates of Partial Retirement," *The Gerontologist* 21 (December 1981): 634–643; and "The Work Ethic and Retirement," in *The Work Ethic—A Critical Analysis,* ed. Jack Barbash et al., (Madison, Wis.: Industrial Relations Research Association, 1983), 87–100.
86. Robert C. Atchley, *The Sociology of Retirement* (Cambridge, Mass.: Schenkman, 1976); and *Aging: Continuity and Change* (Belmont, Calif.: Wadsworth, 1983).
87. Atchley, *The Sociology of Retirement,* chap. 9.
88. Malcom H. Morrison, "Work and Retirement in an Aging Society," *Daedalus* 115 (Winter 1986): 269–293.
89. Herbert S. Parnes, ed., *Work and Retirement: A Longitudinal Study of Men* (Cambridge, Mass.: MIT Press, 1981).
90. Barry Alan Mirkin, "Early Retirement as a Labor Force Policy: An International Overview," *Monthly Labor Review* 110 (March 1987): 19–33.
91. Ibid., 28, table 1.
92. Morrison, "Work and Retirement in an Aging Society," 285–286.

CHAPTER 10

Occupational Trends:
A Look at the Future

THE FOCUS of this final chapter is on changes that are occurring and
will occur in the occupational structure of the United States between
now and the end of the twentieth century. The growth and decline of
particular occupations and industries have implications for occupational
choice, careers, and other topics dealt with in the preceding chapters.
The main task of this chapter is to identify these changes and examine
their implications.

THE SIZE, SEX, AND RACE COMPOSITION
OF THE LABOR FORCE

In 1980 there were 102,830,000 Americans employed in the labor force.
By 1990 that number is expected to grow to 118,315,000, an average increase of 1.4 percent *per year* for the decade. By 1995 the labor force
will number 127,563,000, an average increase of 1.5 percent for each year
between 1990 and 1995.[1]

The dramatic increase in the employment of women discussed in
chapter 7 is expected to continue. While 52.9 percent of all women were
in the labor force in 1983, their participation rate is expected to be at
60.3 percent by 1995 and women will make up slightly more than 45 percent of the entire labor force. The biggest increase will occur among

women ages thirty-five through forty-four; by 1995, 82.8 percent of women in this age group are expected to be in the labor force.[2]

The black labor force will also grow in the years ahead. There were 10,900,000 in the labor force in 1980. By 1990 they will number 13,600,000 and will increase to 14,800,000 by 1995. The participation of black women in the labor force is expected to increase at much the same rate that it will increase for white women. In 1980, 53.2 percent of black women (compared to 51.2 percent of white women) were in the labor force. By 1995, 61.2 percent of black women and 60.0 percent of white women will be in the labor force.[3]

THE INDUSTRIAL COMPOSITION OF THE LABOR FORCE[4]

The U.S. Department of Labor classifies occupational activities by the industries in which they are performed. Table 10.1 presents data on the number of persons employed in different industries in 1980, the number expected to be employed in 1990 and 1995, and the projected average annual rate of change between 1980–1990 and 1990–1995. In interpreting these data, it should be kept in mind that projections are based on the assumption of modest economic growth during the period under consideration.

Agriculture and private household employment are the only categories expected to experience an actual *decline* in the absolute number of people employed. The decline in agriculture will occur largely because of increased productivity resulting from technological advances and the growth of large-scale corporate agribusiness (see chapter 6).

Growth in mining will come mainly through increases in employment in oil and natural gas drilling. Employment in stone and clay mining and quarrying will actually decline an average of 4.1 percent per year between 1980 and 1995. The overall modest growth in the number of persons employed in mining activities will occur primarily because of improvements in mining technology.

Employment in construction is expected to grow through the 1980s as a result of new home construction necessary to meet the housing needs of new households. Although the formation of new households will slow down in the early 1990s, employment in construction will continue to increase because of an expected growth in the demand for new commercial and business buildings and the increased need for maintenance, remodeling, and repair of existing buildings.

During the late 1970s and early 1980s there has been a great deal of discussion among leaders in business and finance, as well as politicians and economic policymakers at the federal level, about the decline of American manufacturing industries. The mass media often portray the situation as one in which the majority of manufacturing jobs are on the verge of completely disappearing. Such portrayals and predictions are clearly exaggerated. As table 10.1 indicates, employment in the manufacture of both durable and nondurable goods will increase, but it will increase at a lower rate than the growth of the labor force as a whole.

The durable and nondurable goods manufacturing categories include particular industries that will experience a good deal of variation in their rates of growth and decline. For example, within the durable goods category, employment in the manufacture of guided missiles and space vehicles is expected to grow by an average of 5.4 percent per year between 1980 and 1995. The manufacture of computers and related equipment is another area in which substantial growth is expected. Between 1980 and 1995 employment will increase by an average of 7.9 percent per year. Employment in the manufacture of electronic components of all kinds will increase by 5.7 percent per year during this period. The manufacture of scientific equipment and devices used in the control of manufacturing processes will see a rise of 6.5 percent per year in employment for the period 1980–1995, and employment in the manufacture of medical and dental equipment will increase by an average of 8.7 percent per year. Despite the "bright spots" a number of industries will experience minimal growth and actual declines. Employment in the manufacture of wooden containers will decrease by − 5.3 percent on the average during each year between 1980 and 1995 as synthetic containers become more common and economical. Employment in the manufacture of radio and television receivers will increase by a very modest 0.9 percent per year reflecting the continued dominance of the market for these goods by foreign manufacturers.

The difficulties of the steel and automobile industries have been publicized extensively in recent years. Recent declines in employment among steel and automobile workers illustrate the poor prospects for these industries. Between 1972 and 1983, employment in basic iron and steel production decreased from 772,000 to 485,000 workers, or a drop of 37.2 percent. During this same period, employment in motor vehicle manufacturing decreased 6.2 percent, from 808,000 to 758,000 workers.[5] Between 1979 and 1983, some 219,000 workers in primary metals industries (mostly steel) lost their jobs. As of January 1984, 37.7 percent were unemployed and another 15.6 percent had taken early retirement or had given up looking for work. During this same time period (1979–1983) 224,000 automobile workers lost their jobs. In January 1984, 24.0 percent of them were unemployed and an additional 13.1 percent had retired early or had quit looking for work.[6]

Employment prospects in nondurable goods manufacturing is less

Table 10.1
Employment and Increase or Decrease in Employment
for Major Industry Groups, 1980-1995

Industry	Employment (in thousands)			Average Annual Percent Change	
	1980	1990	1995	1980-90	1990-95
Agriculture	2,860	2,652	2,550	-0.8	-0.8
Mining	723	781	864	0.8	2.0
Construction	5,865	6,963	7,925	1.7	2.6
Manufacturing	20,673	22,236	23,491	0.7	1.1
Durable goods	12,423	13,550	14,496	0.9	1.4
Nondurable goods	8,250	8,686	8,995	0.5	0.7
Transportation	3,250	3,450	3,594	0.6	0.8
Communications	1,362	1,687	1,950	2.2	2.9
Public utilities	966	1,064	1,093	1.0	0.5
Trade	22,493	26,355	28,545	1.6	1.6
Finance, insurance, and real estate	5,702	7,113	7,585	2.2	1.6
Services	21,097	27,863	31,290	2.8	2.3
Private household	1,598	1,400	1,346	-1.3	-0.8
Government	16,241	16,750	17,230	0.3	0.6
Total	102,830	118,315	127,563	1.4	1.5

Source: U.S. Bureau of the Census, Statistical Abstract of the United States, 1985 (Washington, D.C.: U.S. Government Printing Office, 1984), 405, table 679.

favorable than for durable goods, and here too there is considerable varia-tion from one industry to another. The average percent *decline* per year in employment expected to occur between 1980 and 1995 for several of these industries is: dairy and bakery products, − 4.8 percent; tobacco products, − 4.5 percent; leather tanning, − 6.8 percent; and leather prod-ucts, − 4.2 percent. Among the major nondurable goods manufacturing industries, only magazine and book printing and publishing stand out as an area expected to experience growth. Between 1980 and 1995 em-ployment in this industry is expected to grow by an average of 4.9 per-cent per year.

The transporation industry will also be one that experiences minimal growth. Railroad transportation in particular will offer poor employment prospects. Employment here is expected to decline by an average of -4.7 percent for each year between 1980 and 1995.

Employment in communications is projected to experience substan-tial growth as a result of an anticipated increase in demand for all kinds of communications services. Employment in radio and television broad-casting, in particular, is expected to average a growth rate of 7.3 percent per year. Employment growth in public utilities industries (mainly gas and electricity) is expected to be very small.

Wholesale and retail trade is an area where the overall growth rate will be at about the average for all industries. However, the growth of employment in restaurants is expected to increase at a higher than average rate. Employment here will increase by an average of 4.4 percent per year between 1980 and 1995.

Employment in the finance, insurance, and real estate industries will increase at a rate slightly above the average for all industries but within this grouping there will be uneven growth. Employment growth in credit agencies and financial brokerage agencies will be well above the average with an average increase of 6.0 percent per year for the period 1980–1995.

Overall, the "service" industry will experience a growth rate well above the average for the entire labor force. This industry category, however, includes a great variety of work activities that will have different growth patterns and offer very different career opportunities. During the period 1980–1995 the greatest growth is expected in "miscellaneous business services" (e.g., accounting, engineering, and legal services) which are projected to increase by an average of 7.9 percent per year. Employment in hospitals is expected to grow at an average rate of 6.2 percent per year and all other medical services are expected to increase by an average of 8.3 percent each year. Much of this growth will be in response to the medical care needs of the growing elderly population. However, it is possible that pressures to reduce the cost of health care may result in slower growth here.[7]

During the early 1980s the demand for elementary and secondary school teachers was quite low. Between 1979 and 1982 the number of people employed as teachers actually declined by -1.7 percent. However, between 1985 and 1992 the number of teachers will increase by 8.7 percent. The greatest growth will be among elementary school teachers (an increase of 15.3 percent) while secondary school teachers will decrease by -3.6 percent.[8] Employment in private elementary and secondary educational institutions will also increase by 4.1 percent between 1980 and 1995.

THE OCCUPATIONAL COMPOSITION OF THE LABOR FORCE

In chapter 6 we identified and discussed the long-term shift of the American labor force from agricultural to industrial and service occupations (see table 6.1). As the preceding section indicated, agricultural employment is expected to continue to decline somewhat through the mid-1990s. While industrial employment will increase slightly, it is clear that the really substantial growth will be in service occupations. This shift from the production of *goods* to an emphasis on the delivery of *services* is often referred to as the development of a *postindustrial society*.

The term is an unfortunate one because it implies the disappearance of goods-producing industries, which is clearly not the case. What is important about postindustrial society is the change that is occurring in occupational skills and resources that are needed.

Industrial society produced wealth in the form of tangible things like capital goods and manufactured products. In a postindustrial society, greater value is placed on output in the form of less tangible assets such as *knowledge* and *innovation.*[9] Where industrial society required workers with physical strength and manual and technical skills, postindustrial society has created a demand for the *knowledge worker.* A command of abstract, theoretical knowledge and analytic skills, as well as the ability to apply knowledge to the solution of new problems are the kinds of competencies that are coming to be valued.[10] The importance of education in producing these competencies is obvious but nonetheless crucial. In order to be valued and rewarded in a postindustrial society, future workers will not only need mathematical, scientific, and communications skills, they will also need the ability to think in analytic and innovative ways.

An examination of changes occurring and expected to occur in particular occupations can provide a more detailed picture of how the labor force is changing and how it will change in the years ahead. There are two basic ways to look at the growth of occupations. One is to identify the change in the absolute *number* of jobs in an occupation. The other is to identify the *rate* (in terms of a percentage increase) at which new jobs are being created in an occupation.

OCCUPATIONS WITH HIGH NUMERICAL GROWTH

Table 10.2 lists the twenty occupations that are expected to have the greatest increase in the absolute number of new jobs created between 1984 and 1995. They are listed in rank order from the largest to the smallest number of new jobs created.

There are at least seven occupations in this list (cashier; janitor, cleaner, and maid; waiter and waitress; nursing aide, orderly, and attendant; general office clerk; and the two food preparation categories) that are prime examples of dead-end, low-wage, secondary labor market occupations or, at most, occupations in the lower tier of the primary labor market (general office clerks). These seven service occupations will account for 2,446,000 of the new jobs created between 1984 and 1995. Clearly, many new jobs will offer few long-term career opportunities of the kind associated with professional and managerial employment. This projection is consistent with information on the kinds of new jobs that were created in the early 1980s. According to a report issued in late 1986

Table 10.2
The Twenty Fastest-Growing Occupations, Based on
Increase in the Absolute Number of Jobs, 1984-1995

Occupation	Number (thousands)		Change, 1984-1995	
	1984	1995	Number	Percent
Cashier	1,902	2,469	566	29.8%
Registered nurse	1,377	1,829	452	32.8
Janitor, cleaner, and maid	2,940	3,383	443	15.1
Truck driver	2,484	2,911	428	17.2
Waiter and waitress	1,625	2,049	424	26.1
Wholesale trade salesworker	1,248	1,617	369	29.6
Nursing aide, orderly, and attendant	1,204	1,552	348	28.9
Retail salesperson	2,732	3,075	343	12.6
Accountant and auditor	882	1,189	307	34.8
Elementary school teacher	1,381	1,662	281	20.3
Secretary	2,797	3,064	268	9.6
Computer programmer	341	586	245	71.8
General office clerk	2,398	2,629	231	9.6
Food preparation worker, not fast food	987	1,205	219	22.1
Food preparation worker, fast food	1,201	1,417	215	17.9
Computer systems analyst	308	520	212	68.7
Electrical and electronic engineer	390	597	207	52.8
Electrical and electronic technician	404	607	202	50.0
Guard	733	921	188	25.6
Automotive and motorcycle mechanic	922	1,107	185	20.1

Source: George T. Silvestri and John M. Lukasiewicz, "Occupational Employment Projections: The 1984-1995 Outlook," *Monthly Labor Review* 108 (November 1985): 42-57.

by the Joint Economic Committee of Congress, there were 6.7 million new jobs created in the United States between 1979 and 1984. About 22 percent (or 1.5 million) of those jobs were at or below the federal minimum wage of $3.35 per hour. About 58 percent of all new employment during this time period paid annual wages of less than $7,000.[11] The creation of new jobs through economic growth often is stressed by policymakers as a solution to the problem of unemployment and a way of creating career opportunities for members of minority groups (see chapter 8). However, the expansion of low-wage service jobs is unlikely to address these problems in a meaningful way.

Several of these fastest growing jobs, such as nurses, accountants and auditors, teachers, computer programmers and systems analysts, and electrical and electronic engineers and technicians, are examples of relatively good-paying, primary labor market occupations. These professional, semiprofessional, and technical occupations will offer significant career opportunities to educationally prepared college graduates. Professional, managerial, executive, and administrative jobs are expected to grow by 22 percent between 1984 and 1995. In addition, technicians

Table 10.3
The Twenty Fastest-Growing Occupations, Based on
Rate of Growth (percent increase), 1984–1995

Occupation	Number (thousands)		Change, 1984–1995	
	1984	1995	Number	Percent
Paralegal	53	104	51	97.5%
Computer programmer	341	586	245	71.8
Computer systems analyst	308	520	212	68.7
Medical assistant	128	207	79	62.0
Data processing equipment repairer	50	78	28	56.2
Electrical and electronic engineer	390	597	206	52.8
Electrical and electronic technician	404	607	202	50.7
Computer operator (except peripheral equipment)	241	353	111	46.1
Peripheral computer equipment operator	70	102	32	45.0
Travel agent	72	103	32	43.9
Physical therapist	58	83	25	42.2
Physician assistant	25	35	10	40.3
Securities and financial services salesworker	81	113	32	39.1
Mechanical engineering technician	55	75	20	36.6
Lawyer	490	665	174	35.5
Correction officer and jailer	130	175	45	34.9
Accountant and auditor	882	1,189	307	34.8
Mechanical engineer	237	317	81	34.0
Registered nurse	1,377	1,829	452	32.8
Employment interviewer	72	95	23	31.7

Source: Same as table 10.2.

and related technical support workers are expected to increase by 29 percent.[12]

OCCUPATIONS WITH HIGH GROWTH RATES

Table 10.3 lists the twenty occupations that are expected to have the highest *rates* of growth between 1984 and 1995. They are listed in rank order of their projected percentage increase. Many of these occupations are comparatively quite small. Although their growth will not create large numbers of new jobs, they represent occupations that offer expanding opportunities for those in them.

What is striking about this list is the extent to which computer-related occupations are represented. Five of the top ten occupations deal with computers in some manner. Employment in computer occupations has grown rapidly since the mid-1960s. Future growth in employment here is expected to result from the application of computers to new areas, the expansion of existing computer systems, and the adoption of more comprehensive computer systems by more small- and medium-size businesses.

In addition to computer-related occupations, other scientific and technical occupations will experience substantial growth. These include electrical and electronics engineers and technicians as well as mechanical engineers and technicians. The rise here will come in part from the employment of engineers to design new computers, but it will also reflect the need to employ engineers in the design of new products and production methods. Although not shown in table 10.3, civil engineers are also expected to increase in number by 46,000 between 1984 and 1995.[13] Occupations such as these are prime examples of postindustrial occupations in which knowledge and its application will be so important.

There are four occupations in table 10.3 in the health field (medical assistant, physical therapist, physician assistant, and registered nurse). As noted earlier, a good deal of the growth here will be in response to the health care needs of the growing elderly population. However, cost-containment pressures may lead to an increase in the health care provided on an outpatient basis and in patient's homes. Urgent care centers and "surgicenters" will also continue to grow. Although the number of physicians and surgeons is expected to increase by 23 percent between 1984 and 1995, these trends will increase employment opportunities for other health-related occupations (i.e., those in table 10.3) even more rapidly.[14]

DECLINING OCCUPATIONS

It should be apparent from our discussion of the growth and decline of particular industries that there are also specific occupations that will experience decreases in employment. The twenty occupations that are expected to experience *the greatest rate of decline* (in terms of percentage decreases between 1984 and 1995) are listed in table 10.4.

Although the most rapidly declining occupations are mainly semi-skilled blue-collar occupations, several white-collar occupations are also included. The decline in some clerical occupations will be the direct and indirect result of office automation. This is particularly the case with stenographers, statistical clerks, and central office telephone operators. As professionals and managers increasingly become skilled at using desktop personal computers and executive work stations, the need for support staff will decline. Although not shown in table 10.4, payroll and timekeeping clerks are expected to decline by -5.0 percent between 1984 and 1995, and very low growth rates are projected for file clerks, reservation and transportation ticket agents, traffic, shipping, and receiving clerks, and production, planning, and expediting clerks. These projections reflect the fact that the increased use of computers for the work involved in these jobs will make them less labor-intensive. The increased use of automated teller machines and electronic fund transfers in bank-

Table 10.4
The Twenty Occupations that Will Decrease the Fastest,
Based on Rate of Decline (percent decrease), 1984–1995

Occupation	Number (thousands)		Change, 1984–1995	
	1984	1995	Number	Percent
Stenographer	239	143	–96	–40.3%
Shoe sewing machine operator and tender	33	22	–11	–31.5
Railroad brake, signal, and switch operator	48	35	–13	–26.4
Rail car repairer	27	21	–6	–22.3
Furnace, kiln, or kettle operator and tender	63	50	–13	–20.9
Shoe and leather worker and repairer	43	35	–8	–18.6
Private household worker	993	811	–182	–18.3
Telephone station installer and repairer	111	92	–19	–17.4
Sewing machine operator	676	563	–113	–16.7
Textile machine operator and tender	279	235	–44	–15.7
Textile machine maintenance mechanic	26	22	–4	–14.8
Statistical clerk	93	81	–12	–12.7
Industrial truck and tractor operator	389	342	–47	–11.9
Central office telephone operator	77	68	–9	–11.5
Farm worker	1,079	958	–121	–11.2
College and university faculty	731	654	–77	–10.6
Farm and home management advisor	27	24	–3	–9.6
Metal and plastic extruding and drawing machine setter and setup operator	28	25	–3	–9.1
Textile and garment pressing machine operator and tender	116	106	–10	–8.8
Postal service clerks	317	290	–27	–8.5

Source: Same as table 10.2.

ing also will result in a slower than average rate of growth for bank tellers.[15]

The expected decline in employment in the blue-collar occupations in table 10.4 is due to a variety of factors. The overall decline of rail transportation will be reflected in decreases among railroad brake, signal, and switch operators and rail car repairers. Continuing automation, especially the introduction of computer assisted manufacturing processes, will also reduce the need for workers in many production occupations such as textile machine operators and setup workers in many industries. As a reflection of this change, both programmers and operators of numerical control machine tools are expected to increase 32 percent and 30 percent, respectively, between 1984 and 1995.[16] Computer-aided design (CAD) and computer-aided manufacturing (CAM) have reduced the need for semiskilled machine operators, but increased the demand for workers knowledgeable about the design and operation of these new technologies. The semiconductor and computer industries are as essential to production today as the fractional horsepower motor and the assembly line were in an earlier era.

CHANGING DEMOGRAPHICS: A POSSIBLE LABOR SHORTAGE?

Despite the fact that unemployment has been a major concern among economists and labor force analysts in the 1970s and 1980s, in the last few years of this century and the early 2000s the United States may actually face a labor shortage. The reason for this is ultimately to be found in the changing birthrates of the population. The *baby boom* period of high birth rates (roughly 1945–1960) was followed by a *baby bust* in which birthrates dropped. Between 1965 and 1979, in particular, birth rates decreased significantly. In the early 1980s we began to experience what is sometimes referred to as an *echo boom* as the bulk of the baby boom generation had its children. However, the number of children being born will begin to decrease again around the turn of the century as the smaller, baby bust generation has its children.

These changing patterns of birth rates have implications for the supply of potential workers as well as impacts on the educational system and the supply of military personnel. By 1995, for example, the number of teenaged workers will be 20 percent less than it was in 1975. In 1985, the number of sixteen to nineteen-year-old workers was 20 percent less than it was in 1978 and the number of twenty to twenty-four-year-olds was just beginning to drop.[17]

The number of children between the ages of six and eighteen decreased by forty-five million (a 14 percent decrease) between 1975 and 1985. This resulted in an oversupply of teachers and school buildings nationally. The anticipated rise in the demand for elementary and secondary schoolteachers noted earlier will arise from the need to educate the children who are members of the echo boom generation. The decrease in college and university faculty identified in table 10.4 represents the effects of the baby bust generation. Between 1980 and 1985 the number of eighteen to twenty-four-year-olds dropped 5 percent.[18] The demand for college and university faculty will probably not increase significantly until the early 2000s when the echo boom generation reaches college age.

The declining number of young people will also affect the military services. In 1995 there will be 4.3 million fewer people in the eighteen through twenty-one age group from which the military services recruit most heavily. Currently, the military services recruit about 42 percent of all qualified eighteen-year-old men. In order to maintain the armed forces at present personnel levels they will need to recruit 55 percent of them by 1995.[19] Other options of course might include recruiting women more aggressively or offering larger bonuses or other enticements for reenlistment.

When the majority of the baby bust generation is in its late teens and early twenties, businesses that have come to rely on young, low-wage workers will be affected the most. These include fast-food restaurants, hotels, and all businesses that depend on tourism. Fast-food outlets are already experimenting with the hiring of older, retired workers.[20] By 1995 the number of entry-level workers throughout the labor force will be low. More importantly, as the baby bust generation ages, there may continue to be a shortage of workers. Such trends may stimulate a number of changes. In the early 2000s, a labor shortage could create additional pressures and opportunities for women to enter the labor force. Another possibility would be relaxation of our currently very stringent immigration policies or development of "guest worker" programs designed to supply workers for particular jobs and industries. Finally, a labor shortage could lead to a rethinking of the meaning of retirement and possibly slow down if not reverse the recent trends toward early and partial retirement discussed in chapter 9.

SUMMARY

While the forecasting of social change is a hazardous undertaking, this final chapter nevertheless has attempted to identify some of the major changes taking place in the American economy and labor force and to project those changes into the near future. While the labor force will increase in size, the participation of women and minorities will grow more rapidly than the average rate of growth of the labor force.

In terms of major industrial groupings, agriculture is expected to decrease, as is private household employment. Growth in other industries will be uneven, but employment in communications, finance, insurance, and real estate, and all other service activities is expected to increase faster than other industry categories.

The particular occupations that are expected to grow in the coming years are a peculiar mix. They include many low-wage, secondary labor market, service jobs with few if any career prospects. However, exceptionally strong growth is also projected for jobs that are prototypes of the postindustrial labor force. These include technical, scientific, semiprofessional, and professional occupations. Especially noteworthy are occupations related to health care, computer-related occupations, and those in the electrical and electronics fields. As has been the case in the past, people with the appropriate training and educational credentials will be in a position to take advantage of the growth of these technical and professional occupations while those without the credentials will find their choices limited to service jobs in the secondary labor market.

NOTES

1. U.S. Bureau of the Census, *Statistical Abstract of the United States, 1985* (Washington, D.C.: U.S. Government Printing Office, 1984), 405, table 679.
2. Ibid., 392, table 655.
3. Ibid.
4. Except as otherwise noted, the data in this section are from the source cited at the bottom of table 10.1.
5. Calculated from data in U.S. Bureau of the Census, *Statistical Abstract, 1985,* 412, table 690, and 752, table 1342.
6. Paul O. Flaim and Ellen Sehgal, "Displaced Workers of 1979–83: How Well Have They Fared?" *Monthly Labor Review* 108 (June 1985): 3–16, table 2.
7. Anne Kahl and Donald E. Clark, "Employment in Health Services: Long-Term Trends and Projections," *Monthly Labor Review* 109 (August 1986): 17–36.
8. U.S Bureau of the Census, *Statistical Abstract, 1985,* 140, table 224.
9. John Naisbitt, *Megatrends: Ten New Directions Transforming Our Lives* (New York: Warner Books, 1982).
10. Peter Drucker, *The Changing World of the Executive* (New York: Truman Talley, 1982).
11. Barry Bluestone and Bennett Harrison, *The Great American Job Machine: The Proliferation of Low Wage Employment in the U.S. Economy,* Study prepared for The Joint Economic Committee of Congress (Washington, D.C.: 1986).
12. George T. Silvestri and John M. Lukasiewicz, "Occupational Employment Projections: The 1984–95 Outlook," *Monthly Labor Review* 108 (November 1985): 42–57.
13. Ibid., 52.
14. Ibid., 53.
15. Ibid., 54.
16. William M. Austin, "The Job Outlook in Brief," *Occupational Outlook Quarterly* 30 (Spring 1986): 2–30.
17. Data cited in this paragraph are from Terry Stevenson Supple, "The Coming Labor Shortage," *American Demographics* 8 (September 1986): 32–35.
18. Ibid., 33–34.
19. Ibid., 34.
20. Ibid.

OCCUPATION INDEX

AUTHOR INDEX

SUBJECT INDEX

THE BOOK'S MANUFACTURE

Sociology of Occupations and Professions,
Second Edition, was typeset by
Printech, Inc., Schaumburg, Illinois.
Printing and binding were done by
Braun-Brumfield, Ann Arbor, Michigan.
Cover and internal design by John B. Goetz,
Design & Production Services Co., Chicago.
Text and display types are Electra.